Trump and Hitler

Henk de Berg

Trump and Hitler

A Comparative Study in Lying

Henk de Berg
School of Languages and Cultures
University of Sheffield
Sheffield, UK

ISBN 978-3-031-51832-4   ISBN 978-3-031-51833-1 (eBook)
https://doi.org/10.1007/978-3-031-51833-1

© The Editor(s) (if applicable) and The Author(s), under exclusive licence to Springer Nature Switzerland AG 2024, corrected publication 2024
This work is subject to copyright. All rights are solely and exclusively licensed by the Publisher, whether the whole or part of the material is concerned, specifically the rights of translation, reprinting, reuse of illustrations, recitation, broadcasting, reproduction on microfilms or in any other physical way, and transmission or information storage and retrieval, electronic adaptation, computer software, or by similar or dissimilar methodology now known or hereafter developed.
The use of general descriptive names, registered names, trademarks, service marks, etc. in this publication does not imply, even in the absence of a specific statement, that such names are exempt from the relevant protective laws and regulations and therefore free for general use.
The publisher, the authors, and the editors are safe to assume that the advice and information in this book are believed to be true and accurate at the date of publication. Neither the publisher nor the authors or the editors give a warranty, expressed or implied, with respect to the material contained herein or for any errors or omissions that may have been made. The publisher remains neutral with regard to jurisdictional claims in published maps and institutional affiliations.

Cover illustration: © Alex Linch/shutterstock.com

This Palgrave Macmillan imprint is published by the registered company Springer Nature Switzerland AG.
The registered company address is: Gewerbestrasse 11, 6330 Cham, Switzerland

Paper in this product is recyclable.

The original version of the book has been revised. A correction to this book can be found at https://doi.org/10.1007/978-3-031-51833-1_8

Non ridere, non lugere neque detestari, sed intelligere
Not in order to mock, lament, or execrate, but understand
Baruch de Spinoza

Preface

President Trump was not some kind of Hitler. Adolf Hitler started the Second World War and instigated the Holocaust. Nothing remotely similar can be said of Donald Trump. I do not even believe that President Trump was a convinced racist, although he did systematically exploit racial tensions, as I will argue throughout this book. The two men were not "in essence" the same. Yet there are good reasons to compare their political styles.

Intriguingly, suggestions of a link between the Donald and the Führer go back a long way. As early as 1990, *Vanity Fair*'s Marie Brenner reported that Trump's then wife, Ivana, had said "that from time to time her husband reads a book of Hitler's collected speeches, *My New Order*, which he keeps in a cabinet by his bed".[1] Brenner also related that according to one of his lawyers "Donald is a believer in the big-lie theory", the systematic twisting of facts as explained and practised by Hitler and his Propaganda Minister, Joseph Goebbels.[2] Of course, such incidental remarks are not nearly enough to justify a book-length comparison of Trump's and Hitler's approaches to politics. Nor are several striking but inconsequential biographical parallels: both the US President and the Reich Chancellor had a domineering father and a doting mother; both were non-smokers and virtual teetotallers; and both were germophobes. The main reason why a comparative study of the two men makes sense is the widespread suspicion that there are significant similarities between their uses of incendiary language, scapegoating, establishment-bashing, and other toxic forms of political strategy.

Some Trump-Hitler comparisons are, one may assume, merely the logical outcome of Godwin's law—the idea, first put forward in 1990 by Mike Godwin, that the longer a heated discussion lasts, the higher the likelihood of a Hitler analogy becomes.[3] If you are worried and angry about Donald Trump's anti-democratic tendencies, a *reductio ad Hitlerum* (to use the phrase the philosopher Leo Strauss coined in 1951) might seem a good way to emphasize your abhorrence.[4] Such superficial and rhetorically overblown comparisons are obviously not particularly informative. There have, however, also been serious discussions of the way in which Trump exploited social strains within contemporary America and the way Hitler sought to manipulate Germany in the 1920s and 1930s.

Thus, in his *Washington Post* article "This Is How Fascism Comes to America", the historian and political analyst Robert Kagan points to several important features of Trumpism that equally apply to Hitlerism.[5] President Trump—Kagan writes—transcended his political party, and the allegiance of his supporters was to him rather than to the party or an ideology. His electoral programme was relatively vague and inconsistent, explicit only about what he was against, not about what he was for. He deliberately played on his potential followers' fear and anger, directing their resentment to a range of (as a rule ethnically defined) "others". The proposed remedy for the country's ills was to get tough with such enemies. However much his supporters may have suffered economic dislocation, Trump's message was not primarily an economic one. What he offered was above all an attitude, an aura of strength and national greatness. Moreover, he presented himself as the only one capable of delivering such redemption. In doing so, he in effect invited his followers—as Kagan puts it—to "run roughshod over even the institutions created to preserve their freedom".[6] Finally, Trump's rise was aided and abetted by blinkered conservative politicians harbouring the illusion that they would be able to control him, or who in any case were unwilling or unable to stand up to him. Hence Kagan's conclusion: "This is how fascism comes to America, not with jackboots and salutes [...], but with a television huckster, a phony billionaire, a textbook egomaniac 'tapping into' popular resentment and insecurities, and with an entire political party—out of ambition or blind party loyalty, or simply out of fear—falling into line behind him".[7]

The British historian Richard J. Evans, author of a three-volume standard work on the rise and fall of the Third Reich, has likewise detected alarming echoes of the 1930s in Trump's reign. In an interview with Isaac Chotiner entitled "Too Close for Comfort", he mentions "the stigmatization of minorities", the "hyperbolic and exaggerated language" directed against real or perceived enemies, and the attacks on the judiciary: "if you look at the courts, that's one of the most interesting aspects of what Trump has been doing. He clearly has a contempt for the courts and the law, which echoes that of the Nazis very, very clearly".[8] Moreover, both Trump and Hitler possessed a highly informal management style that created competing competencies and internal rivalries among the people working for them. The result was bureaucratic chaos. More generally, Evans points to today's toxic media climate, "the poisoning of political and public discourse through lies and insults", as being "very similar to the early 1930s in Germany".[9]

In spite of such parallels, there has been no comprehensive comparison of Trump's and Hitler's political styles and of the historical contexts in which they came to power. *Donald Trump in Historical Perspective: Dead Precedents*, a collection of essays edited by Michael Harvey, looks at the American President through the lens of, among others, Plato's tyrant, Machiavelli's political actors, Andrew Jackson, Benito Mussolini, Mao Zedong, and Richard Nixon, but it contains no chapter on Hitler.[10] The closest we get to a systematic exploration of Trumpism and Hitlerism are studies such as Ruth Ben-Ghiat's *Strongmen: How They Rise, Why They Succeed, How They Fall* and Federico Finchelstein's *From Fascism to Populism in History*.[11] Both are brilliant books, but their impressive scope—ranging from Mussolini to Muammar Gaddafi and from Berlusconi to Marine Le Pen—precludes a concentrated focus on Trump and Hitler. Admittedly, many of these two men's political and rhetorical stratagems are not unique to them, but derive from what has come to be called the authoritarian leader's playbook.[12] Yet this does not make a comprehensive and historically detailed comparison of Trump and Hitler any less instructive, especially as few political leaders (with the possible exception of North Korea's Kim dynasty) have relied equally consciously, heavily, and systematically on strategies of self-staging. Trump and Hitler—I will argue throughout this book—are the quintessential political performance artists.

There is a further reason why a single-volume study of the two leaders might prove enlightening. Both appealed to "the people's" so-called common sense (what the National Socialists called *das gesunde Volksempfinden*, the healthy instinct of the people); both claimed to speak in the name of "the people"; and both were extraordinarily successful at gathering a massive following. They were *populists* in this precise sense of the term.[13] Yet we are inclined to see Hitler as a violent autocrat and—from 1933—a murderous dictator (which he was), but not as a populist (which he also was) whose ideas were widely embraced from below as well as being enforced from above. A comparison with Trumpism, I believe, will help us gain a better understanding of the attraction Hitlerism held for so many. This can only be achieved if we understand the popular appeal of Trump; and this, too, is one of this book's aims. Critical studies have understandably focused on the dangers posed by Trump's approach to politics; and the majority of his supporters are usually seen as uneducated and gullible—and in any case largely passive—victims of his confidence tricks. I will try to flip the chessboard, as it were, by exploring not just how Trump conned the people, but also why they embraced his lies actively. We are dealing—I will argue—with a two-way process from which Trump's supporters emerged, in their own perception at any rate, revitalized and empowered. It is this fatal interplay of political deceptions and popular dreams that is at the heart of Trumpism and Hitlerism alike.

This study, then, has three interrelated aims. First, it offers a systematic comparison of Trump's and Hitler's approaches to politics: their various forms of populist self-staging, their conman skills and rhetorical strategies, and their leadership and management styles. This is not to say—the point bears repeating—that I believe that President Trump was a fascist or semi-fascist leader: operating as he did within the confines of liberal democracy, he was on the whole unable to follow through on his authoritarian inclinations and he never built up (and never intended to build up) a terrorist dictatorship as Hitler did. Rather, I see Trump as a "formal" or "formalized" Hitler; in other words, as a politician who used many of the public-relations tools that Hitler employed, but without incarnating the same kind of murderous evil.[14] That even this kind of would-be authoritarianism poses a genuine threat to liberal-democratic values and institutions should be obvious. Second, I will examine the social contexts—the fault lines and tensions in their respective societies—that the two political leaders managed to exploit. Here, I will focus on the relation between identity, dignity, and narrative. This will enable me—third—to throw light on the astounding resonance that Trump's and Hitler's lies found.

A final remark. As phrases such as "the populist leader" are without exception used with Trump and Hitler in mind, I combine them with the pronouns *he*, *him*, and *his*.

Sheffield, UK   Henk de Berg

Notes

1. Marie Brenner, "After the Goldrush", *Vanity Fair*, September 1990. When Brenner asked Trump about Ivana's statement, his response was: "*If* I had these speeches, and I am not saying that I do, I would never read them". The book in question is Adolf Hitler, *My New Order*, edited with commentary by Raoul de Roussy de Sales (New York: Reynal & Hitchcock, 1941; no translator is mentioned). In 2016, Ishi Press International brought out a two-volume reprint.
2. Brenner, "After the Goldrush". I will discuss the concept of the big lie in Chap. 7.
3. See Mike Godwin, "I Seem to Be a Verb: 18 Years of Godwin's Law", *Jewcy*, 30 April 2008.
4. See Leo Strauss, "The Social Science of Max Weber", *Measure: A Critical Journal* 2.2, 1951, pp. 204–30, reprinted as chapter 2 ("Natural Right and the Distinction Between Facts and Values") of *Natural Right and History* (Chicago and London: The University of Chicago Press, 1965; first published 1953), pp. 35–80; the relevant citation is on pp. 42–43. Cf. Michael Lind, "Quit Comparing Trump to Hitler", *Politico*, 8 March 2016. For a discussion of the issues raised by Godwin's and Strauss's ideas, see François De Smet, *Reductio ad Hitlerum. Une théorie du point Godwin* (Paris: PUF, 2014).

5. Robert Kagan, "This Is How Fascism Comes to America", *The Washington Post*, 18 May 2016. Cf. Robert Kagan, "Our Constitutional Crisis Is Already Here", *The Washington Post*, 23 September 2021.
6. Kagan, "How Fascism Comes to America".
7. Kagan, "How Fascism Comes to America". On the hollowing out of liberal democracy from within, and especially on the complicity of traditional conservative politicians in the rise of authoritarianism, cf. Frank Finlay, "Revisiting Sebastian Haffner's Memoir *Geschichte eines Deutschen* in the Context of Contemporary Political Trends", *German Studies Review* 46.2, 2023, pp. 207–25.
8. Isaac Chotiner, "Too Close for Comfort", *Slate*, 10 February 2017.
9. Chotiner, "Too Close for Comfort".
10. Michael Harvey (ed.), *Donald Trump in Historical Perspective: Dead Precedents* (New York and London: Routledge, 2022). Miranda Carter's "What Happens When a Bad-Tempered, Distractable Doofus Runs an Empire?" (*The New Yorker*, 6 June 2018) offers a comparison with Emperor Wilhelm II.
11. Ruth Ben-Ghiat, *Strongmen: How They Rise, Why They Succeed, How They Fall* (London: Profile Books, 2021; first published 2020), and Federico Finchelstein, *From Fascism to Populism in History* (Oakland: University of California Press, 2019 [with a new preface]; first published 2017).
12. Cf. Ben-Ghiat, *Strongmen*, p. 7.
13. As I will discuss the various aspects of Trump's and Hitler's populism throughout this study, I refrain from providing bibliographical references here. For a list of key studies on populism, see Chap. 4, note 18.
14. I borrow the term "formal(ized)" from the German-American thinker Siegfried Kracauer, who in his analysis of Fritz Lang's oeuvre characterizes Haghi (the master spy in Lang's 1928 film *Spione*) as a "formalized"—that is, largely ideology-free—Mabuse (the villain in Lang's 1922 *Dr. Mabuse* and his 1933 *Das Testament des Dr. Mabuse*). See Siegfried Kracauer, *From Caligari to Hitler: A Psychological History of the German Film* (Princeton: Princeton University Press, 1966; first published 1947), p. 150.

Contents

1	**Self-Staging: Aura and Appearance**	1
	Charisma, Aura, Artifice	4
	Confidence Artists	8
	Acting and Role-Playing	10
	Charm, Calm, and Fake Anger	15
	Absolutism	17
	Real and Fake Expertise	19
	Theatre and Politics	24
	Politics as Theatre	29
	Propaganda	33
	Saviour from Above	36
	Another Saviour from Above	41
	Photography	44
	A Long Tie and a Short Moustache	48
2	**Corruption and Money**	69
	Trumpworld: An Embarrassment of Riches	70
	Hitler's Early Profits	76
	The *Reichskanzler* and His Riches	84
	The Paladins' Perks	96
	The Brown Swamp	102
	Two Forms of Corruption	105

3 Enemies, Scapegoats, and Conspiracy Theories — 121
The Community and Its Others — 122
Scapegoats — 125
Populism as Participatory Authoritarianism — 130
The Container Approach — 135
Conspiracy Theories — 141

4 The Establishment, the Elite, and the Experts — 155
The Establishment in the Crossfire — 157
Why Establishment-Bashing Makes Us Feel Good — 162
Can Politics Ever Be the Will of the People? — 166
Are Elites Really That Bad? — 169
Emotion Versus Expertise — 175

5 Identity and Negative Myths — 189
Stories Are Us — 189
Aristotle Was Right — 192
Lie to Me — 194
Collective Identity and Myth — 196
The Myth Gap I: Times of Crisis — 199
The Myth Gap II: Dignity — 203
Filling the Myth Gap I: Conflict-based Storytelling — 207
Filling the Myth Gap II: Negative Myths — 209

6 Leadership Style — 227
Ways of Working — 229
Emotional Distance — 235
Follow the News: Shape the Narrative — 236
Informal Decision-making, Opportunism, Social Darwinism, and the Power of the Will — 239
Divide and Rule — 246
Collaboration, Loyalty, and Self-denial — 248

7 Speeches, Lies, and Narrative (Un-)Truth — 263
Speaking as Performance — 265
Jokes and Insults — 268

Violence and Strategic Controversy	272
Entertainment, Community, and Individual Empowerment	274
Simplicity, Repetition, and Interpretative Openness	278
Making the Country Great Again	281
Emotions and Dreams	287
Extremism and Exaggeration	291
Twitter	294
Narrative (Un-)truth	299
Narrative (Un-)truth, Continued: Truthiness and Group Identity	306

Correction to: Trump and Hitler — C1

Select Bibliography — 323

Index — 327

About the Author

Henk de Berg is Professor of German at the University of Sheffield. He is the author of three other books, including *Freud's Theory and Its Use in Literary and Cultural Studies* (described by Peter Gay as "as good an introductory text as one can possibly hope for"), which received a Choice Outstanding Academic Title Award and has been translated into three European languages as well as Chinese. Among his eight co-edited books are *Modern German Thought from Kant to Habermas* as well as *Tzvetan Todorov: Thinker and Humanist* and *Rethinking Ernst Bloch*. Born in the Netherlands, Henk de Berg has lived in the UK since 1996.

1

Self-Staging: Aura and Appearance

Meeting Hitler and looking into his eyes—the erstwhile Nazi supporter Fridolin von Spaun recalled in an interview with the BBC—"was one of the most curious moments of my life. The gaze, which at first rested completely on me, suddenly went straight through me and into an unknown distance".[1] The storm trooper Otto Wagener, who in the early 1930s served as economic advisor to Hitler, felt as if the Führer's gaze "did not come from his eyeballs" but "from somewhere much deeper: I felt as if it came from infinity".[2] Many other Nazi supporters were likewise captivated by Hitler's "flaming, steel-blue eyes".[3] They were the kind of eyes "such as Frederick the Great must have had", a woman said.[4] For his part, Joseph Goebbels, who joined the National Socialists in 1925 and later became the Third Reich's Propaganda Minister, thought that Hitler's "big blue eyes" were "like stars".[5] Yet, strikingly, there were also numerous Germans who remained immune to the famous stare. One of them even described the Führer's face as completely *nichtssagend*, blank and unimpressive.[6]

This tells us that Hitler's magnetism was not simply a part of his personality. Rather, it emerged in the interaction with his public. As the British historian Laurence Rees puts it, "Adolf Hitler's charismatic appeal was not universal. It was present only in the space between him and the emotions of his audience. Two people could meet Hitler at the same time and one might find him charismatic and the other might think that he was a fool".[7] The magic only worked on those already inclined to embrace Hitler's leadership and ideas. If this was not the case, you were likely to find the man off-putting, or just comical, and his views crass and simplistic.

In later chapters, I will examine the peculiar hopes and fears that predispose people to attribute almost superhuman qualities to certain political leaders. Here, I wish to explore the other end of the mesmeric relation—the actions of the charismatic leader. For the type of charisma that is at issue results from a two-way process. It is the product *both* of the audience's receptivity, their yearning for charismatic leadership, *and* of the politician's artifice, his ability to project a particular image. Hitler applied a range of stratagems to appear charismatic. The same is true of Donald Trump.

The stare is a case in point. Hitler simply "looked fierce" while holding the eyes of the person opposite him much longer than one would normally do. Indeed, the power stare is a well-known parlour trick, akin to the seducer's overlong "romantic" gaze across a room. Donald Trump used the same technique, as his former political advisors Corey Lewandowski and David Bossie reveal in their book on the 2016 presidential campaign. "Sometimes, before Trump did interviews on shows like O'Reilly or Hannity, he'd turn to Hope Hicks or Keith Schiller, his longtime bodyguard, Jason Miller, or Corey or Dave to ask if the stare was up to par that day. 'How's the look?' he'd ask, looking straight through the camera".[8]

The example of Hitler's gaze also makes it clear how little we actually know about him. Few people, I would imagine, are aware that he had blue eyes. Most of us know him from black-and-white photographs, or from films and television series in which the actor playing the Führer has brown eyes. Indeed, we sometimes joke about how "un-Aryan" the leading Nazis looked: commander in chief of the German air force Hermann Göring was seriously obese, Joseph Goebbels was short and club-footed, while Hitler had dark hair and—we mistakenly assume—dark eyes. More importantly, thinking of the Führer we tend to picture a ranting and raving maniac. We see the actor Bruno Ganz in *Downfall*, totally incapable of controlling his emotions. In fact, "one of Hitler's most striking characteristics"—his personal architect Albert Speer wrote after the war—was "self-control".[9] He was an exceptionally devious politician, well able to hide both his feelings and his intentions if the occasion required it.

Our picture of Donald Trump is likewise one-dimensional. Even some of the people who opted to work for him considered their boss something of a political nincompoop. When soon-to-be chief campaign strategist Steve Bannon was told that Trump was thinking of running for President, his sarcastic response was: "Of what country?"[10] Secretary of State Rex Tillerson called Trump "a moron" (with an intensifying adjective) and Secretary of Defence Jim Mattis described him as having the intelligence of "a fifth or sixth grader", while economic adviser Gary Cohn thought him "dumb as shit".[11] The 2019 book *A Warning*, written by "a senior Trump administration official", provides perhaps the fullest collection of anti-Trump tropes. According to the anonymous author, the President was (in alphabetical order): all over the place, baby-like, clueless, confused, crazy, distracted, easily swayed, erratic, forgetful, gullible, haphazard, ignorant, impatient, impulsive, inattentive, incurious, inept, intellectually lazy, irascible, naïve, undisciplined, unfocused, uninformed, unstable, and vain.[12] As we will see, however, Trump possessed some very real skills—perhaps not so much those one looks for in a decent and capable democratic leader, but certainly those that make for a powerful campaigner and wily political operator.

In many ways, there is a world of difference between Hitler and Trump. The German politician was an ideologically committed, anti-Semitic mass murderer, responsible for both the Second World War and the Holocaust. As far as I can tell, the American President had no firm convictions whatsoever. Nor does he appear to have been a committed racist, although—as I will argue throughout this book—he systematically played to white nationalist sentiments. In other respects, however, the two men were surprisingly alike. Above all, both understood the power of *politics as spectacle*, and both worked hard to create a persona adapted to their respective propaganda shows.

Charisma, Aura, Artifice

Using a phrase coined by the early twentieth-century sociologist Max Weber, scholars have described politicians like Hitler as *charismatic leaders*.[13] The authority of such leaders, Weber says, rests on their followers' "devotion" to the leaders' perceived "exceptional sanctity, heroism or exemplary character" and "the normative patterns or order revealed or ordained" by them.[14] By way of example, Weber mentions the sway that Jesus held over the disciples. (The term *charisma*, "divinely bestowed grace", comes from early Christianity.) Thus, the obligation to obey is based not so much on any office that the leader may hold, but rather on "personal loyalty",[15] a loyalty generated by a belief in the leader's assumed exceptional qualities.

Charismatic authority is to be distinguished from what Weber calls *traditional authority*, which rests on "an established belief in the sanctity of immemorial traditions".[16] This is the kind of power held by hereditary monarchs. The charismatic leader's authority is also different from a third source of power that Weber identifies—*legal authority* resting on the rational acceptance of laws. This is the power exercised by leaders and officials in modern democracies.

The advantage of Weber's concept of charismatic leadership is that it enables us—as the British historian Ian Kershaw puts it—to look for "explanations of [Hitler's] extraordinary form of political domination primarily in the perceivers of 'charisma' [...] rather than, in the first instance, in the personality of the object of their adulation".[17] We do not need to assume that Hitler (or Trump) somehow *was* inherently charismatic, and then desperately try to figure out what combination of personal qualities this charisma consisted in. Instead, we can restrict ourselves to the question why and in what ways his supporters *considered* him to be so. For charisma in Weber's sense exists only to the extent that it falls "within the scope of [...] belief", as he puts it somewhat awkwardly.[18] "What is alone important is how the individual is actually regarded by those subject to charismatic authority, by his 'followers' or 'disciples'".[19]

Some have argued that Weber's concept is hard to apply in the context of a modern state. Yet Weber himself stresses that none of his three types of authority is likely to exist in pure form. Real-world authority is usually a mixture of types. Moreover, Ian Kershaw is right when he says that Weber's notion of charismatic power helps us understand "the corrosive impact of that power when superimposed upon a contradictory form of domination—the legal, bureaucratic framework of the German state apparatus".[20]

In addition, as Kershaw also highlights, Weber's theory enables us to bring the intimate relationship between Hitler's peculiar appeal and his social and political environment into sharp relief. From its inception, the Weimar Republic—the democratic Germany that had come into existence after the First World War—suffered from a lack of broad popular support. Mistrust in the newly minted political system and its leaders reached its climax following the collapse of the German economy in 1929/30. Against a backdrop of mass unemployment, governmental paralysis, institutional impotence, and national division, charismatic leadership appeared to offer a way out. In other words, it was precisely the crisis, or perceived crisis, of the modern democratic system that made rational-legal power lose credibility. "Salvation", many people felt, "could only be sought with a leader who possessed *personal* power [...], sweeping away the causes of the misery and the faceless politicians and bureaucrats who prevail over it, and seeming to impose his own personal power upon the force of history itself".[21] A similar point can be made about Trump's America, as I will argue in later chapters.

Yet Weber's approach has two significant drawbacks. First, by shifting the focus so comprehensively to the audience, it loses sight of the ability of charismatic leaders to *make themselves appear* a certain way. Hitler and Trump employed an array of schemes and strategies to project a charismatic image. Their techniques—as we will see—ranged from the highly conscious choice of hairstyle and dress to the equally calculated organization of awe-inspiring mass events. Indeed, both men were media politicians *par excellence*. Few, if any, political leaders have possessed as shrewd an understanding of the power of appearances. Second, Weber's concept of charisma remains virtually contentless and is of little help when analysing the specifics of Hitler's and Trump's self-staging.[22]

A more promising approach is offered by another German thinker, the philosopher and literary critic Walter Benjamin (1892–1940). In a famous essay, written in the 1930s, on the "technological reproducibility" of photography and film, Benjamin uses the concept of the *aura* to designate the ability to evoke a special kind of awe.[23] This can be an attribute of objects, such as certain works of art, but also of people. Benjamin defines the aura, in a way that is not easily understood, as the "unique appearance of a distance, however close it may be".[24] The example he provides is hardly more helpful: "To follow with the eye, while resting on a summer afternoon, [...] a branch that casts its shadow on you is to breathe the aura [...] of that branch".[25]

What, then, is the aura? Imagine that you have just slept with someone you are desperately in love with. It was not just sex—you have made love. Now you are lying next to that person, whose warm body is so close you can touch it. Yet the feeling is so beautiful, so special, that you experience something almost mystical. It feels as though you were transported beyond yourself. The aura is this awe-inspiring combination of proximity and distance. Something is factually close, yet feels far away. The experience is one of quasi-divine revelation, and the result is wonder, awe.

The central tenet of Benjamin's essay is that in the modern world such experiences are slowly disappearing. His focus is on art, which he views as secularized religion. (The religious statues of old, which were seen as embodiments of the divine, have given way to merely artistic, but still awe-inspiring sculptures.) Traditional works of art, such as the *Mona Lisa*, possessed an aura because there was always just one of them. Each was unique in time and space. Photographs and films, by contrast, exist in countless copies and are therefore no longer special and hence no longer auratic.

In addition, we now perceive objects and people in a different way than before. In Benjamin's jargon, "the social basis of the aura's present decay" is to be found in "the desire of the present-day masses to 'get closer' to things spatially and humanly, and their equally passionate concern for overcoming each thing's uniqueness by assimilating it as a reproduction".[26] Mass tourism, posters, and postcards have robbed even the *Mona Lisa* of its awe-inspiring quality. We have reduced the distance between ourselves and our political leaders so much that we know almost everything about them. They, too, are no longer special.

1 Self-Staging: Aura and Appearance

This trend has only increased since Benjamin wrote his essay, when few voters were aware, say, that Franklin Delano Roosevelt was in a wheelchair. A few decades later, much more was known about John F. Kennedy, but not, for example, the fact that he sometimes had to be hoisted onto Air Force One with a hydraulic lift—a kind of cherry picker—because his back pain was so bad he could not walk up the stairs. His many affairs also went largely unnoticed. Nowadays, we ask politicians even about the kind of underpants they wear (as happened with Bill Clinton during a 1994 MTV town-hall meeting) or where they bought them (as was the case with Margaret Thatcher in a 1986 BBC interview).[27] As a result, nothing and no one appears charismatic anymore.

Yet Benjamin also detects a counter-trend, which manifests itself precisely in the political arena. It is not the rebirth of the old auratic forms, though. It is the emergence, or rather the construction, of a new kind of aura, an *artificial* or *fake* one. What we are witnessing—Benjamin says, writing in the 1930s—is the "aestheticization of political life".[28] Its artistic director is "fascism"; its result, a "Führer cult".[29] Employing a term that Benjamin himself does not use, one might say that politics is being turned into a Wagnerian *Gesamtkunstwerk*, a total work of art. National Socialism (or at least an important dimension of it) is a systematic attempt at *Auratisierung*, the auratification of political events, buildings, and above all the Leader.

Drawing on Benjamin's ideas, we can recast Weber's charisma as a specific combination of proximity and distance. In other words, Hitler and Trump are not just charismatic, but *auratic*. They are *close* to the people both literally, when they are pressing the flesh, and ideologically, in that they are populists claiming to speak on behalf of the people. Yet they are also *far away* because they are the Chosen ones, the Saviours who will redeem the people. This aura—Benjamin also tells us—is not inherent in them, but an artificial construct. Hitler and Trump fake their uniqueness.[30]

The question we have to answer is: how exactly did Hitler and Trump create this awe-inspiring image of themselves? How were they able to appear both like all of us and unlike any of us? What were the stratagems they employed, and what personal skills enabled to them to carry off such a massive confidence trick?

Of course, the two men were not merely propagandists. They wielded real power and took decisions with real-world consequences. Hitler moreover, unlike Trump, quickly built up a nation-wide terror machine after he had become Chancellor in 1933. He started a world war and instigated the Holocaust. Yet neither man would have been able to do what he did without his make-believe aura.

Confidence Artists

It is perhaps no coincidence that Hitler's favourite writer was Karl May (1842–1912).[31] One of the most widely read and most widely translated German-language authors of all time, May specialized in adventure stories. His novels are set in exotic far-away places, most notably the American Wild West. Yet they were written and read in a rapidly industrializing and increasingly bureaucratic society. Within this challengingly complex real-world context, they offered reassuringly simple fantasies akin to the political fantasies put forward by populist leaders then and later.

May's fictional world is thoroughly black-and-white. The good guys are under attack from a small but powerful clique of bad guys, who are after money, influence, and status. It is their selfish individualism, moderated only by strategic alliances and nepotism, that threatens to tear the community apart. Fortunately, they can be stopped. Not by the people of good will alone, who themselves are insufficiently powerful against the forces of evil, but by the hero of the story, who takes up the cudgels for right and justice. Such heroes are the focus of May's novels: men like Old Shatterhand in the Wild West series who are not just better scouts and better shots than any other cowboy or "Indian", but superior beings altogether—Heroes and Leaders unlike the world has ever seen.

Much of Karl May's success rested on his claim that his novels were based on a true story—his own.[32] The conceit was that *he* was Old Shatterhand. In reality, May had never even set foot on American soil.[33] What he *had* seen was the inside of a prison cell, or rather several prison cells. He was a convicted thief and fraudster who at various times had impersonated a police officer, a medical doctor, and a seminary teacher.

But he was also a marketing genius who managed to sell millions of Germans on his fake biography.

He had himself photographed in "Old Shatterhand's" cowboy outfit; he showed off the hero's famous *Bärentöter*—or Bear Killer—rifle; and he christened the villa he acquired in 1896 *Villa Shatterhand*. Other marketing tricks included a new generic name for his books (the initial *travel novels* was replaced by *travel stories*) and an autobiographical sketch emphasizing the authentic nature of his fiction. On his lecture tours throughout the German-speaking world, he played the role of the fearless adventurer to perfection. Even the Austrian royal family was taken in.

Hitler attended one of Karl May's lectures in Vienna in March 1912. By then, the author's real biography was widely known. Hitler was unconcerned. During a discussion at the hostel where he was living at the time, he praised May as "a 'magnificent, perfect human being, since he was absolutely singular at describing countries and people from the most remote continents truthfully'. When his colleagues argued that May had never seen the scenes of his novels, Hitler responded 'that this spoke even more in favor of May's genius, because his descriptions are true to nature, and much more realistic than those of all other explorers and travelers'".[34] The statement shows that already early on Hitler preferred narrative truth over factual truth—a topic to which I will return in the final chapter.

The Führer never lost his admiration for the creator of Old Shatterhand. His press secretary, Otto Dietrich, recalled that during the first years of his Chancellorship Hitler re-read "all the volumes of Karl May's Indian tales".[35] In later years, Hitler repeatedly criticized the "timidity" of his generals, who "had not read enough Karl May".[36]

Ideologically, Karl May's influence on Hitler was limited. Indeed, his Vienna lecture was a defence of pacifism, and he rejected anti-Semitism. What resonated with Hitler, we may assume, was the reductive simplicity of May's fiction: the black-and-white vision of society; the identification of complex social ills with the evil actions of concrete individuals; and the exaltation of heroic saviours. Unconsciously, Hitler may also have been attracted to Karl May the confidence artist—the ordinary man who through one-upmanship and the cunning deployment of narrative truth becomes an extraordinary "hero".

Make-believe, then, becomes an instrument of self-glorification. Yet things do not end there. More often than not, deceit turns into self-deceit.[37] At some point, confidence artists start to believe that they actually are superior human beings, if only because their lies are being believed. This generates a strange ambivalence on the part of leaders such as Hitler and Trump. On the one hand, they know full well that the image they project is fake and that they are not the heroes they pretend to be. On the other hand, their very success shows them that they *are* special. As a result, they start to believe their own press.

Finally, the audience are not being robbed or cheated in any straightforward way. They, too, get something out of the trick, which is in essence a transaction. They are given, not merely a dream, but the *power to dream*. The trick works so well because it is enabling, liberating. It shows us that there is a way out of our miserable lives, or at least makes us believe so. In the case of literary fiction, the loss of belief is unproblematic. We just close the book, or we abandon the author altogether. With political beliefs, the awakening tends to be of a ruder sort.

Acting and Role-Playing

Hitler—like Trump, as we will see—possessed all the qualities of a master con artist. To begin with, he had impressive acting skills. Indeed, "[i]n an unguarded moment"—former Reich Finance Minister Lutz Schwerin von Krosigk wrote shortly after the war—he "called himself the greatest actor in Europe".[38] He could imitate voices, accents, and even the sounds of different types of artillery to perfection, and he was a gifted mimic of mannerisms.[39] A former secretary recalled how "he would pretend he was seated at a machine ready to type. He would flex his imaginary sheet of paper, straighten it up carefully, adjust the platen with the knob at the side and then, to the laughter of the onlookers, begin typing with his forefingers, not forgetting to use the carriage lever, space bar and upper case keys as the occasion demanded. He aped the movements so accurately that no professional mime could have done it better".[40]

Most of Hitler's subordinates only saw the entertainment dimension of his "thespian skills",[41] as when he parodied their colleagues (usually in

1 Self-Staging: Aura and Appearance   11

their absence) or world leaders such as Mussolini. On occasion, they would catch glimpses of his political play-acting. Schwerin von Krosigk, for instance, describes how the Führer, almost with tears in his eyes, implored Hjalmar Schacht not to resign as Reich Economics Minister. The moment Schacht had exited the room and closed the door behind him, not a trace was left of Hitler's emotional pain.[42] Yet I doubt whether even the Führer's closest collaborators were aware of the full extent of his chameleon-like character. Certainly, the wider public was not.

What those in Hitler's immediate environment did see was his fundamental mendacity. Yet few, if any, appear to have believed he could be untruthful to *them*. That insight was reserved for outside observers, such as foreign diplomats, though even they usually found out too late. Thus, André François-Poncet, who in the 1930s was the French Ambassador to Germany, remarked in his memoirs that Hitler was capable of uttering complete falsehoods "with an expression of perfect sincerity on his face".[43] Retrospectively, Schwerin von Krosigk, too, observed that the Führer "wasn't even honest towards his most intimate confidants".[44] The overwhelming impression that Hitler's collaborators retained of their boss, however, was that he was an enigma. He "was a master of the art of concealing his intentions", his photographer Heinrich Hoffmann wrote in 1955, and "not for the outside world alone, but also for this immediate entourage".[45] Towards the end of his twenty-year confinement in Spandau Prison, Albert Speer tried to sum up his view of the Führer:

> Recently, in these days full of memories, I have considered how I would probably characterize Hitler today, after the passage of twenty years. I think I am now less sure than I ever was. All reflection magnifies the difficulties, makes him the more incomprehensible. Of course I have no doubts at all about the judgment of history. But I would not know how to describe the man himself. No doubt I could say that he was cruel, unjust, unapproachable, cold, capricious, self-pitying, and vulgar; and in fact he was all of those things. But at the same time he was also the exact opposite of almost all these things. He could be a solicitous paterfamilias, a generous superior, amiable, self-controlled, proud, and capable of enthusiasm for beauty and greatness. I can think of only two concepts that include all his character traits and that are the common denominator of all those many contradictory

aspects: opaqueness and dishonesty. Today, in retrospect, I am completely uncertain when and where he was ever really himself, his image not distorted by playacting, tactical considerations, joy in lying. I could not even say what his feeling toward me actually was—whether he really liked me or merely thought how useful I could be to him.[46]

In his memoirs, Speer highlights "Hitler's remarkable duplicity—indeed, 'multiplicity' would be a better word".[47] Many other former Nazis likewise recalled the Führer's sphinx-like nature. This fundamental impenetrability was an essential element in Hitler's calculated combination of proximity and distance. Just as God is ineffable to the community of believers, so Hitler was beyond comprehension to his *Volk*. You could see and occasionally even touch the Führer, but somehow he remained forever beyond your grasp. This was his Benjaminian aura: he was, or rather he ensured that he came across as, the *unique appearance of a distance, however close it may be*.

Hitler understood that he had to keep up this appearance at any place and at any time. The one thing he could not do was let people see behind the façade. Whatever emotion he was feigning, whatever lie he was telling, he knew he had to be the Führer. That was the one role he could not surrender, the mask he could not take off.

Similarly, Trump was always playing "Trump", selling himself as much as, or even more than, his properties or his policies. That is why he, too, ultimately remained an enigma. As Michael D'Antonio puts it in the postscript to his biography *The Truth about Trump*: "Anyone who tried to grasp the 'real' Trump was likely to fail. As the ninety-two-year-old doyenne of gossip Liz Smith tells me, 'I've known him forever, and I can't figure him out'".[48] In D'Antonio's words, Trump is "Trump the spectacle"; in the words of another biographer, he is "Trump the greatest show on earth".[49]

Trump was well aware of the theatrical dimension of his persona. "The show is Trump", he once said in an interview, adding with characteristic display of confidence that "it is sold-out performances everywhere".[50] In another interview he confessed candidly that for him the only way to get ahead was "to think of yourself as a one-man show".[51] Key to the success of this self-staging was his performative prowess "grounded"—as Timothy

1 Self-Staging: Aura and Appearance 13

L. O'Brien puts it—"in an actor's disciplined ability to always hit his mark, on cue, and an unwavering commitment to staying on message".[52]

This gift for make-believe was accompanied by an astounding ability to be economical with the truth, be it in the form of "truthful hyperbole" (as shameless exaggeration is famously called in Trump's *The Art of the Deal*),[53] hot air, or outright mendacity. For Trump, the use of factual inaccuracies was just another instrument in his public-relations toolkit. "He lied strategically. He had a complete lack of conscience about it", Tony Schwartz, who co-authored (or authored) *The Art of the Deal*, recalled in 2016.[54] As far as one can tell, Trump was not even particularly truthful vis-à-vis his closest collaborators: both his economic adviser Gary Cohn and his lawyer John Dowd thought him simply "a liar" (Cohn added the adjective "professional", Dowd used a stronger word).[55] Chief political strategist Steve Bannon, for his part, "often recounted, with continuing astonishment, the many times the president 'looked me in the eye and lied', and how he invariably did this with maximal sangfroid and aplomb".[56]

In order to be "Trump", Trump fostered an auratic combination of proximity and distance. Unlike many other celebrities, he did not act as a diva. When still a businessman, he was surprisingly approachable. Reporters had no trouble making appointments with him, and ordinary people found him easy to talk to. While he did not like to shake hands— like Hitler, Trump was a germophobe—there was no standoffishness, no condescension. As President, he was inevitably less accessible to the general public, but he retained his deliberately anti-elitist attitude. Staff possessed much easier access to the Oval Office than had been the case with previous Presidents, and he was keen to be seen with "the people", giving his followers the opportunity to take selfies whenever security permitted. Nor did he abandon his plain-fare culinary habits ("I was doing all kinds of beautiful sauces", his first wife, Ivana, once said with some regret, "but Donald eats only steaks and potatoes, so I gave up").[57] Indeed, instead of hiding his predilection for junk food, he flaunted it.

Yet Trump also ensured he was not viewed as just any business leader or President. He was unique, he was Trump. As such, he consistently demanded respect, subordination, and adulation—that is to say, hero-worship. His multiple residences all aimed to inspire awe. Replete with gold and other garish symbols of wealth and power, they were of shocking grandiosity. Before becoming "Mr President", he insisted on being called "Mr Trump", regardless of how long his interlocutors had known him. Even the irreverent Steve Bannon addressed him in this way.[58]

Except when playing golf, Trump almost always wore a jacket and tie. When in August 2014 he took the Ice Bucket Challenge, he was in a suit; and when in February 2017 the *New York Times* published a story claiming he watched television in his bathrobe, he was livid.[59] The newspaper painted a picture of a White House in total disarray, with confused policy-making followed by chaotic implementation processes accompanied by staff infighting, yet the President zoomed in on the mention of his sartorial appearance. The depiction of "Trump" in a bathrobe, he must have felt, had literally exposed him, revealing him as a weak old man—a mere mortal. Through his press secretary Sean Spicer, he informed an incredulous world that he did not wear bathrobes and did not even own such a garment.

Strongman Benito Mussolini regularly appeared in public settings partially disrobed, showing off his physique as a well-built swimmer, a bare-chested muscle man threshing grain, and so on.[60] Hitler, by contrast, made sure he was never seen *sans* suit or uniform. To be anything but fully clothed in public would have drawn too much attention to his corporality: it would have destroyed his auratic transcendence. Moreover, the kind of macho image projected by Mussolini could too easily be mocked. Hitler was well aware of the significant reputational damage that two of the Weimar Republic's most senior politicians—President Friedrich Ebert and Armed Forces Minister Gustav Noske—had suffered when the *Berliner Illustrirte Zeitung* published a photograph of the two men in their bathing suits.

Trump, too, avoided the Mussolini approach. Writer and actress Jenn Hoffman, who was a contestant on season six of *The Apprentice*, recalled the occasion when the candidates went to the beach, all of them wearing beach clothes. Trump was in a suit and tie. "He takes off his shoes and his socks, and he's balancing kind of awkwardly. Then he notices that we're watching him. Sheepish is too strong a word, but he says almost bashfully, 'You can tell I'm not a beach guy'. It wasn't his usual bravado, leaning into it. It was a little quieter, like he got caught being awkward, vulnerable for a second".⁶¹ An Emperor without clothes—both Hitler and Trump realized—is an Emperor without authority.

Charm, Calm, and Fake Anger

Playing a role convincingly and consistently requires enormous self-control. This is not a quality we associate with Hitler or Trump. Hitler in particular we tend to picture as a loose cannon and a raving lunatic. The reasons for this are to be found partly in his public oratory (which I will explore in the final chapter) and partly in his bouts of rage—which, however, were almost invariably faked, as will become clear. We are also understandably disinclined to ascribe to Hitler any qualities we usually view as positive. For fear of glorifying him, we prefer to see the man as crazy rather than cunning, short-fused rather than strategic. In doing so, we fall into the very trap that so many of his contemporaries walked into: that of underestimating him.

Albert Speer addresses this issue in his Spandau diaries: "I get the impression that people are increasingly representing Hitler as a dictator given to raging uncontrollably and biting the rug even on slight pretexts. This seems to me a false and dangerous course. If the human features are going to be missing from the portrait of Hitler, if his persuasiveness, his engaging characteristics, and even the Austrian charm he could trot out are left out of the reckoning, no faithful picture of him will be achieved. Certainly the generals in particular were not overwhelmed by a despotic force for a whole decade; they obeyed a commanding personality who frequently argued on the basis of cogent reasoning".⁶²

Speer's final point makes good sense and applies not just to Hitler's generals, but to all top Nazis. Göring and Goebbels, for example, were very evil people, but they were also extremely gifted and ambitious. Göring was a supremely confident, sharply intelligent, and highly decorated fighter pilot who in the First World War had shot down over twenty enemy aircraft, while Goebbels was a propaganda genius with a PhD to boot.⁶³ Yet both men not only subordinated themselves to Hitler—they venerated him. If Hitler had not possessed a very particular skill set, they would not have accepted the authority of this otherwise undistinguished leader, who was neither an aristocrat, nor an experienced politician, nor an officer (let alone a high-ranking one) and who had no university education.

This point, which goes to the heart of Hitler's success (if one can use that word), is arguably the most commonly misunderstood aspect of his leadership. Let us therefore dwell on it a little longer. Albert Speer was by no means the only one to highlight Hitler's self-control. The Führer's secretary Christa Schroeder likewise stressed his "astonishing self-mastery".[64] Her memoirs recount how "to the end he remained master of his emotions. Should bad news arrive during a private conversation the only clue would be a movement of his jaw and he would carry on calmly".[65] For his part, Hitler's valet Heinz Linge—no frail old man, but a sturdy SS officer—describes the scene following the assassination attempt of 20 July 1944 (dramatized in the 2008 film *Valkyrie* with Tom Cruise): "As I was running to Hitler's bunker, Major von Freyend […] came up at the trot. He was greatly distressed, blood running down his face. Horrified I asked what had happened. He gasped: 'The Führer is alive and is in the small dining room of the bunker'. When I got there Hitler looked at me questioningly with great eyes and noticed my concerned expression. With a calm smile he said: 'Linge, somebody tried to kill me'. His uniform was in ribbons. His hair was singed and hung down in strands. My knees were trembling, but he acted as though nothing had happened".[66] Hitler knew he could not *not* act the Führer. This was perhaps the main reason why he drank hardly any alcohol: he could not afford to lose control.[67]

No one so self-possessed gives in to anger at the slightest provocation, and indeed Hitler did not. The Führer's hysterical outbursts tended to be "carefully staged", as Albert Speer puts it.[68] Albert Krebs—who for a short while was *Gauleiter*, or district leader, of Hamburg, but fell out with the Nazi leadership in 1932—makes the same observation:

> In my presence Hitler never bit the carpet either literally of metaphorically. […] On the other hand he once cursed and raged like a whirling dervish before an assemblage of Hamburg political leaders […] The spittle literally dribbled out of the corners of Hitler's mouth over his jerking chin. But even on this occasion one cannot speak of an actual pathological attack of

rage. A person truly trembling with fury loses control over speech; he can only stammer and spew out words without clearly intelligible connections. Hitler, on the contrary, never for a moment interrupted the best form of propaganda and psychological mass manipulation in his exhortation, though this must have demanded strong mental concentration. I believe that in this instance, too, Hitler was playing the role of a furious thunderbolt-hurling Wotan, rather than that he was driven into fury by bitter disappointment over a defeat of rather customary dimensions.[69]

More often, however, the Führer turned on the charm. He seemed able to endear himself to anyone from ordinary folk to millionaire industrialists and celebrities. Many who had negative preconceptions of him, based either on his public speaking or on stories they had heard, came away with an entirely different impression of him.[70] Of course, none of it was real. Hitler was forever selling his strongest asset—himself. To cite once more Albert Krebs: "He would run down the steps of the Brown House [the Nazi headquarters in Munich] to grasp Count Ernst zu Reventlow's hands in both of his and greet him with 'My dear Count!' while his voice tremoloed with benevolent friendship. Everyone watching this knew that Hitler's true feelings toward the Count had nothing to do with dear benevolence. He wept tears before the mutinous SA men in the Veterans' Hall in Berlin to lead them back to obedient loyalty. He could be a charming conversationalist who kissed the ladies' hands, a friendly uncle who gave children chocolates, a folksy fellow who shook the calloused hands of workingmen and peasants".[71]

Absolutism

A key feature of auratic leaders is that they are always right. Mere mortals reflect and ponder, the Leader knows. They hesitate and vacillate, the Leader is certain. They go back on their decisions, the Leader remains firm.

Such display of undeviating confidence is extraordinarily difficult to carry off. However hard auratic leaders may pretend to be semi-divine superhumans, they are not. All leaders, auratic or not, have doubts, procrastinate, and despair for shorter or longer periods. Hitler and Trump were no exceptions. Their strength lay in their peculiar ability to feign certainty. Each of them managed to convince his followers that he was their rock—the rock on which all criticisms would crack and all attacks would shatter.

Here, they were helped by their fundamentally narcissistic natures. Narcissism in the technical sense is not merely an unhealthy love of self, or a desire to be the centre of attention. It also involves the tendency to take oneself as the yardstick of all experience and evaluation. Narcissism is therefore as a rule accompanied by *dogmatism* as regards one's own views and *intolerance* as regards the views of other people. In a normal context, these are not positive qualities. In the context of political populism, as attributes of auratic leaders, they are signs of strength. This is why—as Laurence Rees puts it—the young Hitler's "ignorant slogan shouting in 1913", before Germany's humiliating military defeat in the First World War and its subsequent social upheaval, "would later be seen as certainty of vision".[72] His youthful "over-confidence would be perceived as a mark of genius", his intolerance as strength of character.[73]

The auratic leader's followers are looking for certainty in uncertain times, for stability in a world in flux. They yearn for *terra firma*, and the Leader creates it, or so they believe. This is the power of the aura: the belief that the Leader knows what is right and acts accordingly. When, in 1932, Hitler rejected the offer to become "merely" Vice-Chancellor, Joseph Goebbels wrote in his diary: "The Führer is very certain of victory. […] That's how I love him most".[74] And after his boss had secured the Chancellorship: "Hitler is tremendously self-assured. Once again, he has been proved right in everything".[75]

This does not mean that the auratic leader's followers never doubt him. Even true believers have crises of faith. The mark of successful leader-conmen is their ability to dispel such doubts, either through real-world results or through persuasion. Thus, most people in Hitler's entourage (let alone the population at large) did not want to go to war in 1939. It was only Germany's rapid early victories that convinced them. Others, such as Albert Speer, allowed themselves to be persuaded: "Any doubts I might have had were quelled by the self-assurance Hitler showed. In those days he seemed to me like a hero of ancient myth who unhesitatingly, in full consciousness of his strength, could enter and meet the test of the wildest undertakings".⁷⁶ According to press secretary Otto Dietrich, even when things were going seriously wrong the magic often still worked. "During the last years of the war many persons came to him beset by doubts; they left him inwardly strengthened and in spite of everything filled with new faith".⁷⁷

There is a particular danger in this kind of absolutism. Not only is it literally inhuman—people are not God—it also gets worse over time. The more a leader like Hitler or Trump believes in himself, the more his followers believe in him. The more his followers believe in him, the stronger the leader's public image becomes. And the stronger the image becomes, the more disinclined the leader will be to compromise. This is why successful auratic leaders become increasingly intransigent.

The auratic nature of Hitler's and Trump's authority also explains why they are by definition unable to pivot to the centre. When a number of conservative politicians decided to help Hitler become Chancellor, they did so in the expectation of containing him. Within a more traditional political framework—they thought—Hitler would automatically become more normal and hence more malleable. The Republican Party appears to have harboured similar illusions about Trump. But auratic leaders cannot thrive, and know they cannot thrive, as ordinary politicians. Their aura requires absolutism; their extraordinariness, extremism. Hence, there was never going to be a democratic Adolf Hitler. If you take away his so-called omniscience and omnipotence, as well as his ruthlessness and anti-Semitism, what is left is not a charismatic democratic politician. What is left is a mediocre painter with no charisma whatsoever. By the same token, Trump could not be both charismatic and centrist. A conventional Trump would not be Trump, but a run-of-the-mill businessman.

Real and Fake Expertise

Acting was the central skill that Hitler possessed as a con artist, but it was not the only one. By all accounts, he had a phenomenal memory. He was able to recall the minutest details of conversations he had had, of rallies at which he had spoken, and even of operas, theatre plays, and films he had seen. His secretary Christa Schroeder describes how he could not only remember the names of people he had encountered years before, but also "exactly the time, place and circumstances under which he had met a person".[78] He was equally strong on technological details and numerical data, impressing experts such as his architect Albert Speer and Finance Minister Lutz Schwerin von Krosigk.[79]

In addition, Hitler possessed a vast knowledge of ships, aircraft, cars, and weaponry, as well as all kinds of military equipment. He was able to summarize long and complex discussions concisely, going straight to the heart of the problem. He was also an accomplished speed reader. Not least, he could size people up quickly and he displayed an almost animalistic instinct to detect fear in a person.

Though these were real skills, the Führer was not above magnifying people's perception of them through a variety of tricks. He would prepare conversations carefully by reading up on the relevant subjects beforehand, and then deliver his knowledge as if it were part of his general education.[80] He would pass off other people's ideas as his own. Equally shamelessly, he would, in true Karl May fashion, describe "from personal experience" all manner of things he had never actually seen. Finally, like many confidence artists, Hitler had the ability to predict the future—after the fact, of course. In November 1939, for example, he escaped an assassination attempt in Munich's Bürgerbräu beer hall because he left the building early. "I had a most extraordinary feeling", he later told Heinrich Hoffmann, "and I don't myself know how or why—but I felt compelled to leave the cellar just as quickly as I could".[81] Hoffmann appears to have taken this "moment of inexplicable intuition"[82] at face value, but there was nothing clairvoyant about Hitler's departure. The decision to return to Berlin by train instead of plane, and hence earlier than planned, had been taken because of bad weather and well before the meeting started.[83]

Like Hitler, Trump had all the skills of a master conman. He never vacillated, at least not in public. Whatever spot he found himself in, he invariably displayed complete certainty. Accusations of adultery, however credible, suspicions of illegal behaviour, however numerous, political investigations, however threatening—nothing seemed to shake him. The journalist Michael Wolff, author of *Fire and Fury* and other books about the Trump administration, has provided the best characterization of this:

The truth would not be shaken loose from him. You could count on him: no matter what the circumstances, Trump would never be beaten into submission. It was his word against, sometimes, everybody else's, but it was his word and he would not waver from it. [...] Very little about him was real, and yet he managed to be at least halfway believed by enough people so that he could continue the con. This was where he really shone: he always stayed in character. When a person who is the target of multiple investigations remains outwardly untroubled, the effect is quite extraordinary. [...] And he carried the total confidence and even serenity of the innocent. [...] "I always win", he frequently declared. "I know how to handle it". Or, another favorite: "I never blink".[84]

Trump's skill set stretched well beyond this apparent sang-froid. He had an extraordinarily retentive memory for both figures and people. *The Apprentice* contestant Omarosa Manigault Newman recalled how Trump always "had a full grasp of the rules and parameters of each task. He knew each of our names and performance histories, show by show".[85] When "there had been a mix-up on one of the episodes where a contestant lost money on the task, [...] Trump repeated a lengthy numbers sequence with no notes in front of him, calculated them in his head in moments, and came to the conclusion that the math-addled contestant should be fired".[86] *Celebrity Apprentice*'s Eden Gaha was likewise struck by Trump's mental acuity and recall: "He could look at a task-sheet for maybe a minute and almost word for word perfectly deliver it in one take".[87]

Trump also possessed a confidence artist's sense of other people's pressure points. "He sizes up people as well as I've ever seen anyone do within three or five seconds", one of his early public-relations managers told business-guru biographer Robert Slater.[88] In Omarosa's words, "Donald Trump was uncannily intuitive and extremely perceptive. He seemed to be able to sense when certain individuals were susceptible to being influenced by his power and abiding by his loyalty demands".[89] Moreover, he could be incredibly charming if the occasion required it. "He could talk to you, and I saw him do it, to famous and important people", Trump's former project manager Blanche Sprague recalled, "and these people felt like they were the only person in the world. It was like he hypnotized them. [...] I don't know how he did it, and I never saw anybody replicate it".[90]

Even the most critical journalists acknowledge that "in person he could seem almost soothing", appearing "charming and full of flattery".[91] They also point out that much of it was transactional: "When he needed help, he could be extraordinarily attentive, but when he did not need anything he had little warmth to spare".[92] Ultimately, it would seem, Trump's likeability was really his ability "to turn on the charm"[93] if and when it was in his interest.

Trump was a one-take actor in real life as well as on television.[94] As Robert Slater presciently put it in 2005: "To understand how Donald Trump functions [...], one should think of him not necessarily as an entertainer, but rather as someone with the skills of an entertainer. Neither he nor some of those who work with him on *The Apprentice* like to hear him described as an actor, perhaps because to do so might appear to denigrate his business acumen. Yet he certainly employs the same skills of an entertainer—especially an actor—and he gets very far with those skills".[95] People close to him suspected that even his frequent inconsistencies and occasional manifestations of wackiness were often carefully staged to throw his opponents off guard or create strategic ambiguity.[96] Certainly many of his outbursts of anger were a way of "playing people", as Tony Schwartz puts it: "Trump would flatter, bully, and occasionally get mad, but always in a calculated way".[97] Two examples may suffice. On one occasion in the early 2000s—Robert Slater recounts—Trump decided to inspect the construction of one of his properties.

> The project manager stood outside the front door, waiting to greet the boss. As he approached his man on the spot, Trump noticed a fault in the construction of the sidewalk surrounding the front door. [...] "I can't believe you approved this", he shouted like a parent scolding a child. "You think I'm going to pay for this fuckin' job? This is supposed to be one solid piece of granite. Who gave out the job? [...] This is the worst job I've ever seen. Go find out the name of the contractor". [...] Walking into the elevator, Trump confided to someone tagging along on the visit that his attack on the project manager was "mostly an act, but I *did* feel that way. It was a

terrible job". Then, as if removing himself from the scene and offering some instant analysis, he suggested, "That's the way I get things done".[98]

When running for President, Trump used a similar ploy to test prospective communications director Jason Miller. The journalist Tim Alberta describes the scene in his book *American Carnage*:

> "You just came over from [Presidential candidate Ted] Cruz? I guess you want to join the winning team, right?" Trump said. "Ted is a little nasty. Sometimes he's nice". Miller didn't speak. "Let's see where your loyalties lie", Trump continued. "Tell me something negative about Ted. Give me some dirt". "I can't do that", Miller replied. "No?" Trump said. "C'mon. You have to give me something". Miller still refused. After two more rounds of this, Trump abruptly turned angry. "OK, I'm not fucking around anymore", he told Miller. "Give me something on Cruz or you're outta here". The room went silent. The assembled cast [...] wore concerned looks. Miller sat speechless, expecting to see security coming for him at any moment. Then Trump broke into a grin. "Right answer!"[99]

Trump developed his ability to play-act early on and retained it his entire life. The one thing he was always capable of was projecting an image, regardless of the circumstances he found himself in. This ability was underpinned by his remarkable self-control, one of his most important—and most often overlooked—attributes. We tend to view Trump (like Hitler) as a loose cannon; in doing so, we ignore Trump's (and Hitler's) calculating nature.

As Gwenda Blair reports, when Trump was in college and "on the squash team, where players were often tardy and had tantrums when they lost, Donald was never late and never had a meltdown".[100] Decades later, when he was billions in debt and his business empire was on the verge of collapse, Trump remained equally calm. "When he said the usual pleasantries, the good-to-see-yous and glad-to-be-heres, he meant them [or appeared to mean them, anyway; HdB] and when he sat down with the bankers and lawyers, he was [a] model of decorum".[101] Where most other businesspeople would have succumbed to stress or panic and thrown in the towel, the future President "showed up every morning at eight a.m. ...

tie tied, suit pressed, focused, and moving forward, and asking, 'What do we do now?'"[102]

Trump carried these skills over into the political arena. This remained hidden, because his spiel was, precisely, to play the anti-establishment berserker. But he was not losing it—he was play-acting. In private, he effortlessly employed a different style. It was the same with off-camera interviews. When he spoke with *The Washington Post*'s Michael Kranish and Marc Fisher, for instance, his voice was calm, even gentle, while "his sentences grew longer and more complex than they'd been in debates or TV appearances".[103] He "never sounded angry", and "[h]is face didn't turn red".[104]

It is these attributes that convinced so many of the people working for Trump that he was their man. Even the ones who ultimately came to the conclusion that he was not suitable to be President could not help but admire his never-die attitude. Trump may have "operated almost entirely off of gut instinct", his former Special Assistant Cliff Sims writes in *Team of Vipers*, yet "he was also the most methodical, patient person I've ever seen in the midst of a crisis—the eye of the storm. And you could bet every penny you had that he was going to get up and go to work the next morning".[105] His political opponents, by contrast, discerned neither Trump's skills nor his underlying resilience—a fatal mistake.

Theatre and Politics

Hitler's and Trump's conmen skill sets played a central role in their unceasing and strikingly successful endeavours to build up and foster a Benjaminian aura. They also possessed the requisite *experience* to play the auratic leader. Of course, it would be anachronistic to view their pre-political life as conscious preparation for the role of "people's politician". But it did provide them with significant insights into the relation between politics, entertainment, and spectacle—insights they would exploit in their political careers.

Retrospectively, then, one can say that Hitler's political apprenticeship began with watching Wagner operas.[106] At a time when television was non-existent and large-scale film viewing just a blip on the horizon,

1 Self-Staging: Aura and Appearance 25

Wagnerian music-theatre provided the future Führer with an understanding of how politics might be conducted—that is to say, populistically abused—in the context of modern mass culture.

Already in his teens, when he was still living in the Austrian city of Linz, Hitler was a fanatical admirer of the German composer. A friend from these early years, August Kubizek, later recalled Hitler's unbounded enthusiasm following a performance of Wagner's *Rienzi*—the story of an ordinary man in medieval Rome who becomes the people's tribune—in Linz's regional theatre some time in 1905. In "a state of complete ecstasy and rapture", the young Adolf "conjured up in grandiose, inspiring pictures his own future and that of his people".[107] Whatever the exact truth of this image, which looks suspiciously like an instance of backward projection, there can be no doubt about Hitler's passionate love for Wagner.[108]

In the years between 1906 and 1913, spent largely in Vienna, Hitler deepened his understanding of the performative aspects of Wagner's operas. Having failed the entrance examination to the Viennese Academy of Fine Arts, he made a living selling home-drawn postcard pictures, and occasionally larger watercolours, of the city's famous buildings.[109] A fair proportion of his income was spent on visits to opera houses as well as to theatres and art galleries.

Hitler was particularly impressed by the work of the Court Opera's internationally renowned stage director-cum-designer, Alfred Roller.[110] In contrast to the traditional, music-focused, Wagner productions of the era, Roller put a strong emphasis on the use of light, colour, and other stage effects, turning the maestro's operas into visual as well as auditory spectacles. Again and again, the young Hitler attended Wagner's music-dramas staged by Roller, while also reading up on the history of theatre and opera production. The result was a thorough familiarity with the secrets of stage design. Albert Speer recalls in his Spandau diaries how Hitler the politician would surprise his fellow National Socialists with his "amazing knowledge of stagecraft, his interest in the diameter of revolving stages, lift mechanisms, and especially different lighting techniques".[111] This knowledge—the historian Brigitte Hamann observes—"clearly influenced the stage-productionlike Nuremberg [Nazi] party conventions and the most varied celebrations and hours of commemoration. Speer's 'domes of light' [at each annual Party rally in the latter half of the 1930s, a massive number of anti-aircraft searchlights pointing upwards produced a *Lichtdom*, or Cathedral of Light] were to continue Roller's 'direction of light'. The sea of red flags, the marching up during the roll of drums and music by Wagner, preferably in darkness, when it was easier to put an audience in a solemn, emotionally charged mood: all this was as if in a perfectly staged Wagner opera, with the Reich chancellor's entrance and speech as the big climax".[112]

The cultural historian Frederic Spotts likewise highlights the relation between Hitler's early encounter with Roller's staging of Wagner and the Führer's later staging of his own appearances. Besides searchlights, among the Führer's "favourite devices was fire, which made figures, banners and flags shimmer in an eerie glow. [...] Torches, bonfires, Bengal lights, fireworks, flares, pyres, flames rising out of enormous braziers all produced a wondrous spell. It was for the sake of such fiery effects and the impact of nocturnal lighting that he saved his favourite ceremonies for night-time. [...] Hitler also calculated the effect of sounds and availed himself not just of music but of sirens, cannon salutes, rifle shots, fanfares, church bells and even the tread of boots and aircraft fly-pasts. [...] He arranged the build-up to his own appearances with the skill of a composer".[113]

For Hitler, then, Wagnerian opera meant more than a certain kind of music, or a certain kind of story. With hindsight, we can see that what he took away from Roller's productions was a practical understanding of the dynamics of large-scale public events, gaining an appreciation of the power of presentation and the mechanics of audience manipulation. We will explore the most famous example—the 1934 Nuremberg Party rally documented in the propaganda film *Triumph of the Will*—further below.

The insights that Hitler gained from his encounter with Wagner's operas stretched beyond what he learned from Roller. He also developed a sense of the entertainment potential, and hence the possible mass appeal, of traditionally elevated—or "tedious"—social activities. This sensibility would prove a massive political advantage in an era characterized by the rise of mass culture. Here, the Führer was far better equipped than establishment politicians, who clung to the performative practices of a bygone age, all the more so as he was not averse to helping himself from the public-relations tool kit of the one political group whose propaganda methods were also attuned to modern times—the communists.

Wagner's *Gesamtkunstwerke*—his "total works of art", which combine poetry, song, and theatre into all-encompassing music-dramas—are like the best Hollywood films. They do not merely aim to interest or engage, they strive to absorb the audience entirely. As the German historian Wolfram Pyta puts it in his masterful study of Hitlerism's *fundamentum in arte*, Wagnerian opera aims to "overwhelm the spectators completely by a comprehensive activation of all the senses so as to induce a state of total artistic intoxication".[114] Executed judiciously, this approach can lead to genuinely impressive artistic productions. Taken to extremes, it is likely to result in the victory of spectacle over art, creating events reminiscent less of art than of rave parties, in which critical appreciation is lost in the ecstasy of depersonalizing immersion.

The philosopher Friedrich Nietzsche was the first to draw attention to this danger. In *The Case of Wagner* (1888), written after his early adulation of the composer had given way to hostility, Nietzsche provides a devastating critique of what he sees as Wagner's pathological desire to psych up the audience and inflame their passions.[115] Wagner realized—Nietzsche says—how music can be used "to excite weary nerves".[116] He went down this route because he wanted to be popular, knowing that such music attracts large audiences and brings in money. Wagnerian opera is a way to achieve public acclaim: it reduces music to an attention-grabbing device. It represents the "over-all change of art into histrionics".[117]

For Nietzsche, then, the corruption of Wagner's art hand goes hand in hand with the corruption of Wagner the artist: "the musician becomes an actor, his art develops more and more as a talent to *lie*".[118] The key passage in *The Case of Wagner* reads as follows:

> You do not know who Wagner is: a first-rate actor. […] The actor Wagner is a tyrant; his pathos topples every taste, every resistance.—Who equals the persuasive power of these gestures? Who else envisages gestures with such assurance, so clearly from the start? The way Wagner's pathos holds its breath, refuses to let go an extreme feeling, achieves a terrifying *duration* of states when even a moment threatens to strangle us—Was Wagner a musician at all? At any rate, there was something else that he was more: namely, an incomparable *histrio* [actor], the greatest mime, the most amazing

genius of the theater ever among Germans, our *scenic artist par excellence*. […] Wagner was *not* a musician by instinct. He showed this by abandoning […] all style in music in order to turn it into what he required, theatrical rhetoric, a means of expression, of underscoring gestures, of suggestion, of the psychologically picturesque.[119]

Nietzsche therefore compares the composer to Cagliostro, the infamous eighteenth-century confidence trickster. Wagner takes us in by selling us on his counterfeit virtues and values—by "rattling about 'devotion', about 'loyalty', about 'purity'".[120] He convinces us because "he says something so often […] till one believes it".[121] He makes us feel good about ourselves because his music exalts us as much as it glorifies him. What Wagnerian opera "offers us is a magnifying glass: one looks through it, one does not trust one's own eyes—everything looks big, *even Wagner*".[122] And he has no need for logic or consistency. "What he envisages first is […] a scene that people—this he thinks through in depth, and […] the rest follows from this, in accordance with a technical economy that has no reasons for being subtle. […] With such a sense of the theater for one's guide, one is in no danger of unexpectedly creating [genuine] drama. Drama requires *rigorous* logic: but what did Wagner ever care about logic?"[123]

Against this backdrop, it is easy to see how the Führer could and would later benefit from his early familiarity with Wagner's artistic seduction techniques. In Wolfram Pyta's phrase, what Hitler learned from the maestro was how to be "a political performance artist".[124] He came to understand the importance of staging and self-staging, the power of spectacle, the allure of immersive events. He experienced people's desire to be ennobled and their willingness to abandon critical reflection. He found out about their need for true German ideals, and he learned how to fake those and inculcate them through repetition. Not least, he became aware of how emotion can overwhelm reason, and how irrelevant logic and consistency are in the context of mass persuasion.

There is one further thing we need to look at—Wagner's desire to overcome the social conflicts and divisions in modern German society. His ultimate aim was to create a sense of community through the medium of art. Transcending class antagonisms and regional differences, his music was to engender a feeling of togetherness among the members of the *Volk*, the German people sharing a common destiny. In the words of the literary scholar Lutz Koepnick, Wagnerian opera's "central task was nothing less than to emancipate individuals from the strictures of their private existences [...] so as to recuperate the foundations of meaningful communality".[125] Its goal was to replace the selfish *I* with a national *we*.

Hitler would translate this rather fanciful artistic project into a much more dangerous—and ultimately murderous—political one. As we will see in later chapters, National Socialism sought to appeal to people across the political spectrum. It was a container ideology, an eclectic mixture of nationalism, socialism, capitalism, racism, law and order, anti-elitism, hierarchism, meritocratic individualism, and reassuring collectivism. What held it all together was the myth of the *Volk* and their auratic Führer. Wagnerian opera provided the blueprint for the creation of this myth. It taught Hitler how to create a community based on emotion rather than reason, on fictional stories rather than factual needs, and on subjugation rather than solidarity.

Politics as Theatre

For Hitler, Vienna was more than Wagner alone. The city also brought him in direct contact with political populism, as well as with mere political chaos.[126] He often attended the sessions of the Austro-Hungarian parliament. With well over 500 seats, it was the largest assembly in Europe, consisting of around thirty parties representing multiple nationalities and ethnicities. One problem was that it had no common language—and no interpreters either. Members were allowed to use German, Italian, Czech, Polish, Ukrainian, Serbian, Croat, Slovenian, Romanian, or Russian. Another problem was that there existed no clear rules of procedure and no time limit to the speeches. There were rows and shouting matches, as well as endless procedural debates and filibusters. On one occasion, Czech nationalists blew whistles and small trumpets, with the parliament's president watching the scene through his binoculars, unable to stop them.

In *Mein Kampf*, Hitler gives a stylized description of his first visit to the assembly: "The intellectual content of what these men said was on a really depressing level, in so far as you could understand their babbling at all; for several of the gentlemen did not speak German, but their native Slavic languages or rather dialects. [...] A wild gesticulating mass screaming all at once in every different key, presided over by a good-natured old uncle who was striving in the sweat of his brow to revive the dignity of the House by violently ringing his bell and alternating gentle reproofs with grave admonitions. I couldn't help laughing".[127]

Hitler claims that it was this "lamentable comedy" that put him off parliamentarianism forever.[128] What seems certain is that it provided him with further insight into the way performance and entertainment can be used to create a populist politics. A contemporary source observed how popular it was to go and watch the assembly, because there the people of Vienna "attend an entertainment for free. The representatives personally 'jumping on' each other compensates the Viennese entirely for theater performances, which they would have to pay for after all if they wanted some entertainment. In Parliament they can have a grand time, 'by the grace of the representatives', and what they get out of it also gives them enough material to amuse their good friends for many an evening in the tavern".[129]

The fact that much of the debate was incomprehensible was actually an advantage to Hitler. It sharpened his sense of the "spectacular" dimension of political messaging. Of course, words are vitally important too in politics. But they are usually part of a larger event that is first and foremost visual in nature. Hence, if the overall optics are not good, the speaker has a serious problem. That is why today's media consultants often watch their clients on television with the sound turned off.[130]

The other instruction in the art of populism that Hitler received in Vienna was provided by Karl Lueger, the city's mayor and the cofounder and leader of the Christian Social Party. It was not Lueger's "programme of social reform, municipal renewal, populist democracy, and loyalty to the Habsburg monarchy all welded together by popular Catholicism"[131] that attracted the future Führer. This political platform he considered insufficiently pro-German and overly pro-Catholic. More consequential was Lueger's anti-Semitism, though even this aspect of the mayor's agenda Hitler would later criticize for being too moderate, "a sham anti-Semitism which was almost worse than none at all".[132] (This says more about Hitler than about Lueger, whose racism was actually quite repulsive.) Lueger's real impact, however, was as a practitioner of mass politics.

He was a brilliant speaker with an extremely strong popular appeal. In Brigitte Hamann's words, "Lueger liked to deliver his speeches in the native dialect, adjusted to the intellectual level of his audience, simplified everything that was complex, and spiced up his speeches with jokes. And he did what yielded the most votes: he attacked his voters' enemies and exacerbated their antipathies, not only against politicians but also against national and religious minorities, 'the rich up there', 'the mob down there', the 'nonbelievers' and the 'foreigners, who take away our women, apartments, work, etc.' He deliberately appealed to emotions and instincts rather than the intellect and critical faculties".[133]

In *Mein Kampf*, Hitler characterizes Lueger's approach by contrasting it with that of Georg von Schönerer's pan-German movement. The latter—he writes—was in the right ideologically, but proved unable to connect with the masses. Overestimating the average person's intelligence, it failed to put its message "in a form suited to the receptivity of the masses, which is and remains exceedingly limited".[134] Schönerer and his fellow pan-Germans were *de facto* elitists. "The only forum to which they really spoke consisted of five hundred parliamentarians".[135] In doing so, they ignored the power of the press and hence of propaganda. They did not understand that what they actually said "was quite unimportant; the important thing was what people read about them".[136]

Moreover—Hitler continues—rather than developing a new philosophy, the pan-German movement fell victim to the influence of "moderate bourgeois elements".[137] As a result, it remained stuck in "mere grumbling and criticizing"; and instead of a radical "faith bordering more or less on religion" arose "an effort gradually to grind off the edges of struggle by means of 'positive' collaboration; that is, in this case, by acceptance of the existing order".[138] In short, Schönerer surrendered to the establishment. Lueger, by contrast, realized that a new movement needs a base of hardcore followers. "He therefore laid the greatest stress in his political activity on winning over the classes whose existence was threatened and therefore tended to spur rather than paralyze the will to fight".[139] In this way, he "ensured himself of a following that was difficult to shake, whose spirit of sacrifice was as great as its fighting power".[140] At the same time, he managed, "with infinite shrewdness",[141] to win over the Catholic Church—a pillar of the establishment and a mainstay in the lives of the mass of the population.

The writer Felix Salten, author of the global bestsellers *Bambi* and the pornographic *Josefine Mutzenbacher*, has given an incisive description of Lueger's populist approach in his book *Das österreichische Antlitz* (The Face of Austria, 1909):

> He takes the Viennese people's fear away. Until then, they were berated. He commends them. The establishment demanded respect of them. He delivers them from all respect for the establishment. The establishment told them that only the educated should govern. He shows them how poorly the educated know how to govern. He, an educated man, a doctor [of law], a lawyer, rips into the doctors, tears the lawyers apart, berates the professors, and jeers at science. He surrenders everything that intimidates and confines the masses, he throws it down, stomps on it, laughing; and the cobblers, the tailors, the coachmen, the greengrocers and shopkeepers rejoice. They roar with enthusiasm and believe that the new age has begun as foretold in the words 'Blessed are the weak in spirit'. He validates Vienna's lower class in all its qualities, its lack of intellectual wants, its distrust of education, its tipsy silliness, its love of street songs, its adherence to the old-fashioned, its over-confident self-satisfaction; and they rave, they rave blissfully when he talks to them.[142]

Felix Salten also draws attention to another aspect of Lueger's populism—the mayor's ability to create a charismatic, or auratic, persona. Lueger played the people's tribune to perfection, with a commanding presence, "the best you can imagine for the role of demagogue".[143] Compared to him, "all previous mayors were nothing but plodding bit players".[144] Lueger was the star and he made sure everybody knew it. He employed a "monarchical technique"[145] to elevate himself above his citizens. "His picture is everywhere. In offices, in class rooms, in restaurants, in theatres, in shop windows. His face is as ubiquitous and familiar as that of the Emperor".[146] Lueger's public events, too, were as grand as that of Franz Joseph, with a massive entourage of deferential civil servants and priests in attendance and a band playing the *Lueger March*. And just as the name of the Emperor was on all state-owned buildings, so that of

Lueger was chiselled into all municipal buildings: *Built under Mayor Dr Karl Lueger*. In brief, Lueger ruled the city not just as a celebrity, but by creating and fostering a celebrity status. His aura—Salten tells us—was as much the cause as the result of his dominance.

Hitler learned as much from Lueger as he did from Wagner. It was only after the First World War, however, that he was able to prove his own suitability for the role of demagogue.

Propaganda

In May 1913, Hitler moved from Vienna to Munich, in the eyes of many the cultural capital of the German Empire. The move also enabled him to avoid the draft. Although born in Austria, Hitler felt German, or rather pan-German. He had no love for the Habsburg monarchy and no desire to serve in its army. In Munich, he continued his modest existence as a painter of postcard pictures and watercolours. His dreams of artistic greatness were not realized: he was competent, especially when it came to the drawing or painting of buildings, but not in any way original.

When the First World War broke out in August 1914, Hitler immediately enlisted in the Bavarian army, delighted with this opportunity to do his bit for the German cause. His Austrian citizenship posed no obstacle in the eyes of a military keen to sign up as many enthusiastic volunteers as possible. He served as a dispatch runner (a somewhat misleading term, as occasionally bicycles were used), carrying messages between command posts. While not a war hero like the flying ace Hermann Göring, Hitler was brave enough, earning first the Iron Cross Second Class and then the Iron Cross First Class. His fellow soldiers thought him a bit strange: Hitler hardly drank and did not visit brothels, preferring to spend his free time drawing or reading. Still, no one who knew him well appears to have disliked him, and he was on the whole well integrated.

The First World War provided Hitler with a sense of meaning and direction, perhaps even with a feeling of being at home in the world. Yet it was only the war's aftermath that put him on the path towards populist demagoguery. Strikingly, he took the first step on this road in a left-wing political context.

A few days before the armistice of 11 November 1918, the Bavarian monarchy of Ludwig III—part of the German Empire but possessing a number of special rights—gave way to a revolutionary republic led by Social Democrats and Independent Social Democrats. In April 1919, this socialist republic was supplanted by a workers' council republic (*Räterepublik*) of communists and anarchists, which ruthlessly eliminated any form of opposition until it was itself suppressed—even more ruthlessly—one month later by the national government using right-wing paramilitary units (*Freikorps*). Hitler cooperated as representative of his army unit first with the socialist regime and then with the communist *Räterepublik*. He very much wanted to remain in the army, and he combined a hatred of the old monarchical system with a vague sympathy for popular uprisings. Of course, this left-wing—or at the very least ideologically ambiguous—stage of his career did not fit his later, more heroically straightforward narrative of his political development. Accordingly, he always kept silent about his short-lived flirtation with the Left.

Among Hitler's duties as unit representative was propaganda: he was expected to inculcate the correct political attitude in his fellow soldiers. His skills in this area must have been apparent, because he was selected for a very similar function by the right-wing post-*Räterepublik* army leadership in Bavaria. This is not as odd as it may sound. For one thing, Hitler's political views—like those of many other people at this tumultuous time—were still in flux, and he was not perceived as a committed left-winger. For another, his German nationalism dovetailed with the counterrevolutionary regime's stance against international Bolshevism.[147]

Hitler was first ordered to take a set of instruction courses, which he did in July 1919, attending lectures on history, politics, and economics. They were and would remain his only formal education after secondary school, which he had left at the age of sixteen. He was particularly impressed with the ideas of the self-styled economics expert Gottfried Feder (1883–1941). Feder castigated finance capitalism—the world of the stock market, of financial speculation—as the greatest threat to social justice, glorifying instead the values of "honest work" in what is nowadays called the real economy. What is more, he saw this social antagonism in anti-Semitic terms—as the opposition between *Jewish rapacious capital* and *German productive capital*.[148] Hitler soaked up these ideas, which would become a cornerstone of the National Socialist world view.

Having completed his training, Hitler was sent to the army camp at Lechfeld, thirty miles west of Munich, to educate the soldiers stationed there in the proper political—nationalistic and anti-communist—cast of mind. In *Mein Kampf*, he describes this five-day period as an unqualified success,[149] but that is an exaggeration. The historian Thomas Weber points out that just as in "a preseason game in sports, in which a weak opponent has been picked so as to boost morale and self-confidence, Hitler and his fellow propagandists were asked to address only the most loyal and committed soldiers".[150] Still, to this audience Hitler was clearly "the star performer",[151] as Ian Kershaw puts it. In their reports, his listeners single Hitler out as by far the best speaker, praising his passion and folksy manner, the clear and concrete nature of his lectures, and the persuasiveness of his message.[152] If Lechfeld was not the propaganda sensation Hitler later claimed it was, it was nonetheless an important stage in his development as a demagogue.

Hitler had demonstrated his politico-rhetorical prowess, but he had not yet entered the political arena proper. This only happened as the result of another assignment. In September 1919, he was ordered to direct his attention to the German Workers' Party, or DAP (Deutsche Arbeiterpartei), a new right-wing extremist grouping founded by Anton Drexler and Karl Harrer. Its main features were patriotism and anti-Semitism; an emphasis on issues of employment and social mobility, though without much in the way of concrete policy proposals; the rejection of any kind of internationalism, including communism and finance capitalism; and—above and beyond these more immediate foci—the vision of an ethnically homogeneous, mutually supportive, classless, and meritocratic German society, the *Volksgemeinschaft*. Instead of merely observing the DAP and reporting back on its activities, as his superiors had told him to do, Hitler ended up joining it as a committed member. This was the beginning of his political career.

Hitler was genuinely attracted to the party's ideology, but he also saw an opportunity to build a successful post-army life for himself.[153] Starting off as the DAP's chief public-relations officer, he rapidly extended his influence. In Thomas Weber's words, it was Hitler who, as "the party's primary 'salesperson'" transformed the DAP from what was essentially "little more than a politicized *Stammtisch*, the meeting of regulars in a pub or beer hall" with an active membership of a few dozen, into a numerically still relatively small, but significant political force in Bavaria.[154] (Hitler's withering, and as usual highly stylized, account of the party's initial amateurism contains some of the few humorous passages in *Mein Kampf*.[155]) In February 1920, the DAP changed its name to National Socialist German Workers' Party, or NSDAP (Nationalsozialistische Deutsche Arbeiterpartei). In July 1921, Hitler took over the chairmanship.

In the months and years to come, Hitler would systematically increase the NSDAP's profile and power, displaying unexpected organizational and leadership talents. From the start, he made sure that the key positions in the party were occupied by people who were personally loyal to him. He built up and fostered a network of social contacts, whom he also tapped for funding. And he developed an array of marketing strategies to make the NSDAP stand out from the other parties and keep it in the news. Above all, he set about turning himself into an auratic Leader.

Saviour from Above

The famous 1935 Nazi propaganda film *Triumph of the Will* provides the best example of Hitler's auratification as the Leader. It illustrates perfectly what Walter Benjamin called "the aestheticization of politics".[156]

Triumph of the Will was directed by Leni Riefenstahl, whose cinematic synthesis of aesthetics and politics would profoundly influence Trump strategist Steve Bannon as well as Roger Ailes, the founder and long-time chairman of Fox News.[157] Ostensibly, the film is a documentary on the *Reichsparteitag* held in the Bavarian city of Nuremberg in 1934, one of the massive party rallies the NSDAP organized each year between 1923 and 1939 to showcase itself (though the 1939 rally, the "Reich Party Congress of Peace", had to be cancelled because Germany had just started the Second World War.) In reality, the film aims above all to glorify the Führer. As Rudolf Heß, Hitler's official second-in-command at the time, exclaims at the end of the film: "The Party is Hitler! Hitler, however, is Germany, just as Germany is Hitler!"

Riefenstahl's film was not simply a propagandistic selection and arrangement of scenes from the rally. Rather, the rally itself—a series of events stretching over an entire week—was organized with an eye to the making of the film.[158] As Susan Sontag puts it in her essay "Fascinating Fascism" (1975): "History became theatre. [...] Everything was designed with the camera in mind. [...] With *Triumph of the Will*, the image is no longer a record of reality; 'reality' has been constructed to serve the image".[159]

Hitler was centrally involved both in the organization of the party congress and in the making of the film. In his Vienna years, large-scale film viewing had been but a blip on the horizon. Now, two decades later, cinema was a mass medium with enormous public-relations potential. The still relatively new German Chancellor was well aware of this. He wanted *Triumph of the Will* to be the modern equivalent of a Wagnerian total work of art. The spectators had to be taken in through an emotionally overwhelming integration of image, word, and music, so that they would see him not merely as just another politician, but as the people's tribune and the nation's saviour—as their Leader, the Führer. The ultimate aim was to convince the audience of Hitler's *aura*.

How does Riefenstahl seek to do this? How does she try to present Hitler as the *unique phenomenon of a distance, however close it may be*? Let us analyse the film's first ten minutes, which contain the most revealing cinematic devices.

The opening sequence shows Hitler's plane flying into Nuremberg, the clouds "draw[ing] apart like a stage-curtain"[160] as the aircraft descends. This arrival from above provides the viewers with the first indication of Hitler's auratic nature. Power resides at the top, as we know from organigrams and league tables. What is more, *God* is traditionally seen as being "in heaven", and the film—here and later—consciously portrays Hitler as a Messianic saviour. Indeed, the descending plane casts a clearly visible cruciform shape over his followers below, the faithful "on earth". Finally, in the 1930s air traffic was still something out of the ordinary. In opting for this mode of transport, Hitler presents himself as a man of the future—even though in reality he had a strong fear of heights and felt more than a little uncomfortable every time he boarded a plane.[161]

Upon landing, Hitler is driven to his hotel, the Deutscher Hof. All along the way, he is greeted by throngs of ecstatic ordinary men, women, and children. Yet the main focus remains on *him*, who as the camera's "privileged object [...] is the ultimately significant spectacle—for the crowds *in* the film and for the spectators *of* the film".[162] Indeed, *Triumph of the Will* centres to such a degree on his person that high-ranking members of the military complained about being underrepresented. In order to placate them, the Führer commissioned Riefenstahl to make a separate film about the army, which resulted in the rather tedious *Tag der Freiheit*, or "Day of Freedom", released a few months after *Triumph of the Will*.

Most of the time, Hitler is filmed from below, the adoring masses looking up to him both literally and metaphorically. His relationship with them in the film idealizes his relationship with the German people in reality. The contrast between his individual agency and their collective subordination reflects—or markets—the newly appointed Chancellor's virtual omnipotence, or rather his striving for it. There is no one like him, the film tells the audience, no one able to do what he does. Yet the crowd is not portrayed as passive. Their enthusiastic support of Hitler makes it clear that he executes what they desire. As Rudolf Heß, addressing Hitler, puts it later in the film: "You are Germany. When you act, the nation acts. When you judge, the people judge". Moreover, the members of the crowd are at peace with themselves and each other. There are no class, gender, or age antagonisms, no loners who do not fit in, and no outsiders—the perfect *Volksgemeinschaft*.

Hitler not only speaks and acts on behalf of his people, he is also personally close to them. As Ian Kershaw observes, right-wing "leadership expectations in the Weimar era broke with traditions of a monarch-subject relationship, replacing it with partly neo-feudal, but partly pseudo-democratic notions of a relationship between leader and 'following' in which the leader represented in an authoritative way the will of the people without standing above and outside it in the fashion of a monarch or dictator".[163] Hitler's populist style represented a deliberate attempt to play to such expectations (as well as to conceal his *de facto* dictatorial desires and powers). In *Triumph of the Will*, this proximity is highlighted when Hitler's motorcade stops for a moment so as to allow a woman with a child on her arm—symbolizing the present and the future of

Germany—to present a bouquet of flowers to the Führer. During and immediately after this scene, the camera zooms in on a few individual faces among the rapturous crowd, thus emphasizing the personal bond between the Leader and each of his followers even more strongly. Today—we may assume without being frivolous—Hitler would have stopped to give his admirers an opportunity to take some selfies.

Yet however close, literally and metaphorically, Hitler is to his people, he remains the unique phenomenon of a distance, a quasi-divine presence. He is filmed in such a way that the sun produces a halo around his head. A similar lighting effect is used with his outstretched right hand, which appears to radiate a supernatural glow. Indeed, just as his descent from the sky aims to signal the arrival of a new Messiah, so his journey into the city centre is meant to evoke Jesus' triumphal entry into Jerusalem.

Riefenstahl even manages to deify Hitler in his hotel. She has him standing at a first-floor window of the Deutscher Hof in images that—in Lutz Koepnick's words—"recall the early Christian metaphor of the *fenestra caeli*, the 'window of heaven' through which one would behold the light of the savior".[164] Strikingly, Hitler does not speak at this point.[165] The camera lingers on a large *Heil Hitler* sign below his window and we see and hear the cheering crowd outside the hotel, but the Führer does not address them. Why should that be so? The answer involves a Wagnerian device—the synthesis of image and sound. There is no need for the Führer to speak, because we can hear his followers. The film amalgamates his visual appearance with the auditory manifestation of the German *Volk*. In other words, not only is Hitler the voice of the people, the people now speak as and for the Führer.

This, incidentally, is one of the dangerous attractions of the populist faith: in glorifying the Leader and his ideology, we glorify ourselves and our biases and prejudices.[166] We submit to the Leader and yet, paradoxically, in doing so we become stronger, elevated by his power that we experience as ours. I will return to this empowering, or rather quasi-empowering, dimension of populism in a later chapter.

There is another reason why Hitler does not speak at this point. When Jesus enters Jerusalem, some of the Pharisees—Jewish believers distinguished by their strict observance of traditional religious law—urge Him to rebuke the disciples, who are cheering Him. But Christ "answered and said unto them, I tell you that, if these should hold their peace, the stones would immediately cry out" (Luke 19:40). Similarly, the *Heil Hitler* sign tells the audience that there is no point in trying to silence Hitler's supporters or even Hitler himself (as the authorities sought to do between 1925 and 1927, when they imposed a public-speaking ban on him). In addition, the film suggests that there is no reason to respect political traditionalists with their "legalistic" objections to the Führer's rule.

Even without these rather subtle points, Hitler would have appreciated the Luegerian dimension of the *Heil Hitler* sign. At an NSDAP meeting in Munich in April 1929, he highlighted how Lueger "upon coming to power in Vienna tried to solidify and immortalize the power of his movement through magnificent buildings, in accordance with the idea that, if words no longer speak, the stones must speak. They chiselled in everywhere: Built under Dr Karl Lueger etc."[167]

In the years to come, the National Socialist regime would produce a range of further films auratifying the Führer. Instead of focusing directly on Hitler himself, however, these productions proceeded by historical analogy. They portrayed heroic figures from Germany's past—such as the playwright Friedrich Schiller, the "Iron Chancellor" Otto von Bismarck, and the scientist Robert Koch—as precursors to its current hero, the Führer. They prompted the audience to view Hitler through a world-historical lens, so that he, too, would be seen as a transformative genius. "The great poets, painters, sculptors, scientists, explorers, politicians and generals honoured in Third Reich cinema were all projections of the Führer, himself exalted in propaganda as a great general, supreme politician, artist and architect of genius".[168] Moreover, these world-historical individuals were depicted as having achieved their goals not with the support of the establishment, but against it. Each of them succeeds "in the face of opposition from a pedantic and uncomprehending society, but always fully conscious of his moral obligation to the German collective spirit".[169]

At the same time, the analogical approach served to justify particular concrete actions on Hitler's part. Thus, *Bismarck* (1940), which focused on the German unification of 1871, implicitly defended bypassing parliamentary procedures and reasoned discussions as the only way to move the country forward. It also suggested the desirability of an alliance between Germany and Russia, which Hitler had in fact just concluded in the form of the Molotov-Ribbentrop pact. Two years after *Bismarck* was released, at a time when the Second World War was beginning to turn sour for Germany, *Der große König* (The Great King, 1942) reminded the German people that Frederick the Great, too, had known military setbacks, but that it had been his personal leadership and intuition that saved the day.

Another Saviour from Above

Trump, like Hitler, possessed no government experience when he took office. However, again like Hitler, he did have some experience in the political arena. He appears to have considered running for President several times, possibly as early as 1987, and he almost ran for New York governor in 2014. In February 2000, he abandoned, at the last minute, his campaign as a Presidential candidate for the populist Reform Party (founded five years before by Ross Perot)—and yet he won the primaries in Michigan and California, where he was still on the ballot.

These forays into the world of politics were universally seen as mere advertising campaigns aimed at drawing attention to Trump the businessman. With the benefit of hindsight, it is more likely that they were genuine political ventures. What is certain is that they provided Trump with important insights into the workings of politics and political campaigning. "Our sources show convincingly"—Allen Salkin and Aaron Short write in their book *The Method to the Madness*—"that these were pursuits on which Trump spent copious time and mental energy. They were major moments in the political education of a future President".[170]

Even more important for Trump's ascendency to the Presidency was his media career. His electoral success rested largely on his skills as a political performance artist. Here, his role as co-producer and host of *The Apprentice* was decisive. He already had fairly extensive media experience when he entered the world of television, having been centrally involved in such spectacles as WrestleMania (the "wrestling matches"—that is to say, highly choreographed pugilistic theatre shows—organized by the World Wrestling Entertainment company)[171] and the Miss Universe pageants. But his real media education was *The Apprentice*, later followed by *Celebrity Apprentice*.

Reality television not merely made Trump known to a much larger audience than ever before. It also made him an expert on the visual dimension of media messaging. As President—Cliff Sims writes admiringly—Trump displayed a professional showman's understanding of "the sets, the graphics, the wardrobe choices, the lighting, and just about every other visual component of a broadcast".[172] In addition, *The Apprentice* prompted Trump to analyse his audience demographically and to adapt his communication strategy accordingly. The journalist Cynthia Littleton reports how Trump would "call NBC's ratings research team at 6 a.m. after each airing to get the earliest numbers, which he would then discuss at length with producers and NBC execs. He proved a quick study in dissecting demographics and using the data to guide the direction of episodes".[173]

Moreover, reality television enabled Trump to deepen his practical grasp of the multi-dimensional nature of public communication. As the television producer Bill Pruitt puts it: "In every reality show or every documentary, for that matter, whether it's *Dancing with the Stars*, *The Voice*, *Real Housewives*, *Amazing Race*, or *The Apprentice*, there's three versions: there's what happens, there's what gets filmed, and there's what gets cut down to 43 minutes and 30 seconds and squeezed between commercial breaks".[174] As we saw earlier, Hitler came to realize that for populists the real audience is not other politicians, but the public at large. Criticizing the elitism of Georg von Schönerer, he wrote in *Mein Kampf* that it is ultimately unimportant what populist politicians say: what counts is "what people read about them".[175] Working on *The Apprentice*, Trump arrived at the same understanding of the difference between reality and reporting, truth and theatre, substance and spin. As a politician, he shrewdly exploited this practical experience, manipulating the news cycle with ready-made soundbites, extravagant and hence "newsworthy" statements, and—above all—carefully staged conflicts.

The attention-generating structure of reality television is underpinned by a distinctive narrative logic—the trials and tribulations of commedia dell'arte-like stock characters, with the villains ultimately meeting their demise and a hero carrying the day. Central to this narrative logic is *conflict*. The story lines are based on a developing series of clashes between characters whom we either boo or cheer. In this sense, reality shows are like the stories told by Karl May and Richard Wagner: they follow what the Swiss psychologist Carl Gustav Jung called an *archetypal pattern*. That is to say, they reflect the human mind's tendency to organize experience according to a set of universal, often binary schemata such as good/bad, man/woman, winners/losers, sin/redemption, and life/death. Grey may be the colour of truth, but black-and-white is the colour of theatrics. This is the most important thing that Trump took away from *The Apprentice*: establishing a rapport with the populace is not about political nuance, but about primal simplicity.

Indeed, Wynton Hall, who co-authored Trump's *Time to Get Tough: Making America #1 Again* (2011), has called him "the number-one applied Jungian psychologist in the country".[176] Trump's earlier *How to Get Rich* (2004), which on the cover promises to reveal the secrets of "the star of *The Apprentice*", even has a short chapter entitled "Read Carl Jung".[177] This is not to imply that Trump possessed a scholarly understanding of Jung's ideas. His insights were intuitive rather than analytical; and his interests were practical rather than theoretical. He used (or abused) Jungian psychology to paint a reductive, primitive picture of American society that touched his electorate on a raw, primeval level. Everything and everyone was simplified to the point where only a few stereotypical characteristics remained. Republican opponents Ted Cruz, Marco Rubio, and Jeb Bush became Lyin' Ted, Little Marco, and Low-Energy Jeb; Hillary Clinton was reduced to Crooked Hillary.[178]

Emblematic of Trump's reality-television approach to politics was the official launch of his Presidential campaign. Normally, politicians announcing their candidacy walk straight up to the podium, or they enter from the wings. Trump did something different.

In the opening scenes of *The Apprentice*, we see Trump in a helicopter, flying towards Trump Tower. He does not take the lift up like ordinary people. He is—literally—above that. It is the show's contestants who have to go up in order to see him. They take the lift up to the boardroom, or at least they are filmed as if they were doing so. (In reality, their apartment and the boardroom were on the same floor.) The phrase *higher up* is not merely a spatial expression: power resides at the top. When announcing his candidacy, Trump used the same Riefenstahlian ploy. Waving and making his trademark thumbs-up gesture, he rode down the escalator in Trump Tower to the hundreds of mere mortals waiting in the atrium below. The country's Saviour had arrived.

Photography

Cinema, as we saw earlier, was central to the Führer's auratification. The same can be said of photography.[179] During the Third Reich, photos of Hitler were everywhere: in official buildings and private homes, on posters and leaflets, on commercial products such as postcards and playing cards, and of course in newspapers, magazines, and books. Like *Triumph of the Will*, they aimed to endow Hitler with the two key features of the auratic leader—proximity and distance. They portrayed him as someone simultaneously like all of us and unlike any of us: man of the people *and* heaven-sent saviour.

In order to ensure the consistency of this message, Hitler worked with only one photographer, Heinrich Hoffmann. There were regular press photographers, of course, and several other leading Nazis had their own personal photographers, but only Hoffmann was given unlimited access to the Führer. Moreover, Hitler personally scrutinized every single one of Hoffmann's photographs before clearing it for publication. Even more than spin doctor Joseph Goebbels, then, it was the couple Hitler-Hoffmann that shaped the visual dimension of the Führer's public persona.

The photographer employed a particular and highly conscious strategy: he aimed to amalgamate Hitler with his best roles. As the media critic Georg Seeßlen puts it in his afterword to Hoffmann's memoirs: "Hoffmann's images of Hitler present neither a 'man' nor a 'role', but rather the perfect in-between: the man who has found his role, and the role that has found its man".[180] The confidence artist is transfigured into the statesman, the commander in chief, the architect, and the artist, but also into a reliable friend, a dog lover, and so on. Accordingly, during the 1932 election Nazi-owned newspapers received instructions such as this: "each day, the front page is to be devoted to a specific, coherent theme (big spread). As follows: Tuesday, 29 March: Hitler—the man; Wednesday, 30 March: Hitler—our comrade (loyal, compassionate, etc.); Thursday, 31 March: Hitler—the fighter (enormous achievements through force of will, etc.); Friday, 1 April: Hitler—the statesman".[181]

The dual nature of Hitler's charisma—its auratic combination of proximity and distance—rests on a constant back-and-forth between its two poles. The ordinariness of his human dimension is negated by his superhuman qualities, while the unrelatability of his superhuman dimension is negated by his human qualities. In philosophical terms, the duality is *dialectical.* The human image prevents Hitler's heroism from becoming inflationary and hence implausible.[182] The superhuman image enables Hitler to place himself above all others and rise above all difficulties. In this way, the Führer can be *our* (proximity) *saviour* (distance).

On the whole, Hoffmann did not proceed by doctoring images, though he knew how to do this. When still in training, he had assisted his supervisor in faking pictures of duelling students. "Each participant"—Hoffmann recalled in the 1950s—"had to be photographed separately in the studio. Then each figure had to be cut out most carefully and pasted on to the photograph of the empty Duelling Hall, which formed the background. Finally this composite picture had to be re-photographed and the net result gave a vivid impression of a furious duel in full progress".[183] When working for the Führer, Hoffmann would resort to such trickery only infrequently. For example, the well-known picture of Hitler cheering the outbreak of the First World War in Munich's Odeonsplatz—one of the most widely reproduced images of the Nazi era—was almost certainly the result of a cut-and-paste job in Hoffmann's studio.[184] Later, the pictures documenting the signing of the Molotov-Ribbentrop pact were doctored at Hitler's request. The Führer considered the cigarette dangling from Stalin's lips incompatible with the solemn nature of the occasion. The offending object was duly airbrushed out.[185]

Yet as a rule Hoffmann simply photographed Hitler "the right way" to begin with. He studiously avoided taking pictures that might make his boss look weak or ridiculous.[186] Hence, ordinary Germans never saw their leader with his reading glasses. "The Führer", Hitler explained to his valet, "does not wear glasses".[187] (His secretaries therefore used custom-made typewriters with extra-large characters for the texts of his speeches.)

As discussed earlier, Hitler was never seen wearing bathing trunks or engaging in sports. Even Eva Braun's small Scottish terriers were banned. "A statesman", Hitler told Hoffmann, "does not permit himself to be photographed with a little dog, however amusingly winning it may be. A German sheepdog is the only dog worthy of a real man".[188]

In addition, the Führer used photography to check how he came across in different types of clothing. Hoffmann would take studio pictures of him in his new suit, uniform, hat, or cap, so as to establish whether these garments worked or not. The same method was employed with haircuts, postures, facial expressions, and rhetorical gestures, as well as with lighting modes and viewing angles. Hitler was a pioneer of the kind of media training that is now *de rigueur* for all politicians and celebrities. The most impressive pictures also made excellent publicity material.

Let us return to the main aim of Hoffmann's work—the creation of the Führer as both man of the people and supreme leader. Hitler's regular-guy image was marketed through photographs advertising his "love" for his mother, "respect" for his father, and the "camaraderie" he enjoyed with his fellow soldiers during the First World War. Other photos would show him relaxing in a garden chair, going for a walk, reading a newspaper, or picknicking. Particularly popular were pictures of Hitler with his dog, as well as snapshots of him with little children. Many of these intimate photographs were collected and sold in themed albums.[189]

Special attention was paid to the captions. Hitler was acutely aware of how the description of a picture could—and usually would—steer people's interpretation of it. Many years later, Donald Trump showed a similar awareness of the relation between caption and image in the case of television. Cliff Sims describes how obsessed the President was with "the 'chyrons', the words displayed at the bottom of the screen that act as headlines for whatever the commentators are discussing. […] When the President would deliver a speech somewhere outside of D.C., the research team would take screenshots of all the chyrons that aired while he was speaking. Then, adding those images to headlines and tweets from influential reporters and pundits, they would race to print out a packet before Trump made it back to the White House".[190] The idea was not just to gauge the reactions to the speech, but also to try and get the various TV networks to change any potentially damaging chyrons.

1 Self-Staging: Aura and Appearance 47

Hoffmann's private—or "privatizing"—photographs of the Führer stage an immediacy that is of central importance to populism. They suggest that there is no gulf between *Volk* and Leader—neither the social antagonisms that separate the people from the old political establishment nor the political structures that traditionally mediate between the base and its elected representatives. The relation between populist leaders and their following is a *personal* one. It transcends party loyalty, party programmes, and party procedures, as well as legal principles (and all too often moral scruples). Hence the National Socialists' most famous self-advertisement, used in the Presidential election of 1932—a poster of the Führer's face against a pitch-black background bearing in white letters the caption "HITLER". No party name and no appeal to political conviction. Just Hitler.

This intimacy, or rather quasi-intimacy, makes it easier to identify with the Leader. He does not represent anyone or anything but the people—not the political system, which is portrayed as corrupt, not the law, which is depicted as mere legalism, but *us*. At the same time, this personalizing approach decomplexifies society, making it look less untransparent, less intractable. Social ills now appear as a problem of people and personalities rather than of supra-individual forces and abstract structures.

This is why populist leaders gain a following not *in spite* but *because* of their lack of detailed policy proposals (a topic I will explore with respect to both Hitler and Trump in later chapters). By eschewing real solutions in favour of radical slogans, they depoliticize politics and replace it with a more attractive-looking proposition—the personal power of the Leader, the triumph of the will.

Of course, this strategy only works—that is to say, it only generates followers—if the Leader is not simply an ordinary man of the people, but a superior one. Hitler had to be made to look not only like all of us, but also unlike any of us. The German people's reaction to him had to be the same as that of Joseph Goebbels in April 1926: "Adolf Hitler, I love you because you are both great and simple at the same time".[191] This superior dimension was constructed by photographs marketing the Führer's "extraordinary" qualities and achievements. Again and again, Hoffmann portrayed Hitler as the great statesman, the great negotiator, the guarantor of peace and prosperity, and—after Nazi Germany had unleashed the

Second World War on the world—the great commander in chief, eager to visit the front (which in reality he was not) just as he had fought on the front lines as an ordinary soldier in the First World War (which he had not). Accordingly, Hoffmann's privatizing photo albums were supplemented by albums celebrating Hitler's "liberation" of the Sudetenland, Hitler's conquest of Poland, Hitler's victory over France, and so on.

This, then, is what Hoffmann and his boss strove for and indeed largely achieved: the creation of the Führer as "simultaneously infallible superman [*Übermensch*] and empathetic fellow human being [*Mitmensch*]", as the media critic Rudolf Herz puts it.[192] It is this dialectical movement—this constant back-and-forth—between proximity and distance, between relatability and venerability, that was at the heart of Hitler's pictorial auratification.

A Long Tie and a Short Moustache

Populist leaders sell themselves more than they do their parties or detailed policy proposals. Hence, their visual appearance is of particular importance to their success. They operate "on a permanent stage", as Claudia Schmölders puts it in her physiognomic biography of the Führer.[193] As we will see in a later chapter, the German dictator opted to dress down to the point of shabbiness and to eschew fancy uniforms and rows of medals (the appearance favoured by his fellow Nazi Hermann Göring) so as to project the image of a man of the people. There was nothing haphazard about his sartorial choices. Each piece of clothing was selected with great care; and the photogenic quality of any new uniform or suit was first tested out in Hoffmann's studio.

President Trump was equally alert to the power of his visual persona. While still a businessman, he had created his own iconic look. Overly long ties made him appear even taller than his six feet two inches.[194] Baggy suits made him look bigger, preventing a beanpole image. For a long time, he combined white shirts and red ties with dark suits; as President, he favoured blue suits, thus evoking the colours of his country's star-spangled banner. This was the outfit he wore when he announced his candidacy.[195] Its colours were matched by those of the podium and the eight American flags lining the back of the stage, and both his wife and his daughter wore white. The result was a highly telegenic colour-me-perfect picture of patriotism.

Trump's trademark physiognomic feature was his artificially yellow hair—striking, immediately recognizable as "Trump", and redolent of gold, hence of wealth and power. When his hair started thinning out, a complex daily comb-over became necessary to preserve this signature feature. As Trump's former lawyer Michael Cohen describes it in his memoir, *Disloyal*: "The operation was much more involved than a simple throw-over of what was left of his hair: the three-step procedure required a flop up of the hair from the back of his head, followed by the flip of the resulting overhang on his face back on his pate, and then the flap of his combover on the right side, providing three layers of thinly disguised balding-male insecurity. The concoction was held in place by a fog of TREsemmé TRES Two, not a high-end salon product. Flip, flop, flap, and there was the most famous combover in the world".[196]

Cohen identifies psychological vulnerability as the reason behind his former boss's "extravagant and obvious overcompensation for his baldness": Trump wanted to appear younger and stronger than he actually was, while at the same time "hiding unsightly scars on his scalp from a failed hair-implant operation in the 1980s".[197] This may well be true. But it was not *just* a matter of personal insecurity. Trump's golden hair was an essential element in his permanent self-advertising campaign and as such possessed clear economic and political relevance. At stake were hardcore business interests, not merely vanity and virility; political propaganda, not merely personal psychology.[198] Trump was fully conscious of this. When Stephanie Clifford—better known under her porn-star name Stormy Daniels—asked him about his hair, he smiled and replied:

"I know. [...] It's ridiculous. Come on. First of all, I have a mirror. Second of all, I have had every celebrity stylist—even Paul Mitchell himself—wanting to give me a make-over. I could have whatever. I could basically have had a head transplant if I wanted, okay?"

"Okay, well, why don't you?"

"Everybody talks about it", he said with an air of in-on-the-joke smugness. "It's my thing. It's *my* trademark."[199]

Hitler, too, engaged in a permanent facial propaganda campaign; and from 1933 onwards, the regime ensured that his visage was ubiquitous.[200] But what about the Führer's moustache, the feature that today makes his face immediately recognizable? Did it play a similar role in his own time?

In his somewhat freewheeling essay "La moustache d'Adolf Hitler", the French writer Alain Jaubert cites Blaise Pascal: "If Cleopatra's nose had been shorter, the face of the world would look very different today".[201] Jaubert then tries to make the opposite case for the German dictator: if Hitler's moustache had been longer, he would not have had the impact on the world that he did. It was only by replacing the elongated moustache he had during the First World War with the shorter variety that he became "the Führer" and hence a world-historical figure. The Hitler moustache created a unique Hitler look.

The idea is tempting, but not true, as historians such as Friedrich Tietjen have shown.[202] Tietjen first disposes of some well-known explanations for Hitler's decision to shorten his moustache. For example, Bridget Hitler (*née* Dowling), who married Hitler's half-brother, Alois, claims in her memoirs that the future Führer stayed with her and her husband in Liverpool between November 1912 and April 1913. She suggested to him that he trim his big moustache, but as usual—she writes—Hitler overdid things.[203] However, there is no proof that Hitler ever even went to England. Equally improbable is the explanation put forward by Alexander Moritz Frey, who served with Hitler during the First World War. According to Frey, Hitler was obliged to change his facial appearance because his long moustache did not fit under a gasmask.[204] This— Tietjen says—make little sense given the shape and size of such contraptions, which at the time were even bigger than today's models.

Most importantly, Tietjen shows that the so-called Hitler moustache was widespread long before Hitler adopted it in the early 1920s. The *toothbrush moustache*, as it was known in the English-speaking world, had been gaining in popularity in the West from the beginning of the twentieth century onwards. Charlie Chaplin sported it as early as 1914. Hence Tietjen's conclusion: Hitler did not create a uniquely Hitlerian feature that was subsequently emulated by others. Rather, he opted for an already existing look. But why this particular one? Hitler's secretary Christa Schroeder writes in her memoirs: "Hitler's nose was very large and fairly pointed. [...] He had wisely grown a small moustache to cover up his very thin lips. During the years of his friendship with Ada Klein [1925–26] he told her: "Many people say I should shave off the moustache, but that is impossible. Imagine my face without a moustache!" and at that held his hand below his nose like a plate. "My nose is much too big. I need the moustache to relieve the effect!"[205]

This still does not answer the question of why Hitler opted for the toothbrush. Here, a closer look at the history of facial hair can help us.[206] In the late nineteenth century, beards were slowly going out of fashion. All across the United States and then Europe, more and more men adopted a clean-shaven look, which was now associated with youth, energy, and discipline. In Germany, this placed particular pressure on Wilhelm II, who had ascended the imperial throne in 1888. Socially awkward and somewhat touchy, alternatingly indecisive and impetuous, and with an (at the time, humiliatingly) crippled arm, the Kaiser yet fancied himself a great military leader and statesman. He loved uniforms, parades, and belligerent speeches, but if he was going to impress the world, he needed a facial appearance to match his fierce ambition. Beards were old-fashioned; the smooth look was too American. Hence, a moustache. But what kind?

Court hairdresser François Haby came up with the perfect solution, the virile, "erect" moustache that would come to be known as the *Kaiserbart*. With its upwardly curved extremities, it was—in the words of the historian Miranda Carter—"the very model of a modern moustache, a controlled riposte to the great bushy, biblical patriarch beards and sidewhiskers of the previous generation".[207] The look soon became popular and was adopted by many; Field Marshal Paul von Hindenburg (Chief of the German Great General Staff from 1916 to 1919 and German President from 1925 to 1934) retained it until his death.

After Germany's defeat in the First World War, the imperial look lost its lustre. Exiled to Holland, even the former Kaiser replaced his martial handlebar with a modest beard. Such was the situation in which Hitler found himself: beards and the *Kaiserbart* were symbols of the past, while the clean-shaven look was still viewed as a foreign invention. This is the reason why he opted for the toothbrush moustache, a look that not long ago had begun to compete with the *Kaiserbart*.[208] As the historian

Christopher Oldstone-Moore puts it in his study *Of Beards and Men*, Hitler realized "that Germany would not rise again by clinging to the past. He knew his country must modernize and that he must present himself as a modern leader. He needed new symbols and a new mustache. The "toothbrush" mustache that he settled on was known before the war as a modern look, becoming popular at the beginning of the twentieth century as larger effusions of hair fell from favor. […] The grandly upturned *kaiserbart*, the drooping walrus of Bismarck, and even the ordinary officer's trim all invoked the failed past. Clean shaving, on the other hand, though admirable for invoking youth and efficiency, also suggested the bland and unromantic modernity of Germany's western rivals. The famous square of dark hair under the nose became the ideal alternative".[209]

Notes

1. Quoted in the BBC documentary *The Dark Charisma of Adolf Hitler: Leading Millions into the Abyss* (2012), written and produced by Laurence Rees. Cf. also Rees's book with the same title (London: Ebury Press, 2013; first published 2012) as well as his 2016 Tans lecture and his conversation with Atticus Mullikin (both available on YouTube). In writing this chapter, I have benefited much from Rees's work, as well as from Ian Kershaw's publications on the image and reality of Hitler's power, including *The "Hitler Myth": Image and Reality in the Third Reich* (new ed. Oxford: Oxford University Press, 2001) and "'Führerstaat': Charisma und Gewalt", in Hans-Ulrich Thamer and Simone Erpel (eds.), *Hitler und die Deutschen. Volksgemeinschaft und Verbrechen* (Dresden: Sandstein, 2011), pp. 58–67. All general historical and biographical information on Hitler and Trump in this and the following chapters comes from the texts listed in the Select Bibliography.
2. Quoted in Claudia Schmölders, *Hitlers Gesicht. Eine physiognomische Biographie* (Munich: Beck, 2000), p. 9.
3. Kurt G. W. Ludecke [= Lüdecke], *I Knew Hitler: The Story of a Nazi Who Escaped the Blood Purge* (London: Jarrolds, 1938), p. 22. Speaking to Hitler, Lüdecke felt "that the whole man was concentrated in his eyes, his clear, straightforward, domineering, bright blue eyes" (p. 25).

4. Quoted in Schmölders, *Hitlers Gesicht*, p. 7.
5. Joseph Goebbels, *Die Tagebücher von Joseph Goebbels*, ed. Elke Fröhlich (Munich: Saur, 1993–2008), vol. 1/I, p. 375 (entry of 6 November 1925).
6. Quoted in Schmölders, *Hitlers Gesicht*, p. 7.
7. Rees, *Dark Charisma*, p. 2.
8. Corey R. Lewandowski and David N. Bossie, *Let Trump Be Trump: The Inside Story of His Rise to the Presidency* (New York: Hachette, 2017), p. 23.
9. Albert Speer, *Inside the Third Reich*, trans. Richard and Clara Winston (London: Weidenfeld & Nicolson, 1995; first published in German 1969), p. 152.
10. Cited in Allen Salkin and Aaron Short, *The Method to the Madness: Donald Trump's Ascent as Told by Those Who Were Hired, Fired, Inspired— and Inaugurated* (New York: All Points Books, 2019), p. 137.
11. Cited in Bob Woodward and Robert Costa, *Peril* (London etc.: Simon & Schuster, 2021), p. 127; Bob Woodward, *Fear: Trump in the White House* (London etc.: Simon & Schuster, 2018), p. 308; and Michael Wolff, *Fire and Fury: Inside the Trump White House* (London: Little, Brown, 2018), p. 304.
12. Anonymous, *A Warning* (London: Little, Brown, 2019), *passim*. The anonymous author later revealed himself to be the Department of Homeland Security official Miles Taylor. See Miles Taylor, "A Statement: Why I'm No Longer 'Anonymous'", *Medium*, 28 October 2020.
13. See, for example, Ludolf Herbst, *Hitlers Charisma. Die Erfindung eines deutschen Messias* (Frankfurt am Main: Fischer, 2010), Wolfram Pyta, *Hitler. Der Künstler als Politiker und Feldherr* (Munich: Siedler, 2015), Christoph Raichle, *Hitler als Symbolpolitiker* (Suttgart: Kohlhammer, 2013), as well as the publications by Kershaw and Rees listed above.
14. Max Weber, *On Charisma and Institution Building: Selected Papers*, ed. S. N. Eisenstadt (Chicago and London: University of Chicago Press, 1968), p. 46.
15. Weber, *On Charisma*, p. 46.
16. Weber, *On Charisma*, p. 46.
17. Ian Kershaw, *Hitler 1889–1936: Hubris* (London etc.: Penguin, 2001; first published 1998), p. xiii.
18. Weber, *On Charisma*, p. 47.
19. Weber, *On Charisma*, p. 48.

20. Ian Kershaw, *Hitler* (Harlow: Longman, 1991), p. 10.
21. Kershaw, "*Hitler Myth*", p. 255.
22. This is not a criticism of historians such as Kershaw, who display a sharp sense of Hitler's strategies of self-promotion. My point is that Weber's definition of charisma is useful only if one implicitly or explicitly goes beyond its conceptual limitations, which is precisely what historians have done. This applies not only to Kershaw, but also to others. Wolfram Pyta, for example, highlights the *Aufführungszwang* to which charismatic leaders are subject—the constant pressure on them to "regenerate their authority through performative acts and the use of mass media as multipliers" (Pyta, *Hitler*, p. 19). Likewise, Christoph Raichle describes the relation between Hitler and his followers as one of "*supply* and *demand*", in which the Führer's self-advertising played a central role (Raichle, *Hitler als Symbolpolitiker*, p. 18).
23. Walter Benjamin, "The Work of Art in the Age of Its Technological Reproducibility" [1939], trans. Harry Zohn and Edmund Jephcott, in Walter Benjamin, *Selected Writings*, ed. Howard Eiland and Michael W. Jennings (Cambridge, Mass., and London: Harvard University Press, 2006), vol. 4, pp. 251–83. Benjamin produced several versions of this text; the 1939 version is the canonical one. The original German text can be found, with extensive English-language commentary, in Henk de Berg and Duncan Large (eds.), *Modern German Thought from Kant to Habermas: An Annotated German-Language Reader* (Rochester, NY: Camden House, 2012), pp. 239–80. On the relevance of Benjamin's concept of the aura to the study of politics, cf. Lutz Koepnick, *Walter Benjamin and the Aesthetics of Power* (Lincoln and London: University of Nebraska Press, 1999).
24. Benjamin, "Work of Art", p. 255 (translation modified). The German reads *einmalige Erscheinung einer Ferne, so nah sie sein mag*. The noun *Erscheinung* ("appearance", "apparition", "phenomenon") evokes the verb *scheinen* (which means both "shine" and "appear" or "seem") and the noun that goes with it, *Schein*.
25. Benjamin, "Work of Art", p. 255 (translation modified).
26. Benjamin, "Work of Art", p. 255.
27. In one form or another, the question has re-appeared in more recent political contexts, including the 2005 Tory leadership debate between David Cameron ("boxers") and David Davis ("briefs") and a 2012 interview with Republican Presidential candidate Mitt Romney, who

was asked what he wears to bed at night ("I think the best answer is as little as possible").
28. Benjamin, "Work of Art", p. 269 (translation modified).
29. Benjamin, "Work of Art", p. 269 (translation modified).
30. On the importance of distance in politics, cf. Rees, *Dark Charisma*, p. 41.
31. The following account draws on Volker Klotz, "Über den literarischen Umgang mit Abenteuern", in *Marbacher Magazin* 21, 1982 (special issue on "Karl May. Das inszenierte Abenteuer"), pp. 2–8, as well as on Gert Ueding (ed. in collaboration with Klaus Rettner), *Karl-May-Handbuch* (third ed. Würzburg: Königshausen & Neumann, 2001), pp. 19–60.
32. Here, I draw on Hans-Otto Hügel, "Das inszenierte Abenteuer", in *Marbacher Magazin* 21, 1982, pp. 10–32, as well as on Ueding (ed.), *Karl-May-Handbuch*, pp. 61–115.
33. Only in later life did May visit the United States and some of the other foreign places described in his novels.
34. Brigitte Hamann, *Hitler's Vienna: A Portrait of the Tyrant as a Young Man*, trans. Thomas Thornton (new. ed. London: Tauris Parke Paperbacks, 2010; first published in German 1996), p. 384, citing an anonymous attendee at the discussion.
35. Otto Dietrich, *The Hitler I Knew: Memoirs of the Third Reich's Press Chief* (New York: Skyhorse Publishing, 2014 [no translator mentioned]; first published in German 1955), p. 123; cf. Hamann, *Hitler's Vienna*, p. 384.
36. Editorial commentary in Adolf Hitler, *Mein Kampf. Eine kritische Edition*, ed. Christian Hartmann, Thomas Vordermayer, Othmar Plöckinger, and Roman Töppel (Munich and Berlin: Institut für Zeitgeschichte, 2016), vol. 2, p. 1628. Ueding (ed.), *Karl-May-Handbuch*, highlights "May's aversion to supercilious officers and the military in general" (p. 286).
37. On the psychology and sociology of conning, cf. Stephan Porombka, *Felix Krulls Erben. Die Geschichte der Hochstapelei im 20. Jahrhundert* (Berlin: Bostelmann & Siebenhaar, 2001), which also contains a section on Hitler (pp. 88–92).
38. Lutz Schwerin von Krosigk, *Es geschah in Deutschland. Menschenbilder unseres Jahrhunderts* (Tübingen and Stuttgart: Rainer Wunderlich Verlag Hermann Leins, 1951), p. 220.

39. Cf. Ernst Hanfstaengl, *Hitler: The Memoir of a Nazi Insider Who Turned against the Führer*, trans. John Willard Toland (New York: Arcade Publishing, 2011, first published in German 1957), pp. 65–66 and 120.
40. Christa Schroeder, *He Was My Chief: The Memoirs of Adolf Hitler's Secretary*, trans. Geoffrey Brooks (Barnsley: Frontline Books, 2012; first published in German 1985), p. 58.
41. Volker Ullrich, *Hitler: Ascent 1889–1939*, trans. Jefferson Chase (London: The Bodley Head, 2016; first published in German 2013), p. 388. Chapter 13 of Ullrich's book provides an excellent overview of Hitler's personal skills, including his acting talent.
42. Schwerin von Krosigk, *Es geschah in Deutschland*, p. 220.
43. André François-Poncet, *Souvenirs d'une ambassade à Berlin. Septembre 1931–octobre 1938* (Paris: Perrin, 2016; first published 1946), p. 228; cf. p. 33. Meeting up with Hitler and trying to read him was thus not the ideal way to gauge his intentions. Indeed, politicians such as Chamberlain would almost certainly have been much better off if they had never spoken to him. Cf. Malcolm Gladwell, *Talking to Strangers: What We Should Know about the People We Don't Know* (London: Allen Lane, 2019), especially pp. 28–45.
44. Ullrich, *Hitler: Ascent 1889–1939*, p. 7, citing Lutz Schwerin von Krosigk's letter to Georg Franz of 13 July 1962.
45. Heinrich Hoffmann, *Hitler Was My Friend: The Memoirs of Hitler's Photographer*, trans. R. H. Stevens (London: Frontline Books, 2011; first published 1955), p. 82.
46. Albert Speer, *Spandau: The Secret Diaries*, trans. Richard and Clara Winston (London: Phoenix Press, 2000; first published in German 1975), pp. 425–26 (entry of 4 May 1965).
47. Speer, *Inside the Third Reich*, p. 55.
48. Michael D'Antonio, *The Truth about Trump* (new ed. New York: Thomas Dunne Books, 2016; first published 2015 as *Never Enough: Donald Trump and the Pursuit of Success*), p. 335.
49. D'Antonio, *Truth about Trump*, p. 211, and Wayne Barrett, *Trump, the Greatest Show on Earth: The Deals, the Downfall, the Reinvention* (new ed. New York: Regan Arts, 2016; first published 1992 as *Trump: The Deals and the Downfall*).
50. Cited in D'Antonio, *Truth about Trump*, p. 204.

51. Cited in Timothy L. O'Brien, *TrumpNation: The Art of Being The Donald* (new ed. New York and Boston: Grand Central Publishing, 2016; first published 2005), p. 216.
52. O'Brien, *TrumpNation*, p. 221.
53. Donald J. Trump, with Tony Schwartz, *The Art of the Deal* (London: Arrow Books, no year; first published 1987), p. 58.
54. Jane Mayer, "Donald Trump's Ghostwriter Tells All", *The New Yorker*, 25 July 2016.
55. Cited in Woodward, *Fear*, pp. 209, 338, 353, and 357.
56. Michael Wolff, *Siege: Trump under Fire* (London: Little, Brown, 2019), p. 75.
57. Norma King, *Ivana Trump: A Very Unauthorized Biography* (New York: Carroll & Graf, 1990), p. 83.
58. "I always call him Mr. Trump. I never call him Donald" (Steve Bannon). Cited in Salkin and Short, *Method to the Madness*, p. 278.
59. The newspaper article in question is Glenn Thrush and Maggie Haberman, "Trump and Staff Rethink Tactics after Stumbles", *New York Times*, 5 February 2017.
60. Cf. Alessandra Antola Swan, "The Iconic Body: Mussolini Unclothed", *Modern Italy* 21.4, 2016, pp. 361–81, and *Photographing Mussolini: The Making of a Political Icon* (London: Palgrave Macmillan, 2020).
61. Cited in Salkin and Short, *Method to the Madness*, p. 107.
62. Speer, *Spandau*, p. 41 (entry of 10 February 1947).
63. Towards the end of the First World War, Göring was put in charge of Fighter Wing 1, the famous "Flying Circus" formerly led by Manfred von Richthofen, the "Red Baron" (so named after the colour of his plane). He received not only the Iron Cross, but also the Pour le Mérite (the "Blue Max"), Prussia's highest military award. At the 1945/46 Nuremberg Trials, his IQ was estimated at 138, well above average.
64. Schroeder, *He Was My Chief*, p. 52.
65. Schroeder, *He Was My Chief*, p. 52.
66. Heinz Linge, *With Hitler to the End: The Memoirs of Adolf Hitler's Valet*, trans. Geoffrey Brooks (London: Frontline Books, 2009; first published in German 1980), p. 156.
67. Cf. Linge, *With Hitler to the End*, pp. 57–58.
68. Speer, *Inside the Third Reich*, p. 152.

69. Albert Krebs, *The Infancy of Nazism: The Memoirs of Ex-Gauleiter Albert Krebs 1923–1933*, trans. William Sheridan Allen (New York: New Viewpoints, 1976; first published in German 1959), pp. 162–63. I will explore another example of Hitler's fake anger in Chap. 2.
70. Cf., for example, Linge, *With Hitler to the End*, pp. 61–62, and Schroeder, *He Was My Chief*, p. 51.
71. Krebs, *Infancy of Nazism*, pp. 160–61.
72. Rees, *Dark Charisma*, p. 10.
73. Rees, *Dark Charisma*, p. 10, and *Dark Charisma* (DVD).
74. Goebbels, *Tagebücher*, vol. 2/II, p. 339 (entry of 13 August 1932). Cf. Dietrich, *The Hitler I Knew*: in autumn 1931, Hitler "spoke of his coming to power as if there could be not the slightest question about it—although to many persons at this time such a thing seemed impossible, and to me it certainly seemed doubtful" (p. 13).
75. Goebbels, *Tagebücher*, vol. 2/III, p. 118 (entry of 29 January 1933).
76. Speer, *Inside the Third Reich*, p. 235. Speer adds the footnote: "And, in fact, nine months previously I had had bas-reliefs portraying the Hercules legend installed on the new Chancellery".
77. Dietrich, *The Hitler I Knew*, p. 103.
78. Schroeder, *He Was My Chief*, p. 53.
79. Cf. Speer, *Inside the Third Reich*, pp. 128 and 210, and Schwerin von Krosigk, *Es geschah in Deutschland*, p. 199.
80. Cf. Frederic Spotts, *Hitler and the Power of Aesthetics* (new ed. New York: The Overlook Press, 2018), p. 234.
81. Hoffmann, *Hitler Was My Friend*, p. 119.
82. Hoffmann, *Hitler Was My Friend*, p. 119.
83. On some level, Hitler may actually have believed that his escape was part of what he called "Providence's plan" for him. As we saw, the belief that confidence artists have in themselves is fundamentally ambivalent. But his appeal to the intentions of Providence was also an attempt at self-auratification. Moreover, as Roger Moorhouse has pointed out, "[e]ach time the story was […] told and retold, it was embellished and gilded a little more". Cf. Roger Moorhouse, *Killing Hitler: The Third Reich and the Plots against the Führer* (London: Jonathan Cape, 2006), pp. 36–58 (55).
84. Wolff, *Siege*, pp. 78–79.
85. Omarosa Manigault Newman, *Unhinged: An Insider's Account of the Trump White House* (London etc.: Simon & Schuster, 2018), p. 30.

86. Manigault Newman, *Unhinged*, pp. 217–18. She then tries to make the case that these skills had somehow disappeared when Trump became President. This strikes me as implausible.
87. Cynthia Littleton, "How Donald Trump Rode Reality TV Fame to a Bid for the White House", *Variety*, 26 April 2016.
88. Dan Klores, cited in Robert Slater, *No Such Thing as Over-Exposure: Inside the Life and Celebrity of Donald Trump* (Upper Saddle River, NJ: Prentice Hall, 2005), p. 34.
89. Manigault Newman, *Unhinged*, p. xxvi.
90. Cited in O'Brien, *TrumpNation*, p. 83.
91. Wolff, *Fire and Fury*, p. 21.
92. Gwenda Blair, *Donald Trump: The Candidate* (New York etc.: Simon & Schuster, 2015), p. 156.
93. BBC reporter Selena Scott, cited in D'Antonio, *Truth about Trump*, pp. 235–36.
94. For some examples, see Michael Kranish and Marc Fisher, *Trump Revealed: The Definitive Biography of the 45th President* (London etc.: Simon & Schuster, 2016), pp. 264–65, and Slater, *No Such Thing as Over-Exposure*, p. 181.
95. Slater, *No Such Thing as Over-Exposure*, p. 15.
96. For some examples, see Blair, *Donald Trump*, p. 175, and Slater, *No Such Thing as Over-Exposure*, p. 35.
97. Cited in Mayer, "Donald Trump's Ghostwriter Tells All".
98. Slater, *No Such Thing as Over-Exposure*, pp. 25–26.
99. Tim Alberta, *American Carnage: On the Front Lines of the Republican Civil War and the Rise of President Trump* (New York: HarperCollins, 2019), p. 337.
100. Blair, *Donald Trump*, p. 14.
101. Blair, *Donald Trump*, p. 165.
102. Kranish and Fisher, *Trump Revealed*, p. 197 (quoting an anonymous source).
103. Kranish and Fisher, *Trump Revealed*, p. 10.
104. Kranish and Fisher, *Trump Revealed*, p. 11.
105. Cliff Sims, *Team of Vipers: My 500 Extraordinary Days in the Trump White House* (New York: Thomas Dunne Books, 2019), p. 32.
106. The following account draws above all on Hamann, *Hitler's Vienna*, Pyta, *Hitler*, and Spotts, *Hitler and the Power of Aesthetics*.

107. August Kubizek, *The Young Hitler I Knew: The Memoirs of Hitler's Childhood Friend*, trans. Geoffrey Brooks (Barnsley: Frontline Books, 2011; first published in German 1953), p. 118. Interestingly, Rienzi ultimately fails, abandoned by his followers.
108. Spotts, *Hitler and the Power of Aesthetics*, makes a case for the historical accuracy of Kubizek's recollection "minus the [...] overwrought verbiage" (p. 227).
109. Hitler also had money from his family. However, he was anything but an assiduous and systematic worker, and he went through occasional periods of genuine hardship, the low point being the autumn and winter of 1909, which he appears to have spent as a homeless person.
110. Early on, Hitler managed to obtain a recommendation letter to Roller, but he was too timid to make use of it. In 1933, shortly after he had become Chancellor, he suggested to Winifred Wagner (the composer's daughter-in-law), who was planning a new production of *Parsifal* at the Bayreuth Festival, that she ask the 69-year-old Roller to design the set. The production took place in 1934. Roller died the following year.
111. Speer, *Spandau*, p. 102 (entry of 11 May 1948); cf. Hamann, *Hitler's Vienna*, p. 67.
112. Hamann, *Hitler's Vienna*, pp. 67–68.
113. Spotts, *Hitler and the Power of Aesthetics*, p. 58.
114. Pyta, *Hitler*, p. 64. My account of Wagner also draws on Koepnick, *Walter Benjamin*, especially pp. 53–82, and the chapter "Richard Wagner and the Framing of Modern Empathy" in Lutz Koepnick, *Framing Attention: Windows on Modern German Culture* (Baltimore: The Johns Hopkins University Press, 2007), pp. 62–94.
115. See Friedrich Nietzsche, *The Birth of Tragedy and The Case of Wagner*, trans. Walter Kaufmann (New York: Vintage Books, 1967), pp. 145–97. The German original can be found in Friedrich Nietzsche, *Sämtliche Werke. Kritische Studienausgabe*, ed. Giorgio Colli and Mazzino Montinari (new ed. Berlin and New York: de Gruyter / Munich: dtv, 1999), vol. 6, pp. 9–53, and vol. 14, pp. 400–409. On Nietzsche's criticism of Wagner, cf. Koepnick, *Walter Benjamin*, pp. 72–73.
116. Nietzsche, *Case of Wagner* (section 5), p. 166 (English) and p. 23 (German).
117. Nietzsche, *Case of Wagner* (section 7), p. 169 (English) and pp. 26–27 (German). The original reads *Gesammtverwandlung der Kunst in's Schauspielerische*.

118. Nietzsche, *Case of Wagner* (section 7), p. 169 (English) and p. 26 (German).
119. Nietzsche, *Case of Wagner* (section 8), pp. 172–73 (English) and pp. 29–30 (German).
120. Nietzsche, *Case of Wagner* (section 3), p. 160 (English) and p. 16 (German).
121. Nietzsche, *Case of Wagner* (section 1), p. 157 (English) and p. 14 (German).
122. Nietzsche, *Case of Wagner* (section 3), p. 160 (English) and p. 16 (German).
123. Nietzsche, *Case of Wagner* (section 9), pp. 174–75 (English) and pp. 32–33 (German).
124. Pyta, *Hitler*, p. 14.
125. Koepnick, "Richard Wagner", p. 64.
126. The following account is based on Hamann, *Hitler's Vienna*, and Pyta, *Hitler*.
127. Adolf Hitler, *Mein Kampf*, trans. Ralph Manheim (Boston and New York: Houghton Mifflin Company, 1999), p. 77; cf. Hamann, *Hitler's Vienna*, p. 120. The German original can be found in Hitler, *Mein Kampf. Eine kritische Edition*, vol. 1, pp. 263 and 265.
128. Hitler, *Mein Kampf*, pp. 77 (English) and vol. 1, p. 263 (German). The German word for "comedy" that Hitler uses is *Schauspiel* (literally, "spectacle" or "drama", "theatre play").
129. Hamann, *Hitler's Vienna*, p. 119, citing *Wien und die Wiener. Ungeschminkte Schilderungen eines fahrenden Gesellen* (p. 137), first published anonymously in Berlin in 1892.
130. Cf. Roger Ailes (with Jon Kraushaar), *You Are the Message* (new ed. New York etc.: Currency Doubleday, 1995), p. 43, and the Canal+ television documentary *Coupez le son! Le charisme politique* (Mona Lisa Productions / Ina, 2007), directed by Thierry Berrod and presented by the Belgian political scientist René Zayan.
131. Kershaw, *Hitler 1889–1936*, p. 35.
132. Hitler, *Mein Kampf*, p. 121 (English) and vol. 1, p. 359 (German).
133. Hamann, *Hitler's Vienna*, p. 284.
134. Hitler, *Mein Kampf*, p. 99 (English) and vol. 1, p. 311 (German).
135. Hitler, *Mein Kampf*, p. 104 (English) and vol. 1, p. 323 (German).
136. Hitler, *Mein Kampf*, p. 104 (English) and vol. 1, p. 323 (German).
137. Hitler, *Mein Kampf*, p. 102 (English) and vol. 1, p. 317 (German).

138. Hitler, *Mein Kampf*, p. 102 (English) and vol. 1, p. 317 (German).
139. Hitler, *Mein Kampf*, p. 100 (English) and vol. 1, p. 313 (German).
140. Hitler, *Mein Kampf*, p. 100 (English) and vol. 1, p. 313 (German).
141. Hitler, *Mein Kampf*, p. 100 (English) and vol. 1, p. 313 (German).
142. Felix Salten, *Das österreichische Antlitz. Essays* (second ed. Berlin: Fischer, 1910; first published 1909), pp. 132–33. My rendering draws on the translation of this passage in Hamann, *Hitler's Vienna*, pp. 284–85.
143. Salten, *Das österreichische Antlitz*, p. 130.
144. Salten, *Das österreichische Antlitz*, p. 140.
145. Salten, *Das österreichische Antlitz*, p. 138.
146. Salten, *Das österreichische Antlitz*, p. 138.
147. It is worth stressing that not all supporters or fellow travellers of the post-1918 Bavarian socialist and communist republics were internationalists. Indeed, Ernst Niekisch—the second executive head of the socialist republic—later became a leading figure in a political movement known as National Bolshevism. Hitler's nationalist orientation was thus by no means unique. More generally, the more extreme varieties of left-wing and right-wing thought are in many respects not as dissimilar as one might think—a topic to which I will return in Chap. 4. One should therefore not overstate the abruptness of Hitler's transition from the Left to the Right.
148. The German terms are *raffendes Kapital* and *schaffendes Kapital*.
149. Cf. Hitler, *Mein Kampf*, pp. 215–16 (English) and vol. 1, p. 579 (German).
150. Thomas Weber, *Becoming Hitler: The Making of a Nazi* (Oxford: Oxford University Press, 2017), p. 106; cf. also p. 107.
151. Kershaw, *Hitler 1889–1936*, p. 124.
152. Cf. Kershaw, *Hitler 1889–1936*, p. 124, referencing Ernst Deuerlein, "Hitlers Eintritt in die Politik und die Reichswehr", *Vierteljahrshefte für Zeitgeschichte* 7, 1959, pp. 177–227 (200).
153. Hitler was demobilized in March 1920.
154. Weber, *Becoming Hitler*, pp. 152 and 117.
155. Cf. Hitler, *Mein Kampf*, pp. 217–24 (English) and vol. 1, p. 581–99 (German).
156. Benjamin, "Work of Art", p. 270 (the original is in italics). Unlike many other Nazi propaganda films, *Triumph des Willens* is widely available on DVD. See, for example, the *Leni Riefenstahl Collection* (Hot

Town, 2009), which also contains Riefenstahl's other National Socialist films, *Der Sieg des Glaubens* (Victory of Faith, 1933), *Tag der Freiheit. Unsere Wehrmacht* (Day of Freedom: Our Army, 1935), and the two-part *Olympia* (1938), on the 1936 Olympic Games in Berlin. My account of Nazi cinema in general and *Triumph of the Will* in particular draws on Kershaw, "Hitler Myth", the chapter "Windows 33/45" in Koepnick, *Framing Attention*, pp. 163–99, Erwin Leiser, *Nazi Cinema*, trans. Gertrud Mander and David Wilson (New York: Macmillan, 1975; first published in German 1968), Steve Neal, "*Triumph of the Will*: Notes on Documentary and Spectacle", *Screen* 20.1, 1979, pp. 63–86, Linda Schulte-Sasse, *Entertaining the Third Reich: Illusions of Wholeness in Nazi Cinema* (Durham and London, Duke University Press, 1966), Philipp Stiasny, "Vom Himmel hoch. Adolf Hitler und die 'Volksgemeinschaft' in *Triumph des Willens*", in Hans-Ulrich Thamer and Simone Erpel (eds.), *Hitler und die Deutschen. Volksgemeinschaft und Verbrechen* (Dresden: Sandstein, 2011), pp. 82–88, and David Welch, *Propaganda and the German Cinema 1933–1945* (rev. ed. London: I. B. Taurus, 2001).

157. Cf. Keith Koffler, *Bannon: Always the Rebel* (Washington, DC: Regnery, 2017), pp. 49 and 136, and Gabriel Sherman, *The Loudest Voice in the Room* (new ed. New York: Random House, 2017), pp. 31 and 63.

158. Cf. Leni Riefenstahl's contemporaneous memoir *Hinter den Kulissen des Reichsparteitag-Films* (Munich: Franz Eher Nachf., 1935), pp. 13 and 31.

159. "Fascinating Fascism" was originally published in *The New York Review of Books* (6 February 1975) and reprinted in Susan Sontag, *Under the Sign of Saturn* (New York: Farrar, Straus & Giroux, 1980), pp. 73–105. The citation comes from the essay's German version, which has a slightly different text: "Verzückt von den Primitiven. Leni Riefenstahl und die bleibende Faszination faschistischer Kunst", *Die Zeit*, 2 May 1975, pp. 17–18 (18).

160. Neal, "*Triumph of the Will*", p. 68.

161. Roger Ailes made use of a similar cinematic device when he produced Richard Nixon's televised state dinner in honour of the Apollo 11 astronauts returning from the moon in 1969. Rather than just focusing on the dinner, he made sure to include a Riefenstahlian presidential arrival. "Cameras captured the president, the first family, and the astronauts descending from the sky in a military helicopter to the parking lot of

the hotel. As they emerged from the cabin, it seemed as if Nixon had also returned from space" (Sherman, *Loudest Voice*, p. 63).
162. Neal, "*Triumph of the Will*", pp. 69–70.
163. Kershaw, "*Hitler Myth*", p. 19.
164. Koepnick, "Windows 33/45", p. 166.
165. On this aspect of *Triumph of the Will*, cf. Koepnick, "Windows 33/45", pp. 169–177.
166. Cf. Émile Durkheim's analysis of religious faith in *Les formes élémentaires de la vie religieuse* (The Elementary Forms of Religious Life, 1912). According to Durkheim, religion is the mode in which society venerates itself. That is to say, religious dogma, symbolism, and practice are the objectified expressions of (frequently opaque and implicit) social norms and values. Endowed with this "objective" power, religion works back on society, binding its members together in a shared social reality, which is continually confirmed and re-confirmed through collective rituals such as thanksgiving and mourning ceremonies.
167. Adolf Hitler, *Reden, Schriften, Anordnungen Februar 1925 bis Januar 1933*, ed. Institut für Zeitgeschichte (Munich etc.: K. G. Saur, 1992–2003), p. 146 (speech of 3 April 1929).
168. Leiser, *Nazi Cinema*, p. 106.
169. Welch, *Propaganda and the German Cinema*, p. 155.
170. Salkin and Short, *Method to the Madness*, p. 5.
171. The company changed names a few times. World Wrestling Entertainment is its current name.
172. Sims, *Team of Vipers*, p. 270.
173. Littleton, "How Donald Trump Rode Reality TV Fame to a Bid for the White House".
174. Cited in Salkin and Short, *Method to the Madness*, p. 90.
175. Hitler, *Mein Kampf*, p. 104 (English) and vol. 1, p. 323 (German).
176. Cited in Salkin and Short, *Method to the Madness*, p. 185.
177. Donald J. Trump, with Meredith McIver, *How to Get Rich* (London: BBC Books, 2004), pp. 78–80.
178. Cf. Lewandowski and Bossie, *Let Trump Be Trump*, p. 102.
179. This section is based on Rudolf Herz, *Hoffmann & Hitler. Fotografie als Medium des Führer-Mythos* (Munich: Klinkhardt & Biermann, 1994) and Christina Irrgang, *Hitlers Fotograf. Heinrich Hoffmann und die nationalsozialistische Bildpolitik* (Bielefeld: transcript, 2020) as well as on Joachim Fest and Heinrich Hoffmann, *Hitler. Gesichter eines*

1 Self-Staging: Aura and Appearance   65

Diktators. Bilddokumentation (third ed. Munich: Herbig, 2005), Hoffmann, *Hitler Was My Friend*, and *Das Hitler-Bild. Die Erinnerungen des Fotografen Heinrich Hoffmann. Aufgezeichnet und aus dem Nachlass von Joe J. Heydecker* (St. Pölten—Salzburg: Residenz Verlag, 2008).
180. Georg Seeßlen, "Bilder eines Un-Menschen, Un-Bilder eines Menschen", in Hoffmann, *Das Hitler-Bild*, pp. 213–39 (226).
181. Cited in Herz, *Hoffmann & Hitler*, p. 197, and in Milena Greif's editorial photo commentary in Hoffmann, *Das Hitler-Bild*, p. 76.
182. Cf. Seeßlen, "Bilder eines Un-Menschen", p. 227.
183. Hoffmann, *Hitler Was My Friend*, p. 21.
184. Cf. Thomas Weber, *Hitler's First War: Adolf Hitler, the Men of the List Regiment, and the First World War* (New York etc.: Oxford University Press, 2011; first published 2010), p. 17 and plate 1, as well as Sven Felix Kellerhoff, "Berühmtes Hitler-Foto möglicherweise gefälscht", in *Die Welt*, 14 October 2010. The Nazis used the photograph in a variety of ways, including as one of their *Zigarettenbilder*, small images that were enclosed in cigarette packets and for which there existed albums similar to those used for stamp collections.
185. Occasionally, Hoffmann was obliged to perform the same operation retrospectively; namely, when re-using photographs depicting Hitler with people who had fallen out of favour.
186. The few exceptions only saw the light of day after 1945.
187. Linge, *With Hitler to the End*, p. 56. Photographs of Hitler with his reading glasses can be found in, among others, Fest and Hoffmann, *Hitler*, and Hendrik van Capelle and Arie Pieter van de Bovenkamp, *Hitler 1889–1945. Een tiran in beeld* (new, revised and extended ed. Ede: De Lantaarn, 2019).
188. Hoffmann, *Hitler Was My Friend*, p. 198.
189. Books for children, such as Johanna Haarer's popular *Mutter, erzähl von Adolf Hitler!* (Mommy, Tell Us about Adolf Hitler!, 1939), tended to use stylized drawings instead of photographs.
190. Sims, *Team of Vipers*, pp. 270–71.
191. Goebbels, *Tagebücher*, vol. 1/II, p. 76 (entry of 19 April 1926).
192. Herz, *Hoffmann & Hitler*, p. 332.
193. Schmölders, *Hitlers Gesicht*; the citation comes from the blurb.
194. In January 2018, Trump went a step further, claiming—through White House physician Dr Ronny Jackson—that he was six feet three inches. This spurious claim came to be known as *girtherism*, in analogy to

Trump's equally spurious *birtherism* contention. Cf. Adam Gabbatt, "A Tall Tale? Accuracy of Trump's Medical Report—and New Height—Questioned", *The Guardian*, 17 January 2018.
195. Cf. Blair, *Donald Trump*, pp. ix and xii.
196. Michael Cohen, *Disloyal: A Memoir* (New York, NY: Skyhorse Publishing, 2020), p. 177; cf. Wolff, *Fire and Fury*, p. 79.
197. Cohen, *Disloyal*, pp. 177–78.
198. During the years he hosted *The Apprentice*, Trump apparently spent $70,000 on hairstyling, which (through his production company) he deducted as business expenses from his taxable income. See James B. Stewart, "Trump Took $70,000 in Tax Deductions for Hair Care. Experts Say That's Illegal", *The New York Times*, 6 October 2020.
199. Stormy Daniels, with Kevin Carr O'Leary, *Full Disclosure* (London: Macmillan, 2018), p. 123.
200. See Schmölders, *Hitlers Gesicht*, as well as "Hitlers Gesicht", in Hans-Ulrich Thamer and Simone Erpel (eds.), *Hitler und die Deutschen. Volksgemeinschaft und Verbrechen* (Dresden: Sandstein, 2011), pp. 36–42. Schmölders uses the phrase *faziale Kampagne*.
201. Alain Jaubert, "La moustache d'Adolf Hitler", in *La moustache d'Adolf Hitler et autres essais* (Paris: Gallimard, 2016), pp. 9–31 (9). The citation comes from Pascal's *Pensées* (written ca. 1657–62; published posthumously in 1670).
202. See the lecture series *Führerbart und Volkskörper—Hitler, wie ihn keiner kennt* by Friedrich Tietjen, available on YouTube.
203. Tietjen's reference is to Bridget Hitler, *The Memoirs of Bridget Hitler* (London: Duckworth, 1979). The book was published posthumously; the original manuscript was entitled *My Brother-in-Law Adolf*.
204. Tietjen's reference is to Hans-Albert Walter, *"Der Meisterzeichner von Nachtstücken und Traumgesichten". Alexander Moritz Frey—wiederzuentdecken* (Frankfurt am Main: Büchergilde Gutenberg, 1988), esp. pp. 245–54 ("Der unbekannte Gefreite"). The journalist and writer Alexander Moritz Frey (1881–1957) served in the List Regiment as a medical assistant. When the Nazis came to power in 1933, he emigrated to Austria; after the *Anschluss* of 1938, he moved to Switzerland.
205. Schroeder, *He Was My Chief*, p. 49. In 1927, Adelheid ("Ada") Klein became secretary to Max Amann, managing director of the Eher-Verlag, which had published *Mein Kampf*.

206. The following account is based on Christopher Oldstone-Moore, *Of Beards and Men: The Revealing History of Facial Hair* (Chicago and London: The University of Chicago Press, 2016).
207. Miranda Carter, *The Three Emperors: Three Cousins, Three Empires and the Road to World War One* (London: Fig Tree, 2009), p. 173. One is reminded of Nietzsche's remark that "the gentlest and most reasonable of men can, if he wears a large moustache, sit in its shade, as it were, and feel safe there: ordinary people will see him as the extension of a large moustache—that is to say, as a military type, easily angered and occasionally violent—and they will treat him accordingly". See Friedrich Nietzsche, *Daybreak: Thoughts on the Prejudices of Morality*, trans. R. J. Hollingdale (Cambridge: Cambridge University Press, 1997; first published in German 1881), p. 171 (translation modified). The German original can be found in Friedrich Nietzsche, *Sämtliche Werke. Kritische Studienausgabe*, ed. Giorgio Colli and Mazzino Montinari (new ed. Berlin and New York: de Gruyter / Munich: dtv, 1999), vol. 3, pp. 247–48 (book 4, entry 381).
208. Cf. Oldstone-Moore, *Of Beards and Men* (p. 317, nt. 17, and p. 319, nt. 44), which references an American newspaper article reporting on letters written to the *Berliner Tageblatt*: "'Toothbrush' Mustache: German Women Resent Its Usurpation of the 'Kaiserbart'" (*New York Times*, 20 October 1907).
209. Oldstone-Moore, *Of Beards and Men*, p. 229.

2

Corruption and Money

Among Trump's loudest rallying-cries was his pledge to "drain the swamp". Indeed, the promise to do away with the web of corruption, grifting, nepotism, and financial dependence purportedly characteristic of "the system" is a staple of all populisms. The irony is that populist movements, if and when they come to power, tend to be swampier than their establishment opponents. What is even more ironic, or maybe just tragic, is that so many people do not seem to care.

The illegal graft—perhaps one should phrase matters more cautiously and say: the immoral lining of one's own pockets—is there for everyone to see. Yet the populist electorate are not particularly bothered. To them, the dubious conduct of their political heroes on the one hand and that of traditional politicians on the other fall into different categories. Apparently, there is corruption and then there is corruption. Before we address this paradox, let us have a look at the kind of misbehaviour that is at issue, starting with Trump and his associates.

Trumpworld: An Embarrassment of Riches

The line separating Donald Trump's job as President from his interests as a celebrity businessman was worryingly thin. Indeed, there are plenty of critics who have argued that it was more than a little porous, or simply non-existent.

Upon becoming President, Trump divested himself of his business interests by transferring ownership of the Trump Organization to Donald Trump Jr, Eric Trump, and the company's CFO, Allen Weisselberg. But how clean a break between economics and politics is it, when the new owners are two of Trump's children and one of his former employees; when the President is kept fully abreast of the company's "profitability reports and stuff like that";[1] and when Don Jr and Eric continue to support their father politically on Twitter and by acting as his surrogates on television? There were other ways, too, in which the links between the Trump Organization and the Trump Presidency seemed not to have been fully severed. The Trump hotel in Washington, for example, "raked in cash" due to the "high demand on the part of Republicans, lobbyists and foreign governments", according to *The Washington Post*.[2] There may well have been further economic connections, or entanglements, between the Trump Organization and domestic and foreign entities. Unfortunately, we have no way of knowing, because Trump—breaking with a decades-long tradition—refused to release his tax returns.

It may be that none of this was illegal. Some critics have argued that Trump was in violation of the US Constitution's emoluments clause, which prohibits government employees from accepting, without the consent of Congress, any gift, emolument, office, or title from a foreign state.[3] Others, including the US Department of Justice, disagreed.[4] But regardless of the legal aspects of the situation, the ethical questions it raises are obvious.

How little Trump achieved in draining the swamp becomes apparent when we take stock of the conduct of some of the people around him.[5]

Ivanka Trump—the self-described "First Daughter"[6]—never fully divested herself of her business interests, even though she was an official, and particularly close, Advisor to the President. She held a large number of trademarks across the world "on items ranging from mousetraps to aromatherapy stoves"[7]—trademarks approved by foreign governments. Her interactions with foreign leaders therefore raise serious questions concerning possible conflicts of interest. (Less seriously, the same interactions generated a host of Internet memes, most notably after Ivanka's somewhat awkward attempt to insert herself into an informal gathering of world leaders at the 2019 G20 summit in Japan. Under #unwantedivanka, a slew of photoshopped pictures had Ivanka sitting next to Churchill, Roosevelt, and Stalin at Yalta, crossing Abbey Road with the Beatles, and attending a range of other historic events.) That she was allowed to act as White House adviser at all was due to a re-interpretation of the US anti-nepotism statute of 1967, which prohibits the President from appointing relatives. On the day her father was sworn in, the US Department of Justice's Office of Legal Counsel released a memorandum stating that the statute, while valid for the various agencies of the executive branch, did not actually apply to the White House itself.[8]

This new interpretation of the statute seems to have been conceived largely with Ivanka's husband, Jared Kushner, in mind. Kushner was made Senior Advisor to the President, tasked with developing a Middle Eastern peace plan. But his portfolio expanded rapidly. As Vicky Ward puts it in her 2019 book *Kushner, Inc.: Greed, Ambition, Corruption*, Trump's leadership style and preference for informal decision-making processes (a subject I will explore in a later chapter) "enabled a 'floater' like Kushner, whose job was undefined, to weigh in on any topic in front of Trump and have far more influence than he would have had in a top-down hierarchy"—a situation "which led to his unofficial title as 'Secretary of Everything'".[9] Yet Kushner's position was at least as problematic as that of his wife.

A son of the seriously wealthy real-estate developer Charles Kushner, Jared took over the running of Kushner Companies following his father's criminal conviction in 2005. (Charles Kushner was jailed for preparing false tax returns and trying to influence a witness—his sister—by setting her husband up with a prostitute.) The company almost immediately took a major hit due to the financial crisis of 2008. Particularly badly affected was a 41-floor office building located at 666 Fifth Avenue,

New York, for which Kushner Companies had paid the enormous (and largely borrowed) sum of 1.8 billion dollars.

As with Ivanka Trump's divestment of her business interests, Jared Kushner's divestiture can be called "limited"[10] at best: his considerable assets—"valued between $167.5 and $569.5 million"[11]—were now held in trust by family members. Moreover, Kushner was not exactly forthcoming or transparent when filling in the required disclosure forms upon entering the White House. According to *Bloomberg*, he "had to file more than 40 updates to disclosures about his assets and liabilities, as well as three about contacts with foreign persons".[12] Because of his continued proximity to Kushner Companies, and above all because there were indications that he continued to cast about for domestic and foreign investments in the substantially leveraged 666 Fifth Avenue Building, Kushner was initially denied access to highly classified information. It appears that his security clearance only came through after intervention by his father-in-law, the President.[13]

More recently, in June 2019, *The Guardian* reported that a company partially owned by Kushner had received $90m from unknown offshore investors.[14] The company in question was Cadre, an online real-estate broker and investment fund that was cofounded by Kushner and in which he still owned a stake worth up to $50 million (a fact initially omitted from his financial disclosure forms—an oversight that was rectified only after it had been revealed by *The Wall Street Journal*). Cadre's investment arm was managed by an offshore Goldman Sachs entity in the Cayman Islands and owned by another such vehicle; Cadre proper benefited from annual fees and a profit-sharing arrangement. It was through this channel that the $90 million of foreign money reportedly found their way to the company. While such a set-up is not illegal, it does not make for transparency—and again raised the question whether Kushner was vulnerable to foreign (or, for that matter, domestic) influence.

All this would have been bad enough, but the situation was aggravated by Kushner's near total lack of qualifications for a job that prominently included brokering peace between Israel and the Palestinians. In *Kushner, Inc.*, Vicky Ward cites the then White House counsel Don McGahn as commenting on Kushner's potential appointment in the following terms: "You know the real reason there's an anti-nepotism law? [...] It's not so much about corruption—though it is, partly—as it is about incompetence. You can't fire family, as a general rule".[15] Ward also reports that Kushner was nicknamed the "clown prince", while Ivanka's office in the West Wing was apparently known as HABI, or the Home of All Bad Ideas.[16]

Finally, both Jared Kushner and Ivanka Trump were not particularly well aligned with the President's ideological agenda. They appear to have been globalists rather than economic nationalists, and they were much more liberal on immigration and LGBTQ+ rights than Donald Trump in his stated policies. This has raised the suspicion that both saw their roles largely "as a networking opportunity", as one of Vicky Ward's sources puts it.[17] But regardless of whether or not they influenced Trump in any meaningful way, and regardless of how indispensable or otherwise they were as White House advisors, their continued involvement in the business world did not exactly help drain the Washington swamp.

If Trump, his daughter, and his son-in-law conducted themselves in a fashion that was "merely" ethically dubious, others in the President's orbit strayed into outright criminality.[18]

In December 2017, Trump's first National Security Advisor—occupant of one of the most important positions in any administration—pleaded guilty to lying to the FBI about his paid consultancy work for the Turkish government and his contacts with Russian Ambassador Sergey Kislyak. Obama had warned Trump against appointing Michael Flynn ("He'll cause you nothing but problems")[19] but the President-Elect had ignored that advice, going instead with "Jarvanka's"[20] rather less well-informed recommendation. Trump should have taken his predecessor's advice. "Arguably", a judge told Flynn at a hearing in December 2018, "you sold your country out".[21] Trump granted Flynn a federal pardon in November 2020. A less prominent foreign-policy advisor to the Trump campaign, George Papadopoulos, was likewise convicted of lying to the FBI about his contacts with foreign nationals (a Maltese man and a Russian woman who both claimed to have connections to Russians with "dirt" on Democratic Presidential candidate Hillary Clinton.) Trump granted Papadopoulos a federal pardon in December 2020.

Trump's former campaign manager Paul Manafort was charged with multiple crimes relating to his political consultancy work in Ukraine (among others for Viktor Yanukovich, the country's pro-Russian President until 2014). The charges included money laundering, tax evasion, and bank fraud; later, witness tampering and obstruction of justice were added. According to the prosecutors, Manafort had raked in 60 million dollars from his Ukrainian clients between 2010 and 2014, spending much of it on a host of luxury items including a now infamous ostrich bomber-jacket worth $15,000 (an item described by *The Washington Post*'s fashion critic Robin Givhan as "an atrocity" and "a garment thick with hubris").[22] He had offered his services to Trump for free, though less—one suspects—out of the kindness of his heart than in the hope of financial gain further down the road: his lavish lifestyle was hard to maintain and he "was drowning in debt at the time".[23] He was sentenced to seven and a half years in jail. Trump granted Manafort a federal pardon in December 2020.

Trump's personal lawyer, Michael Cohen, likewise found himself in court. He was convicted of tax fraud, bank fraud, and lying to Congress, as well as of violating campaign-finance laws while buying off the porn star Stormy Daniels and the model Karen McDougal, who both had claimed to have had an affair with Donald Trump. Cohen was sentenced to three years in jail. According to *Bloomberg*, "a cascade of discoveries" also made it clear "how Cohen sought to profit from Trump's victory. Companies including AT&T and Novartis AG paid him at least $2.4 million after the election for his insights into the Trump administration".[24] As with Manafort ("I didn't know Manafort well. He wasn't with the campaign long"), Trump sought to minimize Cohen's importance to him: "He was a lawyer for me, one of many. [...] Didn't do big deals, did small deals. Not somebody that was with me that much. [...] I would see him sometimes, but when I had deals and big deals I had outside lawyers, and I have a lot of inside lawyers, too, in addition to Michael".[25] In fact, deciding on a personal lawyer, a campaign manager, and a national-security advisor is crucial to anyone running for President. And for someone avowedly focused on draining the swamp, Trump displayed either considerable insouciance or an astonishing lack of judgement (or both) in making these decisions.

The ethical and legal transgressions extended well beyond the circle of people involved in Trump's campaign. Several of his Cabinet members, too, engaged in seriously swampy behaviour. Let us review the most egregious cases.[26]

Health Secretary Tom Price was forced to resign over his wasteful use of private jets at the expense of the American taxpayer. Among other things, he had flown to Philadelphia for $25,000 when a standard commercial flight would have cost him $400, and to Nashville for $17,760 when a regular ticket would have been $200. "Tom Price", Alexander Nazaryan writes acerbically in his 2019 book *The Best People: Trump's Cabinet and the Siege on Washington*, "would leave Washington in disgrace. Whether he returned to [his home in] Atlanta in first class or coach could not be determined, nor whether decency compelled him to pay for the flight out of his own pocket".[27]

Scott Pruitt, whom Trump had chosen to lead the Environmental Protection Agency (EPA), lasted a little longer than Price, but he, too, was eventually obliged to throw in the towel over his misuse of taxpayer money. Indeed, his conduct made "Tom Price's grotesque abuse of government services seem like the theft of a pencil sharpener", as Alexander Nazaryan puts it.[28] To the delight of corporate lobbyists and climate-change deniers, Pruitt's time as head of the EPA consisted largely of endeavours to *get rid of* environmental-protection regulations. This led seven hundred employees to leave the agency in the first year of his tenure. But the EPA's time of dearth was Pruitt's time of plenty. He increasingly "[took] on the trappings of a third-world dictator", ranging from "[ordering] his subordinates to drive him around Washington so he could find an overpriced Ritz-Carlton moisturizer he was fond of" and "spending nearly $10,000 on decorating his own office" to "[surrounding] himself with an army of nineteen security officers".[29] Pruitt resigned in July 2018.

Faced with fifteen government investigations into his conduct, Ryan Zinke stepped down as Trump's Interior Secretary in January 2019. He, too, had on multiple occasions preferred private planes and helicopters to considerably cheaper options. (This is not to suggest that he ought to have continued using the mode of transportation of his first day at work, when he had arrived at the Department on horseback, wearing a cowboy hat, a windbreaker, and jeans.) As was the case with Pruitt—Nazaryan writes—Zinke's "actions consistently favored corporate concerns. It was the latter that were going to fund future political ambitions, which Zinke harbored just as much as Pruitt. He turned the Interior Department into a reverse philanthropy, one that gave away to oil and gas companies natural treasures that belonged to the American people".[30] And, again like Pruitt, he was brought down by his hubris and disregard for the taxpaying public. With Zinke unwilling to change his ways, the number of stories and reports about his conduct began to grow, as did the number of official investigations. Finally, Donald Trump—refusing as always to let anyone steal his limelight, even if only through negative media coverage—had had enough. On 15 December 2018, he tweeted that "Secretary of the Interior @RyanZinke will be leaving the Administration at the end of the year after having served for a period of almost two years".

For the purposes of this chapter it does not matter whether these various manoeuvres are illegal or just immoral. What matters is that they are the exact opposite of Trump's promise to drain the swamp. The type of populism we are dealing with is (among other things, of course) irredeemably kleptocratic in nature. This applies to National Socialism, too. Even the supposedly ascetic Adolf Hitler was no exception.[31]

Hitler's Early Profits

Adolf Hitler tried hard—and successfully—to project an image of himself as a kind of warrior-monk. This is the reason he kept his relationship with his steady girlfriend, Eva Braun, a secret from all but his closest associates. He presented himself as a man of the people; even more so, as essentially classless—as someone with no other ties and no other loyalties than to the *Volk* as a whole. Here—he managed to make the German people believe—was a man devoted body and soul to his mission, a leader without the materialism and corruption of lesser mortals. The reality was rather different.

It is true that Hitler's private life was not as extravagant as that of the Supreme Commander of the German air force, Hermann Göring. Nor was it as licentious as that of Propaganda Minister Joseph Goebbels. Nonetheless, the Führer did quite well out of his political career, and he had no compunction about using state funds for personal ends.

The early origins of Hitler's wealth are to be found in the sales of *Mein Kampf*—his combined autobiography and political manifesto—and the financial support from a number of rich benefactors.

Following his failed attempt at a *coup d'État* in November 1923, Hitler was sentenced to five years' incarceration in Landsberg Prison in Bavaria. He would in fact be released in December 1924 for what the Court considered his good conduct. In Landsberg Prison, Hitler embarked on *Mein Kampf*. Contrary to what is often assumed, his fellow prisoner—subsequently his private secretary and then Deputy Leader of the Nazi Party—Rudolf Heß played little or no role in the process. Hitler wrote the book on his own, even typing up large parts of the manuscript himself. The writing stretched into the post-Landsberg era. The first volume was published in July 1925; the second volume (for which Hitler could call on the help of a typist) came out in December 1926.

Mein Kampf was not an immediate commercial success. Initially, it sold neither particularly well nor particularly badly. In 1930, sales boomed. In that year, the publisher brought out a single-volume *Volksausgabe* (a popular—or people's—edition), which at eight Reichsmarks was considerably cheaper than the two-volume edition, which sold at a price of twenty-four Reichsmarks. A second factor was even more important. In 1930, Hitler's National Socialist German Workers' Party (Nationalsozialistische Deutsche Arbeiterpartei, or NSDAP) won a major election victory. From a mere also-ran, it became the second largest party in the German parliament, the Reichstag. Hitler and his ideas were now the object of considerable national attention. Three years later, when Hitler had become Chancellor, there was an even bigger sales boom: in 1933, the publisher shifted a million copies of *Mein Kampf*.

During the National Socialist reign, a range of strategies were employed to boost sales even further. A short documentary film, *Das Buch der Deutschen* (The Book of the Germans, 1936), featured people from all walks of life reading *Mein Kampf*, suggesting that no self-respecting German could do without Hitler's book. The Reich Estate of German Industry—the nazified successor to Germany's industrialists' associations—was pressured to provide every former soldier who had become disabled during the First World War with a copy. The various Party organs were likewise leaned on to ensure that their members possessed the book. Booksellers were obliged to sell only new, not second-hand, copies. An array of expensive leather-bound gift and jubilee editions were produced. Later, when the war had started, a lightweight *Tornisterausgabe*—or knapsack edition—for soldiers was added to the mix. There was even a state-subsidized Braille edition for the blind. The famous *Mein Kampf* wedding present, however, which registry offices were supposed to buy for all newlyweds, was not nearly as widespread as later mythology would have it. The majority of local authorities felt that they could not afford the expense. Still, by 1945 a total of well over twelve million copies of Hitler's book had been sold.

Unlike many other authors, Hitler had no running battles with his publisher: he himself was the sole shareholder of Franz Eher Nachfolger GmbH. The NSDAP had bought Eher, which published the *Völkischer Beobachter*, Bavaria's main anti-Semitic newspaper, in 1920. But it had done so with borrowed money. The NSDAP's then chairman, Anton Drexler, had refused to dig into the Party's coffers for what he considered an unnecessarily risky undertaking. The next year, Hitler personally paid off the entire loan, acquiring all shares in both the publishing house and the newspaper. He had little trouble in doing so. Due to the growing inflation, the Reichsmark had lost much of its value. For ordinary Germans, this was obviously bad news. For financial speculators and people in possession of significant amounts of foreign currency, gold, or valuables, it was excellent news. Hitler was one of these *Inflationsgewinnler*. He benefited from donations from both foreign backers and wealthy German donors.

This significant level of outside funding was one of the main differences between the NSDAP and many of the other right-wing extremist groups that sprang up after the First World War and then folded for lack of money. The authorities were well aware of this. An official memorandum on the Nazi party, written shortly after the coup attempt of 1923, stated: "Just like war, a revolution requires: 1. money, 2. money, and 3. money. Without money, no revolution".[32] Yet the authorities did not know exactly how much money Hitler and the NSDAP possessed, nor where it came from. Donations often found their way to the Nazis through slush funds. Hitler himself systematically dispensed with receipts when receiving hard cash or expensive jewellery, something which allowed him to hide such gifts from Party oversight as well as from the tax office. He also tended to treat the Party's coffers as his own, regularly helping himself to a few thousand extra Reichsmarks in order to finance his luxurious lifestyle (a topic to which we will return shortly). The disbursements were entered in the books as "additional expenses for PR purposes"; the recipient was not mentioned.

Foreign money was particularly welcome. Especially during the hyperinflation of 1922/1923 even small amounts of foreign currency literally amounted to gold dust. Through various go-betweens, the National Socialists received donations from Italian fascists, ethnic German *Sudetendeutsche* in Czechoslovakia, anti-communist *émigré* Russians, and a host of other foreign sources. There are even indications that the US car manufacturer Henry Ford may have subsidized the rising Nazi movement. Hitler himself denied this more than once. But, then, the whole point of this type of payment was precisely to keep it secret. After all, the Party did not want the money to be taxed, nor did it want political opponents to accuse it of being in the pay of a foreign entity.

The American industrialist and the German politician were certainly well aligned ideologically. Henry Ford was viciously anti-Semitic. His four-volume *The International Jew* (1920–1922)—a reprint of articles originally published in his weekly newspaper, *The Dearborn Independent*—put forward many of the same conspiracy theories and racial prejudices that were central to Hitler's world view. It evoked such fantasies as the Jewish desire for world domination, the Jewish essence of communism, and the parasitical nature of Jewish life. The book's German translation was a massive success in *völkisch* circles. Hitler, too, was an admirer; a large Ford portrait adorned one of the walls of his study in the NSDAP's Munich headquarters. He praised him in *Mein Kampf* as the only American capable of resisting the so-called baleful influence of Jewish financiers.[33] Hitler was impressed by Ford in another respect, too: the cheap Model T car seems to have been the main inspiration behind the idea of the *Volkswagen*, or people's car. (Although Hitler supported the idea as early as 1934, the car did not see mass production until after the Nazi era.) In 1938, the National Socialist government awarded Ford the prestigious Grand Cross of the Order of the German Eagle.

Until 1933, domestic financial support for Hitler, while anything but negligible, was not massive. This was not unproblematic, as the Party's expenses were considerable. From the start, Hitler thought big. Moreover, he was exceedingly media-savvy. More than most, he realized that propaganda is not simply a matter of selling one's existing strengths as best as possible. Rather, it is the selling—the advertising—itself, if it is done in the right way, that creates those strengths. As the Thomas theorem in sociology goes: if people define a situation as real, then that situation is real in its consequences. In other words, if the voters *think* a party is strong, then that party has a good chance of becoming strong. As we saw in the first chapter, Hitler's sense of theatrical make-believe was a potent weapon in his practical political arsenal. But his political *Gesamtkunstwerke* cost large sums of money, even as early as the 1920s. The extravagant party conferences with their pomp and circumstance, in particular, were extremely expensive.

It was thus a matter of great regret to Hitler that initially German big business did not contribute to the National Socialist cause in any substantial way. That only happened from 1933 onwards, as we will see later. Business-related money came from the owners of small and medium-sized companies, most of them based in Bavaria. A rare exception was the industrialist Fritz Thyssen, chairman of the board of Vereinigte Stahlwerke, an iron and steel conglomerate that included his own Thyssen & Co. His most significant donation came in 1928, when he helped finance the so-called *Braunes Haus*, the Nazi party's headquarters in Munich. It is unclear exactly how much money Thyssen donated to the Nazis, but the sum must have been considerable: the transformation of the former Barlow Palace into the National Socialist HQ was a major operation. Located in the poshest area of Munich, the three-floor Brown House sported two big bronze doors, a large entrance hall, wood-panelled rooms with expensive leather chairs, and a restaurant in the basement. From today's perspective, it may have been "a building of tasteless grandiosity", as the British historian Ian Kershaw puts it,[34] but it certainly made an impression at the time. "[O]nly the Swastika flag floating over the roof", wrote Kurt Lüdecke, one of Hitler's early fundraisers, "convinced me that this was not a cardinal's palace or a Jewish banker's luxurious residence".[35]

It is only fair to add that in later years Fritz Thyssen broke with Hitler. Appalled by the increasingly vicious nature of the Nazis' anti-Semitism, opposed to the war in Poland, and no longer willing to defend the Third Reich's (pseudo-)legality, he fled Germany in 1939. He went first to Switzerland, then to France. After the invasion of France in 1940, he was arrested and taken back to Germany, where he was incarcerated, initially in a mental asylum and subsequently in various concentration camps, throughout the war. He died in 1951. In 1929 or 1930, he had explained to the journalist Rosie Waldeck why he was unworried about Hitler's more extreme pronouncements. You had to take Hitler seriously, he had said, but not literally. "Good God", Thyssen told Waldeck, "a leader of the masses on the make has to say many things".[36]

Among Hitler's early domestic benefactors were a significant number of women. Many of them moved in the upper circles of German society; several were aristocrats. They tended to be of a certain age. Their relationship to the young man was that of mother, mentor, and (as far as we can tell, Platonic) mistress. These women shared many of his ideas, but they were also keen to impress their upper-class friends and display this bad boy of German politics in their salons. Hitler for his part was only too happy to play mad, bad, and dangerous to know. He consciously combined revolutionary ruffianism with old-style Viennese charm. He would turn up to soirées with a trenchcoat over his evening dress (which made him look like a Chicago gangster), a holstered pistol, and a heavy dogwhip—as well as a bouquet of flowers for the hostess. He usually left early, sometimes after a deliberately engineered confrontation or faked outburst of anger, to ensure that the remaining guests would then talk about him and him only.

The most influential and enthusiastic of his female champions were Helene Bechstein, who was married to the piano manufacturer Carl Bechstein; Elsa Bruckmann, a Romanian princess by birth; the American Helene Hanfstaengl, wife to the well-connected art-print publisher Ernst Hanfstaengl (himself a strong supporter of Hitler); and Winifred Wagner, who was married to Richard Wagner's son. They provided Hitler with an entrée to Germany's *haute volée*—to its aristocracy, wealthy industrialists, high-ranking military officers, publishers, and public intellectuals. They also acted as his etiquette tutors. This was no idle task, since by no means all of Hitler's social unconventionality and awkwardness was feigned. His table manners, for instance, left much to be desired. At multi-course dinners, he did not know how to use the various sets of cutlery properly, and as a virtual teetotaller he had a tendency to sweeten his wine with sugar. His clothes and speech were not always appropriate either, and here too the *grandes dames* delighted in educating their wild boy. Last but not least, they sponsored Hitler financially, often with inflation-resistant *objets d'art* and jewellery.

The NSDAP in the 1920s may have struggled to finance its large-scale campaigns and lavish conferences, but this did not prevent its leader from living the high life. Nor was he in any way inhibited by the fact that ordinary Party members often had to make real sacrifices just to pay their membership fees. The royalties from the sales of his autobiography-cum-manifesto, foreign and domestic donations, money for speeches and newspaper articles, and the unabashed appropriation of Party funds—all combined to make Hitler a millionaire even before he became Chancellor in 1933.

As early as 1925, only a few months after his release from Landsberg Prison and before the publication of the first volume of *Mein Kampf*, Hitler bought a top-of-the-line Mercedes. His second-hand Selve ("a rattling monster", according to Ernst Hanfstaengl)[37] was in his eyes no longer suitable for a man of his standing. The 1923 coup attempt and subsequent trial had, after all, put him firmly on the national political map. Even more than his old vehicle, his new car set him apart from the communist leaders, who tended to travel by bus, tram, and train. A chauffeur was of course *de rigueur*. Hitler also hired a bodyguard and employed Rudolf Heß as his private secretary. In addition, he engaged a secretary to type up the manuscript of the second volume of *Mein Kampf*. Their combined salaries ran to 800 Reichsmarks per month. The average monthly salary in Germany at the time was 120 Reichsmarks. The ex-convict could even afford to rent a holiday home, Haus Wachenfeld near Berchtesgaden in the Bavarian Alps. In 1929, he moved from his modest flat in Munich's Thierschstraße to a nine-bedroom luxury apartment in Prinzregentenstraße, one of the city's four "royal avenues". Two maids did the housekeeping. Here, Hitler was joined by his half-niece, Geli Raubal, with whom he maintained an erotically tinged—though probably not sexual—relationship.[38]

By the late 1920s, the failed painter had become so rich that he was in a position to start accumulating expensive canvasses by rather more gifted artists. His taste remained bourgeois, though. His preference was for the nineteenth century; the Expressionism of contemporaries such as Marc and Kandinsky was for him "nothing but lame daubing".[39] (His literary taste was equally dubious: his favourite authors were Karl May and Edgar Wallace.) Over time, his collection of works by Carl Spitzweg—the painter best known for *The Poor Poet* of 1839—would grow to be the largest in the world.

The King of Munich, as Hitler came to be called, was not merely relying on his manifold income streams. He was also helped by the fact that he paid almost no taxes. As the journalist and author Wolfgang Zdral puts it, the future leader of Germany was "an ordinary tax dodger".[40]

It appears that before 1924 Hitler was not on the tax office's radar. From then on its officials and Hitler were fighting a running battle, with queries, reminders, fines, and appeals. The tax office wanted to know how he could afford his various luxuries, starting with his brand-new 20,000-Reichsmark Mercedes. Hitler evoked an advance for *Mein Kampf*, bank loans, and debts. He portrayed himself as a struggling political writer who spent most of his extremely modest means in pursuance of his profession. While claiming manifold tax reductions and exemptions for his so-called job-related expenses, including those for his bodyguard and driver, he was careful to mention only those sources of income that he knew the authorities could check, which meant almost exclusively the profits from Eher (his publishing house) and the royalties from *Mein Kampf*. At a conservative estimate, he seems to have declared as little as ten per cent of his actual income.

The tug-of-war came to an end in 1935. Already in 1933, shortly after he had become Chancellor, Hitler was exempted from paying taxes.[41] But this exemption covered only his salary and expense allowance, not any other income. Moreover, he had been informed that he still owed 405,494.40 Reichsmarks in back taxes. Hitler felt that some political pressure was called for. On his instigation, an official from the *Reichsfinanzministerium* discreetly intervened with the tax office. Early

1935, the new leader of Germany was officially fully tax-exempt. The outstanding 405,494.40 Reichsmarks were cancelled into the bargain.

The *Reichskanzler* and His Riches

The year 1933 was not just a political, but also a financial milestone for Hitler. Almost immediately, the newly appointed Reich Chancellor began to use his position to amass an enormous personal fortune. From now on, the money would no longer come in by the hundreds of thousands, but by the millions, and all of it tax-free. Within less than a decade, the supposedly selfless servant of Germany was one of the richest people in Europe.

More conscious than ever before of the power of propaganda, he continued to foster an image of simplicity and sobriety. In a well-publicized act of seeming self-denial, the National Socialist Chancellor waived his salary (as Donald J. Trump would do many years later). But his generosity did not last long. When following the death of President Hindenburg the functions of *Reichspräsident* and *Reichskanzler* were merged into one, Hitler, encouraged by the fact that he was tax-exempt, had a change of heart. From 1935, he collected both salaries—without making this public, of course.

The central factor in Hitler's advancement from millionaire to multi-millionaire was the *Adolf-Hitler-Spende der deutschen Wirtschaft*, or Adolf Hitler Fund of German Trade and Industry. Before 1933, most leading German industrialists did not support the Nazi cause except with occasional small donations that were given more or less indiscriminately to all political parties as a kind of insurance policy. Now a rethink seemed in order (if one abstracts from moral considerations, that is). Partly on their own accord and partly under pressure from the new regime, Germany's captains of industry—led by Gustav Krupp von Bohlen und Halbach, head of the Reich Estate of German Industry—agreed to a special corporate tax to support the nation's "reconstruction". Many of them were still sceptical about the NSDAP, but they had been given assurances by Hitler that the National Socialist order would not actually be economically socialist.[42] So the representatives of concerns such as AEG, IG Farben,

Krupp, Siemens, and Vereinigte Stahlwerke went along with the proposal that all German companies, banks, and farming enterprises contribute 0.5 per cent of their annual wage costs to the fund. In total, this new income stream would generate the colossal sum of 700 million Reichsmarks.

The Adolf Hitler Fund did not carry its name for nothing: the money was put at the Führer's personal disposal. Unsurprisingly, Hitler, who had never been inclined to account for his expenditure to anyone, did not want the NSDAP's treasurer to administer the money. That would have been too official. Rudolf Heß and Max Amann—the managing director of Eher publishing house—were likewise deemed unsuitable. Heß was too scrupulous and correct, Amann too untrustworthy and corrupt. The Führer settled on Martin Bormann, Heß's chief of staff. With a tendency to bullying behaviour and sexual harassment, Bormann was a particularly unpleasant person to work for. But he was an excellent organiser with an eye for detail and a near-photographic memory. He was also completely ruthless. Bormann would ensure that the fund for national reconstruction was used "appropriately"; that is, to fulfil the Führer's every wish and whim.[43]

Hitler possessed one further major income stream. It was linked to his private photographer, Heinrich Hoffmann. Hoffmann, who started working for him in the early 1920s, played a central role in his life. As we saw in the first chapter, the photographer was vital to the Führer's political *Selbstinszenierung*, his strategy of self-promotion through the mediagenic projection of a powerful populist persona. In addition, it was in *Photohaus Hoffmann* that Hitler first met Eva Braun, who worked there as photo-laboratory technician and sales assistant. But Hoffmann's activities also provided Hitler with an important source of income.

Together with Max Amann and Hermann Esser and financially supported by Fritz Thyssen, the two men founded the *Illustrierter Beobachter*, a weekly magazine that served as tabloid version of the NSDAP's more serious, or at least more tedious, *Völkischer Beobachter*. Hoffmann provided the photographs; Hitler wrote lucrative political columns. But the enterprising photographer also developed a number of business schemes that enabled him to benefit more directly from his connection to Hitler and which generated much larger sums of money. The Führer, who received a share in the profits, was the happy co-beneficiary of these ventures. To begin with, Hoffmann, who was Hitler's only official photographer, began selling his boss's pictures to national and international journals and magazines on a massive scale. The more fame and notoriety the politician achieved, the more the demand for pictures went up and the more wealth the photographer accumulated. A second scheme involved the sale of Hitler-themed photo albums. Hoffmann even set up his own publishing house to produce them. Between them, these relatively slim volumes (they did not exceed 100 pages) sold in the hundreds of thousands at a price of ten to thirteen Reichsmarks.

Of course, in addition to fulfilling an economic purpose, the albums also had a clear propaganda function. Carefully selected and captioned, the photographs were meant to combine, or reconcile, the two key elements of political populism—anti-elitism and people's community on the one hand and cult of the leader on the other hand. They portrayed Hitler simultaneously as someone like all of us, a man of the people, and someone unlike any of us, a leader above the fray. A good example is *Hitler wie ihn keiner kennt* (The Hitler Nobody Knows, 1932)—a rather misleading title given the fact that the album seeks to convey the very ideas that the National Socialists had been propagating right from the start. It contains photos with captions such as: "Hitler's mother. This old photograph [...] is now his most precious possession"; "Reply to the system. You say: we are staying whatever the cost. I say: we will beat you whatever it takes"; "Son of the people. No one is loved more by the German workers than Adolf Hitler"; and "Adolf Hitler's life is simplicity itself. He never drinks a drop of alcohol and he doesn't smoke".[44] The free press is a prominent target as fake news: "Relaxation. [...] Reading opposition newspapers, he enjoys the falsehoods they tell about him: champagne boozing sessions, Jewish girlfriends, luxury villa, French money..." and "With his sister. Reading the newspaper reveals lies, lies, and more lies, but the truth is unstoppable. The belief in the Führer is stronger than the power of the press".[45]

Hoffmann sold not only Hitler's photographs, but also his old watercolours. He even produced an expensive coffee-table book with facsimile reproductions. But his masterstroke was the suggestion to Hitler that the

Führer enforce the copyright on the use of his image on postage stamps. The royalties ran into the tens of millions of Reichsmarks.

The Führer's fortune enabled him to live a life of plenty that ordinary Germans could only dream about. In James Pool's summary: "Hitler enjoyed all the benefits of great wealth. He was surrounded by servants who catered to his every need. He had several private chauffeurs, his own pilot, a fleet of custom-made Mercedes automobiles, and several personal airplanes. His private railroad cars were equipped with all the luxuries fit for a king. Fine antiques and handcrafted furniture filled his three homes. [...] All three of his homes contained libraries filled with rare books, which together made up one of the best rare book collections in Germany".[46] And then, of course, there were his paintings, as we saw earlier. "Hitler had so much money to spend on his private art collection by 1938 that he employed two major art dealers, in addition to [Heinrich] Hoffmann, to purchase paintings for him. [...] He now owned Leonardo da Vinci's *Leda and the Swan, A Self-Portrait* by Rembrandt, *The Dancing Children* by Watteau, [and] *The Honey Thief* by Cranach the Elder".[47]

There was nothing too small or too big that the Führer could not get if he wanted it. He only had to drop a hint and his attendants—or, in the case of more extravagant wishes, Martin Bormann—would make things happen. Yet Hitler remained strikingly modest where his clothes were concerned. Frequently, his outfit was unfashionable, ill-fitting, and cheap. In a memoir first published in 1949, Hitler's valet Karl Wilhelm Krause ascribes his master's dress sense to a combination of impatience, idiosyncrasy, and lack of interest in sartorial matters.[48] This is almost certainly a misapprehension, as Krause's memoir itself implicitly makes clear.

According to Krause, Hitler's "civilian clothes were so worn out that even a lowly office clerk would not have worn them, unless it was perhaps just for work".[49] Coats and hats were often bought off the rack. He "wore all his clothes loose, sort of hanging around his body. You can well imagine all the criticism I had to listen to. From all sides, even in letters written by ordinary people—they all reproached me".[50] Krause was equally embarrassed about the Führer's uniform caps. "I often commented to him how 'that really looks like a postman's cap' or 'engine drivers might wear such *lids* on their heads, but certainly nobody else'. [...] Once, at a Party convention, I had removed the wire bow from his cap, and it really looked considerably better. He didn't notice this immediately. Only once we were already on our way, did he realise that the wiring was missing. I was totally convinced that he would throw me out of the car right then and there. [...] I do believe, however, that everyone made fun of how he wore his cap. It was the same story with his shoes and boots. He simply couldn't bear parting from his old high boots. [...] These boots, as well, were the talk of town, what with their unsightly folds".[51] Krause also relates how Hitler tended to combine light suits with black socks and black shoes—something which looked "just awful".[52]

It is of course possible that such predilections were mere personal quirks. Their systematic nature, however, suggests otherwise. Hitler's choices all express, or rather project, an unpretentious and unprivileged persona. *Kleider machen Leute* (Clothes Make the Man, 1874) is the title of Gottfried Keller's well-known novella in which a poor tailor achieves social standing due to his fine clothing. Hitler gave this idea a populist twist by dressing down to the point of shabbiness. The reactions that Krause cites show that the people were indeed taken in by this piece of sartorial trickery.[53]

Among Hitler's more extravagant wishes two stand out. First, there was the conversion of his rustic holiday retreat, Haus Wachenfeld on the Obersalzberg near Berchtesgaden in the Bavarian Alps, into a quasi-royal residence. Hitler had bought Haus Wachenfeld, which he had been renting since the late 1920s, in 1933. "Even before Hitler set eyes on the place", Cris Whetton writes, "the area had long been a retreat for the rich; attracted by its thermal springs, beauty, and isolation, Bavaria's kings chose [it] as their summer residence. By 1923, when Hitler first visited, it had become the favourite location for the summer homes of wealthy industrialists such as [Carl] Bechstein".[54] The conversion of the "little cottage of the People's Chancellor", as Haus Wachenfeld was called on German postcards, took place in several stages and was a massive undertaking.

Named the Berghof, the new building was several times the size of the old chalet. It had two upper floors, an enormous sun terrace, thirty spacious rooms, several dining rooms, a modern kitchen, a dental surgery, and a barber's shop. All guestrooms had a bath made of Italian marble as well as a radio. Hitler and Eva Braun each had their own private room (a huge study with seating area for the Führer, a sitting room for his girlfriend), bedroom, and bathroom. Their bedrooms were separated only by a small storage room with two connecting doors. Eva, a photography aficionado, also had her own darkroom. The so-called Great Hall on the ground floor included a conference area, a huge electronically retractable picture window, and an oversized globe that seems to have been the inspiration for one of the most iconic scenes in Charlie Chaplin's film *The Great Dictator*. Two tapestries on opposite sides of the hall hid a film projector and a wide screen. The walls were adorned with paintings by German and Italian masters. A bronze bust of Richard Wagner by the National Socialist "heroic-realist" sculptor Arno Breker completed (perhaps one should say, marred) the art collection. The basement comprised several large storage rooms and a garage, but also a bowling alley—Hitler was a keen bowler as well as a film buff—that doubled up as a shooting range, which Hitler spurned but Eva Braun enjoyed using.

The Führer did not leave things there. The private and political dimensions of his life had always been one, and he wanted the Berghof to serve as a place where he could plan his projects and discuss them (to the extent that he was capable of discussion) with his subordinates. The idea was that he would hold court at the Berghof and receive his ministers and generals as well as foreign leaders and diplomats there. He wanted, in effect, to have his own supersized Camelot. This required an array of additional buildings and security measures. The latter were needed anyway, as the place had become too much of an attraction for celebrity-obsessed tourists.

Martin Bormann was chosen to construct what in essence would be the Reich's second seat of government after Berlin. He took to the task with gusto—and an iron fist. (His tyrannical regime would eventually earn him the nickname "Napoleon of the Obersalzberg".)[55] He started off by buying up large stretches of land. Owners who refused to sell were threatened with forced eviction or a one-way ticket to a concentration camp. He then embarked on what his biographer Jochen von Lang calls an "insane building spree", though—as von Lang stresses—there can be no doubt that the work was done with Hitler's assent.[56] The result was a small private village with staff quarters, SS barracks with drill ground and gym, a communication centre, a cinema, a hotel, a nursery, a grocer's shop, a post office, and a teahouse, as well as a farm, a greenhouse (for the Führer's vegetarian meals), and even an apiary with a hundred hives. Forest paths were turned into asphalt promenades, and new interconnecting roads were added. The entire area was cordoned off with an elevated barbed-wire fence and declared *Führersperrgebiet*—or prohibited area for private use of the Führer only—*Obersalzberg*. Just three other high-ranking Nazis—Hermann Göring, Hitler's architect Albert Speer, and Bormann himself—likewise possessed houses within this area. An auxiliary branch of the Reich Chancellery in Berlin and a small airfield were constructed just outside Berchtesgaden, which itself was home to a brothel for additional entertainment. During the war, a miles-long network of bunkers and tunnels was built under the Obersalzberg, while the Berghof was covered with camouflage nettting.

Bormann's most insanely grandiose project was the erection of a building on the top of the Kehlstein mountain, located some 2,600 feet above the Berghof. Known as the Eagle's Nest in the English-speaking world, the Kehlsteinhaus was Bormann's present for the Führer's fiftieth birthday in 1939—an expression of sycophancy vis-à-vis his master and a form of one-upmanship vis-à-vis the Führer's other henchmen. The highly challenging project involved tunnelling deep into the mountain, drilling a vertical shaft to the top, and then installing a lift. Several workers lost their lives during the construction work. Although the Kehlsteinhaus is usually called a teahouse, it was really more of a luxury restaurant—built at the price of thirty million Reichsmarks.[57] It was used mostly to impress foreign dignitaries. Hitler himself was not a keen visitor; he disliked the height and the thin air. In addition, he was worried about accidents, such as the lift being struck by lightning, and about assassination attempts in what was an extremely confined and exposed space.

The small Obersalzberg community served as a substitute home for Hitler, who had no emotionally satisfying family life and no real friends. It grounded him and provided him with a psychological balance of sorts. At the same time, there was a specific public-relations dimension to the various architectural designs. The Berghof itself, in particular, was not simply built to furnish the Führer with a combined luxury villa and Alpine seat of government and stun his visitors with mere grandiosity. As

Despina Stratigakos has shown in her magisterial *Hitler at Home*, it was also developed to reflect his newly minted image as a more traditional politician, or at least as someone who was up to the task of leading Germany and whom foreign leaders would take seriously.[58] After all, Hitler had assumed the Chancellorship only recently, and before that he had been more of a revolutionary leader than a party politician. That outsider status had helped propel him to power, but now he had to prove that he could hold his own on the world stage. Indeed, even a year after he had become Chancellor, during the Night of the Long Knives in 1934, Hitler had had a significant number of high-ranking fellow Nazis murdered because he considered them a threat to his control of the Party. This had once again made him look like a Chicago gangster (even though effective propaganda had convinced many Germans of the so-called necessity of this butchery). An update to his image was thus called for. Architecture was one of the means to achieve it.

The Berghof, then, was designed—in Despina Stratigakos's words—"to convey the 'new' Hitler—not the ex-corporal who roused rebels in beer halls or the dictator who cut down his opponents in cold blood, but rather a powerful, cultivated, and, above all, trustworthy statesman. It was the stage on which he performed this new role and invited others to respond to him accordingly".[59] There was a secondary function, too. The upgraded and extended private space was meant to reconcile Hitler the propagandist of community, of "blood and soil", with Hitler the lone, unencumbered warrior. It did so by creating a domestic environment for him, while at the same time stressing his image as a world leader. In this sense, the Berghof fulfilled essentially the same function as Hoffmann's photo albums and was, indeed, the topic of several of them. The message was sold to a variety of journals and magazines, including foreign ones ranging from *Vogue* to the *American Kennel Gazette* ("Hitler Says His Dogs Are Real Friends").[60]

For this reason, Hitler himself was centrally involved in the architectural minutiae. He was not simply indulging in a favourite pastime, as is suggested by his professional architect Albert Speer, who in his 1969 memoir *Inside the Third Reich* pours scorn on what he clearly sees as his master's impulsive dabbling.[61] Hitler was helped by interior designer Gerdy Troost and architects Alois Delgado and Roderich Fick, but the original plans were his. The result was an image of Germanness, social and historical rootedness, cultural refinement, strength, and, inevitably, Führer cult.

Let us look at some of Despina's Stratigakos's examples. To begin with, "the Great Hall's impressive proportions and striking panoramic views [...] reinforced the image of a man of power, vision, and substance" as did the "scale of the furniture. [...] On the southern end of the hall, a fireplace almost tall enough for a man to stand inside evoked a luxurious version of a medieval hearth. [...] On the eastern wall stood a massive cupboard over fifteen feet long and ten feet high designed by Leonhard Gall to hold Hitler's certificates of honorary citizenship—a prominent symbol in the room of the German people's devotion to their leader. How that 'devotion' had been won was suggested by the cupboard's most unique [and to my mind rather lugubrious] feature: five large bronze knobs [...] in the shape of heads, representing [...] a Wehrmacht soldier, a girl in the League of German Girls, the Führer himself, a boy in the Hitler Youth, and an SA man".[62] A library on the first floor—filled mostly with literary classics, books on history, architecture, art, and music, as well as expensive rare editions—suggested erudition and cultivation. On the ground floor, the same function was fulfilled by a large book case, which among others contained a multivolume encyclopaedia, and by Hitler's collection of German and Italian masters.

The paintings were not only meant to give the lie to views of the Führer as an uncultured rabble-rouser. They also addressed possible questions about his sexuality. The flipside of Hitler's image as a warrior-monk was the suspicion that he was—to use an old-fashioned expression—not the marrying kind. It did not help that SA leader Ernst Röhm, for a long time one of the Führer's closest associates but then purged during the Night of the Long Knives, had been gay.[63] The paintings, Despina Stratigakos makes clear, aimed to dispel similar rumours about Hitler. "In the apparent absence of a flesh-and-blood female companion, sensual representations of women in the Great Hall, placed prominently near the fireplace and often visible in published photographs—such as the reclining nude goddess in *Venus and Cupid* by the Italian Renaissance painter and Titian pupil Paris Bordone, and Anselm Feuerbach's 1862 portrait of his model and muse *Nanna*, said to have been Hitler's favorite painting—[...] reinforced Hitler's heterosexual bachelor domesticity as well as his cultural sophistication".[64]

The oversized globe symbolized Germany's self-confidence as a global power. It was "twice as large as the commercial standard", though care had been taken to ensure that globe and base together remained "some four inches shorter than Hitler himself".[65] Finally, there is one other feature of the Berghof to which Stratigakos draws attention—its combination of "traditional materials and craftsmanship" with "the latest technological comforts and conveniences", such as a film projector and screen, a radio, and a record player.[66] This linking of tradition and modernity, of rootedness in the past and orientation towards the future, was central to the National Socialists' self-perception and constituted one of the reasons for its appeal in the confused interwar period with its manifold hopes and fears.

Many guests were taken in by the veneer of respectability. Having visited the Berghof in September 1936, the former British Prime Minister David Lloyd George, for instance, praised Hitler in the *Daily Express* "as 'the George Washington of Germany' and 'a born leader of men' who had brought freedom and prosperity to a peace-loving country".[67] The incumbent Prime Minister Neville Chamberlain was likewise duped. Two weeks after his visit to the Berghof in mid-September 1938, he signed the Munich peace accord with the supposedly trustworthy Führer, whose aims—Chamberlain believed—were "strictly limited" to the *Sudetenland* part of Czechoslovakia.[68] "In spite of the harshness and ruthlessness I thought I saw in his face", he wrote to his sister, "I got the impression that here was a man who could be relied upon when he had given his word".[69] Other foreign dignitaries included the former British King Edward VIII and his future wife, Wallis Simpson; the British fascist leader Oswald Mosley, his wife Diana Mitford Mosley, and her improbably named sister Unity Valkyrie Mitford;[70] Benito Mussolini; the Italian Foreign Minister Count Galeazzo Ciano, who was Mussolini's son-in-law and carried the derisive sobriquet "the little Duce"; and Tsar Boris III of Bulgaria. In addition, various German generals, ministers, and high-ranking civil servants were invited to receive the full treatment of Hitler as a global player. After all, they too had to be convinced of the Führer's suitability for office.

Hitler's attempt to project a more statesmanlike image did not exclude using the threat of force if he thought it would further his cause. In February 1938, he invited the Austrian Chancellor Kurt Schuschnigg to the Berghof with the express intention of browbeating him into accepting the National Socialists' plans for Austria, such as the appointment of Arthur Seyß-Inquart as Interior Minister. Hitler first ensured that the reception committee included two particularly fierce-looking German generals as well as a number of Austrian Nazis whom Schuschnigg had prosecuted. During the meeting itself, he employed one of his favourite techniques, the fake outburst of anger, unleashing a torrent of accusations on his hapless counterpart and suggesting that Germany would occupy Austria if Schuschnigg did not give in. After the lunch break, he continued in the same vein. Finally, with Schuschnigg down but not yet out, Hitler delivered the *coup de grâce*. Seemingly on the verge of losing it completely, he shouted that he needed to confer with General Keitel. He and Keitel then retired to a separate room, where they engaged in some friendly small talk. After about ten minutes, Hitler returned to his by now seriously intimidated guest. Three days later, Schuschnigg acceded to the National Socialists' demands.

For a short while, though, it looked as if Schuschnigg had lost the battle, but won the war. Believing that a German occupation was now off the cards, he decided to put a shrewdly crafted referendum question to the Austrian people which he hoped would confirm his country's territorial integrity and independence from Germany. This time, Hitler was genuinely irate. Abandoning his original idea of a steady growing-together of the two countries, he ordered an invasion. To his surprise, the German troops were met with nothing but cheers of jubilation that often bordered on the hysterical. The Nazis then proceeded to organize their own plebiscite. Over 99% of Austrians and Germans voted in favour of the *Anschluss*, the full integration of Austria into the Reich. This was a stunning result even if one takes into account that people of Jewish descent had not been allowed to participate. (Indeed, many of them were verbally and physically abused following the invasion—a prelude of what was to come.) There had also been a further piece of election fraud: the ballot paper's circle for *Ja* had been made significantly larger than that for *Nein*.

Still, if Austria was the first victim of Hitler's territorial ambitions, it was to a large extent a willing victim.

The *Anschluss* provided the stimulus for Hitler's second extravagant wish—the construction of a Führer Museum in the Austrian city of Linz. Although born in Braunau am Inn, another town in what was then the Austro-Hungarian Empire, Hitler viewed Linz, where he had spent a large part of his youth, as his hometown. Overwhelmed by the ecstatic welcome he received when officially announcing the *Anschluss* in Vienna on 15 March 1938, with almost a quarter of a million Austrians shouting "one people, one Reich, one leader", the narcissistic Führer decided to bestow the greatest honour on Linz that he could think of. He would gift the city a monument to its most famous son—Adolf Hitler. The monument was to take the form of an art gallery that, inevitably, was to be the greatest in the world, surpassing even the Louvre in splendour. More than that, the Führer Museum was only part of a much larger project. Hitler planned to turn Linz into one of the Reich's cultural capitals, with a gigantic university, a gigantic theatre, a gigantic concert hall, a gigantic cinema, a gigantic stadium, and a host of other manifestations of his gigantomania. The plan was never realized. Even in his final days, Hitler could do no more than stare wistfully at a mere scale model of a city that never was and never would be. Yet the initial efforts show how much money he was willing to invest in what was essentially a vanity project.

A special task force was set up to collect the art-works for the Führer Museum. Fanning out all over Nazi-occupied Europe, the *Sonderauftrag Linz* acquired thousands of paintings, etchings, sculptures, and tapestries from Czechoslovakia, France, Belgium, Holland, and other countries. (George Clooney's 2014 film *The Monuments Men* tells the story of the earliest attempt on the part of the Allies to recuperate this art.) In total, the task force spent well over seventy million Reichsmarks—and that was only a fraction of what the full-scale cultural metropolis would have cost.

The figure is misleading in other respects, too. The *Sonderauftrag Linz* did not always pay for the art it was accumulating. Sometimes, it confiscated or looted it outright. More importantly, the very distinction between buying and stealing is problematic in this context. As the journalist and author Wulf Schwarzwäller observes, "Hitler wanted to give the operation at least a thin veneer of legality in order not to look like a common thief and plunderer in the eyes of the world".[71] This explains why not all the art was simply expropriated. But how much of a free and fair economic exchange could there be when behind every transaction was the implicit (or explicit) threat of retaliation in case of non-compliance? More often than not, an offer made by the Nazis was an offer you could not refuse. Hence prices were frequently absurdly low. To insist on the formal legality of such sales is to abandon all sense of historical justice.[72] Finally, the market value of artistic masterpieces has increased dramatically since the 1930s and 1940s. In 2018, for instance, van Gogh's *Vue de l'asile et de la Chapelle de Saint-Rémy sold for a little under 40 million dollars*, while Matisse's *Odalisque couchée aux magnolias and* Monet's *Nymphéas en fleur* each cost over 80 million dollars.[73] Still, the Linz project illustrates well how much Hitler was driven by avarice and self-love rather than a desire to do good for his people. Even the Führer's architect Albert Speer was struck by the extent to which his master's "passion for building for eternity left him without a spark of interest in traffic arrangements, residential areas and parks. He was indifferent to the social dimension".[74]

The Paladins' Perks

The National Socialists promised to make Germany a fairer and more equal society. The system, they claimed, was broken and only Hitler could fix it and lift the country out of the morass of elitism and exploitation, of crime and corruption, in which it threatened to go under. Yet Hitler had no compunction about using Party and state funds for personal ends. In fact, once the NSDAP had come to power, all high-ranking Nazis began to feather their own nests. Luxury villas and grandiose official residences were among the most prized rewards for loyal service.[75] Propaganda Minister Joseph Goebbels, for instance, possessed multiple homes, including an estate consisting of "an ample country house with about thirty rooms, a service building with about forty rooms, and a garage complex".[76] His multimillion-Reichsmark official residence in Berlin included such extravagances as "a marble-topped rosewood dresser in Louis XVI style that cost 30,000 marks, and an eighteenth-century

Aubusson carpet costing 283,450 marks".[77] He also owned a range of expensive limousines and sports cars as well as various motor yachts.

Goebbels's real love however, if one can put it that way, was women. In spite of his clubfoot and diminutive appearance (he stood barely over five feet tall), he had always been an inveterate womanizer. Once appointed Propaganda Minister and Head of the Reich Film Chamber, he acquired virtually unlimited power over Germany's actresses as well as over his female employees, and he harassed them relentlessly. Should a woman show herself unreceptive to his advances, he would resort to the Harvey Weinstein method, threatening to ruin her career, or worse. This predatory sexual behaviour earned him the nickname *der Bock von Babelsberg*, or the Goat of Babelsberg, after the place where the studios of the—nazified—leading German film company, Ufa, were located.

A special case was Goebbels's liaison with Lída Baarová. With her dark hair and size-zero figure, the beautiful Czech actress was "more like the femmes fatales officially frowned upon by the regime than like the image of the 'German woman' held up as a model".[78] Yet in autumn 1936 she and the Propaganda Minister fell madly in love. The problem was that Goebbels's wife, Magda, did not want a triangular relationship. She was willing to put up with her husband's many affairs (she had a few herself), but only if they were short-lived. When she found out how serious things were between Goebbels and his latest girlfriend, she turned to the Führer for help. Hitler immediately realized the gravity of the situation. Nazi propaganda had created a picture of the Goebbelses and their children as the ideal German family, and of the blonde and blue-eyed Magda as the ideal German wife. Moreover, with Hitler keeping Eva Braun out of the public eye, Magda often acted as the Reich's unofficial First Lady. Resolutely, the Führer forced his Propaganda Minister to break it off with Baarová. Conscious as always of the power of images, he also obliged Herr and Frau Goebbels to pose for a joint reconciliation photograph at the Berghof so as to put an end to any rumours that were going round. Lída Baarová, meanwhile, returned to Prague. Her German film career was over.

The story tells us something important about Hitler. Hitler is usually seen as a prude, and no doubt correctly so. What the Baarová affair shows is the extent to which he was able to subordinate personal preference to political purpose. The Führer never intervened in any of Goebbels's erotic escapades. Even the dalliance with Baarová he tolerated for several months. It was only when the affair threatened to become a public-relations disaster and hence a political problem that Hitler put a stop to it. For him, Goebbels was above all a valuable strategic asset. If short-lived extramarital affairs helped keep the Propaganda Minister content and in line, then so be it.

What is more, Goebbels's erotomania could always be used against him, and the Führer was never unhappy about having an additional hold over his underlings. Nor was he in any way averse to exploiting such pressure points actively and ruthlessly if it suited him. The fate of Ernst Röhm is a case in point. For many years, the homophobic Hitler blithely ignored the SA leader's homosexuality. But when in 1933/1934 Röhm's socialist revolutionary vision clashed with Hitler's "democratic" approach, the Führer had his old friend killed. Chief among the charges, or rather *post factum* justifications, were Röhm's so-called sexual deviance and debauchery—a focus that had the added benefit, as critics of the regime noted at the time, of "diverting the attention of the great mass of the public from the political background to the action, and at the same time elevating Hitler's standing as the cleanser of the Movement".[79]

The most obvious example of Nazi corruption is furnished by Hermann Göring.[80] A highly decorated First World War fighter pilot, Göring was universally admired for his personal bravery and enjoyed real popularity among ordinary Germans. He was called *der Eiserne* (the iron man) or, after his early dashing appearance had given way to obesity, *der Dicke* (the fat man). The latter nickname was not pejorative, but rather a term of endearment based on his perceived good nature and joviality. What is more, he managed to present himself "as the champion of national solutions against the corrupt self-interest of the old elites and big business".[81] Yet he was one of the most selfish and greedy National Socialists of them all. His attitude and sense of entitlement made Joseph Goebbels seem little more than middle management.

Hermann Göring possessed over twenty properties—official residences, castles, country estates, and hunting lodges.[82] The most extravagant of these was Carinhall, an enormous country house named for his deceased first wife. Located in Schorfheide Forest about 40 miles north of

Berlin, it had a huge entrance hall that simultaneously served as an art gallery, a reception room, a banquet hall, a library, a hairdressing salon, medical and dental surgeries, a gymnasium that doubled up as a cinema, two mini-casinos, a sauna, and a swimming pool (with sculptures) as well as guests rooms and servant quarters. Space had even been created for a supersized model railway—Göring's favourite toy.[83] The electronically retractable picture windows commanded imposing views of the forest and the nearby lakes. Though officially a state park, the surrounding area was to all intents and purposes Göring's personal property.

The wider estate was home to a tennis court, several boathouses, and an air-raid shelter as well as further servant quarters, barracks for Göring's security personnel, outbuildings for his horse-drawn carriages, and stables. The estate's most extravagant feature was a lion cage: Göring owned several cubs. Even before building Carinhall, the animal-loving *Reichsforstmeister* (Reich Master of the German Forests) and *Reichsjägermeister* (Reich Master of the Hunt) had "made the Schorfheide a sanctuary for the deer, the buffalo, the elk, and the wild horse"[84] while also making German hunting laws much more restrictive, banning the use of devices such as claw traps, and outlawing vivisection. These measures formed a shockingly odd contrast with his attitude vis-à-vis the Jews and other so-called *Untermenschen*. Yet the fascination that Nazis such as Göring and Hitler had with the animal kingdom was not merely an idiosyncrasy. In a twisted way, it was also a manifestation of their social Darwinist view of culture as an extension of nature.

Göring's extravagance extended to other areas of life, too. His second wedding, to the actress Emmy Sonnemann in 1935, was so lavish that the British Ambassador to the Reich, Sir Eric Phipps, felt as if the German monarchy had been restored and the Crown Prince were getting married. For his part, the American Under Secretary of State Sumner Welles, who met the former fighter pilot a few years later, was struck by the man's jewellery—a ring with six large diamonds on one hand and a huge emerald ring on the other. Equally excessive was Göring's appetite for expensive wines and fine food. When Joseph Goebbels ordered all luxury restaurants in Berlin closed following his Total War speech of 18 February 1943, Göring immediately intervened to try and save his favourite establishment, Horcher. It was eventually allowed to stay open as a private Luftwaffe club.

Göring amassed official titles—together with matching uniforms, which he designed himself—the way other people collect stamps. So extreme was his title mania that even other leading Nazis made fun of it. Hitler, for example, liked to annoy the self-important Reich Master of the German Hunt by addressing the Berghof's humble beekeeper as Reich Master of Beekeeping. Göring's fondness for medals was another object of mockery. Foreign Minister Joachim von Ribbentrop disparaged the bemedalled Commander of the Luftwaffe as a walking Christmas tree, while Joseph Goebbels joked that Göring "worshipped fantastic uniforms and orders to such a degree that he had even pinned a medal on his pyjamas".[85] Hitler enjoyed the joke so much that "he commissioned Hoffmann to make a splendid medal out of gold and silver paper and to hand it to Göring together with a florid citation".[86]

Of Göring's multiple boats and ships, his luxury yacht *Carin II* would gain post-war fame. Requisitioned by Field Marshal Montgomery, it was gifted to the British royal family, who renamed it first the *Royal Albert* and then the *Prince Charles*. In 1960, Göring's widow, Emmy, started legal proceedings and managed to reobtain the yacht, which had been registered in her name. She immediately sold it to a Bonn-based printer, who rechristened it *Theresia*. In 1973, he in his turn sold the yacht to the *Stern* journalist Gerd Heidemann, who gave it its original name back. Less than a decade later, the same Heidemann became a global celebrity when he purchased the find of the century, the Führer's personal diaries, from the antiques dealer and collector of Nazi memorabilia Konrad Kujau. For several weeks, the diaries held the world in rapt attention—until it was discovered that they were a forgery, courtesy of Konrad Kujau.[87] Heidemann had used the *Carin II* as a magnet for former Nazis whose memories he wanted to tap into. It was they who unwittingly set him on his ill-fated quest for the Hitler diaries.

Last but not least, there was Göring's massive art collection, most of it acquired through confiscation and forced sales. Indeed, Göring was Hitler's main rival when it came to robbing occupied Europe of its cultural treasures. Both men relied on a special task force led by the National Socialist "court philosopher" Alfred Rosenberg, the *Einsatzstab Rosenberg*, which organized and carried out the looting.[88] (Hitler in addition had his own *Sonderauftrag Linz*, as we saw earlier). Through the offices of the *Einsatzstab Rosenberg*, "in Paris alone some 38,000 homes owned by Jews were sealed and their contents confiscated, stored and catalogued".[89] All in all, Rosenberg "managed to send some 26,000 railroad cars full of looted works and furniture from France to Germany".[90]

Only a fraction of the money for Göring's royal lifestyle came out of his own pocket. Most of his extravagances were officially state-subsidized, or paid for through a circuitous self-appropriation of state funds. He also benefited from more conventional forms of corruption and bribery. Already as an ordinary member of parliament in the late 1920s and early 1930s, Göring had gratefully accepted money and gifts from companies such as Lufthansa and BMW. A few years later, things got worse. In 1936, he was put in charge of the Four-Year Plan, Hitler's scheme to achieve national self-sufficiency and put the economy on a war footing—a scheme that was continued into the war itself. In this capacity, Göring was the most important decision-maker in all matters of manufacturing and heavy industry as well as the economic areas that were now being squeezed, such as housing. (He never achieved full control however, the Nazi state being less of a totalitarian monolith than a polycratic dictatorship consisting of competing fiefdoms.) Göring abused his position of power shamelessly. If business leaders wanted to have something done, or undone, an expensive gift or a financial contribution to the Reich Plenipotentiary of the Four-Year Plan was often a successful way of achieving it. As a result, there quickly developed a whole "system of routine present-giving"[91] that Göring used to finance his high-living.

Hitler, Goebbels, and Göring were by no means the only ones to benefit personally from their political functions. Martin Bormann and Albert Speer, for example, did the same. But the corruption extended far beyond the small circle of top Nazis. Senior army officers, high-ranking NSDAP members, even local Party bosses and functionaries with friends in high places—they all swam in the brown swamp.[92]

The Brown Swamp

Corruption is not simply about illegal or immoral self-enrichment. It is also about loyalty. The powerful keep their underlings in a position of dependence by rewarding them for their services, dangling potential rewards in front of them, and allowing them to enrich themselves. The Führer himself valued loyalty above all else. As with Trump, that loyalty was largely a one-way street: Hitler first and foremost wanted the others to be loyal to *him*. The similarity between the two leaders extends beyond their personal dispositions. However significant and substantive the differences between Hitlerworld and Trumpworld may be (and they obviously are), their organizational structures are akin. They are characterized by overlapping areas of responsibility, informal lines of communication with "access" being the most valuable commodity, and competing fiefdoms. In this environment—which I will examine in a later chapter—patronage becomes an essential tool to build the alliances needed to push through policies and advance personal interests.

There is of course nothing unusual or immoral about rewarding loyal subjects, subordinates, or employees for services rendered. Hitler's practice, however, differed in important respects from that of, say, the Prussian kings. First, he often, though with varying degrees of success, tried to keep it secret. Second, his "rewards" were prospective rather than retrospective in nature. In the words of the historian Norman Goda, "Hitler took no chances that his gestures would be misinterpreted as altruistic gifts or rewards for deeds already done; on the contrary, he took pains to enunciate clearly to each recipient that *he* was the initiator in the gift-giving relationship and that a future obligation of unquestioned loyalty went with the gifts".[93] Third, Hitler's power display was—one suspects—partly motivated by the insecurity of the social upstart, rather than the confidence of the ruling class. After all, he was not an aristocrat or a professional politician, and he had not been an officer in the army. He never even went to university. Hitler had something to prove.

Rewards and gifts—that is to say, bribes—came in different shapes and sizes. They took the form of financial contributions, tax exemptions, promotions, jobs, sinecures, and material objects ranging from bottles of expensive wine and hard-to-obtain foodstuffs to full-blown landed estates. There were no official guidelines for this dispensation of wealth, even though Hitler frequently tried to give his donations the appearance of legality (while at the same time restricting awareness of his actions to as few people as possible—a delicate balance).

One might think that at least one social group would be immune to corruption—the German officer corps. They prided themselves on their integrity, their sense of honour, and their other "Prussian" virtues. Yet they, too, were completely absorbed into the system of patronage and fealty.[94]

Hitler's first steps on the way to corrupting his army officers were his bequests to *Reichspräsident* Field Marshal Paul von Hindenburg in 1933 and Field Marshal August von Mackensen in 1935. The former was allowed to double the size of his estate at public expense; the latter was given a new, 3084-acre estate. Both men were also made tax exempt.

There were several reasons for this largesse. Hitler was using the two highly admired war veterans "as a public yet harmless link to the traditional past".[95] But his very public show of respect was also meant to divert attention away from controversial political events, or at least to ensure that the two men refrained from criticizing them. Von Hindenburg's bequest coincided with the crucial early stage of the National Socialist dismantling of Weimar democracy (such as the outlawing of political parties), while von Mackensen's bequest came hard on the heels of his expressed discomfort at the murders committed during the Night of the Long Knives. Finally, Hitler almost certainly wanted to create a precedent. If the only two surviving Field Marshals from the First World War considered it appropriate to accept such lavish gifts from the Führer, then why should other German officers feel uncomfortable about doing the same?

Hitler did not in any way deceive himself about his motives, as is apparent from his private comments recorded by Major Gerhard Engel. The Führer "does not demand from a general that he be a National Socialist, but he does demand [...] that politically he submit completely to the state leadership and blindly execute orders that the state leadership desires. This will be easier for each, even against inner conviction, if he has received corresponding honors [*Ehrungen*] from the chief of state and through this must feel himself automatically bound".[96]

Among the senior officers who allowed themselves to be corrupted was the intrepid tank commander General Heinz Guderian. A notoriously blunt man who even got himself temporarily suspended for insubordination, he "became remarkably cooperative during and after the acquisition of his [2,313-acre, 1.24-million Reichsmark] estate"[97] in occupied Poland in October 1943. Tellingly, he rediscovered his old rebelliousness "after his estate had been lost to advancing Russian troops and his wife had been made a refugee".[98]

An equally outrageous case of avarice was that of Wilhelm Keitel, universally known as Hitler's "Lakaitel" (a pun on the word *Lakai*, or lackey). In spite of his obsequiousness, even he had occasional disagreements with the Führer. Yet the monocled Chief of the High Command of the German Armed Forces not only happily accepted Hitler's standard present for his generals' sixtieth birthday, a tax-free lump sum of 250,000 Reichsmarks. Inspired by Guderian's example, he also entered into negotiations with the Führer's representative, the Head of the Reich Chancellery, so as to obtain a further financial donation that would allow him to extend his existing estate by purchasing an enormous stretch of state-owned land. There followed a protracted correspondence in which Keitel, shamelessly and pettily, even balked at having to pay the administrative fees. He eventually received well over 700,000 Reichsmarks (Hitler also paid the fees). General Field Marshal Wilhelm Ritter von Leeb, finally, provides the clearest evidence that Hitler was seeking less to reward already-loyal officers than to silence potential opposition to his leadership. Von Leeb was (moderately) sceptical about National Socialism and had voiced (muted) criticism of the army's role in the mass murders of Jews in Lithuania. Hitler gifted him 638,000 Reichsmarks for an estate as well as the customary milestone birthday present of 250,000 Reichsmarks.

Other social groups also got on the gravy train. In the aftermath of Hitler's assumption of power in January 1933, hundreds of thousands of early NSDAP members were rewarded with civil-service jobs, often regardless of their qualifications or abilities. Party members who already held such positions were promoted for purely political reasons. In addition, many political opponents were bought off to ensure their cooperation. (More recalcitrant enemies were dealt with rather more harshly, with many being forced to emigrate or sent to concentration camps.) As Hitler consolidated his position, a significant number of the Nazi hierarchy began feathering their own nests, from local and district Party bosses up to junior and senior ministers.

Before coming to power, Hitler had railed against Germany's "swamp"; after assuming power, he showed no interest in actually doing away with it. He knew that followers able to enrich themselves were happy followers. In this regard, he was like "a political gang leader",[99] as the historian Frank Bajohr puts it in his study of Nazi corruption. Hitler purposefully built up and fostered a network of loyal "clients", while also allowing his henchmen and their subordinates to do a little grifting of their own. Hence Bajohr's conclusion: "At the top of the Third Reich's institutionalized corruption was Hitler himself [...]. Yet one should not see his endeavours to ensure the personal loyalty of the other leading Nazis through a system of patronage as evidence of a National Socialist monocracy. Rather, his system existed *in addition* to the many other nepotistic structures and forms of corruption that permeated the entire NSDAP".[100]

Two Forms of Corruption

Both Donald Trump and Adolf Hitler railed against "the system" and promised to drain the swamp. Central to Trump's 2016 *Contract with the American Voter*—his "100-day action plan to Make America Great Again"—was his pledge to restore "honesty and accountability" to politics and "clean up the corruption and special interest collusion in Washington, DC".[101] *Mein Kampf* castigated the Weimar Republic for having "delivered the civil service to party corruption".[102] In 1943, a proud SS judge claimed: "No other regime in the world has ever engaged in such a total and radical fight against corruption in its manifold manifestations as has National Socialism".[103] The Party philosopher Alfred Rosenberg wrote a book entitled *Der Sumpf* (The Swamp, 1930) against Weimar democracy,[104] and the Nazis made frequent use of campaign posters with texts such as *Gegen Korruption wählt Nationalsozialisten, Hitlerbewegung!* (Against Corruption, Vote for the National Socialists, the Hitler Movement!). Upon coming to power, they even introduced a compulsory *Eintopf*, or stew—a one-pot meal that all German families had to eat several times a year instead of the traditional Sunday roast. The money saved through this "meal of sacrifice" went to the *Winterhilfe*, the National Socialist support for the less fortunate. "Again and again, [official] photographs and news reels would show the Third Reich's leadership eating their own one-pot meals".[105]

Given the propagandistic importance that both Hitler and Trump placed on their promise to fight systemic corruption, it is astounding that their supporters continued to stand with them even after it had become obvious that the swamp was not actually being drained. Why should this be so?

Of course, corruption is by its very nature not always clearly visible. But on some level the people usually do know. They may not be familiar with the details, but they cannot *not* notice if and when something is not quite right. Moreover, from time to time there will be trials of officials who have abused their position for personal gain. Yet by and large the people put up with the newly minted corruption. There are several reasons for this.

To begin with, the occasional court cases give the impression that something is being done to address the problem. The Nazis even orchestrated well-publicized show trials of corrupt officials to prove how serious the new regime was about the issue. More importantly, the leader always stands away from whatever untoward behaviour is going on. Trump, as we have seen, systematically downplayed or denied his links with politically inconvenient minions. He was like T. S. Eliot's ginger mystery cat: when a crime has been discovered, Macavity is never there. In this, he was helped by his outsider status, which, moreover, he continued to foster even after his election. He was Trump and not the Republican Party, which he was happy to criticize publicly when it served his purpose.

Hitler benefited from the same disjunction between his person and the Party. *Wenn das der Führer wüsste* (If only the Führer knew) was a familiar phrase in the Third Reich—as if Hitler himself had nothing to do with the crimes and corruption of his underlings and would put a stop to this sort of behaviour if he were aware of it. This image of Hitler as a leader above the fray was a calculated PR effect, as we saw earlier. The Führer deliberately and systematically projected a populist persona.

In addition, economic success tends to silence critical voices. The German economy improved significantly after the shock of the 1929 Wall Street Crash had been absorbed, while Trump was able to build on the economic upturn that had begun to develop under Obama after the 2008 financial crisis had worn off. If you are doing better yourself, then why should you be overly concerned about other people earning a little on the side? In such circumstances, corruption is merely a blemish on an otherwise positively experienced social order.

There is yet another, more fundamental reason why supporters of populist leaders are not put off by the corruption of the new kleptocracy. As the philosopher Jason Stanley has argued in his book *How Fascism Works*, from a populist perspective corruption "is really about the corruption of purity rather than of law".[106] According to Stanley, when populist leaders and their followers are talking about corruption, what is actually at issue is "corruption in the sense of usurpation of the traditional order".[107] Thus, Stanley says, to many white Americans Obama was corrupt because he had usurped a position—the Presidency—that was not his to take. By the same token, Mexican immigrants are seen as benefiting from a corrupt system because they are enjoying rights that—it is felt—they should not possess. The same goes for the "biased" (that is, independent) judges who protect non-white immigrants and the "partisan" (that is, fair-minded) politicians who support progressive immigration policies. They, too, are part of the swamp. By contrast, the actual corruption of the populist nomenclature is viewed as an unfortunate side-effect of the all-important culture war that is the ongoing process of taking back one's country. Alternatively, it is viewed as "just a matter of the chosen nation taking what is rightfully theirs".[108]

The political scientist Peter Beinart has elaborated on Stanley's ideas, using a lead story on Fox News as an example.[109] On 21 August 2018, Fox—unlike most other news outlets—did not lead with Michael Cohen's bombshell statement that Donald Trump had told him to use campaign funds to pay off two of Trump's mistresses. Fox led with the death of Molly Tibbetts, a white woman from Iowa who allegedly had been murdered by an undocumented Mexican immigrant, Cristhian Rivera. Now, you might think that Fox was merely trying to divert attention from Trump's corruption. According to Beinart, however, there is more to it. Taking his cue from Stanley, he argues: "In the eyes of many Fox viewers, I suspect, the network isn't ignoring corruption so much as highlighting the kind that really matters. When Trump instructed Cohen to pay off women with whom he'd had affairs, he may have been violating the law. But he was upholding traditional gender and class hierarchies. [...] The Iowa murder, by contrast, signifies the inversion—the corruption—of that 'traditional order'. [...] By allegedly murdering Tibbetts, Rivera did not merely violate the law. He did something more subversive: He violated America's traditional social and sexual norms". The same way of looking at things explains the popularity of Trump's characterization of Hillary Clinton as corrupt, as well as the enthusiastic *Lock her up!* chants of his supporters. "For many Americans, female ambition—especially in service of a feminist agenda—in and of itself represents a form of corruption."

What is the occasional infraction of the law by your own kind if your country is being robbed by immigrants before your very eyes? What are a few peccadillos on the part of your leaders if they are the ones standing up for you? What counts is taking back control. Everything else is a sideshow. Hence Beinart's conclusion: what is really at stake for Trump's voters is "the corruption of America's traditional identity. And in the struggle against that form of corruption—the kind embodied by Cristhian Rivera—Trump isn't the problem. He's the solution".

It is possible to take Stanley's and Beinart's ideas one step further. Those of a populist cast of mind tend not merely to *ignore* accusations of financial impropriety and nepotism. Such accusations are actually likely to *increase their partisanship*. After all, the charges are as a rule put forward by members of the old establishment, who in the populist eye are nothing but a bunch of self-righteous judges, holier-than-thou politicians, and legalistic officials. This is what has been called *negative partisanship*. In the words of the political commentator David Frum: "The concept's authors, Alan Abramowitz and Steven Webster, observed that while many Americans do not identify as Republican or Democrat, virtually all Americans dislike one of those parties much more than they dislike the other. Trump cannily exploited negative partisanship to consolidate political support he could never have attracted for his own agenda or his own merits".[110] Or, as the radio broadcaster Hugh Hewitt (quoted by Frum) put it: the fact that there is so much support for Donald Trump "doesn't mean his supporters aren't critical. They are. Of many things. But [...] Trump [...] has all the right enemies".[111]

In short, if you have a strong enough hatred for the system (or, in the case of Nazi Germany, what is left of it), then the populist leader is your man, whatever he or his followers are up to in their "private" lives. What is more, anyone who criticizes him is the enemy, both because such critics usually are representatives of the old "legalistic" system and because they threaten to discredit the all-important project to make America (or Germany) great again. In this environment, any criticism of corruption is tantamount to criticism of the Cause.

Notes

1. Eric Trump, cited in Jennifer Calfas, "Eric Trump Says He'll Give the President Quarterly Updates on Business Empire", *Fortune*, 24 March 2017.
2. "Trump's D.C. Hotel Has Raked in Cash—and Only at the Cost of America's Dignity", *The Washington Post*, 18 May 2019. The article goes on to say: "T-Mobile executives spent nearly $200,000 there as they sought approval for a merger with Sprint. A variety of foreign countries have held events at Trump International. The Trump Organization says it donates all the profits it makes from foreign governments. But the president, who has refused to divest from his company, undoubtedly still benefits from high, price-driving demand at his landmark property, not to mention the profits domestic lobbyists produce. For those seeking to influence the Trump administration, padding the president's wallet with conspicuous spending at his hotel must seem like a viable strategy". Cf. Tara Subramaniam, "Fact-Checking Eric Trump's Claim the Trump Organization Has No Business Ties Overseas", *CNN*, 3 November 2019.
3. Cf. Norman L. Eisen, Richard Painter, and Laurence H. Tribe, *The Emoluments Clause: Its Text, Meaning, and Application to Donald J. Trump* (The Brookings Institution, 2016).

4. Cf. the overview in Kathleen Clark, "The Lawyers Who Mistook a President for Their Client", *Indiana Law Review* 52.2, 2019, pp. 271–303.
5. The following account is based primarily on *Bloomberg*'s "Trump Team's Conflicts and Scandals: An Interactive Guide" and Vicky Ward, *Kushner, Inc.: Greed, Ambition, Corruption: The Extraordinary Story of Jared Kushner and Ivanka Trump* (New York: St. Martin's Press, 2019).
6. Cf. Ward, *Kushner, Inc.*, p. 138, and Bob Woodward, *Fear: Trump in the White House* (London etc.: Simon & Schuster, 2018), p. 145: "'You're a goddamn staffer!' Bannon finally screamed at Ivanka. 'You're nothing but a fucking staffer!' […] 'I'm not a staffer!' she shouted. 'I'll never be a staffer. I'm the first daughter'—she really used the title—'and I'm never going to be a staffer!'".
7. *Bloomberg*'s "Trump Team's Conflicts and Scandals".
8. Daniel L. Koffsky, *Application of the Anti-Nepotism Statute to a Presidential Appointment in the White House Office: Memorandum Opinion for the Counsel to the President*. Cf. Josh Gerstein, "DOJ Releases Overruled Memos Finding It Illegal for Presidents to Appoint Relatives", *Politico*, 3 October 2017.
9. Ward, *Kushner, Inc.*, p. 125, referencing Kevin Liptak, "Trump's Secretary of Everything: Jared Kushner", *CNN*, 4 April 2017.
10. Ward, *Kushner, Inc.*, p. 237. Cf. John Cassidy, "Jared Kushner's Trumpian Divestment Strategy", *The New Yorker*, 10 January 2017.
11. Ward, *Kushner, Inc.*, p. 121, referencing Darla Cameron, Amy Brittain, and Jonathan O'Donnell, "What Jared Kushner Still Owns", *The Washington Post*, 21 May 2017.
12. *Bloomberg*'s "Trump Team's Conflicts and Scandals". Cf. Jessica Kwong, "New Jared Kushner, Ivanka Trump Financial Disclosure Revisions Show 'Pattern of Trouble with Their Filings', Watchdog Says", *Newsweek*, 4 April 2019, and Kara Scannall, "Background Check Chief Has 'Never Seen' Mistakes and Omissions at Level of Jared Kushner Forms", *CNN*, 13 February 2018.
13. In August 2018, Kushner Companies finally managed to lease 666 Fifth Avenue to Brookfield Assett Management for a period of 99 years. See Charles V. Bagli and Kate Kelly, "Deal Gives Kushners Cash Infusion on 666 Fifth Avenue", *The New York Times*, 3 August 2018. The same article reports that "Brookfield is one of the world's biggest real estate companies, and […] Qatar Investment Authority […] is the

second-largest investor in the company [...] That has raised questions given Jared Kushner's portfolio in the White House, which includes the Middle East. Brookfield has said that the Qataris had no knowledge of the deal before its public announcement".

14. Jon Swaine, "Company Part-Owned by Jared Kushner Got $90m from Unknown Offshore Investors since 2017", *The Guardian*, 10 June 2019. All data in the text are taken from this article as well as from Vicky Ward, "Jared Kushner May Have an Ethics Problem—to the Tune of $90m", *The Guardian*, 15 June 2019.
15. Ward, *Kushner, Inc.*, p. 119.
16. Ward, *Kushner, Inc.*, pp. 206 (referencing Desmond Butler and Tom LoBianco, "The Princes, the President, and the Fortune Seekers", *Associated Press*, 21 May 2018) and 131.
17. Ward, *Kushner, Inc.*, p. 74.
18. In what follows, I draw on *The Mueller Report, Presented with Related Materials by The Washington Post* (London etc.: Simon & Schuster, 2019) as well as on the sources mentioned in note 5 further above.
19. Ward, *Kushner, Inc.*, p. 103, referencing Kristen Welker, Peter Alexander, Dafna Linzer, and Ken Dilanian, "Obama Warned Trump against Hiring Mike Flynn, Say Officials", *NBC News*, 8 May 2017.
20. According to Michael Wolff in *Fire and Fury: Inside the Trump White House* (London: Little, Brown, 2018, pp. 66–82), this was Steve Bannon's nickname for Jared Kushner and Ivanka Trump. Before the publication of that book, the sobriquet used by people around the couple appears to have been "Javanka". Cf. Eve Peyser, "Is it 'Javanka' or 'Jarvanka'? An Investigation", *Vice*, 10 January 2018.
21. Cited in *Mueller Report*, p. 538.
22. Robin Givhan, "Paul Manafort's Ostrich Jacket Pretty Much Sums Up Paul Manafort", *The Washington Post*, 2 August 2018.
23. *Mueller Report*, p. 618.
24. *Bloomberg*'s "Trump Team's Conflicts and Scandals".
25. Philip Bump, "A Brief History of Trump Playing Down His Relationships with Politically Inconvenient People", *The Washington Post*, 11 October 2019 and Brooke Singman, "Trump Rips Cohen for 'Flipping', Praises Manafort in Exclusive FNC Interview", *Fox News*, 23 August 2018.
26. The following overview is based on Alexander Nazaryan, *The Best People: Trump's Cabinet and the Siege on Washington* (New York and

Boston: Hachette, 2019) as well as *Bloomberg*'s "Trump Team's Conflicts and Scandals".
27. Nazaryan, *Best People*, p. 133.
28. Nazrayan, *Best People*, p. 156.
29. Nazrayan, *Best People*, p. 165, 172, 162, and 165.
30. Nazaryan, *Best People*, p. 189.
31. The following two sections ("Hitler's Early Profits" and "The *Reichskanzler* and his riches") are based primarily on Wulf Schwarzwäller, *The Unknown Hitler* (New York: Berkley Books, 1990; first published in German 1986), Henry Ashby Turner, Jr., *German Big Business and the Rise of Hitler* (New York: Oxford University Press, 1985), Cris Whetton, *Hitler's Fortune* (Barnsley: Pen & Sword, 2004), and Wolfgang Zdral, *Der finanzierte Aufstieg des Adolf H.* (Vienna: Ueberreuter, 2002). I also found the following two books by James Pool useful, even though they are not always entirely reliable: *Who Financed Hitler: The Secret Funding of Hitler's Rise to Power, 1919–1933* (rev. and updated ed. New York etc.: Pocket Books, 1997) and *Hitler and His Secret Partners: Contributions, Loot and Rewards, 1933–1945* (New York etc.: Pocket Books, 1997). Specifically on *Mein Kampf*, I have made use of the editorial introduction to Adolf Hitler, *Mein Kampf. Eine kritische Edition*, ed. Christian Hartmann, Thomas Vordermeyer, Othmar Plöckinger, and Roman Töppel (Munich and Berlin: Institut für Zeitgeschichte, 2016), vol. 1, pp. 7–84, as well as of Sven Felix Kellerhoff, *"Mein Kampf". Die Karriere eines deutschen Buches* (Stuttgart: Klett-Cotta, 2015) and Othmar Plöckinger, *Geschichte eines Buches. Adolf Hitlers "Mein Kampf" 1922–1945* (updated ed. Munich: Oldenbourg Verlag, 2011).
32. Cited in Zdral, *Der finanzierte Aufstieg*, p. 8.
33. See Adolf Hitler, *Mein Kampf*, trans. Ralph Manheim (Boston and New York: Houghton Mifflin Company, 1999), p. 639: "It is Jews who govern the stock exchange forces of the American Union. […] only a single great man, Ford, to their fury, still maintains full independence". For the German original, see Hitler, *Mein Kampf*, vol. 2, p. 1619. From the early 1930s onwards, the reference to Ford was replaced by the phrase "only few still maintain full independence". Why this happened is unclear.
34. Ian Kershaw, *Hitler 1889–1936: Hubris* (London etc.: Penguin, 2001; first published 1998), p. 343.

35. Kurt Ludecke [= Lüdecke], *I Knew Hitler* (New York: C. Scribner's Sons, 1938), p. 390.
36. R. G. Waldeck, *Meet Mr. Blank* (New York: G. P. Putnam's Sons, 1943), p. 49, cited in Pool, *Who Financed Hitler*, p. 121.
37. Ernst Hanfstaengl, *Hitler: The Memoir of a Nazi Insider Who Turned against the Führer*, trans. John Willard Toland (New York: Arcade Publishing, 2011; first published 1957), p. 44.
38. Geli Raubal would commit suicide in 1931 under circumstances that have never been fully cleared up.
39. Henry Picker, *Hitlers Tischgespräche im Führerhauptquartier* (Munich: second ed. Propyläen, 2009), p. 203 (entry of 27 March 1942, early afternoon). The German reads "ein einziges verkrüppeltes Gekleckse". The word *verkrüppelt* (crippled, deformed, stunted) has connotations of degeneracy and later on in his monologue Hitler goes on to castigate modern art as "Jewishized". His photographer Heinrich Hoffmann reports the Führer as saying: "I cannot abide [...] paintings in which you can't tell whether they're upside down or inside out, and on which the unfortunate frame maker has to put hooks on all four sides, because he can't tell either!". See Heinrich Hoffmann, *Hitler Was My Friend: The Memoir of Hitler's Photographer*, trans. H. R. Stevens (London: Frontline Books, 2014; first published 1955), p. 171.
40. Zdral, *Der finanzierte Aufstieg*, p. 17.
41. On Hitler's tax exemption, I have also drawn on Ralf Banken, *Hitlers Steuerstaat. Die Steuerpolitik im Dritten Reich* (Berlin and Boston: de Gruyter, 2018), pp. 228–32.
42. In his continued attempts to win big business over to the cause, Hitler had been making the same promise before, notably in a secret 1927 pamphlet for industrialists and in his 1932 speech at the Düsseldorf Industrie-Klub. He was, of course, simultaneously wooing the workers with a much more employee-friendly, socialistically tinged programme.
43. On Bormann, I have also drawn on Jochen von Lang (with the assistance of Claus Sibyll), *The Secretary: Martin Bormann: The Man Who Manipulated Hitler*, trans. Christa Armstrong and Peter White (New York: Random House, 1979; first published in German 1977).
44. Heinrich Hoffmann, *Hitler wie ihn keiner kennt. 100 Bild-Dokumente aus dem Leben des Führers* (Berlin: Zeitgeschichte, 1935 [orig. published 1932]; digital reprint London: Ostara Publications, 2019), pp. 4,

25, 54, and 69. The captions are by Baldur von Schirach, the leader of the Hitler Youth, who was married to Hoffmann's daughter, Henriette.
45. Hoffmann, *Hitler wie ihn keiner kennt*, pp. 40 and 45.
46. Pool, *Hitler and His Secret Partners*, p. 140.
47. Pool, *Hitler and His Secret Partners*, pp. 142–43.
48. See Karl Wilhelm Krause, "The Valet of Hitler: In the Shadow of Power [1949]", which is part 1 of Herbert Döhring et al., *Living with Hitler: Accounts of Hitler's Household Staff*, trans. Eva Burke (Barnsley: Greenhill Books, 2018), pp. 17–91.
49. Krause, "Valet of Hitler", pp. 36–37.
50. Krause, "Valet of Hitler", p. 37.
51. Krause, "Valet of Hitler", p. 38 (translation modified).
52. Krause, "Valet of Hitler", p. 39.
53. Admittedly, the allusion to *Kleider machen Leute* is slightly misleading. In Keller's novella, Wenzel Strapinski—the well-dressed but penniless tailor—is eventually found out. Supported by his fiancée and future wife, who does not forsake him even after he has been exposed, he only achieves genuine wealth through hard work, clever business dealings (bordering, the story suggests, on exploitation), and speculation.
54. Whetton, *Hitler's Fortune*, p. 239. On Hitler and the Obersalzberg, I have drawn on Hendrik van Capelle and Arie Pieter van de Bovenkamp, *De Berghof. Het Adelaarsnest, Hitlers verborgen machtscentrum* (Hoevelaken: Verba, 2003; first published 1985) and *Hitler 1889–1945. Een tiran in beeld* (new, revised and extended ed. Ede: De Lantaarn, 2019), chapter 14 ("Hitler op de Obersalzberg", pp. 238–301), as well as Herbert Döhring et al., *Living with Hitler* and Albert Speer, *Inside the Third Reich*, trans. Richard and Clara Winston (London: Weidenfeld & Nicolson, 1995; first published in German 1969).
55. Bormann's other nicknames included *braune Eminenz* (Brown Eminence) and *Herrscher über alles* (Lord of Everything).
56. Von Lang, *Secretary*, p. 93.
57. Today, the building is once again being used as a restaurant. It attracts hundreds of thousands of visitors a year.
58. See Despina Stratigakos, *Hitler at Home* (New Haven and London: Yale University Press, 2015).
59. Stratigakos, *Hitler at Home*, p. 85.
60. Cf. Stratigakos, *Hitler at Home*, pp. 194–244.
61. See Speer, *Inside the Third Reich*, pp. 135–36 and 142.

62. Stratigakos, *Hitler at Home*, p. 85; cf. also the illustration on p. 86.
63. Ernst Röhm was one of only a handful of people who addressed Hitler using the personal pronoun *du* (the familiar German form of "you", comparable to the French *tu*) instead of the formal *Sie* (comparable to *vous*).
64. Stratigakos, *Hitler at Home*, p. 94.
65. Stratigakos, *Hitler at Home*, p. 86; cf. also the illustration on p. 252.
66. Stratigakos, *Hitler at Home*, p. 89.
67. Stratigakos, *Hitler at Home*, p. 82, citing David Lloyd George's article "I Talked to Hitler" in the *Daily Express* of 17 September 1936. A reprint of the article can be found in Anson Rabinbach and Sander L. Gilman, eds., *The Third Reich Sourcebook* (Berkeley, Los Angeles, and London: University of California Press, 2013), pp. 77–78.
68. Ian Kershaw, *Hitler 1936–1945: Nemesis* (London etc.: Penguin, 2001; first published 2000), p. 112, citing Gerhard L. Weinberg, *The Policy of Hitler's Germany: Starting World War II, 1937–1939* (Chicago and London: University of Chicago Press, 1980), p. 438. Cf. Stratigakos, *Hitler at Home*, pp. 90 and 265 as well as the illustration on p. 91.
69. Kershaw, *Hitler 1936–1945*, p. 112, citing Neville Chamberlain's letter to his sister Ida of 19 September 1938.
70. Unity Mitford was something of a Hitler groupie in the 1930s. She was sometimes called Unity Mitfahrt because of her constant desire to be on the Führer's side (the German words *Mitfahrt* and *mitfahren* mean "lift" and "ride along with somebody"). Eva Braun was bitterly jealous of her Nordic-looking competitor. On 3 September 1939, the day that Britain declared war on Nazi Germany, Unity Mitford shot herself in the head. She survived, but the bullet remained lodged in her brain. Nine years later, she succumbed to meningitis at the age of 33.
71. Schwarzwäller, *Unknown Hitler*, p. 185.
72. Paradoxically, less vulnerable—especially non-Jewish German, but occasionally also foreign—sellers and art dealers could often demand inflated prices. The reason for this is that, in addition to Hitler, a number of other high-ranking Nazis were avid collectors too. This competition drove up prices. A special case is that of the Dutch art dealer and master forger Han van Meegeren, who managed to sell a fake Vermeer to Hermann Göring. After the war, van Meegeren was arrested on charges of collaborating with the enemy for allegedly having sold part of the Dutch national heritage to the Nazis. Faced with the prospect of

a long prison sentence or even the death penalty, he realized that there was only one way out: he confessed to being a systematic art counterfeiter. See Edward Dolnick, *The Forger's Spell: A True Story of Vermeer, Nazis, and the Greatest Art Hoax of the Twentieth Century* (New York: HarperCollins, 2008) and Jonathan Lopez, *The Man Who Made Vermeers: Unvarnishing the Legend of Master Forger Han van Meegeren* (Boston and New York: Houghton Mifflin Harcourt, 2008).

73. See Nate Freeman, "The 20 Most Expensive Artworks Sold at Auction in 2018", *Artsy*, 24 December 2018.
74. Speer, *Inside the Third Reich*, p. 127.
75. The following account draws on Peter Longerich, *Goebbels: A Biography*, trans. Alan Bance, Jeremy Noakes, and Lesley Sharpe (London: Vintage, 2016; first published in German 2010) and Ralf Georg Reuth, *Goebbels*, trans. Krishna Winston (London: Constable, 1993; first published in German 1990).
76. Longerich, *Goebbels*, p. 405.
77. Reuth, *Goebbels*, p. 250.
78. Reuth, *Goebbels*, p. 216.
79. Kershaw, *Hitler 1889–1936*, p. 520, citing the *Deutschland-Berichte der Sozialdemokratischen Partei Deutschlands (Sopade), 1934–1940*, ed. Erich Rinner (Frankfurt am Main: Petra Nettelbeck/Zweitausendeins, 1980), vol. 1, p. 249 (report of 21 July 1934).
80. The following account draws on Volker Knopf and Stefan Martens, *Görings Reich. Selbstinszenierungen in Carinhall* (eighth, updated ed. Berlin: Ch. Links, 2019), Guido Knopp (in collaboration with Friedrich Scherer, Gerlinde Preis, and Gundula Bavendamm), *Göring. Eine Karriere* (second ed. Munich: Goldmann, 2007), Roger Manvell and Heinrich Fraenkel, *Goering: The Rise and Fall of the Notorious Nazi Leader* (London: Frontline Books, 2011; first published 1962), and Richard Overy, *Goering: Hitler's Iron Knight* (new ed. London and New York: I. B. Tauris, 2012; first published 1984).
81. Overy, *Goering*, p. 73.
82. For a full list, see Knopf and Martens, *Görings Reich*, pp. 168–69.
83. In fact, there were two such model railways in Carinhall, one in the attic and one (which was added later and was even larger and even more technologically advanced) in the cellar.
84. Manvell and Fraenkel, *Goering*, p. 119.

85. Henrik Eberle and Matthias Uhl (eds.), *The Hitler Book: The Secret Dossier Prepared for Stalin*, trans. Giles MacDonogh (London: John Murray, 2005; first published in German 2005), p. 12.
86. Eberle and Uhl (eds.), *Hitler Book*, p. 12.
87. Even the eminent British historian Hugh Trevor-Roper, who had been asked to authenticate the diaries, was taken in. Kujau was a professional handwriting and art counterfeiter. Although many of his forgeries were fairly crude, he had a real knack for "selling" them (in both senses of the word). Among other things, he copied a painting by Julius Engelhard, pretended it was a Hitler painting of Eva Braun, and then managed to convince his prospective buyer of its authenticity by showing him the Engelhard painting and accusing Hitler of plagiarism. See Manfred Bissinger, *Hitlers Sternstunde. Kujau, Heidemann und die Millionen* (Hamburg and Zürich: Rasch und Röhring, 1984) and Robert Harris, *Selling Hitler: The Story of the Hitler Diaries* (London: Arrow Books, 1996; first published 1986).
88. Alfred Rosenberg was the author of the infamous 700-page *Der Mythus des 20. Jahrhunderts. Eine Wertung der seelisch-geistigen Gestaltenkämpfe unserer Zeit* (The Myth of the Twentieth Century: An Evaluation of the Spiritual-Intellectual Confrontations of Our Age, 1930), which put forward a metaphysical and pseudo-religious interpretation of history as the struggle between a Nordic-Aryan "soul" (a concept meant to synthesize biological race and psychological disposition) and a Jewish-Semitic one. Despite its confusing and confused line of argument, it was one of the most successful philosophical books of the Nazi era. Among Rosenberg's other, equally anti-Semitic, works were *Der Sumpf. Querschnitte durch das "Geistes"-Leben der November-Demokratie* (The Swamp: Cross-Sections through the "Spiritual" Life of Weimar Democracy, 1930) and *Der Bolschewismus als Aktion einer fremden Rasse* (Bolshevism as Action of an Alien Race, 1935). He was sentenced to death at the 1945/1946 Nuremberg trials.
89. Manvell and Fraenkel, *Goering*, p. 284.
90. Manvell and Fraenkel, *Goering*, p. 284.
91. Overy, *Goering*, p. 232.
92. The following section ("The Brown Swamp") is based on Frank Bajohr, *Parvenüs und Profiteure. Korruption in der NS-Zeit* (Frankfurt am Main: Fischer, 2004; first published 2001), Norman J. W. Goda, "Black

Marks: Hitler's Bribery of His Senior Officers during World War II", *The Journal of Modern History* 72, 2000, pp. 413–52, Lothar Gruchmann, "Korruption im Dritten Reich. Zur 'Lebensmittelversorgung' der NS-Führerschaft, *Vierteljahrshefte für Zeitgeschichte* 42.4, 1994, pp. 571–93, and Gerd R. Ueberschär and Winfried Vogel, *Dienen und Verdienen. Hitlers Geschenke an seine Eliten* (second, rev. ed. Frankfurt am Main: Fischer, 2001).
93. Goda, "Black Marks", p. 418.
94. Nor, of course, did their self-ascribed virtues prevent them from becoming complicit in the worst crimes the world has ever seen.
95. Goda, "Black Marks", p. 430.
96. Goda, "Black Marks", p. 423, citing Hildegard von Kotze (ed.), *Heeresadjutant bei Hitler 1938–1943. Aufzeichnungen des Majors Engel* (Stuttgart: Deutsche Verlags-Anstalt, 1974), p. 86 (entry of 22 July 1940). The German original can also be found in Ueberschär and Vogel, *Dienen und Verdienen*, pp. 72–73.
97. Goda, "Black Marks", p. 451. Ironically, or tragically, the rightful Polish owners of the estate, who were evicted, came from a family "who in the past had faithfully served the King of Prussia; some of them had even been officers in the Prussian army" (Ueberschär and Vogel, *Dienen und Verdienen*, p. 173).
98. Goda, "Black Marks", p. 452.
99. Bajohr, *Parvenüs and Profiteure*, p. 142.
100. Bajohr, *Parvenüs and Profiteure*, pp. 191–92.
101. Donald J. Trump, *Contract with the American Voter*, 2016 (available at https://cdn.factcheck.org/).
102. Hitler, *Mein Kampf*, p. 518 (English) and vol. 2, p. 1307 (German).
103. Bajohr, *Parvenüs and Profiteure*, p. 137, citing Konrad Morgen, "Der Korruptionsverbrecher", *Kriminalistik. Monatshefte für die gesamte kriminalistische Wissenschaft und Praxis* 17.2, 1943, pp. 117–19 (117).
104. See note 88.
105. Ueberschär and Vogel, *Dienen und Verdienen*, p. 68.
106. Jason Stanley, *How Fascism Works: The Politics of Us and Them* (New York: Random House, 2018), p. 26.
107. Stanley, *How Fascism Works*, p. 26.
108. Stanley, *How Fascism Works*, p. 27.

109. Peter Beinart, "Why Trump Supporters Believe He Is Not Corrupt", *The Atlantic*, 22 August 2018. All citations in the main text come from this source.
110. David Frum, *Trumpocracy: The Corruption of the American Republic* (New York, NY: HarperCollins, 2018), p. 26.
111. Frum, *Trumpocracy*, p. 16, citing a Tweet by Hugh Hewitt of 17 August 2017.

3

Enemies, Scapegoats, and Conspiracy Theories

By far the most striking—and the most abhorrent—aspect of Hitlerian and Trumpian populism is its focus on enemies. Hitler had a visceral hatred for the Jews, and anti-Semitism was central to National Socialist ideology. Trump's 2016 campaign was not merely built on an anti-establishment message, it also played on white-nationalist xenophobia. Even before launching his bid for the Presidency, he jumped on the bandwagon of *birtherism*, the conspiracy theory that Barack Obama was not born in the United States and hence had no right to be President. When, on 16 June 2015, Trump officially announced that he would be running, he focused prominently on the importance of preventing Mexican immigrants from coming into the country: "When Mexico sends its people, they're not sending their best. [...] They're sending people that have lots of problems, and they're bringing those problems with us [the use of "us" instead of "them" is a revealing slip that points to the calculated nature of Trump's attempt to blame outsiders for America's problems: he knows full well that these problems are not simply the result of the actions of others]. They're bringing drugs. They're bringing crime. They're rapists. And some, I assume, are good people". The need to build a wall on the border with Mexico subsequently became a staple of his campaign and indeed of his politics—a concrete symbol of his administration's us-versus-them approach in both domestic and foreign affairs.

So far, so obvious. But how exactly does this creation of what the French call an *adversaire repoussoir*—an opponent as a foil—work? What are its socio-psychological "benefits"?

The Community and Its Others

The first thing to note is that the designated internal enemies are a relatively small group. Jews made up less than one per cent of 1920s Germany. In today's United States, Mexican immigrants are far outnumbered by the rest of the population. True, in addition to these core enemies, there are associate enemies, as it were. Indeed, its ability to blend different foes into one is a key feature of Hitlerian and Trumpian populism, as we will see later on in this chapter. Moreover, through his frequent dog-whistle swipes at African Americans, Trump actually denigrated a pretty large proportion of the population. The point, however, stands: the people who are being painted as the real threat and who are therefore in real physical danger—say, of being deported—are relatively small in number. In other words, the majority of the population feel safe.

This is not a trivial point. It is one of the features that set this type of politics apart from the strongman rule of (let us take an extreme example) Stalin. Under Stalinism, the secret police might knock on anybody's door at any time. In the words of Alexandre Kojève, who once explained the *modus operandi* of the Stalinist system to his fellow philosopher and fellow Russian *émigré* Isaiah Berlin: "In a society in which you have very severe rules, however abstruse, for example a law which states that everybody had to stand on their heads at half past three, everybody would do this, to save their lives. But that was not enough for Stalin. That would not change things enough; Stalin had to squash his subjects into a dough, which he would knead in any way he wanted. There must be no habits, no rules which people could rely on: otherwise things would remain unmalleable. But if you accuse people of breaking laws that they did not break, of crimes that they did not commit, of acts which they could not even understand—that would reduce them to pulp. Then nobody would know where they were, nobody was ever safe, since whatever you did, or did not do, you still might be destroyed. That creates real 'anomie'. Once you have that kind of jelly, you can shape it as you choose from moment to moment. The goal was not to let anything set".[1]

There is a terrible truth to the Russian joke that under Stalin there were only three categories of citizens: detainees, former detainees, and future detainees. Stalin above all put *fear* into his people. His reign was based on Caligula's *oderint dum metuant*, "let them hate me, as long as they fear me". This was not the case with Hitler. Hitler above all offered his people *security*. As long as you were not part of the clearly delineated risk group (which first and foremost included the Jews, but also for example the communists), he would keep you safe, or so people felt—safe from the Jews and the communists, from criminals and corrupt politicians, from gang violence and the threat of unemployment, and from the foreign powers seeking to destroy Germany. Of course, if you *were* part of the risk group, things looked rather different. Moreover, the "benefits" that Hitler bestowed on his country were possible only because of the thoroughly evil nature of his reign. There never was (and there was never going to be, whatever the circumstances) a good National Socialist dimension as distinct from a bad National Socialist dimension. But precisely this far too many Germans refused to see. They only saw the "benefits". They felt safe again, proud again.

Under Stalinism, *you* are the target. The leader is potentially always out to get you. With Hitler, and indeed with Trump, *others* are the target. The leader is there to protect you from the hostile Other that he and his followers have conjured up in the first place.[2]

There is a further advantage to focusing on a small group of enemies only. They can be looked upon as being eminently defeatable as well as extremely dangerous. This conception relies on three mechanisms: foreignization, criminalization, and dehumanization.[3]

Thus, the enemy is not merely small in number, it is also *foreign*, alien, and hence up against the full might of our nation. Moreover, as outsiders they are as a rule perceived as being physically different from us: they have large noses, they smell funny, they have a different skin colour—whatever real or imagined characteristics work best. This makes them even easier to defeat, because anyone can recognize them as "other". Second, they are *criminals*. They operate outside the law, if indeed they are not fully paid-up members of a criminal organization. This is a message the National Socialists kept driving home, as in this newsreel that was broadcast shortly after the German invasion of Poland in September 1939: "The hardest problem for our civil administration in occupied territory is the Jewish question. [...] This Eastern Jewish subhumanity is the source of the international criminals that plague the West. It has supplied Western democracies with pickpockets, procurers, dealers of girls and narcotics, and manipulators of international finance and the press".[4] Similarly, the Trump administration not infrequently depicted refugees and migrants trying to cross the border into the United States as being really MS-13, ISIS, drug traffickers, rapists, and murderers. This approach generates a view of the nation's purported opponents as highly dangerous, but not so dangerous that they cannot be dealt with. On the contrary, as criminals these outsiders are a legitimate object of opprobrium of *all* law-abiding citizens, even of those who may not support the populist movement every step of the way.

The third mechanism—*dehumanization*—is even more extreme. Foreigners and criminals are still human beings and as such possess certain rights. But if the threat is more like that of an animal, if we are being threatened by parasites, rodents, insects, or germs, then these rights no longer apply. The National Socialist depiction of the Jews along those lines is too well known to need much exemplification. Most of us have seen the "rats scene" from the infamous propaganda film *Der ewige Jude* (The Eternal Jew, 1940), and we are all familiar with the term *Untermenschen*, "subhumans". President Trump, as I have emphasized repeatedly in this book, was not some kind of Hitler; he was not ideologically anti-Semitic and he had no genocidal impulse, let alone agenda. But this did not prevent him from describing MS-13 members as "animals" (during a White House roundtable discussion of 16 May 2018)[5] and stating that "Democrats [...] want illegal immigrants [...] to pour into and infest our Country" (in a Tweet of 19 June 2018). Such language aims to increase the urgency that the threat be addressed. After all, now we are dealing not merely with foreigners who will take some of our jobs away; not merely with criminals who will do some of us harm. Now our very existence is at stake, as the community as a whole is in danger of becoming "infested". Above all, this kind of language makes it easier to tackle the problem—by treating human beings in an inhuman way.

Of course, there is a contradiction here.[6] Logically, an enemy cannot be strong and weak at the same time. Psychologically, however, this ambiguity (or ambivalence) is a necessary component of populism. Its enemies need to be weak, so that we know we can defeat them. But they also need to be strong, so that we can scapegoat them. This, precisely, is the main function of the "other".

Scapegoats

If people feel that their existence is not what it should be, that their society is going in the wrong direction, then they want that society to change. If change is not forthcoming, they tend to abreact, to lash out. That is what happened in 1920s Germany, and it is what happened in Trump's America. In a later chapter, I will have occasion to explore the political, economic, and cultural roots of this existential malaise. For now, I wish to focus on its socio-psychological ramifications.

What does it mean to abreact? It means first and foremost to release pent-up anger. The photocopier or the soft-drink dispenser is not working properly and you *kick* it. This simple kick is more complex in nature than one might think. First, it shows that you are frustrated—frustrated not simply because you are unable to fix the machine, but also because you do not even understand what is wrong with it. Second, the kick is a desperate last-ditch attempt to get the darn thing to work after all. On the most basic level, the "kicking"—that is to say, the scapegoating—of a specific social group works in the same way.

You have lost your job, or you worry you might lose your job, and you feel that the political system and the mainstream media ignore your plight. This makes you angry. So you want the situation to be different; you want things to be better. But there is nothing you can do. This makes you even angrier. But how to vent this anger? You do not really understand the fluctuations of the economy; indeed, not even economists seem to understand them. Politics, with its behind-the-scenes lobbying and backroom deals, is equally untransparent, as are the workings of the media. In any case, you cannot "kick" the economy, the political system, and the media. So you lash out by personalizing. You point the finger at those greedy bankers and hedge-fund managers. You blame those corrupt politicians. And you turn your back on those politically correct know-all journalists.

The problem is that all this is still relatively impersonal. There is no *typical* banker, politician, or journalist you can picture in your mind—they remain abstract categories. Moreover, they look in many ways like you, and you do not want to kick *yourself*. So you start casting about, unconsciously, for a more clearly recognizable not-you. This is where the real enemy comes in.

A small group of clearly delineated "others" makes the perfect scapegoat. By lashing out at the Jews or at Mexican immigrants, you can *displace* your anger at an abstract system onto concrete, real people that you *can* hurt. In doing so, you can kick-start society, as it were, and get the darn thing to start working again. It is obvious: if those people are no longer there, then you will have your job back and you will be respected again.

You are not only displacing, though. You are also *projecting*; that is to say, you are ascribing your own aggressive drives to someone else. "I hate them" becomes "they hate me". I am not persecuting *them*; rather, it is they who are out to get *me*. This has a double socio-psychological "benefit". For one, you are no longer the bad person—they are. For another, you can now feel justified in persecuting them. After all, they are out to get you.

There are a number of further processes at work. People are seldom completely unaware of the reality of their situation. As a rule, they are at least dimly conscious of the nature of their predicament. Repression, which helps them push back their feelings of helplessness and anger, is therefore usually not enough. It must be supplemented by displacement and projection. But what if these strategies do not suffice either? Then *reaction-formation* comes into play. Reaction-formation is the strange, paradoxical, but actually fairly common process by which an unacceptable emotion is overcome by the unconscious exaggeration of the opposite tendency. Thus, strong anger towards a spouse may be transformed into kindness of a quite excessive, artificial nature. You feel that your husband is not doing enough in the household and this angers you, but instead of discussing the matter with him, you start doing even more yourself—unaware that you are actually just trying to make him feel guilty. Or, with an example from popular culture, a vampire slayer should not love a vampire, so for a long time Buffy unconsciously converts her love for Spike into strong dislike.

It is this process of reaction-formation that explains the viciousness of much anti-Semitic and anti-immigrant sentiment. Vaguely aware that the so-called outsiders are really just like you, but able neither to accept that fact nor to repress it, you unconsciously double-down on the "othering".

There is yet another socio-psychological "benefit" to scapegoating. It welds our own community together. This is particularly obvious with white nationalism. We may be out of a job, poor, and uneducated, but at least we are not "coloured". Or in the case of anti-immigrant sentiment, at least we are true-born, honest Americans. But it goes further than that. It is not merely a matter of perceived racial superiority. Othering also has a pseudo-democratizing effect. As whites, or true-born Americans, we are all equal, because we all share that principal feature that makes our society *our* society, that makes us *us*. Putting America first means putting all Americans—all *Americans*, and *all* Americans—first. By amplifying differences between us and our designated others, we also level differences between ourselves.

This pseudo-democratic element was one of the fatal attractions of National Socialism, too.[7] We tend to think of Hitler's reign as being highly hierarchical in nature, and of course it was. But the claim, as well as to a not inconsiderable extent the self-perception, was that this hierarchy was based on merit. Of course, there was a good deal of wishful thinking in this, as we saw in the previous chapter. But the stated ideal, or hope, existed all the same. As the historian Götz Aly puts it: "The Nazis' racist teachings have been read solely as encouragement for hatred, violence, and murder, but for millions of Germans their appeal lay in the promise of real equality within the ethnic community. Externally, Nazi ideology emphasized differences; internally, it smoothed them over".[8] This happened automatically, as it were. That is to say, it happened because of the very logic of the mechanism I identified above: the more important the external differences are, the less consequential the internal ones become. But, as Aly points out, it was also a goal that the Nazis pursued actively. For example, their "fondness for uniforms is today seen as a manifestation of [...] militarism. But uniforms, whether worn by schoolchildren or Boy Scouts or sports teams, are also a way of obscuring differences between the well-off and their less fortunate peers".[9] In the perception of many of its adherents (though, again, hardly in reality) National Socialism produced a more equal, more equitable society.

It is easy to overlook how important this combination of racial inequality and ethnic-German equality of opportunity was to Hitlerism. But it was there from the very beginning and was never abandoned. It featured prominently in the *25-Punkte-Programm*, the Nazis' 25-point programme announced by Hitler on 24 February 1920, the day the German Workers' Party (Deutsche Arbeiterpartei, or DAP) changed its name to National Socialist German Workers' Party (Nationalsozialistische Deutsche Arbeiterpartei, or NSDAP). Points 4 to 9 read as follows:

4. Only members of the nation may be citizens of the State. Only those of German blood, whatever their creed, may be members of the nation. Accordingly, no Jew may be a member of the nation.
5. Non-citizens may live in Germany only as guests and must be subject to laws for aliens.
6. The right to vote on the State's government and legislation shall be enjoyed by the citizens of the State alone. We demand therefore that all official appointments, of whatever kind, whether in the Reich, in the state or in the smaller localities, shall be held by none but citizens. We oppose the corrupting parliamentary custom of filling posts merely in accordance with party considerations, and without reference to character or abilities.
7. We demand that the State shall make it its primary duty to provide a livelihood for its citizens. If it should prove impossible to feed the entire population, foreign nationals (non-citizens) must be deported from the Reich.
8. All non-German immigration must be prevented. We demand that all non-Germans who entered Germany after 2 August 1914 shall be required to leave the Reich forthwith.
9. All citizens shall have equal rights and duties.[10]

Werner May's popular *Politischer Katechismus für den jungen Deutschen in Schule und Beruf* (Political Catechism for the Young German Man in the Classroom and the Workplace, 1935) explains these six points: "Germany for the Germans! Germany's soil and Germany's labour are the soil and labour of the Germans. For many years, Eastern Jewry was able to pour over the border into Germany and establish itself in a country that did not belong to it and which it began to bleed dry in an outrageous manner. [...] The Third Reich knows no class differences. Whether people work with their head or their hands—they are all equal; but equal rights also means equal duties".[11]

Scapegoating is an extremely pernicious socio-psychological process. Indeed, we have not yet exhausted the list of its dangerous attractions. Among these is also the paradoxical aggregation-and-disaggregation of the enemy. What does this mean?

The evocation of a specific social enemy makes it possible to separate—to disaggregate—the good "others" from the bad ones. After all, it is to be assumed that some outsiders are, to use Trump's phrase, "good people". However, as a collective—in aggregate form, as it were—they threaten our way of life, so the righteous will simply have to suffer along with the wicked. Scapegoating allows us to have our cake and eat it. We do not have to look upon all Jews or all Mexican immigrants as a threat, because our perspective is based on a concept of "the Jew" or "the Mexican immigrant" that is concrete enough for us to be able to picture the enemy in our mind, yet abstract enough for us to isolate the good Jews or immigrants whom we happen to know.

This attitude is of course not logical. But human beings are not robots, and the mind is not a machine. People's thoughts and actions seldom conform to rational standards. Rather, human psychology is to a significant degree based on our ability to "cheat" logic and rationality. We can block out the parts of reality that we do not wish to acknowledge; we can hold contradictory convictions in our mind; and we can switch from one conviction to another depending on context. This is not illogical in a straightforward, Mr Spock-like sense. That is to say, it may in the end be counterproductive (and indeed it usually is), but it is not as if we got nothing out of it. Mental ambivalence allows us to *satisfy a multiplicity of impulses*.

This trick of the mind is highly complex in nature. It relies, as I indicated, on the context-dependent oscillation between abstraction and concretion, concept and reality, the collective and the individual. But it is a duplicitous back-and-forth by which every swing to one side carries over, as it were, some aspects of the other side. Thus, the abstract concept "Mexican immigrant" is based on characteristics that some real-life Mexican immigrants actually possess; say, a criminal past. This is why you support President Trump's anti-immigration policies. On the other hand, most Mexican immigrants you know are not criminals and you do not treat them as such. This is why on a conscious level you do not see yourself as a racist. But, then, given that they fall into the abstract category "Mexican immigrant", you can never be really sure—so on a less conscious level you still see them as "others". This is why you can continue to support the President's anti-immigration stance.

The socio-psychological "benefit" of scapegoating is thus that it allows you to support racist policies while dissociating yourself from racism. You can be a racist without being a racist, as it were. This is also the reason why populist leaders do not have to turn you into a full-blown xenophobe or anti-Semite, and why you do not have to believe everything they say. All that is needed is that a certain abstract concept of "the enemy", a certain framework of suspicion, is activated. In this way, "reasonable" doubt is created both psychologically and socially, giving you enough of an excuse (both in your own mind and vis-à-vis your fellow citizens) to support the populist movement.

A sense of security, the opportunity to abreact, feelings of ethnic superiority, a perceived equality of opportunity, aggregation-and-disaggregation, and dissociation are not the only *faux* benefits that Hitlerian and Trumpian populism offers. There is also its participatory dimension.

Populism as Participatory Authoritarianism

Populist politics are characterized by authoritarianism and a cult of the leader. In some—extreme—cases, when populists come to power and manage to transform their country into a dictatorship, their rule is one of total or near total autocracy. In all cases, populists display contempt for democratic rules and restrictions. What counts is what the leader wants; and what the leader says goes. Populists invert John Adams's phrase that ours should be "a government of laws and not of men", famously cited by Special Prosecutor Archibald Cox after he was fired on the orders of Richard Nixon.[12] In the populists' world view, the country should be ruled by men, or rather by one strongman.

One could be forgiven, then, for thinking that populist movements consist largely of sheep trotting obediently after their shepherd—followers and not independent thinkers, passive drones and not proactive doers. This is a widely held view on the populist-voting electorate: facing major social and economic challenges but lacking in true individuality and unable to turn their situation around, they look to the saviour-leader for their redemption. They are essentially a bunch of deplorables without any will or initiative of their own.

This view is highly misleading. It overlooks one of the principal elements of populism: *populism is an empowerment of the individual.*

Populist movements involve the mass participation of highly active individuals who often operate on their own accord and who receive real benefits from their actions even when their leader is not yet in power and hence not yet able to "save" them. On some level at least, these individuals are not subjugated by the movement, but set free; not subdued, but mobilized; not crushed and homogenized, but given the opportunity to regain their autonomy.

In order to explain this, I will draw on ideas put forward by the Dutch sociologist Erik van Ree in his study *De totalitaire paradox* (1984).[13] Van Ree himself applies his concept of the totalitarian paradox—the "combination of total autocracy, of a deified leader, with an equally excessive participatory democracy"—to what he calls "the terrorist mass democracies of Stalin and Mao".[14] However, many of his ideas have validity for Hitlerian and Trumpian populism as well. Of course, Trump's rule was not totalitarian, and nor was the relation between Hitler and Germany before 1933. I have therefore called the phenomenon at issue *participatory authoritarianism.*

What does participatory authoritarianism consist in? "Ordinary" authoritarianisms—say, the current regime in Iran—have little support among the population. Their citizens are largely passive, resigned to their fate. By contrast, populist authoritarianisms—say, the early stages of the Khomeini regime, before most Iranians realized they had made a terrible mistake—"rely on fanatical and enthusiastic participation of important parts of the active population", as van Ree puts it.[15] They are emancipatory movements aimed at transforming society. True, it is invariably emancipation of a worrying type—"emancipation of one group to the detriment of another, liberation through hatred, reconstruction through destruction".[16] But that does not make the revolutionary fervour any less real.

All of this is not primarily a matter of active involvement in formal democratic procedures. To the extent that it is, democracy is largely seen as a means to an end—an irritant that one will have to continue to live with or (in the more extreme scenario) a ladder to be discarded as soon as one has reached the top. The basic assumption is the idea that change can be brought about by the "will of the people" beyond and indeed against the old social order and the "rigged" political system. Populist movements are fundamentally *voluntarist* in nature.

Before elaborating on this, I wish to have a brief look at the logic underlying populist activism.

The relation between the movement, its members, and the leader rests on a strange circularity. One of the key pillars of populism is the purity of its ideas. Populists despise compromise, doubt, and anything else they see as half-heartedness. This is the so-called democratic dimension of populism—the conviction that society should be the unadulterated expression of the will of the people. However, this dimension immediately gives rise to its opposite—the rejection of democratic pluralism. If society is supposed to express the will of the people, then the question becomes: what exactly is that general will (to use Jean-Jacques Rousseau's phrase), what does it say? Now, if there were different sources of authority, then you would have different interpretations of the general will, which would therefore no longer be pure. Paradoxically, then, it is precisely populism's radical-democratic idealism that requires that there be one authority only, one leader.

Yet this does not reduce the populist-revolutionary fervour. On the contrary. It is precisely populism's radical-democratic idealism that requires, not only that there be one leader, but also that the movement's members actively participate in its advance or consolidation. As part of a movement that aims to reclaim society from the host of private interests to which it has succumbed and which are tearing it apart, you cannot remain one such private interest yourself. In van Ree's words, "to withdraw into your own private sphere, to moan and groan on your own [...], that too runs counter to the [aimed-for] all-encompassing process of social renewal and is therefore at odds with the totalizing ideology you believe in".[17] You, the people, cannot take back control of society if you merely vote for others (which is what you did in the past, if indeed you voted at all). You can only do so if you take back control of yourself and become an independently thinking and acting individual again.

This is the contradiction that characterizes the populist uprising: it is an attempt to find individuality in and through a mass movement, autonomy in and through dependence, and freedom in and through subservience. Of course, this cannot work, but that should not prevent us from taking both parts of the equation seriously—the perceived benefits as well as the real costs.

So, whereas in the past you took little or no interest in politics, you now go to rallies or at least you watch them on your TV, computer, or mobile phone, or you listen to them on the radio. You read the leader's proclamations in the form of pamphlets or Tweets, and you may buy some books by the movement's spokespeople. You follow the news as reported by the media that are aligned with the movement. You join the Party and perhaps become active in one of its organizations. You express your allegiance through the clothes you wear: a MAGA ("Make America Great Again") baseball cap is not a Nazi uniform, but both tell other people where you stand ideologically.[18] So do insignia, buttons, bumper stickers, and the like. Even voting takes on a different quality. It is no longer a meaningless choice between equally corrupt incarnations of the establishment: now there really is a point to it. And of course the Internet has added a whole layer of political engagement. Facebook, Twitter, and other social media make it possible to become highly active in a way that is relatively unexacting and physically safe. They allow you to opine, comment, and criticize as much as you like and wherever you are—and indeed to rant and rave on the level of a Munich beer-hall conversation.

They also enable the ideologically pure of heart to connect with each other and organize. Last but not least, they are breeding grounds for conspiracy theories (a topic to which I will return).

Populism, then, restores your sense of self-worth. It reactivates your desire to build a genuinely new future for yourself and your family. As we have seen, one of the main converters or switches for this energy is nationalism. The people with whom you are going to build the new future are *your* people, the true patriots. Only this sense of community can overcome the "many-willed-ness"[19] of the existing society. Making society us is therefore first and foremost a matter of making the nation us, or us again. But this can only be done by the nation—the true nation—itself. As Hitler put it after he had been appointed Chancellor in 1933: "Never believe in outside help, help that lies outside our own nation, our own people [*Volk*]. In ourselves alone lies the future of the German people".[20]

The most obvious foil for this nationalism is external in nature: other nations; supranational entities, such as the League of Nations, the United Nations, and the European Union; and international treaties and agreements, such as the Treaty of Versailles and NAFTA. They all threaten us, damage us, exploit us. In order to resist such alien forces, we must put our own country first, because nobody else will. But there are internal foils too. Indeed, the purity of the ideal requires that there be a purge of society; if not a physical one, then at least one on the level of ideas, through criticism. This brings us back to the issue of scapegoats. Populism cannot exist without enemies—and to the mind of the populist there are plenty of candidates.

There is the existing political system with its interminable discussions and, to the extent that it gets anything done at all, its cowardly compromises. There are the system's representatives—the corrupt establishment, the elite, the swamp. There is the old guard—the traditional politicians who cling to conventional beliefs and outdated ideals. There are the faceless bureaucrats, overpaid officials, and self-righteous judges who stand in the way of progress. There are the so-called experts who insist that certain things cannot be done or ought not to be done. There is the fake media, the *Lügenpresse* (the "lying press"),[21] who refuses to see the movement's true greatness and keeps peddling half-truths and full-blown lies. Above all, there are the enemies who are beyond redemption, who live among us or are trying to get into our country, but who can never be us—the foreigners, the immigrants, the Jews. They are the ultimate not-us, the incommensurable Other.

Populist authoritarianism manifests itself to a large extent in this *enemy and scapegoat syndrome*. Yet that does not make its activist dimension any less real. This is the point I have been making: the movement offers its members the opportunity to express what they really feel and to act on what they really believe. This activism is a crucial element in the movement's appeal; to ignore it would be seriously reductive.

It would be equally reductive, however, to ignore the various ways in which the strongman seeks to manipulate his followers' feelings and beliefs and exploit their desire for action. We will have occasion to explore this subject in some of the other chapters, when we will be looking at issues of populist propaganda, rhetoric, and narrative (un-)truth. One manipulative strategy, however, needs to be discussed here—the container approach.

The Container Approach

We have seen that one of the attractions of populism is that it offers us the opportunity to aggregate and disaggregate different people—the "good ones" and the "bad ones"—among one and the same enemy (say, among the immigrants, or among the Jews). Populism performs the same service when it comes to different enemies. That is to say, it makes it possible to supplement our core enemy (the immigrants, the Jews) with a number of associate enemies, whom depending on context and perspective we can either *equate with* or *distinguish from* this core enemy. Hitler's associate enemies included the social-democrats, the communists, establishment politicians, and the *Lügenpresse* or lying press, as well as foreign powers such as France. Trump's associate enemies included African-Americans, the Democrats, establishment politicians, and the mainstream media with its fake news, as well as foreign powers such as China.

Perhaps the best way to picture this mechanism is as a set of shifting concentric circles with an immutable core (the immigrants, the Jews)—a target of which only the bullseye remains fixed, while the rings keep changing positions, or temporarily drop off the board altogether.

The benefit to populist leaders is clear: they can change their focus depending on political expediency. When the National Socialists were competing for votes with the Communist Party of Germany (Kommunistische Partei Deutschlands, or KPD), they presented their communist opponents as being essentially Jewish: "just look at their leaders", "Marx was a Jew", and so on. This narrative continued after 1933, but when Hitler concluded a non-aggression pact with Stalin in August 1939, criticism was moderated, until the German invasion of the Soviet Union in June 1941, when it was resumed with full force. Of course, such shifts can be a bit of a rollercoaster. But people have short memories, and with some fancy rhetorical footwork and enough propaganda this strategy can be a powerful weapon.

The benefit to the leader's followers is equally clear: they can all believe that the leader will deal with their specific enemy of choice. Thus, considerations by different Trump voters might have gone something like this: "Trump is the only one who can stop ISIS from attacking our country"; "Trump may overstate the threat from ISIS, but he's the only one who can prevent our country from being flooded by immigrants"; "I don't agree with everything Trump says about immigrants, but we need someone to shake up the traditional political system, which is totally corrupt"; "Trump will preserve our traditional values by appointing good conservative judges to the Supreme Court"; and so on.

To some extent, such openness is of course characteristic of politics in general. But it is needed much more in the case of populist politics. Populism, after all, is a kind of anti-politics. It is a protest movement that feeds on *opponentism*.

The openness is also much more cynically exploited by populist leaders. Arguably the most important way they do this is by presenting their different chosen enemies as one. They do not simply add up their opponents, as it were, but rather treat them as if they were interlinked manifestations of the same basic social evil. Hitler discusses this container approach quite openly—shockingly openly—in *Mein Kampf*. He writes:

In general the art of all truly great national leaders at all times consists among other things primarily in not dividing the attention of a people, but in concentrating it upon a single foe. The more unified the application of a people's will to fight, the greater will be the magnetic attraction of a movement and the mightier will be the impetus of the thrust. It belongs to the genius of a great leader to make even adversaries far removed from one another seem to belong to a single category, because in weak and uncertain characters the knowledge of having different enemies can only too readily lead to the beginning of doubt in their own right.

Once the wavering mass sees itself in a struggle against too many enemies, objectivity will put in an appearance, throwing open the question whether all others are really wrong and only their own people or their own movement are in the right.

And this brings about the first paralysis of their own power. Hence a multiplicity of different adversaries must always be combined so that in the eyes of the masses of one's own supporters the struggle is directed against only one enemy.[22]

Hitler himself gives a demonstration of this strategy in *Mein Kampf*. Throughout the book, he consistently links crime, prostitution, artistic degeneracy, as well as the mainstream press, establishment politics, and social democracy (which in its turn he identifies with Marxism) to "the Jews".[23] As he presents the matter, all these phenomena were either caused by the Jews, or spread by the Jews, or defended by the Jews, or had succumbed in some other way to the influence of international Jewry. The National Socialists' favourite word for this alleged influence was *Verjudung*, "Jewification" or "Judaization". With roots that go back before the emergence of National Socialism, the term—as the historian Steven Aschheim has noted—not only "reflected the belief that Jews wielded disproportionate influence and occupied (or were about to occupy) pivotal positions of inordinate economic, political and cultural power", but also "connoted a condition in which the 'Jewish spirit' had somehow permeated society and its key institutions, one in which Jewish *Geist* had seeped through the spiritual pores of the nation to penetrate and undermine the German psyche itself".[24] This catch-all term enabled the Nazis to tar their associate enemies with the same brush as their core enemies.

Trump's container approach was less extreme, but he too was adept at linking his associate enemies to his core enemies. Thus, he frequently painted the Democrats as being in cahoots with non-white immigrants, especially with those coming from South America. The Democrats' refusal to fund the Wall, he claimed repeatedly, amounted to an open-door policy that would mean the end of the United States as an independent country. However, at other times (when he needed the Democrats' support, or when he wanted to give centrist voters the impression that he was really on their side), he toned down the anti-Democratic rhetoric. The seemingly unfocussed, meandering style of his speeches, which went from immigration, to the Democrats, to Robert Mueller, to China, to the mainstream media, to fake news, to the Chairman of the Federal Reserve, to James Comey, to Hillary Clinton, and then back to immigration, can at least in part be explained by his desire to blend his and his followers' enemies into one. A more analytical narrative would have collapsed under the weight of its own implausibility. The associative approach, by contrast, evoked a unified image without the speaker's being obliged to embark on the impossible task of actually making the case that these foes were all connected in some meaningful way.

The best example of Trump's linking-together strategy is his demonization of the Squad. In many ways, this quartet of Democratic Congresswomen—Alexandria Ocasio-Cortez, Ilhan Omar, Ayanna Pressley, and Rashida Tlaib—offered an ideal target, a Venn diagram of the kind of people and positions Trump had been railing against ever since he jumped on the birtherism bandwagon and decided to run for President. As young, female, progressive Democrats of colour, they represented precisely the cultural shift that so many of Trump's voters appeared unable to come to terms with. Moreover, Ilhan Omar and Rashida Tlaib were Muslims—another of Trumpism's recurring *bêtes noires*—and Omar was born outside the United States. All Trump had to do, then, was build them up as the face of the Democratic Party. The laws of the media would do the rest. Trump's attacks would catapult the Squad to fame, or notoriety; the Democratic Party would be obliged to defend them (even though the four Congresswomen were significantly to the left of most Democratic voters, let alone the American electorate as a whole); and Trump would emerge—or so he must have calculated—with many more potential votes than before, or at least the Democrats would end up with many fewer potential votes.

The President took to the task with gusto. In three consecutive Tweets, sent on 14 July 2019, he wrote:

> So interesting to see "Progressive" Democrat Congresswomen, who originally came from countries whose governments are a complete and total catastrophe, the worst, most corrupt and inept anywhere in the world (if they even have a functioning government at all), now loudly and viciously telling the people of the United States, the greatest and most powerful Nation on earth, how our government is to be run. Why don't they go back and help fix the totally broken and crime infested places from which they came. Then come back and show us how it is done. These places need your help badly, you can't leave fast enough.

The chain of deliberate associations is clear: Democratic Party, progressive policies, immigration, weak government, corruption, condescending intellectual elitism, lack of patriotism, social anarchy, crime, and infestation. Of course, the President did not discuss the links between these phenomena; Twitter does not lend itself to analysis (which is one of the reasons it was his favourite medium). However, as I remarked above, such lack of discussion only makes the chain appear stronger.

The most striking thing about the series of Tweets is the suggestion that the Congresswomen should go back to where they came from. Now, while Omar was a Somali-born American, Ocasio-Cortez, Pressley, and Tlaib were American-born Americans. Trump's suggestion was therefore based on a false premise, as well as being a xenophobic trope. But precisely the factual inaccuracy and the xenophobia drew even more attention to the Tweets, as Trump knew would happen. Moreover, the four women held very left-wing positions on border security and the Immigration and Customs Enforcement agency (ICE) and were engaged in a dispute with the more moderate Democratic leadership about this. By tweeting about them in the way he did, Trump highlighted their more extreme, or less centric, Democratic stance, while at the same time lumping them together with Trumpism's core enemy, non-white immigrants. He mentioned neither their skin colour nor Omar's and Tlaib's Muslim faith, but he knew there was no need. Both would come out in the media coverage; and the pictures alone would tell half his story.

Trump kept up his attacks in the weeks following his initial Tweets, most prominently at a campaign rally in Greenville, North Carolina (a swing state), on 17 July 2019. Here, he again took aim at the Congresswomen whose "comments are helping to fuel the rise of a dangerous militant hard left". The message was once more that "if they don't like it [here], let 'm leave, let 'm leave". And on 21 July 2019, he tweeted "I don't believe the four Congresswomen are capable of loving our Country". This time, he added—in a perfect demonstration of how populism's enemies are paradoxically both strong and weak at the same time—that Ocasio-Cortez, Omar, Pressley, and Tlaib "are destroying the Democrat Party, but are weak & insecure people who can never destroy our great Nation!"

The belief that there is really just one enemy—that all dangers emanate from a single source—answers a deep psychological need. The philosopher Slavoj Žižek has given the best explanation of this aspect of the container approach, using Steven Spielberg's film *Jaws* as example.[25]

What, Žižek asks, does the shark stand for? Jaws has variously been interpreted as symbolizing natural disaster, immigrants, communism, and capitalism. So which is it? Žižek replies: "none of them and, at the same time, all of them". How does that work? Well, Žižek goes on to say, ordinary Americans, like people all over the world, have a multiplicity of fears. They are afraid that someone might hurt their children. They worry about the number of immigrants coming into the country. They are apprehensive that hurricanes, earthquakes, or floods might wreck their houses. They distrust politicians. They are concerned about the power of big business. "The function of the shark is to unite all these fears, so that we in a way trade all these fears for one alone. In this way, our experience of reality gets much simpler".

According to Žižek, this is precisely what happened during the Weimar Republic. Especially after the Wall Street Crash of 1929, which all but destroyed the German economy, ordinary Germans were in a state of total confusion and helplessness. Many of them had lost their jobs, and those who still had jobs could be let go any time. Their money had lost all its value due to the horrendous levels of inflation. They saw moral degeneracy and corruption all around them. The newspapers appeared to be lying to them all the time, and the political system seemed powerless to do anything about the situation. "How to solve this problem? Simple. You need to generate an [easily intelligible] ideological narrative which explains how things went wrong. [...] Things were OK until Jews penetrated our social body. The way to restore the health of our social body is to eliminate the Jews. It's the same operation as with the shark in *Jaws*. You have a multitude of fears, and this multiplicity of fears confuses you. You replace this confused multitude with one clear figure—the Jew—and everything becomes clear". This is the function of the container approach: it blends a host of abstract and complex threats into a single pseudo-concrete enemy.

The container approach is ideological in nature. An ideology distorts reality. However, it is not simply a ready-made interpretation. Rather, it is an interpretative tool or, to put in in psychological terms, a mindset. It never provides an all-encompassing and fully finalized world view. (If things were otherwise, ideologies would not be adaptable to changing social and historical circumstances, nor would they be able to appeal to large swathes of the population.) Every ideology, Žižek says, acts "as a kind of filter, a frame, so that, if you look at the same ordinary reality through that frame, everything changes". But the frame does not tell us what reality is like, not in any detail anyway. The frame generates possible perspectives on what reality might be like, what might be behind it. Looking through the frame, we start to wonder what particular people might really be after, what particular institutions might really be doing, and what particular events might really mean. "The frame opens the abyss of suspicion".

Conspiracy Theories

It is here that conspiracy theories come into play. Conspiracy theories are the formalized expression of the reign of suspicion: intuitive distrust has become a narrative algorithm.[26] That is to say, conspiracy theories retell history in a different way and in doing so rearrange and reorder our existence. They are a conversion mechanism to transform chaos and confusion into clarity and certainty.[27]

The main aim of conspiracy theories is to make the world less complex. Yet they themselves are a highly complex phenomenon.

Conspiracy theories provide a narrative of us versus them, of good versus evil, by positing a *hidden hand* behind our everyday reality, a reality that we can see but for some reason do not like and hence do not wish to accept as it is. This hidden hand can come in different shapes and sizes—in the guise of Hitler's Jewish world conspiracy, for instance, or McCarthy's communist threat, or Trump's deep state. Yet whatever form conspiracy theories take, they are always curiously paradoxical: they make things more transparent by making them more opaque. Refusing to accept accidents, coincidences, mistakes, ambiguities, and pretty much everything else that makes human life human, conspiracists render life one-dimensional, but they do so by adding a dimension to it. They enlighten through obscurantism.

That may sound counterproductive, silly even; and of course in a way it is. But the approach has enormous psychological appeal. For it dovetails perfectly with our ambivalent state of mind. It speaks both to our fears and to our hopes, both to our ignorance and to our desire for knowledge. The existence of the conspiracy explains our helplessness in the face of a shadowy, scary world *and at the same time* tells us that behind it all there is a pattern we can discover, or have already discovered, and that we can therefore be in control after all.

What is particularly appealing is that conspiracy theories subjectivize, personalize history. They tell you that you are not at the mercy of anonymous forces, but under attack by people and groups of people that you can stand up to and vanquish. So the problem is no longer an economic system that no one knows how to manage—the problem is the capitalist Jew or the Jewish capitalist whom you can bring into line or get rid of. The President's agenda is no longer at odds with abstract legal principles—it is being thwarted by concrete deep-state actors. Social structures have become conquerable enemies.

Conspiracy theories put us back in a position of power. They also exalt us. They make our ordinary lives more interesting and our existence more important, because *we* are the ones in the know. This knowledge, this power elevates us even above the so-called experts.

The problem is that conspiracy theories are seldom completely without "proof". Some Jews were (and are) capitalists; some officials, academics, and actors in 1950s America did have communist sympathies; and some government employees were opposed to Trump's policies. If you take the right (that is to say, the wrong) approach, there is usually enough of a hook to turn such partial and irrelevant truths into one big untruth. Moreover, conspiracies are not always fictitious. Gladio—the network of sleeper spies and secret guerrilla units set up in Western Europe after the Second World War as a resistance movement ready to spring into action should the Soviet Union start an invasion—did exist. So did Nixon's cover-up. So did the public-relations campaign to conjure up an Iraqi WMD threat in the early 2000s, and so did Volkswagen's concerted action to fit their diesel engines with software designed to hide the cars' real carbon-dioxide emission levels. Why, then, should the crash-landed UFO at Roswell or the deep state not also be real? All the more so as we are obliged to take so many things at face value anyway.

Let us be honest: how many of us really have the technological expertise to understand the things involved in putting someone on the moon? The *knowledge* that Neil Armstrong and Buzz Aldrin walked on the moon is ultimately a *belief* in science and social institutions. Hence, there will always be people to whom the "simpler" scenario portrayed in *Capricorn One*—Peter Hyams's 1978 film in which NASA fakes a Mars landing in a television studio—is the more believable one.

Today, the situation is in some ways even more challenging than ever before. We now live in a society saturated with highly realistic fictions. Films, television series, reality shows, and computer games offer us an array of alternative realities, many of them based on "true stories". Ours is forever a polyphonous, polysemous world. What is more, many of these fictions are themselves centred on conspiracies. Oliver Stone's film *JFK* and Breitbart News may belong to different genres and play to different political affinities, but they both suggest possible, if not exactly plausible, *plots*.

These plots (in both senses of the word) can be transposed onto other events and other areas of life. The Internet is the perfect platform for this.

Social media allow the conspiracists to share their ideas, complete with "proof", with the like-minded—quickly, comprehensively, and with little or no interference or oversight. The Internet also brings the like-minded together in chat rooms and a variety of other echo chambers of opinion. And we know from history and scholarly research that being in a group with people like you tends to make you more extreme in your beliefs and actions. Group membership produces not only group think, but also group polarization. Extremism then becomes the norm. You are no longer the odd one out, and your ideas are no longer odd. Nuttiness is the new normal.

In addition, we now live in the age of digital manipulation, from Photoshop to Adobe Voco and beyond. This does not simply mean that dishonest people are now able to fake evidence on a much larger scale and in a much more sophisticated way than Robert Kenneth Wilson, who "photographed" the Loch Ness monster in the 1930s, or Ray Santilli, who "discovered" the alien-autopsy footage in the 1990s. It also—and much more perniciously—means that honest people increasingly doubt the authenticity of evidence that has *not* been faked. Finally, the Internet's unchecked pluralism—or rather mishmash—of speculation, opinion, and fact has undermined the expert's monopoly on truth, making it even harder to refute the conspiracist's claims.

The real problem, however, goes much deeper. The real problem lies in the very nature of narrative itself.

Let us take an example. "Johnny robbed the bank" is a pretty straightforward statement. "We know that Johnny robbed the bank, and we know that Mary was involved as well" is already a good deal less straightforward. Who is we? How do they know? What proof do they have? How was the division of labour between Johnny and Mary? Are they really both guilty? The more information, the more there is room for doubt. This is not just a matter of criminology. That is to say, it is not simply: if there are more clues and more pieces of evidence, then there is more stuff that might turn out to be wrong or exculpatory. It is above all a matter of narratology. It is a question of what one might call the *narrative paradox*.

The German literary scholar Wolfgang Iser has said important things about this.[28] He has made the case that the more details a text provides, the more open to interpretation it becomes. This is what I have referred to as the narrative paradox: more textual density means less textual determinacy. The reason for this, Iser argues, is that the more facts, events, characters, voices, and perspectives a text presents, the more potential narrative connections it generates. These connections need to be made by the reader, and different readers will make different connections. Going from textual element to textual element, they constantly find themselves at narrative junctions at which they can make this *or* that connection, this *or* that causal link, this *or* that inference. Iser therefore calls these junctions *Leerstellen*, gaps or empty spaces.

The point is: the harder you try to preclude possible misunderstandings or refute possible objections, the less likely you are to succeed. To put it in colloquial terms, you will only dig yourself deeper into the hole. Anyone who has ever had an argument with a partner or spouse can testify to this. The more you try to explain, the worse the situation gets. The result is an increasingly frustrating cycle of further explanations and further misunderstandings, interspersed with complaints along the lines of "what are you trying to say?" and "that's not what I meant" or "you just don't understand". That is why a silent embrace and a loving smile are often the better way to go. And that is why the expression is "kiss and make up" and not "make up and kiss". Words will not cut it. "It is quite impossible for the text itself to fill the gaps. In fact, the more a text tries to be precise (i.e., the more [narrative elements] it offers), the greater will be the number of gaps".[29]

Worse, this growth will take place *exponentially*. If you have only a and b, then you are dealing with three elements: a, b, and the relation between a and b. But if you have a, b, and c, then you are suddenly dealing with at least ten elements: a, b, c, a-b, a-c, b-c, ab-c, a-bc, b-ac, and a-b-c.[30]

Iser's argument stretches beyond this straightforward mathematical point, however. He argues that an increase in narrative indeterminacy is not merely the result of an increase in basic data ("Johnny", "Mary", "bank", "robbery", and so on). What is essential, he says, is the way the text presents the connections between them. Here, there are three levels.

First, there are the questions relating to causality and chronology as well as the individual motivations and interpersonal relations of the protagonists. If, for example, a text states "Bob was a little unwell. He didn't go to work", does that mean that he did not go to work *because* he was unwell, or *in spite of the fact* that he was only a little unwell? Or was there no link at all between his indisposition and his absence? The number of such questions becomes even greater if the text does not just tell one story, but presents multiple intersecting story lines—if, say, Bob worked at the bank allegedly robbed by Johnny and Mary. This brings us to the next interpretative level.

On the second level, indeterminacy is related to the number of narrative perspectives and voices in the text. We all know that a Trump rally or a Trump Tweet possessed a different meaning depending on whether it was reported by CNN or by Fox News. Well, the same holds true for the multiplicity of views *within* a report and indeed within any text. The clearest instance of this is when a story is told by multiple narrators, or seen through the eyes of multiple protagonists, as in novels like William Faulkner's *As I Lay Dying* and Gillian Flynn's *Gone Girl* or films like Akira Kurosawa's *Rashomon*. But even if there is just *one* teller or focalizer, the different perspectives still open the door to interpretative uncertainty. For the relation between the characters' perspectives and the teller's perspective is a *Leerstelle*—a narrative gap—too. If, say, a police report reproduces a witness statement but then concludes that the witness is lying, the reader is not obliged to adopt that conclusion. (Note that yet again it is precisely the added textual density—the attempt by the police to make their narrative unassailable—that undermines the text's determinacy.) It is a question of whom the reader chooses to believe.

Let us move on to the third and highest level of indeterminacy. Texts have not only narrators, but also authors. The author is responsible for the text as a whole and everything that is in it. Hence the entire text becomes a *Leerstelle* if the reader does not trust the author.[31]

This has particular relevance in the case of authorial commentary. Authors as a rule provide in-text comments on the events and characters they describe (as in the police report declaring a witness statement a "lie"). Through such evaluations, they attempt to create a particular conception of their text. One might say that they try to get ahead of the reader by removing the text's indeterminacy themselves. The problem is: they can only ever get the reader to respond *to* the comments, not necessarily *in line with* them. Once more it is precisely the added textual density—in this case, the authorial metatext—that engenders interpretative openness. The metalevel comments open up a space for appraisal in that they "permit new gaps to arise in the text. The gaps now no longer lie in the recounted narrative, but between the narrative and the various ways of assessing it".[32] Indeed, the comments' very existence—the fact that the author deemed it necessary to make them at all—"seem[s] to imply other possibilities of evaluation".[33]

What does this somewhat abstract exposition have to do with conspiracy theories? The answer is straightforward enough. Iser's theory explains why it is nearly impossible to refute the conspiracist's claims. The reason is not merely that conspiracy theorists are crazy (although obviously many of them are). Nor is the reason simply that you cannot prove a negative—that there is no real counterargument to claims along the lines of "you cannot prove that the CIA was *not* involved in the assassination of John F. Kennedy". The reason is that the more facts, witnesses, experts, and testimony you include in your anti-conspiracy narrative, the more narrative gaps you produce. In other words, the more extensive, wide-ranging, and detailed your report gets, the more open to interpretation—and hence to doubt—it becomes. There is no way out of the vicious circle of narrative logic.

The situation is even worse than Iser's theory suggests. In addition to the narrative paradox, to which Iser draws attention, there is a psychological dimension to the predicament in which reasonable people find themselves.

The psychological dimension is related to what Freud calls *resistance*, the idea that the closer the psychoanalyst gets to the truth that the patient is trying to repress, the more the patient will push back at the analyst's suggestions. Johnny's "I do not fancy Mary" is therefore just as likely to indicate that he *is* attracted to her as that he is *not* attracted to her. Now, Freud applies the concept of resistance to the workings of the unconscious. But, of course, the same phenomenon occurs on a conscious level. FBI agents know as well as Freudian analysts that the more emphatic the denial, the more there is reason for doubt. The less than intelligent answer "I didn't kill Rick" in response to the question "Where were you Saturday evening?" betrays the murderer, but—and this is the issue under consideration—a more focussed but overly elaborate answer raises suspicions too. The problem is: so does a conspicuously short or seemingly normal answer. And who can tell the difference between conspicuously short and just short, between seemingly normal and normal?

It is all in the mind. It may be true (as Freud is supposed to have said, although there is no evidence that he did say it) that "sometimes a cigar is just a cigar", but (as Freud also recognized) this does not prevent people from looking for possible other meanings. One might call this *paranoia* if it were not for the fact that it is not a medical condition. We all behave in this way. Othello is very much in love with Desdemona, but the moment the seed of suspicion is planted, there is no way he is *not* going to disbelieve what she says. In fact, Iago does not even *plant* the suspicion in Othello; all he does is fan the little flame of doubt that is already there in the Moor's mind. (Otherwise Othello would have disbelieved *him*.) The Moor says to Iago "thou echo'st me / As if there were some monster in thy thought / Too hideous to be shown",[34] but in reality the monster is in his own thoughts. Othello falls victim less to Iago's evil intent than to his own mental disposition—a disposition that is hardly unusual, let alone pathological. If it were any different, it would be hard to explain the play's universal appeal.

This psychological dimension is an additional reason why it is virtually impossible to convince conspiracy theorists that your rational world view is true and that you have no ulterior motives.

There is a final dimension that needs mentioning—language. Narratology and psychology are both underpinned by language. There are no stories without language; there are no thoughts without language. The problem is that all language is inherently contradictory. By definition, any statement can be either true or false. Language can either reveal reality or hide it. At the most fundamental level, therefore, every utterance automatically and by its very nature evokes its opposite. You cannot state "there is no Area 51" without implicitly raising the possibility that there is an Area 51. The news headline "Hillary denies corruption" unavoidably also says "Hillary is corrupt".

This is what the philosopher Jacques Derrida has called the *deconstructive* nature of language. To deny ("I am not a crook") is always also to affirm; to affirm ("I have full confidence in the Secretary of State") is always also to deny. This, then, is the final nail in the coffin of rational argument as a bulwark against conspiracy theories: no linguistic utterance, however factual, is impervious to inversion.

I have spent so much time on these theoretical matters because their relevance stretches far beyond the issue of conspiracy theories. It extends to two further issues that I will be looking at in this book—the workings of the media, and narrative truth. For example, our discussion goes a long way towards explaining why Hillary Clinton's eventual exoneration by the FBI had so little effect. It also explains why fact-checking Donald Trump was in many ways a double-edged sword.

As I hinted earlier, the belief in science and social institutions is crucial to an understanding of things as they really are. This is not because science and social institutions will help convince conspiracy theorists that they are wrong. Our discussion has shown that scientific objections, expert opinions, and government assurances *cannot* achieve this; that, if anything, such arguments are likely to have the opposite effect. What makes the difference is the pre-existing faith in the scientific establishment, political authorities, and so on. Decisive is whether people have a *basic trust* in the world around them or not. That is why it is a key aim of populist leaders to undermine our basic social trust and replace it with *basic distrust*.[35] This is the topic of the next chapter.

Notes

1. Ramin Jahanbegloo, *Conversations with Isaiah Berlin* (London: Phoenix Press, 2000), pp. 64–65. For the sake of clarity, I have made a few minor changes to the original's punctuation.
2. To avoid misunderstanding, this is not to say that the majority of the population in Nazi Germany were somehow not living under a dictatorship, but rather that the system made it possible for them to repress and rationalize away the existence of dictatorial rule. As a result, large swathes of the population did not experience the same kind of fear as people under Stalin did. On this issue, cf. Ian Kershaw and Moshe Lewin (eds.), *Stalinism and Nazism: Dictatorships in Comparison* (Cambridge: Cambridge University Press, 1997), Richard Overy, *The Dictators: Hitler's Germany, Stalin's Russia* (New York: W. W. Norton, 2004),

Laurence Rees, *Hitler and Stalin: The Tyrants and the Second World War* (London: Viking, 2020), and Robert S. Robins and Jerrold M. Post (eds.), *Political Paranoia: The Psychopolitics of Hatred* (Yale: Yale University Press, 1997), especially chapters 10 and 11.

3. The following discussion leans on Leo Löwenthal's classic *Prophets of Deceit: A Study of the Techniques of the American Agitator* (1949), reprinted in Leo Lowenthal [= Löwenthal], *False Prophets: Studies on Authoritarianism* (Brunswick, NJ, and London: Transaction Publishers, 2016), pp. 1–171 (especially pp. 59–73, "The Helpless Enemy").

4. German newsreel of September—October 1939. See the Edition Salzgeber DVD *Harlan. Im Schatten von Jud Süss* (2009), directed by Felix Moeller.

5. A few days later, on 21 May 2018, the White House even released a short press statement entitled "What You Need to Know about the Violent Animals of MS-13", the text of which uses the word *animals* eight times.

6. Cf. Lowenthal, *False Prophets*, pp. 65 and 75–76.

7. Cf. Götz Aly, *Hitler's Beneficiaries: How the Nazis Bought the German People*, trans. Jefferson Chase (London: Verso, 2016; first published in German 2005 and—revised and extended—2006).

8. Aly, *Hitler's Beneficiaries*, p. 30.

9. Aly, *Hitler's Beneficiaries*, p. 30. One could speculate if the MAGA ("Make American Great Again") baseball cap does not fulfil a similar function. Baseball is in many ways the quintessential American sport and is often used as a metaphor for the American way of life with its purported democratic camaraderie and honest competition. Accordingly, the baseball cap could be seen as the symbol of this idealized democratic and meritocratic America.

10. Jeremy Noakes and Geoffrey Pridham (eds.), *Nazism 1919–1945: A Documentary Reader, vol. 1: The Rise to Power 1919–1934* (new ed. Exeter: University of Exeter Press, 1998), pp. 14–15. The German original can be found in Albrecht Tyrell, *Führer befiehl... Selbstzeugnisse aus der "Kampfzeit" der NSDAP* (Bindlach: Gondrom Verlag, 1991), pp. 23–24.

11. Werner May, *Politischer Katechismus für den jungen Deutschen in Schule und Beruf* (Breslau: Heinrich Handels Verlag, 1935), p. 17. This is the fourth—revised and expanded—edition of a book originally entitled *Deutscher Nationalkatechismus*.

12. The phrase comes from the seventh essay in John Adams's *Novanglus Essays* (1774/75) and was incorporated into the Constitution of the Commonwealth of Massachusetts of 1780 (part 1, article 30). On Cox's citation, cf. Ken Gormley, *Archibald Cox: Conscience of a Nation* (Reading, Mass.: Addison-Wesley, 1997), p. 358: "Cox [...] dictated a one-sentence statement to [his assistant] Jim Doyle, who typed it on his manual typewriter. It would be Cox's final statement as Watergate special prosecutor: 'Whether ours shall continue to be a government of laws and not of men is now for Congress and ultimately the American people'".
13. Erik van Ree, *De totalitaire paradox. De terroristische massademocratie van Stalin en Mao* (Amsterdam: Van Gennep, 1984). The formulations in this section are mine, but the ideas are taken from van Ree.
14. Van Ree, *De totalitaire paradox*, p. 14.
15. Van Ree, *De totalitaire paradox*, p. 10.
16. Van Ree, *De totalitaire paradox*, p. 10.
17. Van Ree, *De totalitaire paradox*, p. 14.
18. Cf. note 343.
19. The phrase *many-willed-ness* comes from Friedrich Nietzsche, *Beyond Good and Evil: Prelude to a Philosophy of the Future*, trans. Helen Zimmern (Mineola, NY: Dover, 1987), p. 80 (section 208).
20. Adolf Hitler, *Reden 1920–1945* (no date and publisher given): speech of 10 February 1933, delivered in the Berlin Sportpalast (no page numbers given).
21. Though not coined by the National Socialists, the term *Lügenpresse* was a staple of Nazi propaganda. Today, the word enjoys a certain popularity among far-right circles in Germany.
22. Adolf Hitler, *Mein Kampf*, trans. Ralph Manheim (Boston and New York: Houghton Mifflin Company, 1999), p. 118. For the original German, see Adolf Hitler, *Mein Kampf. Eine kritische Edition*, ed. Christian Hartmann, Thomas Vordermayer, Othmar Plöckinger, and Roman Töppel (Munich and Berlin: Institut für Zeitgeschichte, 2016), vol. 1, pp. 353 and 355.
23. See, for example, Hitler, *Mein Kampf*, pp. 56–65 (English) and 208–31 (German). Hitler of course does the same in his speeches, as does National Socialist propaganda generally.
24. Steven E. Aschheim, *Culture and Catastrophe: German and Jewish Confrontations with National Socialism and Other Crises* (New York: New York University Press, 1996), p. 45. For a more extensive discus-

sion, see chapter 3 of Aschheim's book, "'The Jew Within': The Myth of 'Judaization' in Germany", pp. 45–68.

25. See the Channel 4 DVD *The Pervert's Guide to Ideology* (2013), presented by Slavoj Žižek and directed by Sophie Fiennes. All citations in the main text come from this source. The word *pervert* in the title is used in a psychoanalytical sense and denotes someone who has a non-normalized and hence ideology-critical view of society. Žižek, too, uses the word *container*, but in a slightly different context and with a slightly different focus: "every ideology [...] always has to also work as an empty container open to all possible meanings. It's [...] that gut feeling that we feel when we experience something pathetic [that is, pathos-laden] and we say 'oh my God, I am so moved, there is something so deep'. But you never know what this depth is. It's a void".

26. The phrase *reign of suspicion* comes from the philosopher G. W. F. Hegel, who used it in the section of the *Phenomenology of Mind* (1807) that explores the Terror, the period immediately following the French Revolution.

27. On conspiracy theories, see David Aaronovitch, *Voodoo Histories: How Conspiracy Theory Has Shaped Modern History* (London: Vintage, 2010; first published 2009), Richard Hofstadter, *The Paranoid Style in American Politics and Other Essays* (New York: Vintage, 2008; selection of essays first published between 1952 and 1965), Peter Knight, *Conspiracy Culture: From the Kennedy Assassination to The X-Files* (London and New York: Routledge, 2000), Daniel Pipes, *The Hidden Hand: Middle Eastern Fears of Conspiracy* (New York: St. Martin's Griffin, 1996) and *Conspiracy: How the Paranoid Style Flourishes and Where It Comes From* (New York: The Free Press, 1997), Cass R. Sunstein: *Going to Extremes: How Like Minds Unite and Divide* (Oxford and New York: Oxford University Press, 2011; first published 2009), and Pierre-André Taguieff, *L'imaginaire du complot mondial. Aspects d'un mythe moderne* (Paris: Mille et une nuits, 2006), as well as the study edited by Robins and Post cited above. Specifically on National Socialist conspiracy theories, see Richard J. Evans, *The Hitler Conspiracies: The Third Reich and the Paranoid Imagination* (London: Allen Lane, 2020).

28. See Wolfgang Iser, *Prospecting: From Reader Response to Literary Anthropology* (Baltimore: The Johns Hopkins University Press, 1989), especially pp. 3–30. My argument in this section is arguably more an adaptation and extrapolation than an explication of Iser's theory. Above

all, Iser restricts himself to literature. This focus also explains the array of literary-theoretical concepts that he adopts or proposes (implied reader, schematized aspects, and so on) and which I ignore for the sake of clarity.
29. Iser, *Prospecting*, p. 9.
30. I have used the phrase "at least" because one could also have relations such as ab-bc.
31. I leave aside such possible distinctions as *implied author* versus *empirical author* so as to not to complicate matters unnecessarily.
32. Iser, *Prospecting*, p. 13.
33. Iser, *Prospecting*, p. 13.
34. William Shakespeare, *Othello*, ed. E. A. J. Honigmann, The Arden Shakespeare (London etc.: Bloomsbury, 2009), p. 215 (III.iii.109–11).
35. For the distinction between *basic trust* and *basic distrust*, see Erik H. Erikson, *Childhood and Society* (new ed. New York and London: W. W. Norton, 1993; first published 1950), especially pp. 247–51.

4

The Establishment, the Elite, and the Experts

In his landmark study *Childhood and Society* (1950), the psychologist Erik H. Erikson describes *social trust* as the most fundamental feeling that human beings need if they are to find their place in the world.[1] It is the inner conviction that our social environment means well, that the world is a good place to be, and that we are a meaningful part of it. Such trust starts to develop immediately after birth, when the child "finds that more and more adventures of the senses arouse a feeling of familiarity [...]. Forms of comfort, and people associated with them, become [...] an inner certainty as well as an outer predictability".[2] This "consistency, continuity, and sameness of experience" is the basis for a secure identity—a psychological make-up that enables us confidently to address the challenges we encounter in life. This sense of security also gives us the confidence to absorb any anomalous experiences that might defy our familiar framework. Hence it is vital that this "basic trust [...] maintain itself throughout life".[3]

What happens if this basic confidence in the world is not acquired? Or if it is shattered by a comprehensive transformation of our familiar surroundings? Then, Erikson says, *basic mistrust* develops. Such mistrust is characterized by a blurring of "the borderlines between senses and physical reality, between words and social meanings".[4] Our sense of reality is impaired. Instead of taking the world as it is, we begin to suspect that nothing is as it seems and that people do not mean what they say. This basic mistrust tends to generate two equally problematic defence mechanisms.

For one, we may project our feeling of not being safe, of not fitting in, onto others. That is to say, we may externalize our subjective fear of a "hostile" world by unconsciously transforming it into an objective danger that—we have come to feel—other people represent. In this type of projection, we ascribe to the world the negativity that is really in us. The first targets are as a rule our parents. Subsequently, other authority figures, and sometimes even friends and colleagues, are likely to be viewed with suspicious eyes. We start to believe that everyone is out to get us.

For another, we may engage in introjection and "feel and act as if an [assumed] outer goodness had become an inner certainty".[5] If generated by basic mistrust, introjection leads to an over-identification with idealized others. Desperate for security in a world we experience as hostile, we unconsciously start casting about for substitute parents—say, "exceptional" political leaders—who possess the knowledge and confidence we yearn for. What results is a fusion of their identity and ours in which any realistic appreciation of these "heroic" others has given way to uncritical adulation.

Introjection is the flipside of projection. The more (imaginary) enemies we have, the more our need for (idealized) saviours grows. No one can bear to live in an exclusively hostile environment. Thus, our world view becomes black-and-white.

It seems to me that this is what happened both in Hitler's Germany and in Trump's America. People's familiar surroundings were uprooted by a massive transformation of labour, gender relations, their nation's place in the world, and much else besides. The next chapter will explore the reasons, different but not dissimilar, behind this social upheaval in the two societies at issue. The present chapter looks at two other questions. First, I will examine how basic mistrust undermines society's authority figures, the ruling elite. What, in other words, is wrong with the establishment when looked at from a populistically mistrustful perspective? Second, I will look at the question of how populist mistrust leads to a blurring of inner experience and outer reality. Why, in other words, does populism entail a denial of facts, and hence a rejection of expert knowledge? In both cases, I will also be investigating the ways in which populist leaders exploit and enhance their followers' anxieties and animosities.

The Establishment in the Crossfire

What is wrong with the establishment? Above all—so populists say—the establishment are disconnected from us, from the lived reality of ordinary folk. They are too far removed from us, and therefore do not understand us. That is why they cannot and do not represent us and why they consistently ignore our wishes. They systematically disregard the will of the people. Specifically, they are too international, too global, too cosmopolitan. Instead of caring about their own folk, they are jetting around the world, without any real roots anywhere and without any real attachments to anyone. As a result, they have no sense of community and no sense of tradition. The things that sustain and support *us* and that *we* rely on in our daily lives—stable social relations, established patterns of behaviour, historical continuity, a dependable hierarchy of parents and children, of husband and wife—are to *them* an irrelevance at best and at worst an impediment.

However—populists go on to say—if this natural order is uprooted, we will be uprooted too. If this order disappears, our community will disappear with it. Yet the establishment do not care. Worse, they think that *we* are the ones in the wrong. They see us as discriminatory, even racist, whereas it is really *they* who elevate themselves above others and feel superior—these know-all liberals, the so-called elite, who do not live where we live and do not have to go through what we are going through.

There is another set of accusations that populists level against the establishment. To the populist mind, the establishment are solely aiming for power and self-enrichment. Behind their highfaluting phrases, there is nothing but greed and corruption. They are only ever out for themselves and their own little clique. That is why they are globalists favouring international trade agreements: because laissez-faire capitalism generates the most money (for them, that is). And that is why they have their G20 summits and Davos conferences: not to protect *us* and improve *our* way of life, but to protect *themselves* and further *their* agenda. Because these people are all connected. They are like members of a crime syndicate, who are all in it together. One hand washes the other.

This is why—to the populist mind—the system is rigged. The elite are all shielding each other. They are like a cat with nine lives, or rather like Hydra, whose heads keep growing back (which is why we need a Hercules to save us). This is why they want to keep the existing social order in place, why they are ultimately all wishy-washy revisionists. A little bit of tinkering here and there to ensure that the system keeps working, but nothing too radical, nothing outside the box. Much sophisticated talk, but little social transformation. Plenty of reflective argument, but no real action (unless the banks or other big corporations need rescuing, of course). This is their silent motto: nothing politically incorrect in word, nothing politically inconvenient in deed.

Finally, the establishment—so the populist says—can always rely on the experts, the bureaucrats, the judges, and the mainstream media, because they too are in on it. They are just another part of the establishment whose aim it is to protect this pseudo-democracy so as to prevent it from becoming a real democracy, a society ruled by the people for the people. They are the gatekeepers—of knowledge, of power, of wealth. We by contrast, the so-called deplorable conservatives or conservative deplorables, we are the real revolutionaries. We want to make the system work for everyone.

It is important to realize that such populist ideas are not mere ravings. They may be wildly oversimplified, but it is not as if they had no basis in reality whatsoever. It is indeed true that a disproportionate amount of power and wealth resides with a small group of corporations and billionaires. It is equally true that the adverse effects of globalization tend to hit traditional communities hardest; that mainstream politics is reformist rather than revolutionary; and that many liberals have little patience with people who cling to old-fashioned preconceptions and outdated prejudices. Of course, this does not mean that the populists are right. It is vital, however, to understand where they are coming from, if only because otherwise we will not be able to develop a counterstrategy.

To put it differently, the Eriksonian model we looked at in the previous section explains why we sometimes develop social mistrust. It also explains how this mistrust may shape our world view. But it does not imply that suspicion is never justified. If there is a tectonic shift in our social environment, then inner experience and outer reality no longer coincide. In that case, we cannot continue to rely on our old certainties but instead must re-examine our relationship with the world. We must establish how to respond to the new situation. Should we adapt our familiar framework, or should we alter our social surroundings? Or should we try and do both?

In order to make that decision, we cannot simply take the world as it presents itself to us. We must find out exactly what has changed, and why—and whether these changes are good or bad. Social mistrust is thus not necessarily pathological. This also applies to our view of our elders and betters. There is nothing inherently wrong or outlandish about questioning the power of the establishment.

A cursory glance at some philosophical positions should convince us of this and help us gain a better understanding of populism's anti-establishment message. Marxist thought, in particular, has a proud tradition of social criticism along the lines outlined above, albeit at a rather higher level of sophistication. This should not come as a surprise. After all, Marxism was born of a sustained reflection on the transformation of the old feudal order into a new, class-based, capitalist system—a massive social upheaval in which, as the 1848 *Communist Manifesto* puts it, "all that is solid melts into air".[6]

This new capitalist system, Marx and Engels write, "wherever it has got the upper hand, has put an end to all feudal, patriarchal, idyllic relations. It has pitilessly torn asunder the motley feudal ties that bound man to his 'natural superiors', and has left remaining no other nexus between man and man than naked self-interest, than callous 'cash payment'. It has drowned the most heavenly certainties of religious fervour, of chivalrous enthusiasm, of philistine sentimentalism, in the icy water of egotistical calculation. It has resolved personal worth into exchange value, and in place of the manifold inalienable chartered freedoms has set up that single, unscrupulous freedom—free trade. [...] All fixed, fast-frozen relations, with their train of ancient and venerable prejudices and opinions, are swept away, all new-formed ones become antiquated before they can ossify. [...] To the great chagrin of reactionaries, it has drawn from under the feet of industry the national ground on which it stood. All old-established national industries have been destroyed or are daily being destroyed. [...] It has agglomerated population, centralized means of production, and has concentrated property in a few hands".[7] Modernity, Marx and Engels conclude, "is like the sorcerer who is no longer able to control the powers of the nether world which he has called up by his spells".[8]

In this new world, there are still winners and losers, rulers and ruled. It is the ruling elite—Marx and Engels write in *The German Ideology*—who determine the ideological climate: "The ruling ideas are nothing but the expression of the dominant material [that is, economic] relationships; they are the dominant material relationships in the form of ideas. In other words, they are the expression of the relationships that make one class the ruling one and are therefore the ideas of its dominance".[9]

Other left-wing philosophers have expressed similar ideas. Jean-Paul Sartre's friend Paul Nizan, for example, devoted an entire book—*Les chiens de garde* (The Watchdogs, 1932)—to the mainstream thinkers of his day, whose sole function, Nizan claimed, is "to explain, to fortify, and to propagate the half-truths manufactured by the bourgeoisie and so useful in consolidating its power".[10] They are there to guard the interests of the ruling elite against the legitimate claims of ordinary people, whom they are neither interested in nor know anything about. They "appear not to know how men are constructed; they appear to be unfamiliar with the things men eat, the houses in which they live, the clothing they wear, the manner in which they die, the women they love, the work they perform; with the things they do on weekends, the way in which they nurse their illness, their weekly schedules, their incomes, the newspapers and books they read, the spectacles designed for their entertainment, their films, their songs, their proverbs".[11]

Nizan's fellow French philosopher Louis Althusser took things even further. In the 1960s and 1970s, he argued that existing class and power relations are perpetuated by "ideological state apparatuses" (such as schools, political parties, cultural institutions, and the media) and "repressive state apparatuses" (such as the courts, the police, and the army).[12] The latter secure by force—ranging "from the most brutal physical force, via mere administrative commands and interdictions, to open and tacit censorship"—the continued existence of society's property relations, which are "relations of exploitation".[13] The ideological state apparatuses in their turn cover up and distort our reality in such a way that we embrace this exploitative state of affairs and recognize that we must obey our elders and betters. As a result, our behaviour is reduced to "the inscription in life of the admirable words of the prayer: '*Amen—So be it*'".[14]

Left-wing critiques of the structural imbalance of power in modern capitalist society are by no means restricted to continental European thought. The best-known instance from the English-speaking world is Charles Wright Mills's *The Power Elite* of 1956.[15] Rejecting the optimistic view of American society as consisting of a multiplicity of powerful groups that keep each other in check, Mills argued that America is characterized by a concentration of power in the hands of a select number of people. They occupy the top positions in the federal bureaucracy, the large corporations, and the military, which themselves have become increasingly centralized and powerful. It is this elite who run the show in the United States. What is more, this elite do not make decisions with the common good in mind. They are guided by a "higher immorality": their only aim is to increase the power of their own institutional unit.[16]

These are all ideas that many liberal intellectuals not only are familiar with, but also have a great deal of sympathy for. Moreover, it is not difficult to think of further philosophical and sociological theories akin to the representative examples given above.[17] The point is that the populist and the liberal critiques of modern society are not as dissimilar as one might think. National Socialism was not called National *Socialism* for nothing. Indeed, several influential Nazis, Joseph Goebbels among them, were originally quite close to Marxist ideology. Even Hitler had a left-wing spell of sorts, as we saw in the first chapter.

This is not to say—the point bears repeating—that the populists are right. It does mean, however, that liberals are wrong when they dismiss the populist critique of the establishment as something not worth discussing, or when they treat the populist voter as someone not worth arguing with. Rather, liberals should take populism's anti-establishment message seriously, analyse it, and show why this type of social criticism is mistaken. This is what I wish to do now.

Why Establishment-Bashing Makes Us Feel Good

What are the socio-psychological "benefits" of establishment-bashing? Why do populist leaders engage in it, and what do their followers get out of it?[18]

As I will argue in the next chapter, populism is born of a desire for social wholeness. It rests on the belief that one can achieve a sense of belonging in and through one's racial or national community. Of course, the yearnings in question are largely unconscious, or at least pre-reflective; they are not philosophical deliberations. The same goes for the phenomenon that goes hand in hand with these yearnings—the evocation of an enemy. In reality, society is never whole, never one. It is heterogeneous, consisting as it does of a multiplicity of groups with different value systems, world views, and interests. At times, these groups may overlap; at other times, they may be opposed to one another. How, then, does one create a homogeneous community, a holistic *us*? Or, to put it in the populist's terminology: how does one "regain" it? How do we take back control and make Germany or America great again? The answer is: by excluding from our imagined community[19] anyone who does not fit our populist criteria.

The excluded others are above all our core enemies; say, the Jews, or Mexican immigrants. But they also include the establishment—these know-all liberals who know so little about us ordinary folk and care even less. They are the ones who got us into this mess in the first place and are unable or unwilling to lift us out of it. Their globalism threatens our nation's identity; their progressivism threatens its time-honoured values; and their greedy collusion makes a mockery of its democratic institutions. And nobody should believe that the conservative members of the establishment are any better: what they lack in self-righteous progressivism they make up for in patrician smugness. The entire establishment are antithetical to the people. None of them are us.

The first thing that criticizing the establishment achieves, then, is that it helps us construct our identity. Rather than trying to come to terms with society's pluralism and its many overlapping identities, we create a simple dichotomy of those who belong to the community and those who do not, of "the people" on the one hand and the establishment (as well as other enemies) on the other hand. Dividing society into *us* and *them* enables "us" to imagine a homogeneous community: because "they" are not really part of it. They should be locked up or deported, or should never have been allowed to enter in the first place.

It is this ideological borderline that provides us with a cultural identity, just as the nation's physical borders delimit our community as a geographical entity. This, by the way, is why Trump's promise to build the Wall resonated with so many voters, and why fact-based criticism of such a barrier's effectiveness proved futile. His supporters heard above all a pledge to protect America's traditional identity, not some policy proposal to improve the country's borders.

The key division between us and them is underpinned by a range of further distinctions, such as Christian/un-Christian, Caucasian/non-Caucasian (or Aryan/Jewish) as well as honest/criminal, decent/corrupt, meritocratic/elitist, and national/international. It is these distinctions that enable us to imagine our social environment as a safe, familiar place where we can be at home.

Populist leaders set themselves up as the spokespersons for this *us*. They invariably claim that they act as advocates, not for this particular interest group or that particular interest group, not for this political party or that political party, not for this set of policy proposals or that set of policy proposals, but for the (true) community as a whole. They claim that they *are* the people—that the people speak through *them*.

As the theatre expert Bernd Stegemann has pointed out in an insightful book about the populist's "staging" of politics, there is an important difference here with the liberal way of speaking. Liberals speak, or claim to speak, in the name of abstract principles. They place themselves above the electorate, like a professor leading a discussion among students. However, Stegemann says: "The strategic advantage of taking this neutral position turns into a clear disadvantage when confronted with populists. People who feel they are under siege are not looking for explanations by some higher authority claiming to represent universal reason and 'demonstrating' that things are not as bad as they seem. The liberal way of speaking only feeds the already existing suspicion vis-à-vis an elite that has isolated itself from ordinary people".[20]

Populist leaders seek to *erase* the distance between themselves and the electorate. As Hitler put it in one of his best-known speeches, delivered at the Siemens factory in Berlin on 10 November 1933:

> I have grown up from among yourselves. I was once a worker like you, I served in the war for four and a half years among you. I speak now to you, to whom I belong, with whom I still feel myself united, and for whom at the end of the day I fight. [...] I wage that fight for the millions of our honest, industrious, working, producing people. [...] I was in my youth a worker as you are; through industry, through learning, and—I may say—through hunger, I slowly worked my way up. But in my innermost being I have always remained what I was. [...] For many centuries, foreign countries always counted on having allies in Germany. First it was princes, men without character who, cold as ice, betrayed their peoples. Then it was parties, world views. Always they had their allies. Now I want to show our enemies that they no longer have any allies in Germany. Today, it is the German people who are allied with themselves. [...] I am the guarantor in Germany that this community shall not favour one section of our people over another. You can look upon me as the man who does not belong to any class, who belongs to no rank, who stands above all that. I have nothing but the ties that bind me to the German people. For me every German is equal. What interest have I in the intellectuals, the bourgeoisie, or the proletariat? I am interested only in the German people. To the people alone I belong, and for the people I fight.[21]

It is not necessary for populist leaders to be working class or middle class, or to pretend that they are. All they need to do is convince "the people" that they are on their side. Populism is not anti-hierarchical and hence not anti-elitist as such. What the populist electorate want is that society is genuinely meritocratic, not "rigged" against them, and that their leaders represent *them* and *their* values, not some "globalist clique". This is why it was sufficient for Trump to claim "I am your voice".[22] As a famously rich New York businessman, he knew that any attempt to present himself as an ordinary worker would be futile. So he turned a

4 The Establishment, the Elite, and the Experts 165

potential weakness into a strength: "Nobody knows the system better than me, which is why I alone can fix it".[23]

By criticizing the establishment as out of touch and ridiculing established policies as half-hearted, populist leaders clear the field for their own, more radical, solutions, which they present as simply common sense. It is here that Hitler's and Trump's outsider status comes into play. It is—so their followers believe—precisely because Hitler and Trump are not tied in with the existing political structures that they know what the real problems are. It is precisely because they are not trying to be politically correct that they have the courage to speak out and call a spade a spade—a Jew a Jew, an illegal immigrant an illegal immigrant. And it is precisely because they are not party politicians but leaders above the fray that they refuse to agree to the kind of backroom compromises that merely perpetuate the status quo.

Here, the populist leader's unvarnished, aggressive, and frequently outright offensive language plays an important role. To many, this way of speaking indicates a lack of personal and political sophistication. To the populist electorate, it is a sign of honesty and independence of mind. The populist leader "tells it as it is". Other politicians keep beating about the bush, desperately afraid to upset anyone. Hitler and Trump have the courage of their convictions. They may sometimes overdo things, but at least they are not cowards and cry-babies like those establishment politicians.

There is, then, a strong emotive dimension to establishment-bashing. By denouncing the system, the elite, and so on, populist leaders establish an emotional rapport with their followers. They create what Bernd Stegemann has called a *Gefühlsgemeinschaft*, a community of feeling.[24]

Populist voters feel let down by the establishment. The traditional political parties, the mainstream media, the intelligentsia—none of them seem to care about ordinary folk. This perception is exacerbated by the bureaucratic nature of modern states—a phenomenon to which the German sociologist Max Weber already drew attention in the first decades of the twentieth century. The feeling that many people have is: if there is any support for us at all, it does not derive from a genuine understanding of our problems. We are merely asked to fill in the various sections of our unemployment-benefits form, whereas "what would really help is if they finally got rid of all those immigrants who are stealing our jobs". It is this sense of cultural alienation that Hitler and Trump exploit when railing against the establishment. Their message is: I am with you, I understand you, I care about you. This enables their followers to recapture their moral worth. They are being told: you are not a basket of deplorables on whom the establishment rightfully looks down; rather, the establishment are a bunch of despicables for whom we rightfully show contempt.

There is a final socio-psychological "benefit" to establishment-bashing. It helps create a reassuringly simple picture of the world. It does so in two ways.

First, it divides the world into two clearly distinct groups, the good guys (us, the people) and the bad guys (them, the establishment as well as other enemies). This is an enormous—and enormously comforting—reduction of social complexity. We now know whom to trust and whom not to trust. Moreover, we are no longer subject to anonymous social and economic forces that we do not know how to control. Instead, we are facing concrete bad actors that we can identify and bring into line. Second, because the establishment are the bad guys, there is no reason to listen to their so-called experts. The eggheads are merely the intellectual watchdogs of the existing system.

The populist criticism of the establishment, then, produces not merely a Manichaean view of society, but also a kind of wilful ignorance. Before pursuing this particular aspect further, I wish to answer the question of why the populist's establishment-bashing is misguided.

Can Politics Ever Be the Will of the People?

According to populists, the nation is a homogenous entity, or will be so once more after it has been made great again. As such, it possesses a unified will, and it is this *general will* (to use Jean-Jacques Rousseau's term) that should determine how society is organized. The people are one, and their will should be respected.

In other words, there should be a seamless transition—populists say—from the people to politics, from civil society to the political system. The ideal is that people and leadership, nation and government, flow into

4 The Establishment, the Elite, and the Experts 167

each other, as it were. If there is any deformation of what the people want, then the system is unjust, "rigged". If political compromises are made, then the people are being sold out. Right are only those decisions that the people agree with. Anything standing between the people and their political self-organization—certain political parties or political parties *tout court*, expert committees, or legal principles—is a form of alienation that must be overcome.

This view, which can also be found in certain varieties of Marxism, is fundamentally mistaken. To begin with, no society is able to take decisions without internal disagreement. The idea that "politics" (with all that it entails: factionalism, partisanship, bickering, and trade-offs) can ever be supplanted by some kind of harmonious social self-organization based on consensual decision-making is illusory. Even if everyone subscribed to the same ideology (something that is assumed in the populist vision of a homogeneous community, but which is unlikely enough in itself), even then the decisions that are needed would still have to be negotiated in some way or other. There are two reasons for this, as the political philosopher Isaiah Berlin has shown.[25]

First, no ideology can ever be so specific as to generate not only a set of general ideals (social equality, national self-determination, global dominance, and so on) but *also* a blueprint of all concrete instantiations of these ideals *and* a plan detailing the goals and interim goals that must be achieved in order that these instantiations become a reality. Second, no society, however ideologically unified, can ever be so homogeneous that all of its members would want to solve its problems in the same manner.

In other words, there is always a gap between a society's ultimate end (say, social equality) and the way to achieve it—a gap filled with interim ends that by necessity remain arguable and negotiable. At any of the many intermediate levels between everyday conduct and ultimate end, there is the question: what do we do now? No general principle or scientific calculation can ever answer that question for the people involved (though of course each faction among the people will *claim* that its answer is more in line with society's general principles, or more strongly based in scientific evidence, than is the answer provided by the other factions).

For this reason, there can never be an end of "politics". Nor can there ever be a properly working grassroots democracy, in which all people are centrally involved in all political decisions. Such a system would simply be impossible to create. It would require representative bodies, committees, and delegations—that is to say, intermediate organizations in which not all people would be able to participate continually. Yet not even the inhabitants of a small village would be able to set up camp in the market square to engage in daily political discussion. This is a problem that cannot be solved with referenda, if only because it is impossible to hold a referendum on every single political issue of the day.

In brief, there will always have to be some form of political representation; that is to say, a political system that does not coincide with "the people". The disjunction of civil society and politics—a disjunction that populists decry as alienating and unfair, as evidence of a "rigged" system—is an ineliminable dimension of liberal democracy.

Not only is elimination of the gap between civil society and political system not possible—it is not even desirable.[26] If important public questions are *not* mediated by representative political bodies that remain essentially "alien" to civil society, but instead are settled by grassroots discussions, so that the result can truly count as a decision "by the people", then any criticism of that result becomes a criticism of the people. To disagree with the outcome of a parliamentary process is merely to dissent from a political resolution. To disagree with the un-alienated expression of the will of the people is to oppose the community—it is to be a dangerously subversive element, an "enemy of the people".

The essential distinction, then, is this. Representative democracy, which is based on what the German sociologist Niklas Luhmann has called "legitimation through procedures",[27] requires you to accept the institutional framework that generates political decisions. Radical or grassroots democracy, which posits the identity of the content of the decisions with the will of the people, requires you to agree with the decisions themselves.

This is why the ideal of merging civil society and political system is so dangerous. If such a thing were to happen, it would automatically lead to what the Germans call *Gesinnungsterror* (the enforcement of conviction, the attempt to frighten people into conformity, ideological bullying). Freedom of expression can only be safeguarded if political legitimacy is *not* founded on ideological homogeneity, in which people and leadership, nation and government, flow into each other. The way to achieve that is precisely by retaining liberal democracy's manifold mediating institutions—its political parties, expert committees, independent judiciary, and so on. This system of checks and balances is the best and indeed the only guarantee of democratic pluralism, not *in spite* but *because* of the fact that it generates discussions and disagreements, compromises and trade-offs.

Are Elites Really That Bad?

To the populist mind, the establishment is the enemy. The community should be founded on the people and their leader, not on "elitist" institutions such as parliament or Congress, the courts, the media, the scientific community, or the cultural intelligentsia—unless these are ideologically aligned with the leader, directing their efforts towards implementing his agenda and attacking his enemies. In fact, non-aligned mediating institutions are a *good* thing. They are no obstacle to democratic governance, and those who occupy the key positions in them—the "elite"—are no self-serving clique who have nothing to recommend them.[28]

The American Founders were aware of the need for an interlocking arrangement of checks and balances. They wanted the populace to restrain the potential overreach of political leaders, and political leaders to curb potential excesses of the populace. They also realized that neither power was able to achieve this on its own and that therefore a system of mediations—of shock absorbers and transmissions, as it were—between the voters and the government was required. These mediating institutions in their turn were also meant to balance each other.[29]

Thus, an independent judiciary and legally enshrined rights protect individuals and minorities from the "tyranny of the majority", to use a famous phrase from Alexis de Tocqueville's *De la démocratie en Amérique* (Democracy in America, 1835 and 1840).[30] Without such buffers, there can be no freedom and no security. Without them, witch hunts and ethnic cleansing are just around the corner, as the case of Nazi Germany makes abundantly clear. For the sad truth is that human beings are not reliably humane. While not incapable of doing good, they are persistently inclined to do evil. As Freud teaches us, judging by our unconscious desires we are "a gang of murderers".[31]

Moreover—as Freud also teaches us—group participation tends to amplify our destructive urges.[32] Groups or crowds are seldom better than their constituent members and usually a good deal worse. Without institutional safeguards, they are our unconsciousness unleashed, our drives writ large.

According to Freud, "crowds are more intolerant, more irrational, more immoral, more heartless, above all more uninhibited, than individuals. But the crowd, as crowd, invents nothing; it only liberates, distorts, exaggerates, the individual members' traits".[33] The crowd is characterized by a double identification. Its members identify with each other, and together they identify with the crowd's leader or ideology. This leads to a double renunciation of responsibility. Individually, the members dissolve their ego-identity and reflective ability into the collective, because—as Freud puts it—each of them "feels the need of being in harmony with [the others] rather than in opposition to them".[34] Collectively, they surrender their ego-ideal, their conception of what is morally good, to the leader. This twofold libidinous attachment—to the group and the leader—allows them to drop their inhibitions, to "let go".

What Freud tells us, then, is "that love relationships (or, to use a more neutral expression, emotional ties) also constitute the essence of the group mind".[35] But the erotic union that is at issue is not a beneficial one. It does not so much offer temporary respite from moral obligations, institutional constraints, and public debates—it replaces them altogether. It is the ecstasy of thousands of screaming Nazis welcoming their Führer, the union of "one people, one Reich, one leader". What we are dealing with is "a regression of mental activity to an earlier stage such as we are not surprised to find among savages or children".[36] It is the "revival of the primal horde".[37]

Those who think that this is too pessimistic only need to look at today's social media to see that group behaviour is at the very least fraught with danger. Twitter, in particular, tends to unleash the worst in people, with angry mobs persecuting opponents in veritable witch hunts. Even the collective pursuance of admirable goals tends to assume a totalitarian shape. Woe betide anyone who challenges the justness of a cause. For the

4 The Establishment, the Elite, and the Experts 171

super-ego spurned is just as wrathful as any other unconscious drive unleashed and then blocked. Putting one's trust in "the wisdom of crowds"[38] is not a safe bet.

People are fickle and impressionable. They often pursue, lemminglike, the same misguided goal, or they pursue, equally lemminglike, the same desirable goal with unreasoning haste and unrelenting intolerance. Institutions are a good thing because they slow down and interrupt the crowd's tendency to rush to judgement; because they insert rationality and facts into often highly emotional public debates; and because they insist on proper procedures when the crowd is clamouring for immediate action. This is not to say that—for example—an independent judiciary always gets it right, or that a free press always behaves responsibly. But on the whole we are much better off with them than without them.

There is another problem. People are not very good at focusing on the long term. They want to see results today rather than tomorrow, and they are disinclined to make instant sacrifices, such as paying higher taxes, for future objectives. This problem is aggravated by the relative frequency of election cycles. There are good reasons for this frequency and we would abandon it at our peril, but it does render long-term planning extremely difficult. The problem is exacerbated even further by today's 24/7 news cycle and the demand for instant policy generated by social media.

Populism offers quick and easy fixes. But most social problems are complex and persistent, and their solution often goes against people's immediate interests as well as against their common-sense perception of the situation. Politics can therefore only be successful if it is not a mere function of "what the people want". As Fareed Zakaria puts it in his prescient 2003 book on the dangers of illiberal democracy, *The Future of Freedom*: "Governments will have to make hard choices, resist the temptation to pander, and enact policies for the long run. The only possible way that this can be achieved in a modern democracy is by insulating some decision-makers from the intense pressure of interests groups, lobbies, and political campaigns—that is to say, from the intense pressures of democracy".[39]

If people do think long-term, they tend to focus on a single issue at the expense of other challenges. A good example is the Extinction Rebellion movement. The problem is that we are not facing a single challenge, but many different ones. In addition, there is never a single way to address each of these manifold challenges. Possible solutions to society's problems are invariably open to debate.

What makes the matter even more difficult is that many future objectives cannot easily be combined. Freedom is good and equality is good, but it is not easy to enhance both at the same time, as the debate surrounding affirmative action shows. To believe that one can simply "add up" the things that need to be done, in order then to work through that list, is to fall victim to what the British philosopher Roger Scruton has called the *aggregation fallacy*. This way of thinking "is replicated whenever the desire for good things impetuously cancels any attempt to understand the connections between them. As people aspire to one good thing after another, they project their hope away from themselves, imagining it to be realized in some future human condition. As a result they add one good to another in an ever-expanding wish-list. And because each good has been taken from its context and transferred to an imaginary world, the result is almost certain to involve aims that cannot be advanced together".[40]

What liberal democracy requires, then, is a way to negotiate between these contexts and conflicts. What is needed is a mechanism for compromise. The key question is perhaps most apparent when social movements become political parties, as happened in the case of the Greens in Germany: how to ensure that your ideals become a political and hence a social reality. Looking back on his time as Environment Secretary in the German federal state of Hesse in the mid-1980s, when the grassroots of his Green Party were vociferously demanding the immediate shutdown of all nuclear power stations, Joschka Fischer said in 2011: "However impressive your marches and demonstrations are, you always run into the problem of implementation. In the end, the question is: who is going to implement the things you want?"[41]

As Jonathan Rauch puts it in his powerful critique of political *disintermediation* (the replacement of committee-based deal-making by forms of direct democracy): the fact of the matter is "that governments, and thus democracy, won't work if leaders can't make deals and make them stick".[42] In this regard, Rauch says, domestic politics is like foreign affairs. Both require that we acknowledge "the reality of trade-offs. We live in a world of second and often third choices, and in order to govern one must make decisions and engage in practices which look bad up close and are hard to defend in public [say, backroom deals in which both parties cross the red lines of their respective electorates, because without such a "sell-out" there would be no deal at all] but which, nonetheless seem to be the best alternative at the time. Always, the realist asks: 'Compared to what?' Principles alone mean little until examined in the light of real-world alternatives".[43]

Deal-making and trade-offs require both formal and informal structures. That is to say, they require political parties, expert committees, and a legislature, but also networks of inter-party and cross-party political allies and personal friends. The second category may sound shady, and it is true that informal forums inject an element of intransparency into the political process. Yet they play a vital role in controversial negotiations because they also insert trust into the process and make it easier to reach workable majorities. They make compromise more likely.

The same applies to closed-door negotiations generally. To cite Jonathan Rauch: "As recently as the early 1970s, congressional committees could easily retreat behind closed doors and members could vote on many bills anonymously, with only the final tallies reported. Federal advisory committees, too, could meet off the record. Understandably, in the wake of Watergate, those practices came to be viewed as suspect. Today, federal law, congressional rules, and public expectations have placed almost all formal deliberations and many informal ones in full public view. One result is greater transparency, which is good. But another result is that finding space for delicate negotiations and candid deliberations can be difficult. Smoke-filled rooms, whatever their disadvantages, were good for brokering complex compromises in which nothing was settled until everything was settled; once gone, they turned out to be difficult to replace. In public, interest groups and grandstanding politicians can tear apart a compromise before it is halfway settled".[44]

The *disappearance of social trust in the establishment* and the accompanying trend towards *disintermediation* are processes that started well before the twenty-first century. Fuelled by the rise of social media, they have reached worrying heights in the last decade or so. The problem is that they produce a vicious circle. As Rauch points out, they generate a "chaos syndrome [that] is self-reinforcing. It causes governmental dysfunction, which fuels public anger, which incites political disruption, which causes yet more governmental dysfunction".[45]

It is this chaos and politophobia[46] that populist leaders exploit. This is what Trump was doing in the United States, and it is what Hitler did in Weimar Germany. Hence, instead of embracing the call for more direct democracy (more referenda, more directly elected officials, more public oversight, and so on) we should restore liberal democracy's *representative* dimension to its rightful place.

What about the populist charge that the establishment are an unpatriotic transnational clique? Well, it is true that national establishments possess numerous international links and often have an internationalist outlook. But national problems often require global solutions. Climate change, migration, and international terrorism cannot be addressed successfully on the level of individual countries. The same applies to the question of how to protect the welfare state in the era of globalization.

Moreover, precisely because they are less parochial, the "elite"—the very establishment politicians, mainstream journalists, academics, and writers whom Hitler and Trump denigrated—tend to be less prejudiced. Intercultural knowledge and the ability to speak multiple languages contribute to a less blinkered view of one's own nation, its customs, and its place in the world. Admittedly, the English-speaking world has some catching-up to do in this regard. Its deeply problematic tendency towards monolingualism is illustrated well by the fact that in 2006—only three years after the invasion of Iraq—the American Embassy in Baghdad counted merely six fluent Arabic speakers among its one thousand employees.[47] America's (as well as Britain's) lack of knowledge about Iraq's religious and ethnic divisions also did not aid their efforts to win the peace.[48] Still, major television channels such as CNN—the main target of Trump's scorn for the establishment media—employ an impressive range of multilingual journalists.

The much-maligned establishment has one further thing going for it—its expertise. In the modern world, forms of specialist knowledge are vitally important. Yet populists rail against the "so-called experts" almost as often and vociferously as they denigrate the establishment in general. How is this to be explained?

Emotion Versus Expertise

In the preface to the paperback edition of his book *The Death of Expertise*, Tom Nichols cites a reviewer who had criticized him "by asking, with a complete lack of irony: 'What have experts done for us in the past fifty years?'".[49] The question reminds one of a scene in Monty Python's film *Life of Brian*. Bombarded with a whole list of Roman innovations, an unfazed Reg (John Cleese's character) replies: "All right, but apart from sanitation, medicine, education, wine, public order, irrigation, roads, a fresh-water system, and public health, what have the Romans ever done for us?"[50]

Despite its obvious advantages, expert knowledge does not enjoy a universally good reputation. In particular, science and facts seem to hold little sway over people with populist tendencies. Indeed, the populist electorate frequently exhibits outright scorn for specialist knowledge. In the run-up to the referendum that would take the United Kingdom out of the European Union, the British Conservative politician and pro-Brexit campaigner Michael Gove famously declared that "people in this country have had enough of experts". The sad truth is that he was not wrong. Where does this anti-expertise sentiment come from? And why and how do populist leaders seek to exploit it?

At first sight, it might appear strange that the populist electorate should be so scornful of science and other forms of knowledge. After all, if you feel that your life is being uprooted, you want to know why this is happening. The problem is that the experts to whom you might turn for an explanation are among the chief agents of the very development—the world's increasing globalization and automation—that threatens your traditional existence. Even if they are critical of this social transformation, they still benefit from it. At the very least, they are not impacted by it the same way you are.

Your trust in the world as a place where you can be at home has turned into social mistrust. Society has become a scary place, like a country under occupation, full of enemies and people collaborating with the enemy. You are no longer really sure why people are saying what they are saying.

The populist rejection of science and expertise, then, is not simply a matter of ignorance. True, understanding specialist knowledge requires a certain level of education. But how many of us have a thorough grasp of the ramifications of TPP and NAFTA, or the history of globalization? Listening to the experts is above all a matter of social trust. Besides, there are plenty of cases where the experts disagree, so that listening to "the experts" frequently means listening to those experts that you trust because they are aligned with your overall world view, while ignoring other experts. We should also acknowledge that even "the best and the brightest"[51] in their field can get it seriously wrong.

In any case, it is naïve to assume that all that is needed is to educate the populist electorate by enlightening them as to "the facts". Indeed, providing them with fact-based explanations and encouraging them to address their predicament rationally will only heighten their inner turmoil. Human beings are not machines. Paraphrasing the psychoanalyst Bruno Bettelheim, one might say that to try and get the populist electorate to accept expert findings is to ignore expert findings of how the human mind works.[52]

People who feel that the ground is shifting under their feet are above all looking for stability and certainty. Specialist knowledge, however, is fundamentally provisional and often comes with a variety of caveats. Niklas Luhmann was fond of quoting the conclusions of a study of the relationship between scale and social organization: "Other things being equal, the above statements [...] are true. [...] Other things are never equal".[53] Specialist knowledge offers probabilities rather than certainties.

Under stress, the human mind tends naturally towards black-and-white views and simple explanations. This is one of the reasons why conspiracy theories are so attractive, as we saw in the previous chapter. Complexity, by contrast, is confusing. Moreover, an awareness of nuance, or a recognition that there might not be a clear solution, has a paralyzing effect. If you feel the time is out of joint, you want to set it right. You want action, not talk. But, as Hamlet knew, the native hue of resolution is sicklied o'er with the pale cast of thought. Hence, the more accurately an explanatory framework reflects the world's complexity, the less appealing it becomes psychologically.

Stress and alienation are antithetical to complexity and nuance. They are also antithetical to reason. When we are anxious, rational insights lose their grip on us. Feelings take over. Economists may tell us that GDP is going up, but if we are not experiencing the benefits, we will continue to feel that the economy is doing badly. Statistics may indicate that immigrants commit fewer crimes than the rest of the population, but if we feel threatened by them, it is unlikely we are going to see them as good people (with the exception of "some of them", to quote Trump). In times of economic or cultural crisis, emotion will always trump expertise. This may not be a good thing, but it is a fact—an expert finding.

We should not be surprised by this. Nor should we feel superior to the "ignorant" populist electorate. All of us have fears and phobias that cannot be made to disappear by rational insight. I am afraid of flying. When getting on a plane, I can tell myself a hundred times that "this is safer than crossing the street", but it still feels as though I were about to commit suicide. Other people are afraid of heights, insects, or public speaking—all things that present no objective danger to them whatsoever. They, too, are not swayed by experts telling them this.

In times of crisis, we fall back on emotions that we experience as gut truths. "With less immigration, there would be less crime and less unemployment"—that feels good, that feels right. Psychologists and behavioural economists call this the *affect heuristic*. As Daniel Kahneman explains in *Thinking, Fast and Slow*, the affect heuristic is a method of understanding whereby "judgments and decisions are guided directly by feelings of liking and disliking, with little deliberation or reasoning".[54] This does not mean that you do not engage in any reflection at all, but rather that your arguments tend to follow your emotions. It is no longer the analysis that determines the outcome, but the outcome (which you have already arrived at on emotional grounds) that steers the analysis. "Your political preference determines the arguments that you find compelling. If you like the current health policy, you believe its benefits are substantial and its costs more manageable than the costs of alternatives. […] Your emotional attitude to such things as irradiated food, red meat, nuclear power, tattoos, or motorcycles drives your belief about their benefits and risks".[55]

The comedian Stephen Colbert has popularized the term *truthiness* for this kind of felt truth. What makes such gut instincts, or rather gut insights, extraordinarily difficult to refute is that we experience them as "just common sense". Common sense may be the metaphysics of the Stone Age, as the philosopher Bertrand Russell once said,[56] but it is our default method of understanding when we are afraid and overloaded with (real and fake) information.

Felt truth is so powerful because it is interconnected with two things that are themselves closely connected—stories and identity. It is this nexus that makes us experience our gut insights as common sense.

Stories are more potent than statistics. Human beings are storytelling animals.[57] They view the world through the prism of stories, not charts, tables, and formulae. This is why television spots urging us to donate to a good cause rely on mini-narratives; why reports about the deaths of Eric Garner, George Floyd, and Jacob Blake move us more than does the mere number of African Americans killed by the police; and why politicians with a vague but persuasive-sounding project tend to win against politicians with a laundry list of specific policy proposals. The most important story for each of us is the one that constitutes our identity, the story we tell when someone asks "Tell me about yourself". It is the story of me—not an isolated me, but me in my social relations (as John Donne wrote, "no man is an island, entire of itself").[58] Now, if I view the world through stories, and if the most important story I have is that of me and my community, then my judgements and decisions concerning that world will first and foremost be guided by that narrative identity. One might call this the *identity heuristic*.

The identity heuristic feels like common sense because it rests on the norms, values, and experiences that I share with my community. It is what "we believe".[59] This is the main reason why experts hold so little sway over us. Our common sense is inextricably bound up with our identity and all that it entails—our social life, our status, and our self-esteem. Faced with a choice between our beliefs (that is to say, our identity) and evidence to the contrary, we tend to reject the evidence as one-sided, biased, fake news, Democrat propaganda, a Jewish ploy, or what have you. We say "this is my story and I'm sticking to it".[60]

4 The Establishment, the Elite, and the Experts 179

This tendency is particularly strong when we feel that our community is somehow under attack. When threatened, we pull together, because being in a group offers protection. This self-solidification of the group has a double effect. For one, we are now even more inclined to stick to our shared "truths". Should we have any doubts, we will certainly not express them publicly, if indeed we do not repress them altogether.[61] After all, we do not want to be ostracized. For another, we become even more disinclined to distrust outsiders and their motives, including any expert that is not "one of us".

We feel—and are—under attack when we are at war. Similarly, we feel that we are being attacked when we find ourselves in a culture war (regardless of whether we use that term or not). As I will explain in the next chapter, this is the experience many people had in Weimar Germany, as well as the experience of many people—Trump's supporters above all—in today's America. This sense of beleaguerment changes the nature of politics and with it the role and perception of expert knowledge.

The sociologist William Davies has made a number of highly perceptive points about this in his book *Nervous States: How Feeling Took Over the World*.[62] In a culture war, Davies says, politics is seen in militaristic terms. It becomes one of the means by which we fight that war. This fight takes place not only on the level of ideas, but also on that of emotions: "War elevates feeling to a status it doesn't have during terms of peace, in two senses. First, our emotions and physical sensations acquire a fundamental value. Courage, stamina, optimism and aggression are crucial resources in battle. Fear, pain and pessimism are deliberately triggered in the enemy. All the same things that experts pledge to disregard [...] become instrumental when war breaks out. Second, feeling becomes a navigational aid and source of information, rather as one might feel one's way through a darkened room. Where there is an absence of commonly agreed facts, each side has to rely on a combination of private intelligence and instinct".[63]

Why are there no commonly agreed facts? Because in war—William Davies says—knowledge, too, becomes a weapon. Facts are being used to rouse one's own side and discredit the other side, or they are being manufactured for that purpose. As a result, the ideal of objectivity evaporates. People no longer strive for it, and they no longer believe in it. The experts have become the enemy (unless they are on your side and confirm what you believe already). The information gap this produces is filled by feeling; that is to say, by emotions pure and simple and by emotion-driven conceptions, or misconceptions, of reality. One might say that emotions are the new facts.

By way of example, Davies mentions the controversy surrounding the number of people that attended Donald Trump's inauguration in January 2017. Following the ceremony, White House Press Secretary Sean Spicer described the audience as "the largest [...] to ever witness an inauguration, period". This was hardly the case. CNN and other television networks broadcast images showing clearly that the crowd at Barack Obama's 2009 inauguration had been significantly larger. Factually, Sean Spicer's statement was patently absurd, and he got a good deal of flak over it. However, for Trump—as well as, one suspects, his followers (perhaps even including Spicer)—this was not about the old facts, but the new ones.

In Davies's words: "Within the media's seemingly factual statements about crowd sizes, Trump saw injustice, elitism and persecution. 'They demean me unfairly', he told an ABC News interviewer a few days later, before leading him to a wall-mounted photograph of the inauguration, apparently showing the vast size of the crowd from a more accurate angle. 'I call it a sea of love', he said, gesturing to the image. 'These people travelled from all parts of the country—maybe the world—to get here. And they loved what I had to say'. For Trump, this was no mere disagreements over 'facts'. It was an opposition between two emotions: the arrogant sneer of his critics and the love of his supporters".[64]

Against this backdrop—Davies suggests—White House Advisor Kellyanne Conway's claim that Sean Spicer had merely provided "alternative facts" and Spicer's own claim that "sometimes we can disagree with the facts" actually made some kind of weird sense.[65] To say this is not to endorse their position. It is to explain why their way of looking at things—their emotive epistemology—resonated with Trump's supporters.

There is one final point to which Davies draws attention. It is the new role that the leader assumes in conditions of war. With objectivity gone, the mind's main function is no longer to represent the world as it is. It is to act on it. Accordingly, the war leader—the brains behind the troops— "is not an observer, but a protagonist. [...] The crucial psychological

4 The Establishment, the Elite, and the Experts 181

attribute of such a figure is not honesty but 'resolution', not the capacity to provide accurate reports on the world, but to dominate it".[66] This is the fundamental difference between the expert and the leader: "Expert knowledge takes the form of a promise: trust me, these are the facts. [...] The basic injunction of any leader is *follow me*".[67]

Let us now move on from William Davies's insights and ask ourselves the question: how do populist leaders exploit the gut insights of their base? What do they get out of denigrating expert knowledge?

First, it enables them to create a community of people who share a "common sense" of the world and its ills. The Nazis called this frame of reference *das gesunde Volksempfinden*, the healthy instincts of the people. Shared emotions and prejudices are powerful unifiers, much more so than are cold truths. By ridiculing the experts and playing to the common people's *docta ignorantia*—their aversion to the intellectual's claim to knowledge[68]—charismatic leaders establish an emotional rapport with their supporters. What emerges is a community of believers led by the charismatic leader as Messiah. In this way, the leader sets up a new political and cultural arena, with two opposing camps: those who are in the faith and those who are not.

Second, expertise-bashing helps populist leaders clear the field for any unfounded views they wish to propagate and any controversial actions they plan to undertake. Ignoring expert advice is typical of the populist's approach to decision-making. Thus, President Trump was not particularly keen on reading memos or even listening to other people's views. Nor was Adolf Hitler. The British historian Laurence Rees recounts an instance of this. "When [...] in 1935 Martin Bormann sent a paper on youth issues to Hitler, he received a reply on 5 June from Fritz Wiedemann, Hitler's adjutant, which said, 'I am returning to you the enclosed memorandum. The Führer received it but then gave it back to me at once unread. He himself wishes to deal with this question in his major speech at the next Party Rally and does not want his thinking to be influenced in any way from any quarter'".[69]

Populists do not merely *ignore* expert advice. They actively *discredit* fact-based opposition to their ideas and projects. By openly undermining any experts contradicting them—be these experts intelligence-community officials, scientific advisors, judges, journalists, or historians—populist leaders set themselves up as the only arbiters of truth. In doing so, they clear the way for their own, wholly unfounded, claims; say, the claim that certain "outsiders" (the Jews, Mexican immigrants, or whoever it may be) present an imminent danger to the nation. This makes it easier to sell measures such as curtailing the freedom of the press, building a wall, or leaving the Paris climate accord.

Disagreeing with the facts allows populist leaders to present their own *alternative facts* and tell a story of their own. Conversely, spinning their own story "de-facts" the world and enables them to create a new perceptual reality. As we saw earlier, the kind of story that populists tell is intimately connected to "the people's" sense of identity. The next chapter will explore this connection in more detail.

Notes

1. See Erik H. Erikson, *Childhood and Society* (new ed. New York and London: W. W. Norton, 1993; first published 1950).
2. Erikson, *Childhood and Society*, p. 247.
3. Erikson, *Childhood and Society*, p. 250.
4. Erikson, *Childhood and Society*, p. 248.
5. Erikson, *Childhood and Society*, pp. 248–49.
6. Karl Marx, *Selected Writings*, ed. David McLellan (Oxford etc.: Oxford University Press, 1977), p. 224. For the German original, see Karl Marx and Friedrich Engels, *Werke* (Berlin: Dietz, 1965–90), vol. 4, p. 465.
7. Marx, *Selected Writings*, pp. 223–25 (translation modified); Marx and Engels, *Werke*, vol. 4, pp. 464–67.
8. Marx, *Selected Writings*, p. 226 (punctuation modified); Marx and Engels, *Werke*, vol. 4, p. 467.
9. Marx, *Selected Writings*, p. 176 (translation modified); Marx and Engels, *Werke*, vol. 3, p. 46. There is a one-sidedness to this citation of which Marx and Engels were well aware. It resides in the fact that the statement ignores the heterogeneity of the ideological superstructure, as well as the complexity of its interactions with the material basis. Here, as elsewhere in their work, Marx and Engels are "bending the stick" (to use Lenin's phrase) by overstating the opposite of what they are seeking to refute. In other words, their emphasis on the social force of economics is meant to

counterbalance their philosophical opponents' emphasis on the primacy of ideas.
10. Paul Nizan, *The Watchdogs: Philosophers and the Established Order*, trans. Paul Fittingoff (New York and London: Monthly Review Press, 1971; first published in French 1932), p. 92. For an attempt to update Nizan's ideas for the media age, see Serge Halimi, *Les nouveaux chiens de garde* (second, revised and extended ed. Paris: Raisons d'agir, 2005) and the eponymous film based on it (Epicentre Films, 2012; dir. Gilles Balbastre and Yannick Kergoat).
11. Nizan, *Watchdogs*, p. 29.
12. The classic statement is Althusser's 1970 essay "Idéologie et appareils idéologiques d'État". See Louis Althusser, "Ideology and Ideological State Apparatuses: Notes towards an Investigation", in Louis Althusser, *Lenin and Philosophy and Other Essays*, trans. Ben Brewster (New York: Monthly Review Press, 2001), pp. 85–126.
13. Althusser, "Ideology", p. 101 (in the original in italics).
14. Althusser, "Ideology", p. 123.
15. See Charles Wright Mills, *The Power Elite* (Oxford etc.: Oxford University Press, 2000; first published 1956).
16. "The Higher Immorality" is the title of the final chapter of Mills's book (Mills, *The Power Elite*, pp. 343–61).
17. Here, one might think of Antonio Gramsci's notion of hegemony, or of Michel Foucault's reflections on the link between power, knowledge, social discourse, and subjecthood (a link that becomes visible in—say—the erstwhile medicalization of homosexuality and the accompanying discrimination of gays as somehow "sick"). Another example would be the various feminist critiques of patriarchal structures and male-dominated perspectives in contemporary society.
18. In what follows, I have benefited much from Roger Eatwell and Matthew Goodwin, *National Populism: The Revolt against Liberal Democracy* (Harmondsworth: Penguin, 2018), Dirk Jörke and Veith Selk, *Theorien des Populismus* (Hamburg: Junius, 2017), Benjamin Moffitt, *The Global Rise of Populism: Performance, Political Style, and Representation* (Stanford: Stanford University Press, 2016), Cas Mudde and Cristóbal Rovira Kaltwasser, *Populism: A Very Short Introduction* (Oxford: Oxford University Press, 2017), Jan-Werner Müller, *What Is Populism?* (new ed. Harmondsworth: Penguin, 2017), Bernd Stegemann, *Das Gespenst des Populismus. Ein Essay zur politischen Dramaturgie* (third ed. Berlin:

Theater der Zeit, 2017), Hans Wansink, *De populistische revolutie* (Amsterdam: Prometheus, 2017), and Peter Wierenga, *Ik brul, dus ik ben. Denkers over populisme* (Amsterdam: Boom, 2017).
19. Cf. Benedict Anderson, *Imagined Communities: Reflections on the Origin and Spread of Nationalism* (rev. ed. London and New York: Verso, 2006).
20. Stegemann, *Das Gespenst des Populismus*, p. 54.
21. Adolf Hitler, *Reden 1920–1945* (no date and publisher given): speech of 10 November 1933, delivered at the Siemens factory in Berlin (no page numbers given).
22. Donald Trump, nomination-acceptance speech at the Republican National Convention in Cleveland, Ohio, 21 July 2016.
23. Donald Trump, nomination-acceptance speech at the Republican National Convention in Cleveland, Ohio, 21 July 2016.
24. Stegemann, *Das Gespenst des Populismus*, p. 54.
25. See Isaiah Berlin, "Does Political Theory Still Exist?", in Isaiah Berlin, *Concepts and Categories: Philosophical Essays* (second ed. Princeton, NJ: Princeton University Press, 2013), pp. 187–225.
26. Here, I follow Hermann Lübbe, *Praxis der Philosophie, praktische Philosophie, Geschichtstheorie* (Stuttgart: Reclam, 1978), especially pp. 61–93.
27. See Niklas Luhmann, *Legitimation durch Verfahren* (new ed. Frankfurt am Main: Suhrkamp, 1983).
28. In what follows, I have benefited much from Richard Pildes, "Romanticizing Democracy, Political Fragmentation, and the Decline of American Governance", *Yale Law Journal* 124.3, 2014, pp. 804–52, Jason Grumet, *City of Rivals: Restoring the Glorious Mess of American Democracy* (Guilford, Connecticut: Lyon Press, 2014), Jonathan Rauch, *Political Realism: How Hacks, Machines, Big Money, and Back-Room Deals Can Strengthen American Democracy* (2015; available at https://www.brookings.edu/books/political-realism/) as well as "How American Politics Went Insane", *The Atlantic*, July / August 2016, Carlo Strenger, *Diese verdammten liberalen Eliten. Wer sie sind und warum wir sie brauchen* (Berlin: Suhrkamp, 2019), and Fareed Zakaria, *The Future of Freedom: Illiberal Democracy at Home and Abroad* (New York and London: W. W. Norton, 2003).
29. Early nineteenth-century thinkers such as Alexis de Tocqueville and G. W. F. Hegel formulated important ideas about this issue that have acquired a renewed vigour in our populist age. On Hegel, cf. my article

"Hegel's View of Modern Society", *Publications of the English Goethe Society* 81.1, 2012, pp. 1–11.
30. See Alexis de Tocqueville, *Democracy in America and Two Essays on America*, trans. Gerald E. Bevan (Harmondsworth: Penguin, 2003), especially chapters 7 and 8 in part 2 of volume 1.
31. Sigmund Freud, *The Penguin Freud Library*, trans. Angela Richards and James Strachey (Harmondsworth: Penguin, 1990–93), vol. 12, p. 86. The citation comes from Freud's *Zeitgemäßes über Krieg und Tod* (Thoughts for the Times on War and Death, 1915).
32. See above all his *Massenpsychologie und Ich-Analyse* (Group Psychology and the Analysis of the Ego, 1921), translated in Freud, *Penguin Freud Library*, vol. 12, pp. 91–178.
33. Peter Gay, *Freud: A Life for Our Time* (New York and London: W. W. Norton, 1988), p. 405.
34. Freud, *Penguin Freud Library*, vol. 12, p. 121.
35. Freud, *Penguin Freud Library*, vol. 12, p. 120.
36. Freud, *Penguin Freud Library*, vol. 12, p. 148.
37. Freud, *Penguin Freud Library*, vol. 12, p. 155.
38. Cf. James Surowiecki, *The Wisdom of Crowds: Why the Many Are Smarter Than the Few* (London: Abacus, 2007; first published 2004).
39. Zakaria, *The Future of Freedom*, p. 242 (I have corrected a typographical error in the original).
40. Roger Scruton, *The Uses of Pessimism and the Dangers of False Hope* (London: Atlantic Books, 2012; first published 2010), p. 154.
41. See the X-Verleih DVD *Joschka und Herr Fischer. Eine Zeitreise durch 60 Jahre Deutschland* (2011), directed by Pepe Danquart. Just as his party, Fischer had a long learning curve. He had originally been an anarchistically inclined squatter, not averse to the occasional street fight with the police. He entered parliament in 1983; one and a half years later, he caused a major scandal when he addressed the parliamentary chairman with the immortal words "With respect, Mr. Speaker, you are an asshole [*Mit Verlaub, Herr Präsident, Sie sind ein Arschloch*]". In 1998, Fischer became Foreign Secretary in Gerhard Schröder's coalition government.
42. Rauch, *Political Realism*, p. 2. For the term *disintermediation*, see Rauch, "How American Politics Went Insane".
43. Rauch, *Political Realism*, p. 7.
44. Rauch, "How American Politics Went Insane". Cf. chapter 5 in Grumet, *City of Rivals*, which bears the apt title "The Dark Side of Sunlight".

45. Rauch, "How American Politics Went Insane".
46. This is my term. Jonathan Rauch uses the word *politiphobes* to refer to those who "believe that obvious, commonsense solutions to the country's problems are out there for the plucking" but not seized upon because "politicians are corrupt, or self-interested, or addicted to unnecessary partisan feuding". His reference is to John R. Hibbing and Elizabeth Theiss-Morse, *Stealth Democracy: Americans' Belief about How Government Should Work* (Cambridge etc.: Cambridge University Press, 2002). See Rauch, "How American Politics Went Insane".
47. See James A. Baker, III, Lee H. Hamilton, et al., *The Iraq Study Group Report: The Way Forward—A New Approach* (New York: Vintage, 2006), p. 92.
48. Cf. Baker, Hamilton, et al., *Iraq Study Group Report*, p. 10.
49. Tom Nichols, *The Death of Expertise: The Campaign against Established Knowledge and Why It Matters* (new ed. Oxford: Oxford University Press, 2019), p. xiv. In addition to this book, the following account also draws on William Davies, *Nervous States: How Feeling Took Over the World* (London: Jonathan Cape, 2018) and Sara E. Gorman and Jack M. Gorman, *Denying to the Grave: Why We Ignore the Facts That Will Save Us* (Oxford: Oxford University Press, 2017).
50. See the Columbia TriStar DVD *Life of Brian* (2003; the film came out in 1979), directed by Terry Jones.
51. Cf. David Halberstam, *The Best and the Brightest* (New York: Ballantine Books, 1993; first published 1969), the classic study of the failures of the American policy elite leading up to and during the Vietnam War.
52. Cf. Bruno Bettelheim, *The Uses of Enchantment: The Meaning and Importance of Fairy Tales* (Harmondsworth: Penguin, 1991; first published 1976), p. 49.
53. For example, Niklas Luhmann, *Ökologische Kommunikation. Kann die modern Gesellschaft sich auf Gefährdungen einstellen?* (second ed. Opladen: Westdeutscher Verlag, 1988), pp. 161–62, citing Gerald D. Berreman, "Scale and Social Relations: Thoughts and Three Examples", in *Scale and Social Organization*, ed. Fredrik Barth (Oslo: Universitetsforlaget, 1978), pp. 41–77 (77).
54. Daniel Kahneman, *Thinking, Fast and Slow* (Harmondsworth: Penguin, 2012; first published 2011), p. 12.
55. Kahneman, *Thinking*, p. 103.

56. Russell's phrase is sometimes also cited as "Common sense is the metaphysics of savages". Cf. Ray Monk, "The Dark Side", in *What Philosophers Think*, eds. Julian Baggini and Jeremy Stangroom (London and New York: Continuum, 2003), pp. 161–70 (168).
57. Cf. Jonathan Gottschall, *The Storytelling Animal: How Stories Make Us Human* (Boston and New York: Mariner Books, 2013; first published 2012).
58. The citation comes from John Donne's *Devotions upon Emergent Occasions* of 1624.
59. In the final instance, science, too, rests on the consensus of the scientific community, but it has rather more robust and explicit methods of verification and falsification before it gets to that final instance.
60. Gorman and Gorman (*Denying to the Grave*, p. 123) use the phrase "That's My Story and I'm Sticking to It" as heading for a section on confirmation bias, our tendency to focus on information that confirms, rather than refutes, our beliefs.
61. I will come back to this combination of psychological ambivalence and social dissimulation in the final chapter.
62. See William Davies, *Nervous States: How Feeling Took Over the World* (London: Jonathan Cape, 2018).
63. Davies, *Nervous States*, p. 125.
64. Davies, *Nervous States*, p. 4. Davies's suggestion on the same page that Trump actually "*did* see a densely packed crowd" almost certainly underestimates Trump's salesmanship and his awareness of the distinction between factual truth and PR.
65. Conway made her claim on Chuck Todd's *Meet the Press* on 22 January 2017; Spicer's claim was made at a press conference the day before.
66. Davies, *Nervous States*, p. 147.
67. Davies, *Nervous States*, p. 148.
68. The term *docta ignorantia*, which I have used somewhat loosely, comes from the late Medieval philosopher Nicholas of Cusa, or Cusanus. According to Cusanus, God is fundamentally unknowable. To believe otherwise is to fall victim to pseudo-knowledge. The only real knowledge we can possess is the *knowing ignorance* that acknowledges that the truth is beyond our reach.
69. Laurence Rees, *The Dark Charisma of Adolf Hitler: Leading Millions into the Abyss* (London: Ebury Press, 2013; first published 2012), p. 156.

5

Identity and Negative Myths

Who am I? What does it mean to be me? The answer to this abstract philosophical question—the most fundamental question that a human being can ask—takes us straight to the most concrete political decisions that people can make. For the answer is not: I am a set of statistical facts about age, gender, occupation, or what have you. The answer is that I live in and through stories. The answer is that I am a story.[1]

Stories Are Us

What does it mean to say that human beings are stories? It means three things.

First, it means that we are not static entities. We live not simply in the present, but we know that we are coming from somewhere and that we are going somewhere. This is one of the key differences between human beings on the one hand and stones, plants, and animals on the other hand, which is why Existentialist thinkers—such as Jean-Paul Sartre—have made it the cornerstone of their philosophy. Human beings never simply coincide with what they are at any given moment. They are also their past and their future. Their past is always with them in the form of memories, guilty feelings about mistakes they have made, and regrets about what might have been. They always project themselves into the future, because they have plans, they worry about what might happen tomorrow, and so on.

Thus, when someone asks me "who are you?", I tell a story, the story of my life. I say something like: "My name is Henk de Berg and I was born in 1963. I'm originally from Holland but came to the UK in 1996". Being the nerdy academic that I am, I will in all likelihood go on to describe the papers I am hoping to complete in the not too distant future. The same understanding of *narrative identity* is behind standard job-interview questions like "what experience do you have?" and "where do you see yourself in five years' time?".

It is such stories that make us *us*. This is the reason why the replicants in Ridley Scott's classic science-fiction film *Blade Runner* have artificial childhood-memories implanted in them. Without these, they would not be genuinely humanoid. (I say *humanoid*, but if replicants have memories, both artificial and real ones, and if they are able to project themselves into the future, with the ability to act on that basis and choose their destiny freely—as Rutger Hauer's replicant character Roy Batty does at the end of the film—are they then not really just like us?).[2] The narrative nature of identity is also the reason why Alzheimer's is such a terrible disease. If people lose that "stretching" into the past and into the future, if the ability to tell that story slips away from them, then they lose their identity.

Second, we are also the stories that *other people* tell about us. I may say "I am the greatest writer that ever lived", but if no one believes me—that is to say, if other people tell a different story about me—then I have a problem with my identity. This is what the famous phrase "L'enfer, c'est les Autres"—Hell is other people—from Jean-Paul Sartre's theatre play *Huis clos* (No Exit, 1944) refers to. Confined for all eternity to an infernally hot lounge room, all three characters in Sartre's play are guilty of evil acts, yet have a story to justify their actions. Garcin has physically abused his wife and has betrayed his war comrades. Estelle has drowned her illegitimate child und pushed her husband to suicide. Inès is responsible for the death of the husband of her lesbian lover, who in her turn ended up committing suicide. Yet all three claim that they are victims in one way or another and therefore not really responsible for their actions. However, each protagonist's attempt at self-justification comes up against the disbelief of the other two, who see the evil deed for what it is. Garcin's, Estelle's, and Inès's self-serving stories founder on the suspicion of their little community. This, then, is what Sartre is saying: the stories that other people tell about us can validate our identity, but they can also undermine it and make our lives a living hell.[3]

Third, through the perspective of stories, we know not only ourselves, but also the world around us. Historians, scientists, and journalists rely on narratives and narrative devices when answering questions such as: why did the French Revolution occur; how did the universe come into existence; and what happened at Chappaquiddick? Entrepreneurs and politicians do the same. So do we, ordinary people. We say "Peter is such a horrible person. Do you know what he did?"—and then we tell the story. To quote the title of a book by the German philosopher Wilhelm Schapp, human existence is *in Geschichten verstrickt*, inextricably bound up in stories.[4] In other words, I am not simply my own story (as told by myself and others), but a story that interlinks with other stories. My story is interwoven with the stories of my community—the stories told by its members about themselves, the others, and the community as a whole.

In a manner that is largely unconscious, I combine such stories into the narrative of me. If, however, one of these stories contradicts that narrative, I tend to re-interpret it so as to make it fit. Alternatively, I might simply ignore it ("slavery was a long time ago and has nothing to do with me") or reject it as untrue ("claims of institutional racism in the police are totally exaggerated"). Narrative identity does not rest on historiographical truth or scientific validity. People who are part of—and hence tell—a different story may know better, but "this is my story and I'm sticking with it".[5] On an abstract level, the facts arguably remain the same. On a concrete existential level, they assume very different meanings. What is a manifestation of deep-rooted sexism from one narrative perspective is harmless boys-will-be-boys locker room talk from another. Depending on the story, my wealth may be the result of hard work, the exploitation of the proletariat, or white privilege.

We have seen that existentially significant identity is narrative identity. But we have seen something else as well: narrative identity is fundamentally tension-laden. On the one hand, I am the story that I and others tell about me. My own narrative needs to be validated by other people, as we saw with Sartre's *Huis clos*. On the other hand, I am disinclined to assimilate stories that other people tell and which do not fit a more or less positive narrative of me. Under normal circumstances, this tension can be used productively. With a socially responsible and psychologically bearable combination of acceptance and rejection of outside opinion, we develop a more realistic and less self-absorbed view of who we are.

In times of social upheaval, this give-and-take is much harder. When all that is solid is melting into air, we cling all the harder to old convictions. When we feel that our entire way of life, our whole culture, is at stake, our first goal is to remain who we are and protect our identity. So we band together with like-minded people and wall ourselves off from those who are "not like us". And we tell our story as *we* see it. We speak, but we no longer listen. We want to dominate the conversation to ensure that society is about us again, so that we can be the people who (we keep telling ourselves) we have always been. This is why all culture wars are story wars.

Aristotle Was Right

Stories are what makes us us. That is why stories are all around us. Even our fictions are stories. Novels, plays, operas, Hollywood films, television series, and online games à la *World of Warcraft*—they are all story-based. What is more, they are almost all *proper* stories: they have "a beginning, a middle, and an end",[6] as Aristotle famously put it.

Despite multifarious attempts to disrupt the traditional forms of artistic creation, Aristotle's basic narrative principle still reigns supreme. The failure of avant-gardism is perhaps the most striking feature of the evolution of aesthetic communication. Dadaism has become entirely historical. The French *nouveau roman* ("new novel"), with its incomprehensible anti-plots or no-plots, was and is read by academic specialists only. Experimental films—say, Alain Resnais's *Last Year in Marienbad*, which consists of multiple iterations of the same unintelligible scenes—appeal merely to a handful of hardcore film buffs while annoying everybody else. As a rule, we only embrace narrative devices such as flashbacks and telling-the-story-backwards provided we can still wrap our heads around the overall story as a meaningful series of events.

By the same token, a painting resonates with us only to the extent that we can "picture" it in narrative terms. No one gets anything out of Mondrian's *Compositions* without understanding their place in art history, which is the "story of art". A Mark Rothko only comes to life in and through our interpretations, or the interpretations of art critics. The moment a Vermeer is shown not to be by Vermeer, but a forgery, we view it in a different light, both artistically and financially.[7]

Hence today, in a world saturated with images, the word is as powerful as ever before. For ultimately it is the narrative that defines the image, not the other way round. Is a video showing a group of policemen beating a defenceless Rodney King proof of police brutality or not? One would have thought that the answer was obvious. Yet lawyers for the policemen told a different story, one that somehow managed to convince the members of the jury that what they were seeing was an act of self-defence. The video did not speak for itself. No image ever does. Today, the majority of people view such videos differently not because the images have changed, but because the overall cultural narrative is finally shifting towards a greater awareness of the depth and persistence of racial bias in American society, including in the police. We live in what the French thinker Guy Debord has called a *society of the spectacle*, in which images generated by the media, advertising, and popular culture are all-pervasive.[8] However, such a society is of necessity also a society of narratives—of true stories, false stories, and (as we will see further below) myths.

Let us return to Aristotle's narrative precept. The French experimental filmmaker Jean-Luc Godard was once asked whether his movies actually had a beginning, a middle, and an end. He replied: "Yes, but not necessarily in that order".[9] That was witty, but his anti-order is not what people are looking for. Human beings want genuine order, because they are forever in search of meaning. More than anything else, they want to make sense of the messy reality that is their existence. This is where stories—proper stories—come in. As Jonathan Gottschall puts it in his brilliant book *The Storytelling Animal*: "The storytelling mind is a crucial evolutionary adaptation. It allows us to experience our lives as coherent, orderly, and meaningful. It is what makes life more than a blooming, buzzing confusion".[10]

However, Gottschall goes on to say, there is a catch. Because it is so averse to uncertainty, the mind has a tendency to see meaningful patterns even when there are none. It does so particularly in times of social or psychological crisis. The most dangerous outcome of this tendency are conspiracy theories.

More generally, the mind—as we observed in the previous section—tends towards reassuring self-deception. For this reason, popular fiction is seldom utterly pessimistic and usually positively upbeat. The mind craves certainty, stability, security. Thus, in detective stories the killer normally gets caught. Villains-as-heroes are as a rule loveable rogues, while the actual bad guys get their comeuppance. The majority of sitcoms are about true friends or harmonious families. Romantic comedies have a happy end. High art fulfils an important cultural function by challenging such rose-tinted simplifications, but it is not something that human beings can live with on a daily basis. Ultimately, we want to be lied to as much as we lie to ourselves.

Lie to Me

In his book *All Marketers Are Liars / Tell Stories*, advertising guru Seth Godin explains the commercial success of Banquet's Crock-Pot Classics: "It turns out that millions of Americans feel guilty about the fact that they no longer cook dinner for their families. They were raised to believe that a home-cooked meal = love = family = healthy and in our modern world, they can't find the time or the energy to pull it off. A lot of these people own Crock-Pots, the electric slow-cooking device used for making soups and stews. John Hanson of Banquet introduced Crock-Pot Classics, saying, 'Banquet Crock-Pot Classics contain all of the high-quality ingredients needed for a slow-cooked meal—like tender meats, fresh vegetables, hearty potatoes and perfectly seasoned sauces—and are ready to cook with less than five minutes of preparation. At the end of the day, Banquet Crock-Pot Classics welcome home families with the inviting aromas of a slow-cooked meal'. In other words (if Banquet had stated the real deal): 'Here's a bunch of stuff, preserved by chemicals and freezing. Dump it all in the pot, turn it on and you'll end up with something we could have just as easily precooked for you and sold frozen, ready for the microwave'".[11]

What can we learn from this example? First—Godin says—we can see that the culinary facts do not really matter. Crock-Pot Classics contain a whole range of artificial colourings and flavourings, but that is not what its customers are buying. What they are buying is an atmosphere or rather a story, a story about family and togetherness, wholeness and wholesomeness.

Banquet's customers are buying a world view, a perspective on themselves, their family, and their place in the world. Ultimately, they are buying an identity. But—this is Godin's second point—they are not acquiring a *new* identity. On the contrary. Successful advertising is not about *changing* our world view, but *reinforcing* it. As Godin puts it, "*great stories agree with our worldview*. The best stories don't teach people anything new. Instead, the best stories agree with what the audience already believes and makes the members of the audience feel smart and secure when reminded how right they were in the first place".[12] Hence his advice to marketers: "Don't try to use facts to prove your case and to insist that people change their biases. You don't have enough time and you don't have enough money. Instead, identify a population with a certain worldview, frame your story in terms of that worldview and you win".[13]

This takes us to the third and final point that Godin makes; namely, the insight that "*consumers are complicit in marketing*".[14] They believe because they want to believe. They buy the product because they have already bought into a specific view of themselves and the world. If that view is wrong (or one-sided, or racist, or what have you) and marketers are merely seeking to reinforce it, then one might say that they are lying, or at least that they are not trying very hard to find out and communicate the truth. But by the same token one might say that it is the *customers* who are deceiving themselves, not unlike the protagonists in the play by Sartre we looked at earlier. "Successful marketers are just the providers of stories that consumers choose to believe".[15]

Godin's observations are particularly relevant to the study of populist electioneering. As Laurence Rees and other historians have made clear, Hitler's ideas resonated with so many people because he only ever reinforced what they already believed; he never sought to convince them of anything new.[16] His skill was in connecting with his audience's preconceptions and prejudices ("some Jews have far too much power in Germany") and then taking them well beyond that ("Germany is being bled dry by the Jews, who are nothing but parasites"). As Nicholas O'Shaughnessy puts it in his landmark study *Selling Hitler*, the psychological process at issue can best be conceived as a "partnership in wishful thinking in which the masses were self-deluded as well as other-deluded".[17] In other words, the German population—the target of Hitler's political advertising—was "more co-conspirator than victim", while the advertising itself was above all "an invitation to share in the creation of a hyperbolic fiction".[18] This holds true not only for 1920s and 1930s Germany, but also for Trump's America, as we will see now.

Collective Identity and Myth

Stories that create and foster a collective identity are called *myths*.[19] Myths are neither fact-orientated historiographical accounts nor free-wheeling literary fictions, but rather hybrids of both. Their overarching function is to unite us and make *e pluribus unum*.[20] They do so by recounting and reimagining the community's origins, positing a set of group features, validating certain norms, values, and ideals, and encouraging particular forms of behaviour. "Myths", Jonah Sachs writes in his book *Winning the Story Wars*, "provide *story, explanation*, and *meaning* in a single neat package".[21] Among the examples he gives is the American dream: "*Story*: America was clawed from the tyranny of British class and privilege and formed into an exceptional nation by men who believed in liberty, merit, and self-discipline. *Explanation*: That's why opportunity for success and prosperity is open to every American. *Meaning*: So if you work hard, you too will be rewarded".[22]

Viewed positively, myths bind the community together. However, there are real dangers to the mythological imagination. Myths have the capacity to overpower our critical faculties. They appeal to the heart rather than to the mind, so we are always in danger of losing ourselves in them, just as we may lose ourselves in the emotions generated by crowd behaviour.[23] This is all the more dangerous as myths themselves are collective in nature. Their strength is also their weakness: they bring us together by stressing our commonalities while passing over, or papering over, our differences. Hence, they can spurn us on and make us stronger by giving us a sense of a shared destiny, but they can also overwhelm us and weaken our individuality by imposing a reductive one-size-fits all framework on our (inevitably diverse) community.

The American dream, for instance, is essentially a white Anglo-Saxon myth. It ignores the existence of Native Americans and glosses over the role of slavery in US history. This does not mean that it cannot serve a positive purpose. If the American dream is understood as an appeal to bring about the level playing field it talks about, then there is no reason to reject it. A good example is Martin Luther King's "I Have a Dream" speech of 28 August 1963: "When the architects of our republic wrote the magnificent words of the Constitution and the Declaration of Independence, they were signing a promissory note to which every American was to fall heir. This note was the promise that all men [...] would be guaranteed the unalienable rights of life, liberty, and the pursuit of happiness. It is obvious today that America has defaulted on this promissory note in so far as her citizens of color are concerned. [...] We refuse to believe that there are insufficient funds in in the great vaults of opportunity of this nation. [...] So I say to you, my friends, that even though we must face the difficulties of today and tomorrow, I still have a dream. It is a dream deeply rooted in the American dream [...] I have a dream that my four little children will one day live in a nation where they will not be judged by the color of their skin but by the content of their character".[24]

If, by contrast, we take the myth of the American dream at face value, then we lose sight of that need for social change. We think that we are there already, that all we have to do is live the dream. Accordingly, unemployment and poverty are seen as the result of a failure of character, not of structural inequality or discrimination. By the same token, affirmative action is seen, not as an attempt to facilitate the American dream, but as an attempt to undermine it by allowing people to cheat.

Myths become dangerous if we refuse to acknowledge the discrepancies between mythological imagination and sociological reality; that is to say, if we refuse to examine their interpretative dimension. Yet that is precisely what myth invites us to do. It presents historically and socially specific imaginations as if they reflected some unchanging and unchangeable natural order. Myth transforms culture into nature.

The French thinker Roland Barthes has said important things about this in his bestselling *Mythologies*, first published in 1957.[25] His best-known example is the cover of an issue of the magazine *Paris Match* depicting a young black soldier saluting the French flag. The story that the image tells us, Barthes argues, is a prime example of the mythological imagination: France is a colour-blind Empire whose children embrace the global projection of her military might wherever they are from. In other words, the image tells us that French colonialism is nothing controversial, nothing to worry about. It is just how things are: "*look at this good Negro who salutes like one of our own boys*".[26] In this way, Barthes says, the mythological imagination takes us in. The myth of the French *mission civilisatrice* makes me—an ordinary French person—feel good about myself and the world. It tells me that colonialism "is natural and *goes without saying*: I am reassured".[27] This is the dangerous temptation of myth: it invites us to view what are really social power-relations and human actions as facts of life, as eternal verities.

Myths, then, are collective constructions of identity that work rather like the individual's construction of identity. Both are largely unconscious processes that have a tendency towards reassuring self-deception. Both are subject to various forms of unintentional but "useful" forgetting. And both tend to ignore or supress any stories that do not fit the mythological narrative.

This does not mean—the point bears repeating—that myths are always a bad thing. They can play a positive role in our lives if they act as a kind of collective *ego-ideal*, to use a psychoanalytical term. Understood in this way, myth represents our better collective self. It is who and what we want to be and hence who and what we want to strive towards, because we know we are not there yet (as exemplified by Martin Luther King's "I Have a Dream" speech).

Admittedly, putting the matter like this is a simplification. Strictly speaking, the ego-ideal is a value-neutral concept; its content can be positive *or* negative. It is thus entirely possible to think of collective ego-ideals that are racist or otherwise immoral in nature. The myth of the West's civilizing mission—what Rudyard Kipling called "the white man's burden"[28]—is a case in point. Myths can "sell" forms of social injustice as aims that are worth striving towards. Such *negative* collective ego-ideals are characterized by a strong emphasis on hierarchy (the distinction between classes, genders, ethnicities, and the like) and exclusivity (the presumed superiority of one's own community). They blossom when the community's traditional myths become frayed.

The Myth Gap I: Times of Crisis

With the unravelling of time-honoured constructions of collective identity, there emerges what Jonah Sachs has called a *myth gap*.[29] A myth gap is "the space between the realities of our moment in history and the shared stories to which we turn for explanation, meaning, and instruction for action".[30] It "arises when reality changes dramatically and our myths are not resilient enough to continue working in the face of that change".[31]

Under normal circumstances, myths bind the community together. In a time of crisis, when things are falling apart, we still want to be together. Indeed, because we are scared, we are more in need of security, of a place where we can be ourselves, than ever before. We are also angry. "Why is this happening to me? And why are so many other people not affected, or even benefiting? It's just not fair". So we start casting about for someone to blame, an enemy we can vanquish. It is at this point that the mythological imagination turns negative.

The old myths have lost their persuasiveness. Too big is the gulf that separates their imagined world from our everyday experience. As a result, negative myths arise—stories that construct our identity in a more selective and more antagonistic manner. Our community becomes smaller and hence "safer", because those whom we blame for the crisis are no longer considered part of it. They are no longer us, but an incommensurable non-us, an enemy we have to beat. They are now the Other. Hence, Germany is no longer all Germans, but all "Aryans"—and the Jews are the enemy. The United States is no longer all people living on its soil, but only "true-blood" Americans—with illegal immigrants as their core enemy.

Like all myths, negative myths are hybrids of factuality and fiction. They are neither reality descriptions nor fairy tales, but rather mixtures of the two. Their truth-value, if the term is applicable at all, is not a straightforward scientific one. Moreover, again like myths in general, they are heavily emotive in nature, appealing to the heart rather than to the mind. This is what makes them so dangerous. As Alex Evans puts it in his book *The Myth Gap*: "Too often, political progressives try to fight these hugely resonant stories with policy memos. Their hope appears to be (against all evidence to the contrary) that rational arguments and empirical data will win out against powerful narratives of "us versus them", or corrupt politicians only out to line their own pockets, or conspiracies to falsify climate data. This was the mistake made by the ineffectual campaign to persuade Britons to remain in the EU. It was the mistake made by US climate campaigners in 2009, when they were routed by climate deniers and the Tea Party. And it was the mistake that paved the way for Donald Trump to win the US presidency in 2016".[32] I will return to this issue in the final chapter, which deals with narrative (un-)truth.

It is the gap caused by the unravelling of the United States' most powerful myth—the combined stories of America's "manifest destiny" and the American dream—that provided an opening for Donald Trump's populism. The United States was instrumental in the West's victory over communism, but 9/11 put a real dent in its post-Cold War triumphalism. The humiliatingly unsuccessful wars in Afghanistan and Iraq, as well as the equally unconvincing interventions in Libya and Syria, eroded its geopolitical confidence still further. Finally, the rise of countries such as China and Russia marked, if not the decline of the United States, then at least the emergence of a multipolar, "post-American", world order.[33]

At the same time, accelerating globalization and the accompanying outsourcing of production to lower-wage countries wreaked havoc on significant parts of the American economy. Perhaps even more devastating was the impact of automation and robotization. Previously solid working-class and middle-class jobs were no longer secure. A new kind of underclass came into existence, impoverished, without health insurance, and often addicted to alcohol or painkillers. The financial meltdown of 2008 generated both a cataclysmic economic recession and the widespread perception that the government, while keen to bail out the big corporations, was unwilling to extend the same level of support to ordinary Americans. Income disparities grew exponentially, and many parents worried that their children would do worse than they themselves had done.

Just as powerful as these geopolitical and economic developments was a double-layered cultural shift. Its first layer was the increasingly diverse make-up of the United States, which was at odds with the myth of America as an essentially white Anglo-Saxon country. Its second layer was the accompanying perception among significant swathes of the white working and middle classes that they were being discriminated against in favour of people of colour. In the terminology of their most extreme representatives, they were being "replaced". This perception was intensified by the belief that the social challenges they faced were being ignored or minimized by mainstream liberals and mainstream conservatives alike. It was heightened even further by an aversion to a "political correctness" that—so it was felt—shielded anyone but "us", ordinary hard-working white folk.

Together, these geopolitical, economic, and cultural shifts all but undid the traditional—mythical—understanding of what it means to be an American.

Comparable, though more violent, historical developments created an even more acutely felt myth gap in the Weimar Republic. In 1871, after a successful war against France, the German Empire was founded. A massive economic upturn ensued. The rapid extension of trade and industry went hand in hand with an unprecedented rise in infrastructure and construction projects. Its innovations in technology, chemistry, and medicine put the new state at the forefront of scientific research and development. On the eve of the First World War, the German Empire was among the strongest economies in the world.

It is true that the large-scale industrialization process was accompanied by poverty and other social problems. Yet earlier rural life had in many ways been worse; now, at least, people could hope for a better future.[34] In addition, workers were protected by a nascent social-security system that provided them with health insurance, accident and disability insurance, and pensions. Last but not least, the Empire, which had become not only an economic powerhouse but also a military superpower, engendered a strong sense of national pride.

All this came to an abrupt end in 1918, when the country lost the First World War. The defeat was all the more crushing as military and political propaganda had left the German population wholly unprepared for it. The humiliation was compounded by the harsh conditions of the Treaty of Versailles, which placed the entire responsibility for the war on Germany and imposed punishing reparations. In addition, the German army and navy were to be significantly reduced in size, while the air force had to be disbanded altogether. The country was stripped of 13% of its territory, which amounted to one tenth of its population, as well as all its foreign investments and a large proportion of its manufacturing plants and livestock.

The erstwhile proud Empire, authoritarian but stable, was now in total chaos. The Allied naval blockade, which continued for several months after the armistice of November 1918, was causing disease and starvation on a massive scale. Law and order were breaking down. Right-wing and left-wing militias, as well as criminal gangs, roamed the streets. In 1919, following the violent suppression of a number of communist uprisings, the Empire officially gave way to the Weimar Republic. Yet few people embraced the newly minted democracy. Even most of its supporters were mere *Vernunftrepublikaner*, "rational republicans" acting out of political necessity only.

Weimar democracy struggled to command respect to the very end. It proved unable to allay the widespread fears of a communist take-over along the lines of the Russian revolution of 1917. An array of extremist right-wing associations and political parties sprang up, competing (and occasionally collaborating) with each other while engaging in violent confrontations with left-wing opponents. There were two attempts at a *coup d'État*—one led by the monarchists Wolfgang Kapp and Walther von Lüttwitz in 1920 and one led by Hitler's National Socialists in 1923—and hundreds of political assassinations. Between 1923 and 1925, France and Belgium occupied the Ruhr, Germany's industrial heartland, because the country had defaulted on its reparation payments. The population was shocked and outraged: not even during the war had foreign troops set foot on German soil. It was a humiliating reminder of the republic's political and military weakness.

Even more catastrophic were two economic crises. In 1922/23, growing inflation gave way to unheard-of levels of hyperinflation. Ordinary products and foodstuffs now cost trillions of Reichsmarks, obliging many to resort to medieval bartering. The workers suffered horribly, while middle-class Germans saw their savings wiped out almost overnight. A currency reform (November 1923) and a restructuring of the reparation payments coupled with significant American loans (August 1924) inaugurated a period of economic stability and relative prosperity, but only a few years later disaster struck again. In 1929, the Wall Street Crash caused a worldwide recession. Germany was hit particularly hard. Unemployment skyrocketed and poverty gripped the nation. Weimar democracy, with its constant changes of government, appeared weaker than ever. Radical solutions were called for—or so many people felt.

The main beneficiary of this extremist atmosphere was Hitler's Nazi Party, which went from 2.6% of the vote in 1928 to 18.3% in 1930. In 1932, its share of the vote went up even further, to 37.3%, making it the largest party in the German parliament. In January 1933, Hitler was appointed Chancellor. The Nazi era had begun.

The Myth Gap II: Dignity

The political, economic, and cultural developments I have just outlined should not be understood in a merely cumulative fashion. They point beyond themselves to something deeper. Both in the case of America and that of Germany, what we are dealing with are depth-psychological, perhaps one should even say anthropological, issues. Ultimately, what is at stake is people's *identity*.

For human beings to exist, certain material conditions need to be in place. We need food, water, clothing, and shelter. As society develops technologically, so do our material needs. Things that once were luxuries, or did not even exist, become necessities. In addition to such material requirements, people have immaterial needs. We need to find our place in the world, a place where we can be at home. People are social beings. What is more, they are capable of choice, not animals moved by instinct; their social environment is a dynamic and evolving set of interactions and institutions, not a herd. Our sense of belonging is thus not a given, but won over time; once won, it can also be lost again. We acquire this feeling of being at home through our family, our friends, our work and colleagues, and larger collective affiliations such as our country, which unites us historically, culturally, and linguistically. Without these, the world would remain alien to us and we would be overwhelmed by its complexity and unpredictability.

Feeling at home is not just a matter of security, however. It is also about being accepted for who we are. That is to say, it is also about *dignity*.

The contemporary thinker who has highlighted this dimension of human existence most forcefully and convincingly is Francis Fukuyama. Taking inspiration from the philosophies of Plato, Hegel (1770–1831), and Alexandre Kojève (1902–1968), Fukuyama argues that the human psyche consists of three parts—desire, reason, and what Plato calls *thymos*, a sense of self-worth.[35] "*Thymos* is something like an innate human sense of justice: people believe that they have a certain worth, and when other people act as though they are worth less [...] they become angry. The intimate relationship between self-evaluation and anger can be seen in the English word synonymous with anger, 'indignation'. 'Dignity' refers to a person's sense of self-worth; 'in-dignation' arises when something happens to offend that sense of worth. Conversely, when other people see that we are not living up to our own sense of self-esteem, we feel *shame*; and when we are evaluated justly (i.e., in proportion to our true worth), we feel *pride*".[36]

Self-esteem comes from within, but it is not pre-given. It is mediated through our relationship with other people. It is therefore misleading to say that it is innate. What is innate is the potential for it. As Fukuyama puts it in a less misleading passage: "It is not enough that I have a sense of my own worth if other people do not publicly acknowledge my existence. Self-esteem arises out of esteem by others".[37] Our inner sense of dignity requires external recognition.

The idea dovetails with that put forward by Sartre in *Huis clos*, which we examined at the beginning of this chapter.[38] This should not come as a surprise. For what is the demand that other people recognize our dignity other than the demand that they accept us for who we are, that they respect our identity? Dignity is really a proud sense of one's identity. Hence, if other people acknowledge our dignity, they validate our identity. By contrast, if they believe that we do not deserve the worth we ascribe to ourselves, or if they think that they can just trample on it, they offend and undermine our sense of who we are.

Thymos is an extremely strong motivator. It can overcome the desiring part of the psyche that needs nourishment, as when someone goes on hunger strike. It may also overwhelm the rational, calculating, part of the psyche, as when we lash out against a mean-spirited superior who is in a position to sack us. The most iconic examples are to be found in westerns such as John Sturges's classic *The Magnificent Seven*, in which a group of downtrodden Mexican villagers, ignoring the rational cost-benefit analysis favouring self-preservation, throw caution to the wind and rise up against the much more powerful bandit Calvera and his men. (In accordance with a somewhat problematic ethnic trope, they then seek help from a group of courageous American gunslingers led by Yul Brynner—an obvious metaphor for America's "manifest destiny").[39]

Thymos, Fukuyama points out, also transcends economic desire. Thus, while there were and are economic components to the civil-rights movement's fight for equality, ultimately the movement is about human dignity. The legalization of gay marriage has had economic implications, but mere economic equality could have been achieved through civil unions. Gay marriage is really about full social acceptance of gay identity. Even seemingly purely economic issues—say, the demand for higher wages—as a rule have a strong thymotic dimension.

In spite of the recent rise of identity politics, many liberals still vastly underestimate the role that thymos plays in life in general and politics in particular. They ascribe Trump's victory largely to the economic deprivation of his base, to be countered by various "plans" and "programmes".

Hitler's rise to power, too, is often seen as having its roots in economics, specifically the devastating repercussions of the Wall Street Crash. Such views rely on a reductive—economistic and rationalistic—concept of human nature. As the cognitive scientist George Lakoff puts it in an incisive critique of his fellow progressives: "If we just tell people the facts", so progressives tend to believe, "they'll all reach the right conclusions. But we know from cognitive science that people do not think like that."[40] Yet many progressives cling to this belief all the same, which blinkers "Democratic politics in a very important way. It is assumed that voters will vote their self-interest. [...] People do *not* necessarily vote in their self-interest. They vote their identity. They vote their values. They vote for who they identify with. They may identify with their self-interest. That can happen. It is not that people never care about their self-interest. But they vote their identity."[41]

This, then, is the situation in America and post-Imperial Germany. It is not just that many people's economic fortunes have taken a nosedive, leading to unemployment and poverty. It is not just that there have been major political changes that many people do not agree with. It is not just that many people have witnessed a range of cultural developments that they resent. What has happened in the eyes of large swathes of the population is that *they can no longer be who they are*. The ground has collapsed under their feet. They have lost all sense of belonging. "We don't know where we stand anymore. We don't count anymore. We have been abandoned. We no longer recognize where we are. We are strangers in our own country". It is their identity that has been destroyed.

A myth gap has emerged. To a significant proportion of the population, the optimistic stories they have been telling about themselves—about who they are and where they are going—seem mere illusions now. The equally upbeat stories that establishment politicians have been telling about them, validating their sense of identity, likewise ring hollow. It is this myth gap—the collapse of the American dream and the German dream, respectively—that explains Donald Trump's and Adolf Hitler's electoral success.

Filling the Myth Gap I: Conflict-based Storytelling

Donald Trump's and Adolf Hitler's electoral appeal lies not in their concrete campaign promises, which in any case are few and far between.[42] What they offer is a story of their electorate's identity, a new myth aimed at restoring "the people's" sense of dignity and destiny. By embracing this myth, their voters impose a new narrative structure on their uprooted lives.

The myths put forward by Trump and Hitler have a peculiar characteristic: they are *negative myths*. They explain why things have gone so disastrously wrong, and they do so by identifying a clear culprit, an enemy. Of course, they also promise to make things right again. But their oppositional thrust is significant. Much of their popularity derives from this against-ism, which is a much stronger unifier than any positive vision. After all, it is easy to agree on what is not working, but a good deal less easy to agree on what it should be replaced by. Moreover, the blame for what has gone wrong is placed not on abstract structures, but (as we saw in previous chapters) on concrete adversaries—the Jews, Mexican immigrants, establishment politicians, and so on. They are made responsible for everything that ails the country. This construction-and-demonization of an Enemy lends Trump's and Hitler's mythological imagination a dimension that is almost religious. Their myths are a kind of secular theodicy: they solve the problem of evil in the world.[43]

In foregrounding conflict, Trump and Hitler are applying a fundamental narrative principle first highlighted by Aristotle: fictional stories are built on problems.[44] If there is no problem, then there is no story (or at best some tedious avant-garde anti-story, which comes to the same thing). The more classic—that is to say, the more unforgettable—a story is, the more this principle applies. In Agatha Christie's stories, the problem is usually a murder, which is solved when the murderer is apprehended. In *The Magnificent Seven*, the problem is the exploitation of a Mexican village, which is overcome when Calvera and his men are eliminated. Sitcoms like *Friends* are likewise based on the principle "problem occurrence + problem resolution". Even so-called reality television follows this pattern. The producers of series such as *Big Brother* and *Love*

Island quickly discovered that merely showing attractive or famous people did not do it for the viewers. So they started to script and edit the programme so as to create narrative arcs based on conflict.

The mind thinks in stories, or at least that is its default position. Stories impose an intelligible structure on a chaotic and unpredictable reality. Literature and film teach us that the most popular stories are those that centre on conflict. This explains much of the appeal of tabloid newspapers, which thrive on reporting—or at any rate writing about—rows and fights between celebrities. More significantly, it goes a long way in explaining the attraction of Trump's and Hitler's negative myths. Both leaders display a shrewd understanding of the power of conflict in narrative.

Trump honed his storytelling skills first as a businessman and then as host of *The Apprentice*, a reality TV show that revolves entirely around problem-solving and competition. This experience is at the root of his approach to politics. He urged his staff early on "to think of every day as an episode of a reality show in which he defeated his enemies".[45] It is worth recalling that his chief political strategist, Steve Bannon, also had hands-on experience of conflict-based storytelling.[46] Before joining the 2015/16 Trump campaign, he led Breitbart News—the Internet-based media outlet best known for its unapologetic right-wing views and unrelenting attempts to unleash a culture war on America—and made documentaries such as *Border War* (2006, about illegal immigration), *Battle for America* (2010, on the Tea Party's assault on establishment politics), and *Generation Zero* (2010, a critique of Wall Street-style capitalism). Prior to that, Bannon was involved in a company whose activities centred on the massively multiplayer online role-playing game *World of Warcraft*.[47]

Hitler, for his part, drew inspiration from Wagner's operas, with their clashes between outsider heroes and establishment villains. As the British historian Ian Kershaw observes, "for Hitler, Wagner was more than the music alone".[48] What struck a chord with Hitler was the composer's vision of "a world of Germanic myth, of great drama and wondrous spectacle, of gods and heroes, of titanic struggle and redemption, of victory and death. It was a world where the heroes were outsiders who challenged the old order, like Rienzi, Tannhäuser, Stolzing, and Siegfried; or chaste saviours like Lohengrin and Parsifal. […] And it was a world created with grandiose vision by an artist of genius, an outsider and revolutionary, all-or-nothing refuser of compromise, challenger of the existing order, dismissive of the need to bow to the bourgeois ethic of working for a living, surmounting rejection and persecution, overcoming adversity to attain greatness".[49] The most obvious example of Hitler's awareness of conflict as a narrative device is of course his autobiography-cum-manifesto, which is not called *Mein Kampf* for nothing. Indeed, his own original title was even more explicitly against-ist: *4½ Jahre Kampf gegen Lüge, Dummheit und Feigheit. Eine Abrechnung*, or "Four and a Half Years of Struggle against Lies, Stupidity, and Cowardice: A Reckoning".

Filling the Myth Gap II: Negative Myths

What are the main features of Trump's and Hitler's negative myths?[50]

To begin with, there are the against-ist elements we explored in the third and fourth chapters—the focus on enemies and scapegoats, and the vilification of the establishment, the elite, and objective knowledge. There, we also examined how Trump and Hitler combine their core enemies—Mexican immigrants and the Jews, respectively—with various associate enemies. It is this container approach that enables them to conjure up the image of a single Enemy of mythical proportions. Thus, Trump links Mexican immigrants with criminals, who are being aided and abetted by the open-border policy of the Democratic Party, which has been taken over by radical socialists, who have the support of the fake media. A good example of Hitler's lumping-together approach is his adaptation of the *Dolchstoßlegende*, the conceit that Germany lost the First World War because it was "stabbed in the back" by a cowardly homefront led by Social Democrats, who—this is the National Socialist twist—are basically all Jews, whose rootless internationalism has permeated the Weimar Republic and is behind its unwillingness to resist the Allies' financial exploitation of Germany and its inability to protect the German people's livelihood and values, and this lack of patriotism and of moral fibre in its turn is being heralded by the *Lügenpresse*, the Jewified "lying press".[51]

The conflict, then, is not merely a competition between opposing political parties and policies. It is a political and cultural civil war. (Not for nothing did the Nazis call their rise to power the *Kampfzeit*, or "Time of Struggle"). In this war, the other is not another you, but the very opposite of you, the one who is wiping out your kind. The enemy is the Other, the monster that lives among us. This is the mythical core of the conflict: it is a battle between good and evil. We must slay the monster that is laying waste to our community. And it is the final battle. After this reckoning, we will either rise from the ruins, or we will have perished forever.

The positive mirror image of this society at war with itself is a specific notion of the nation—an America or Germany made whole again. As Nicholas O'Shaughnessy puts it in *Selling Hitler*, the National Socialist myth was above all "a historical narrative of rebirth, a 'decay-regeneration metaphor'".[52] The same is true of Trump's Make America Great Again myth.

This mythical nationalism is based on the evocation of a spurious us, "the people". The nation is not everyone living on its soil, but a segment of it—a large segment, to be sure, but still a segment only. As we saw earlier, negative myths require that our "true" community be smaller than society as a whole, because that feels safer, more familiar. By redefining their respective countries in this way, Trump and Hitler offer their potential voters an easy-to-acquire group cohesion. After all, tribal identities come more naturally to human beings than do Constitution-based ones. In Nicholas O'Shaughnessy's words, "Nazism"—and the same applies to Trumpian populism—"was the antidote for the culturally dispossessed. […] The individual was no longer alone in the world but a member of a group with which he was united by ties of blood, of inherited folk wisdom, culture and history, and by antagonism to all that threatened these things. […] Nazism offered the […] rootless […] a regression to the warm, febrile tribal family".[53]

What we are dealing with is a form of ethno-nationalism. It is true (in my view anyway) that Trump was not a convinced racist. Here, he and Hitler were worlds apart. Yet it is hard to deny that this is the sentiment Trump was playing to—a nationalism centred on a presumed Anglo-Saxon identity. The ethno-national community is composed of those

5 Identity and Negative Myths 211

people who are united by a common ancestry, or more precisely by some vague bogus notion of this commonality.

O'Shaughnessy makes an important point in this context when he points to the shifting geographical spread of the German-speaking lands throughout history.[54] How do you create a national identity when your country has grown out of a long historical process of cross-pollination involving many different ethnicities and cultural traditions? The same question poses itself with respect to the "melting pot" that is the United States. Do you see this diversity as a strength, or do you take refuge in an imagined homogeneity? Trump and Hitler elect to do the latter.

The (true) people are credited with especial decency, common sense, and what O'Shaughnessy terms a "kind of native authenticity".[55] Their grounded, solid character distinguishes them both from the migrant worker's shifty obsequiousness and from the elite's cosmopolitan arrogance. Theirs is a life of honesty and hard work. They know in their guts what is right, whatever the mainstream media, partisan politicians, and corrupt judges are saying. And they possess good old-fashioned values. Not for them the permissiveness of Weimar-era Babylon Berlin—with its gay scene, specialized brothels, drug dens, Satanic rituals, and fetishist pornography[56]—or America's politically correct toleration of everything and anything from abortion to transgenderism.

Hitlerian and Trumpian populism not only glorifies the people's so-called greatness. It also seeks to ensure that there are clear external signs of it. Part of Hitler's and Trump's mythical narrative is therefore the emphasis on military power. This is not merely about having an offensive and defensive capability. It is also about external recognition of one's place in the world. As Trump puts it in his book *Great Again: How to Fix Our Crippled America*: "we have to maintain the strongest military in the world, by far. [...] When people know that we will use force if necessary and that we really mean it, we'll be treated differently. With respect".[57]

Hitler, too, in his public pronouncements stresses the central importance of the military. In *Mein Kampf*, for example, he writes: "No more glorious monument can be dedicated to [Germany's military] than a statement of the truth that it was slandered, hated, combated, and also feared by all inferior peoples".[58] Upon coming to power, he immediately set about restoring his country's military might, in open defiance of the

Versailles Treaty. Now, Hitler always intended to wage war. But his compatriots did not know this. Yet they overwhelmingly supported the build-up of the new Reich's armed forces, including the introduction of compulsory military service. They did so not because they were yearning for war (almost none of them were), but because they wanted to see their national pride restored. And then, of course, there were the endless uniformed Party rallies and military parades. President Trump, meanwhile, had his own big military parade, "Salute to America", on 4 July 2019. In a speech interrupted again and again by the "USA, USA, USA" chants of his supporters, he said that today "we remember that we all share a truly extraordinary heritage. Together, we are part of one of the greatest stories ever told, the story of America".[59]

A great people must have a great history. This is a central feature of Hitler's and Trump's mythical imagination aimed at reviving their supporters' identity. The past—or at least the distant past, before things went all wrong—is a source of pride. Conversely, questioning that past is unpatriotic: it is tantamount to treason.

The propagation of the presumed greatness of German history is a key element in the National Socialists' publicity campaign, and Hitler has little trouble selling it to his nostalgic electorate. Later, when free and fair elections give way to acclamation based on one-party state propaganda backed up by force and repression, it becomes a crucial element of National Socialist education. Thus, Werner May's popular *Politischer Katechismus für den jungen Deutschen in Schule und Beruf* (Political Catechism for the Young German Man in the Classroom and the Workplace, 1935) states:

> Great and glorious is the history of your people, and you can be proud of it. The days of betrayal, the years of shame that Germany had to endure between 1918 and 1933, are a reminder that you must work and create for the resurrection of your fatherland. The great men of your people call you to loyalty! Never forget that a Frederick the Great, a Bismarck, that the heroes of the world war who now sleep in foreign soil or in the depths of the sea were your brothers. In the streets of the cities, in the market places and the villages, the memorials call to you: never forget that we were happy

to shed our blood, for you, for Germany's holy soil, for the good and the life of this great people.⁶⁰

Werner May's words should not be misunderstood as expressing a desire for armed conflict. Hitler carefully kept his intention to go to war secret from the German people. Even in September 1939, when the German army invaded Poland, he claimed that this was a matter of self-defence. Germany was "returning fire", he said when announcing what would be the start of the Second World War. Werner May's reference to war memorials is meant to give the German people a sense of identity. It is not a vow to bring back the past wholesale. The same applies to Donald Trump's defence of Confederate statues, as we will see now.

For the populist, the past represents a source of rootedness and native authenticity. It was a time when you—or your "kind"—still counted and your place in society was still secure. It was a time when other people respected you even if they did not like you. (Hitler's remarks about the German military cited above are telling in this regard.) Of course, this golden era never really existed. The populist's past is an imaginary past. A realistic view of history would not help you regain your dignity. The working and middle classes' factual political weakness during the Kaiserreich, or slavery and its legacy in America, are hardly things to be proud of. What is needed is a *retrospective utopia*, a concept the Nazis took to extremes with their glorious "Aryan past".

What makes this retrotopian vision so powerful—and so hard to refute—is that the people who are seduced by it *know* on some level that it is unrealistic. Perhaps it would be better to say that they are aware of its selective nature. It is a mistake to think of Trump's and Hitler's supporters as devoid of all intelligence, knowledge, and moral sense. They do not want to bring back 1970s medical technology, or live in huts like the Germanic tribes did. Nor are the majority out-and-out racists who think that blacks are inferior to whites, or that all Jews should be killed. (In fact, Nazi propaganda actively sought to enable the German population to rationalize and repress what was being done to the Jews.) The populist leader's retrotopia is akin to a football manager's speech reminding the players of the club's "glory days". It is pep talk telling the team that they can "do it again". No player will take such a picture as an objective history lesson, or as a suggestion to start playing the way football was played thirty years ago.

Let me explain this further by zooming in on Trumpian populism. I believe that the mindset of many Trump supporters can be compared to that of an average 1970s white person who says: "I am not a racist. Look at the parent-teacher association I chair: about one third of our members are black, and I have no problem with that". Fast-forward fifty years and the ratio has been reversed. Now it is the white members who make up one third of the association. But *that* no longer feels right. Now the chairperson feels threatened. The implicit racism that was there from the start comes to the surface: "We are being squeezed out. Next thing you know there'll be none of us left". The chairperson's time is out of joint.

What we are dealing with is not unadulterated racism, but a more subtle form of racism—racist anti-racism. The chairperson wants to be able to say: "African Americans, too, are welcome to join our parent-teacher association". But such an attitude is possible only if the people in charge are white—if the *us* is white folk. That is no longer the case, and it is this that renders our chairperson receptive to the populist's ethno-nationalist message.

Such is the way many Trump voters experience the world. Their identity—they feel—is being whittled away. "We are no longer in charge. We have lost control of our lives". This is why birtherism resonates: it may not be literally true, but somehow Obama feels illegitimate. "We are no longer respected. We do not count anymore". This is why Trumpians are put off by the Black Lives Matter movement: not because they believe that the police always do the right thing, but because they feel that the movement ignores *their* plight. "Even our past is being taken away from us". *Gone with the Wind*—racist. *Baby, It's Cold Outside*—no longer acceptable. Confederate statues—monuments of shame. "So we simply forget about our ancestors?" And so on.

Such ethno-nationalism is deeply problematic, to put it mildly. But we must understand how and why it finds resonance if we are to get a handle on the Trump phenomenon, both philosophically and politically. Not least, we must acknowledge that most people who see things this way are not blind to police brutality, including the killing of African Americans; that they do not think the Confederacy should have won; and that they do not want to reintroduce segregation, let alone slavery. We are not dealing simply with a lack of enlightenment that can be remedied by providing empirical information and moral education. The mythical imagination operates on a different plane than that of facts. In the final analysis, it is about a sense of self-worth. Hence, it can only be countered politically with another form of mythical imagination, one that creates a more positive and more inclusive story of American identity.

There is a clear economic dimension to Trump's and Hitler's mythological imagination, but it is secondary to its cultural thrust. Indeed, economics is seen almost entirely through a cultural lens. Steve Bannon has provided a succinct characterization of this approach: "A country is not an economy. A country is a culture that has an economy".[61] He goes on to say that what is needed is an "American economic nationalism" that "is about the nurturing of an economy that has manufacturing, agriculture—all of that—that can sustain the American family, and therefore, American society".[62] The economistic focus on mere profit and the accompanying glorification of international free trade—he says—are thus a mistake. Once you sever the link between a country's economy and its culture, the social fabric dissolves. "Look at America in 2017. We're so close to losing America as the culture we know [...] That's why there's an opioid crisis. I mean, we have a crisis in the Midwest and with the working class around the country where people have lost their jobs, and now they have to go get government assistance. They lose their dignity. And what do they do? They do opioids and go look at pornography".[63]

National Socialism similarly stresses the interconnection of national culture and economics. Without the right cultural framework, there is no ennobling work, just grubby moneymaking, Werner May declares in his *Politischer Katechismus*, taking up the Nazis' infamous distinction between *Jewish rapacious capital* and *Aryan productive capital.*[64] Conversely, if people cannot participate in the economy, or if their work has no wider social significance, they lose their sense of identity and the community disintegrates. Unemployment means "not being allowed to create, being excluded, being on the sidelines".[65] Accordingly, the Weimar Republic's mass unemployment was responsible for the nation's "financial impoverishment" and "economic weakness", but also for the "debilitation of its soul [*seelische Kraft*]".[66]

Hitler's and Trump's narratives do not propose a transformation of the existing economic system along socialist or communist lines. National "Socialism" is hardly more socialist than American economic nationalism. Big business continues to play a central role, while the workers do not gain any significant influence. Hitler's and Trump's appeal lies above all in the promise to protect ordinary hard-working folk from corporate greed, unfair international competition, and interference by foreign powers. The German historian Karl Dietrich Bracher has described this element of the National Socialist message with especial clarity: "The successful onslaught of National Socialism on the middle classes begun in 1929 was closely connected with the frequently invoked 'anti-capitalist sentiments' of these groups. What they wanted was not socialism but protection of the small property owners against the growing incursion of big capital".[67]

Similarly, Trump's message of economic nationalism is above all a promise to restore the security and dignity of the American worker within a fairer capitalist system. The way to create such a system, a system that works for all Americans and not just the happy few, is—so the message goes—by sheltering it from globalism, be it in the form of financial capitalism à la Wall Street, free-trade agreements such as NAFTA, supranational organizations such as the WTO, or countries like China. As Steve Bannon puts it in a conversation with Keith Koffler, the real enemy is less the Democratic Party, or the old-style Republican Party, than the "Party of Davos" (a reference to the Swiss town that hosts the world's annual top economic forum). This global financial, managerial, scientific, and cultural elite is the driving force behind both political parties' destructive neoliberalism and the root cause of our social ills: "They just live in this kind of globalist reality, the party of Davos [do], where what happens in Shanghai and what happens in Chelsea, and London, and what happens in Paris or the Hamptons is more what drives them than what happens [among average Americans]. [...] The party of Davos—when it's all going right they get all the upside and the little guy gets nothing. He gets more foreign competition. He gets illegal aliens".[68] When things go wrong, the big corporations get bailed out, and the little guy still gets nothing. American economic nationalism therefore means "that we sort out particularly this crony capitalism".[69]

The point I am making is not so much that Hitler's and Trump's anti-capitalist diatribes are not actually all that anti-capitalist. My point is that in the final analysis their economic message is not really an economic one at all. It plays to the voters' desire for fairness, for dignity, for a secure and respectable place in society. Herein lies the mythical power of this aspect of Hitler's and Trump's story-telling: rather than offering the voters a set of policy proposals, it promises to make them full members of the community again.

This point is of such crucial importance that I wish to provide further support for it by citing a number of key passages from Karl Dietrich Bracher's classic study *The German Dictatorship: The Origins, Structure and Consequences of National Socialism*. Bracher lucidly describes the cohesive, identity-creating, force of the Nazis' economic narrative. At the same time, his description implicitly confirms the parallels between then and now that I have drawn. "It was"—Bracher writes—"the rural and urban 'middle classes', in the broad sense of the term, which started and carried out the breakthrough of the NSDAP. The 'panic of the middle classes', which set in with the outbreak of the economic crisis, was sharpened by the fact that the middle class felt threatened not only economically but, more importantly, socially as well. The violent reaction which drove many of its members toward the radical Right arose out of a subjective feeling of crisis in a time of social upheaval in an industrial, democratic age. The power of the old middle class continued to decline within an expanding population; its nervous irritability and susceptibility to radical slogans were the result of this prestige loss as well as of economic plight. Out of a general desire for security after the catastrophe of the inflation, this group, after having for so long maintained an apolitical isolation from democracy, reacted in a markedly political fashion to the new crisis. And that was why it turned to [Hitler's] 'new' party".[70]

The story war over Germany's economic distress was "fought out with particular sharpness in the mixed industrial-agrarian regions".[71] The reason Hitler did so well there lay in the fact that he spoke to the electorate's nationalism as well as their economic needs. More precisely, it lay in his ability to subsume economics into a narrative of values, self-worth, and belonging. His "dual fight of the 'idealistic, national' people against the decadent 'foreign powers' of both proletarian as well as capitalist materialism proclaimed the primacy of national 'idealism' over economic materialism. [...] Therefore, contemporary socialist interpretations which saw the NSDAP in purely socio-economic terms as a reactionary middle class and peasant movement considered only one side of the phenomenon and ultimately failed in the task of unmasking it ideologically and effectively halting its progress. What is important is that National Socialist propaganda [...] brought into play attractions and ties which promised an integration beyond the manifold immediate [that is, economic] interests."[72]

Hitler's mythical synthesis of economic security and national identity put him in an exceptionally strong political position. Broadly speaking, the traditional Right did not have a convincing economic message, while the traditional Left and the communists were seen by many as overly internationalist or simply unpatriotic. Hitler, by contrast, catered to all voters, or at least to a great many of them (all the more so as his lack of concrete policies allowed him to be all things to all people and adapt his message according to audience and circumstance—a topic I will explore in the final chapter). To cite Bracher one more time: "National Socialism's dynamics and appeal [...] did not lie in a socially closed interest movement of the middle classes—that is, a class movement—but, on the contrary, in its emphasis on being a unifying movement of the most varied and antagonistic groups", a movement that exerted a "cohesive force across heterogeneous interests, considerations, and feelings".[73]

Another central feature of Hitlerian and Trumpian mythology is the glorification of the leader. This is an issue I have already examined from several angles. The first chapter, for example, looked at Hitler's and Trump's highly conscious strategies to construct a charismatic—auratic—persona for themselves. Such auratification of the leader resonates with the populist electorate, because the more insecure and beleaguered people feel, the more certainty and protection they require. This is something we saw in the third chapter: the more (imaginary) enemies people have, the greater their need for (idealized) saviours.

The mythological imagination transforms the charismatic leader into an archetypal hero. This process works in two directions. It is on the one hand the effect of concrete "mythologizing" public-relations endeavours; say, Hitler's and Trump's descending-from-heaven stratagem discussed in

5 Identity and Negative Myths 219

the first chapter. On the other hand, it results from a peculiar receptivity on the part of the audience, who—driven by a desperate hope and taken in by the leader's promises and real or perceived successes—*want* him to be their Redeemer. This is why I used the Jungian term *archetypal hero*. Archetypes are primordial images that arise from the mind's tendency to organize experience in specific patterns. It is this archetypal mould, "a kind of [psychological] readiness", as Jung says, that leads humankind "to produce over and over again the same or similar mythical ideas".[74]

The hero archetype is one such primordial image. It can be found in religion, fairy tales, literature, art, and popular culture. But it also manifests itself in real life. Confronted with certain people, we have a propensity to ascribe superhuman qualities to them. If these qualities are positive, they produce hero worship; if they are negative, they lead to demonization and scapegoating. As Jung himself puts it, "the archetypes usually appear in projection; and, because projections are unconscious, they appear on persons in the immediate environment, mostly in the form of abnormal over- or under-evaluations which provoke misunderstandings, quarrels, fanaticisms, and follies of every description. Thus, we say, 'He makes a god of so-and-so', or, 'So-and-so is Mr. X's *bête noire*'. In this way, too, there grow up modern myth-formations, i.e., fantastic rumours, suspicions, prejudices".[75]

There are other archetypes, too; for instance, the wise old man, or the innocent virgin. The important thing is that the qualities we detect in such people are not actually inherent in them. They are attributions, ascriptions. Why certain people, and not others, activate archetypal perceptions in us is a sociopsychological question, one that involves the historical context and the emotional state of society as least as much as the personality and behaviour of the "hero", "wise old man", or "innocent virgin". It also involves the nature and reach of the mythical—that is to say, mythologizing—narrative. The heroic Hitler or Trump is not an objective category, but a subjective one; not an external reality, but an inner certainty. The archetypal hero "dwells nowhere except in the soul of man".[76] People *create* their heroes. "And", as Jung puts it in his conversations with the psychologist Richard I. Evans, "afterward you may discover that it was a hell of a mistake".[77]

Finally, Hitlerian and Trumpian mythology possesses a number of distinctive presentational features. These include the appeal to emotions instead of facts (a topic I touched upon in the previous chapter); the inconsistent line of argument; the use of symbols that encapsulate and enhance the message, such as "Make America Great Again" baseball caps and the Swastika; and the absolute certainty with which the message is expressed, coupled with a complete aversion to political correctness, nuance, and self-criticism. As these are highly complex issues that deserve to be discussed in depth, I will postpone them until the last chapter, which deals exclusively with questions of rhetoric and narrative truth.

For the time being, let us leave mythology behind and turn to reality. What were Hitler and Trump really like? What was their psychological make-up? And how were they as managers, as leaders? The next chapter will seek to answer these the questions.

Notes

1. This is not obvious. For example, Florian Coulmas's recent 140-page *Identity* (Oxford: Oxford University Press, 2019), published in the well-known "Very Short Introduction" series, manages to say next to nothing about the relationship between identity and story-telling.
2. This is less clear in Philip K. Dick's novel *Do Androids Dream of Electric Sheep?* (1968), on which *Blade Runner* is based, even though the novel does mention several times that some androids have false, "synthetic", memories. Yet both the novel and the film confront us with a fascinating paradox. When the cold and distant Rachael, who believes that she is human, finds out that she is a humanoid, she paradoxically becomes *more human* in mind and behaviour. The reason for this, I would suggest, is that she now has a real past. Her new awareness of herself, her heightened existential depth, transforms her. Other texts by Dick—such as his 1956 short story "The Minority Report", which provided the basis for Steven Spielberg's 2002 film *Minority Report*—approach the same issue from the other end by asking to what extent we can still said to be human if the way we project ourselves into the future is predetermined or (which is not quite the same) can be known in advance.

3. Cf. Sartre's remarks on the play reproduced in *Les écrits de Sartre*, eds. Michel Contat and Michel Rybalka (Paris: Gallimard, 1970), p. 101.
4. See Wilhelm Schapp, *In Geschichten verstrickt. Zum Sein von Mensch und Ding* (fifth ed. Frankfurt am Main: Klostermann, 2012; first published 1953); cf. Jonathan Gottschall, *The Storytelling Animal: The Stories That Make Us Human* (Boston and New York: Mariner Books, 2013; first published 2012), p. 1. In the remainder of this chapter, I also draw on Alex Evans, *The Myth Gap: What Happens When Evidence and Arguments Aren't Enough?* (London: Eden Project Books, 2017), Set Godin, *All Marketers Are Liars / Tell Stories* (New York: Portfolio / Penguin, 2009; first published 2005), Dan P. McAdams, *The Stories We Live By: Personal Myths and the Making of the Self* (New York: The Guildford Press, 1997; first published 1993), Jonah Sachs, *Winning the Story Wars* (Boston, Mass.: Harvard Business Review Press, 2012), Annette Simmons, *The Story Factor: Inspiration, Influence, and Persuasion through the Art of Storytelling* (rev. ed. New York: Basic Books, 2006) and *Whoever Tells the Best Story Wins* (New York etc.: Amacom, 2007).
5. Cf. Simmons, *Story Factor*, pp. 53–54.
6. Aristotle, "On the Art of Poetry", in *Aristotle, Horace, Longinus: Classical Literary Criticism*, trans. T. S. Dorsch (Harmondsworth: Penguin, 1984; first published 1965), pp. 29–75 (41).
7. With a fake Vermeer, the price would go down. With a forged minor master, the price would go up if the painter were a famous counterfeiter such as Han van Meegeren.
8. Specifically, Debord claims that these images, far from merely being things in society we look at, interpose themselves between us and society. They are representations *through which* we look at our world. The problem is, Debord says, mediated by images everything becomes a spectacle. Wars become television entertainment; parliamentary democracy turns into a series of propaganda films. What is more, this de-realization of social relations is at the same time their commodification. We become the consumers of our own lives—an existence in which people advertise, buy, and sell themselves, their emotions, and their social relations (a development we can observe today in an extreme form with reality shows, YouTube, TikTok, and so on). See Guy Debord, *The Society of the Spectacle*, trans. Ken Knabb (Berkeley: Bureau of Public Secrets, 2014; first published in French 1967) and *Comments on the Society of the*

Spectacle, trans. Malcolm Imrie (London and New York: Verso, 1998; first published in French 1988).
9. Cited in David Sterritt, *The Films of Jean-Luc Godard: Seeing the Invisible* (Cambridge etc.: Cambridge University Press, 1999), p. 20.
10. Gottschall, *Storytelling Animal*, p. 102. The phrase *blooming, buzzing confusion* was first used by William James in *The Principles of Psychology* (1890) to describe a baby's experience of the world.
11. Godin, *All Marketers Are Liars*, p. 105.
12. Godin, *All Marketers Are Liars*, p. 13.
13. Godin, *All Marketers Are Liars*, p. 41.
14. Godin, *All Marketers Are Liars*, p. 18.
15. Godin, *All Marketers Are Liars*, p. 19.
16. See Laurence Rees's BBC documentary *The Dark Charisma of Adolf Hitler: Leading Millions into the Abyss* (2012) as well as his 2016 Tans lecture and his conversation with Atticus Mullikin (both available on YouTube). I will come back to this issue in Chap. 7.
17. Nicholas O'Shaughnessy, *Selling Hitler: Propaganda and the Nazi Brand* (London: Hurst & Company, 2016), p. 103.
18. O'Shaughnessy, *Selling Hitler*, p. 104.
19. On myth, cf. Wilfred Barner, Anke Detken, and Jörg Wesche (eds.), *Texte zur modernen Mythentheorie* (Stuttgart: Reclam, 2003), Pierre Maranda, *Mythology* (Harmondsworth: Penguin, 1972), and Robert A. Segal, *Myth* (second ed. Oxford: Oxford University Press, 2015).
20. Cf. Gottschall, *Storytelling Animal*, p. 124.
21. Sachs, *Winning the Story Wars*, p. 60.
22. Sachs, *Winning the Story Wars*, p. 60.
23. Cf. the discussion of crowd psychology in the previous chapter.
24. Martin Luther King, Jr., *A Testament of Hope: The Essential Writings and Speeches*, ed. James Melvin Washington (New York: HarperCollins, 1986), pp. 217 and 219.
25. See Roland Barthes, *Mythologies*, trans. Annette Lavers (London: Vintage, 1993; first published in French 1957) and *The Eiffel Tower and Other Mythologies*, trans. Richard Howard (Berkeley, Los Angeles, and London: University of California Press, 1977; first published in French 1957).
26. Barthes, *Mythologies*, p. 124.
27. Barthes, *Mythologies*, p. 143.

28. Rudyard Kipling's poem *The White Man's Burden: The United States and the Philippine Islands* was first published in 1899.
29. See Sachs, *Winning the Story Wars*, especially chapter 3. Cf. Evans, *Myth Gap*.
30. Sachs, *Winning the Story Wars*, p. 58.
31. Sachs, *Winning the Story Wars*, p. 61.
32. Evans, *Myth Gap*, p. 104.
33. Cf. Fareed Zakaria, *The Post-American World* (London: Allen Lane, 2008).
34. What Matt Ridley writes about early industrial England applies equally to the industrializing German Empire: "There are still people [...] who follow Karl Marx in believing that the industrial revolution drove down most living standards, by cramming carefree and merrie yokels into satanic mills and polluted tenements, where they worked till they broke and then coughed their way to early deaths. Is it really necessary to point out that poverty, inequality, child labour, disease and pollution existed before there were factories? In the case of poverty, the rural pauper of 1700 was markedly worse off than the urban pauper of 1850 and there were many more of him. [...] The reason that the poverty of early industrial England strikes us so forcibly is that this was the first time writers and politicians took notice of it and took exception to it, not because it had never existed before". See Matt Ridley, *The Rational Optimist: How Prosperity Evolves* (London: Fourth Estate, 2011; first published 2010), pp. 218 and 220.
35. See especially Francis Fukuyama, *The End of History and the Last Man* (London: Hamish Hamilton, 1992) and *Identity: Contemporary Politics and the Struggle for Recognition* (London: Profile Books, 2018). Cf. also Henk de Berg, *Das Ende der Geschichte und der bürgerliche Rechtsstaat. Hegel—Kojève—Fukuyama* (Tübingen and Basel: Francke, 2007) and "Bonjour Tristesse: Alexandre Kojève's Reading of Françoise Sagan", *Phrasis* 50.1, 2009, pp. 3–20.
36. Fukuyama, *End of History*, p. 165.
37. Fukuyama, *Identity*, p. 10.
38. Sartre took many of his ideas from Hegel and Kojève.
39. Antoine Fuqua's 2016 remake seeks to neutralize the various ethnic clichés.
40. George Lakoff, *The All New Don't Think of an Elephant* (White River Junction, Vermont: Chelsea Green, 2014), p. 15.
41. Lakoff, *All New Don't Think of an Elephant*, p. 17 (emphasis added).

42. Of course, once in power Trump and Hitler enacted a great many concrete policies. But their *electoral appeal* cannot be explained by any concrete plans and proposals. I will return to this issue in Chap. 7.
43. Cf. Gottschall, *Storytelling Animal,* p. 116. Gottschall makes this point with reference to conspiracy theories in general.
44. Here, I draw above all on Gottschall, *Storytelling Animal,* chapter 3.
45. James Poniewozik, *Audience of One: Donald Trump, Television, and the Fracturing of America* (New York: Liveright, 2019), p. 249, referencing Maggie Haberman, Glenn Thrush, and Peter Baker, "The President vs. the Presidency", *New York Times,* 10 December 2017. On Trump's understanding of the relation between aesthetics and conflict, cf. also Omarosa's remarks about her time on *The Apprentice,* in Omarosa Manigault Newman, *Unhinged: An Insider's Account of the Trump White House* (London etc.: Simon & Schuster, 2018), pp. 21–35.
46. See Joshua Green, *Devil's Bargain: Steve Bannon, Donald Trump, and the Nationalist Uprising* (new ed. New York: Penguin, 2018) and Keith Koffler, *Bannon: Always the Rebel* (Washington, DC: Regnery, 2017).
47. The phrase *massively multiplayer online role-playing game* is usually shortened to MMORPG and pronounced *mor-peg*. In Joshua Green's summary, in *World of Warcraft* millions of subscribers battle each other "in the mythical realm of Azeroth, a fantasy world of elves, dwarfs, trolls, goblins, and dragons. Skilled players can win weapons, armor, and gold. These are, of course, *virtual* items acquired and used within the game. Yet ardent enthusiasts were willing to buy them for real money, in the real world, to help them conquer *World of Warcraft*". The company that Bannon was involved in created the opportunity for them to do so. The venture ultimately foundered on a lawsuit brought by players who—understandably—considered this practice unfair. See Green, *Devil's Bargain,* pp. 81–83 (81).
48. Ian Kershaw, *Hitler 1889–1936: Hubris* (London etc.: Penguin, 2001; first published 1998), p. 43. See also my analysis of Karl May's stories in Chap. 1.
49. Kershaw, *Hitler 1889–1936,* p. 43.
50. In addition to drawing on Trump's and Hitler's own pronouncements, I have benefited above all from Nicholas O'Shaughnessy's *Selling Hitler* (see note 17 above) as well as his *Politics and Propaganda: Weapons of Mass Seduction* (Manchester: Manchester University Press, 2004) and *Marketing the Third Reich: Persuasion, Packaging and Propaganda* (Oxford

and New York: Routledge, 2018). I also found the following Trump apologias useful: Newt Gingrich, *Understanding Trump* (New York: Hachette, 2018; first published 2017) and *Trump's America: The Truth about Our Nation's Great Comeback* (New York: Hachette, 2018) as well as Victor Davis Hanson, *The Case for Trump* (New York: Basic Books, 2019).

51. For the National Socialists' use of the terms "Jewification" and "lying press", see Chap. 3.
52. O'Shaughnessy, *Selling Hitler*, p. 157. The phrase *decay-regeneration metaphor* comes from Aristotle A. Kallis, *Propaganda and the Second World War* (Basingstoke: Palgrave Macmillan, 2000).
53. O'Shaughnessy, *Selling Hitler*, p. 193.
54. O'Shaughnessy, *Selling Hitler*, p. 209.
55. O'Shaughnessy, *Selling Hitler*, p. 165.
56. Cf. Mel Gordon, *Voluptuous Panic: The Erotic World of Weimar Berlin* (expanded ed. Los Angeles: Feral House, 2006) and *The Seven Addictions and Five Professions of Anita Berber: Weimar Berlin's Priestess of Depravity* (Los Angeles: Feral House, 2006).
57. Donald J. Trump, *Great Again: How to Fix Our Crippled America* (New York etc.: Threshold Editions, 2016; first published 2015 as *Crippled America*), pp. 32–33.
58. Adolf Hitler, *Mein Kampf*, trans. Ralph Manheim (Boston and New York: Houghton Mifflin Company, 1999), p. 279. For the original German, see Adolf Hitler, *Mein Kampf. Eine kritische Edition*, eds. Christian Hartmann, Thomas Vordermayer, Othmar Plöckinger, and Roman Töppel (Munich and Berlin: Institut für Zeitgeschichte, 2016), vol. 1, p. 725.
59. Donald J. Trump, speech at the "Salute to America" parade, Washington, DC, on 4 July 2019.
60. Werner May, *Politischer Katechismus für den jungen Deutschen in Schule und Beruf* (Breslau: Heinrich Handels Verlag, 1935), p. 31. This is the fourth—revised and expanded—edition of a book originally entitled *Deutscher Nationalkatechismus*.
61. Stephen K. Bannon, cited in Koffler, *Bannon*, p. 95.
62. Stephen K. Bannon, cited in Koffler, *Bannon*, pp. 93 and 95.
63. Stephen K. Bannon, cited in Koffler, *Bannon*, p. 96.
64. May, *Politischer Katechismus*, p. 58. The distinction between *raffendes Kapital* and *schaffendes Kapital* comes from Gottfried Feder, as we saw in Chap. 1.

65. May, *Politischer Katechismus*, p. 59.
66. May, *Politischer Katechismus*, p. 59.
67. Karl Dietrich Bracher, *The German Dictatorship: The Origins, Structure and Consequences of National Socialism*, trans. Jean Steinberg (Harmondsworth: Penguin, 1973; first published in German 1969), p. 201. Cf. O'Shaughnessy, *Selling Hitler*, p. 207.
68. Stephen K. Bannon, cited in Koffler, *Bannon*, pp. 89–90. Cf. the Munk debate *The Rise of Populism: Stephen K. Bannon vs. David Frum*, ed. Rudyard Griffiths (Toronto: Anansi, 2019).
69. Stephen K. Bannon, cited in Koffler, *Bannon*, p. 91.
70. Bracher, *German Dictatorship*, p. 201.
71. Bracher, *German Dictatorship*, p. 201.
72. Bracher, *German Dictatorship*, p. 202.
73. Bracher, *German Dictatorship*, p. 203.
74. Carl Gustav Jung, *Two Essays on Analytical Psychology*, trans. R. F. C. Hull (Princeton: Princeton University Press, 1977; first published 1953, revised and augmented 1966), p. 69.
75. Jung, *Two Essays*, p. 95.
76. Carl Gustav Jung, *The Archetypes and the Collective Unconscious*, trans. R. F. C. Hull (London: Routledge, 1991; first published 1959, revised 1968), p. 6.
77. Richard I. Evans, *Jung on Elementary Psychology: A Discussion between C. G. Jung and Richard I. Evans* (London and Henley: Routledge & Kegan Paul, 1979; originally published 1964 in a shorter version entitled *Conversations with Carl Jung*), p. 71.

6

Leadership Style

Was Trump the laziest President in American history? Listening to his critics, one could certainly get that impression. "I'm sure most older men in retirement homes live more active lives than does Donald Trump", MSNBC talkshow host Joe Scarborough concluded witheringly on *Morning Joe* halfway through the President's four-year term.[1] Even measured commentators have been shocked by the amount of time America's most important senior citizen spent in front of the TV. "It was scary", Bob Woodward writes in *Fear: Trump in the White House*.[2] "Trump didn't show up for work until 11:00 in the morning. Many times he watched six to eight hours of television in a day".[3] On the eve of his inauguration, Trump promised the American people he would "work so hard" for them,[4] but in the years that followed only his supporters saw any evidence of that (or chose to believe him, at any rate).

If he was not watching television, he was reading the papers, ringing up friends, talking to anyone who walked into the Oval Office when he happened to be there, having spur-of-moment bull sessions, and—of course—flooding Twitter with @realDonaldTrump messages. This, at least, is how it has seemed to many. And if he was not engaging in any of the activities above, he was out playing golf. Before taking office, Trump had repeatedly criticized Obama for spending too much time golfing. In office, Trump could be found on the golf course much more frequently than his predecessor.[5]

Institutional structures were largely ignored. There were two organizational charts. "The official org chart"—Trump's former Special Assistant Cliff Sims writes in his memoir—"looked like a typical White House, perhaps just a little more top heavy. The *real* org chart, however, was basically Trump in the middle and everyone he personally knew connected to him—like a hub and its spokes. This exacerbated staff tensions when the official hierarchy was upended by the reality of how Trump operated".[6] The President arrived at his decisions without much serious discussion with representatives of Republican party and state organs, away from administrative channels, and in his own time, which could be either worryingly slowly or scarily impetuously.

White House staffers used the impressive term *Executive Time* for the substantial meetings-free part of Trump's schedule, making his unofficial business sound professional and coordinated.[7] The reality was that the President's governing style was largely free-wheeling, and his working day largely unstructured.

Much the same can be said about Hitler's governing style and working day. Paperwork, office work, and indeed any kind of systematic work had not been his thing when he was still a would-be artist; and this did not change when he entered politics in 1919. Indeed, he retained his unmethodical approach to his duties to the very end. This is how the leading Hitler biographer Ian Kershaw describes the soon-to-be Chancellor's management style in the early 1930s: "Hitler contributed as good as nothing to the running and organization of the massively expanded Nazi Movement. His 'work-style' (if it could be called such) was unchanged from the days when the NSDAP was a tiny, insignificant *völkisch* sect. He was incapable of systematic work and took no interest in it. [...] To call [his office in the Party's Munich headquarters] Hitler's 'work-room' was a nice euphemism. Hitler rarely did any work there. [...] Even the big painting of Frederick the Great [...] could not motivate Hitler to follow the example of the Prussian king in diligent attention to duty. He had no regular working hours. Appointments were there to be broken. [...] Party workers at headquarters [...] could never find a fixed time to see Hitler, even about extremely important business. If they managed, clutching their files, to catch him when he entered [...], he would as often as not be called to the telephone and then apologize that he had to leave and would be back the next day. Should they manage to have their business attended to, it was normally dispatched with little attention to detail. [...] Often he would completely ignore something brought to his attention, deviating at a tangent into some current whim".[8]

Upon becoming Chancellor, Hitler initially forced himself into a more regular working pattern. He soon gave up. A nine-to-five job was not for him. Whenever he could, he would escape to his house in Munich, or to his holiday retreat in the Bavarian Alps. After his modest cottage there had been converted into a palatial residence, this new mansion—the Berghof—became the Reich's real seat of power.[9] It was at the Berghof that Hitler did his scheming and strategizing and took his major decisions. Here, his life was a little more structured, with regular walks and meals at fixed times. Yet his approach to work was as unsystematic as before, and he continued to leave bureaucratic matters, however important, to his underlings.

Hitler as a rule only emerged from his room at around 11.30 a.m. His work schedule was determined more by his inner needs than by organizational necessities. He discussed his ideas, if he discussed them at all, only in a small circle of loyal accomplices. Policy was made without regard for the intricacies of implementation. Administrative processes were left for others to sort out. Paperwork was entirely beneath him. Freedom and flexibility were paramount. At bottom, the Führer remained the anti-institutional bohemian he had always been.

Ways of Working

What are we to make of Trump's and Hitler's leadership style? Can it even be called a leadership style? How can they lead if they are not actually leading? How can they manage (in both senses of the word) without any apparent management skills? They do not even seem to be *trying* to control the party and the state they are supposed to be in control of. How is that possible?

Viewed from a democratic perspective, their leadership style is indeed deeply problematic: it is not just disorganized, but dangerous. The ship of state is steered not by the captain, but by whichever officers happen to be on deck at a particular moment in time. There are no clear lines of communication and hence no transparency and no oversight. There is no genuine political consultation and hence no system of checks and balances. As a result, there is a significant fault line in the way the country is being run. On the one hand, there is the day-to-day management, which is a largely anonymous, bureaucratic affair without much input from the Leader. On the other hand, there are the major decisions, which are highly personal, Bonapartist diktats without much input from political representatives or scientific advisors. These two concurrent processes are fundamentally at odds with each other—a recipe for governmental disorder.

Yet it was precisely its chaotic, non-deliberative nature that made this leadership style so suitable for politicians like Trump and Hitler. They were big-picture men both by inclination and by necessity. Managers who are too hands-on will inevitably get bogged down in the detail of their daily operations: the ability to delegate is a vital requirement for all leaders of large organizations. This is even more the case if your policies are unconventional; if your chief methods of persuasion are force of personality and propaganda rather than reasoned argument and fact-based discussion; and if your aim is to dominate rather than achieve institutional consensus. The moment you engage with the administrative process, you immediately get caught up in the self-referential logic of the system. Bureaucratic assessments require reports, which in their turn need assessing and hence require further reports. Committees generate sub-committees and working groups. Meetings lead to more meetings. Political consultation and expert opinion transform extremism into pragmatism, grand schemes into gradual projects. All this may ultimately contribute to a better—more responsible, more democratic—outcome, but that is not what the Leader is interested in most (or, in the case of Hitler, at all).

In the classic British sitcoms *Yes, Minister* and *Yes, Prime Minister*, quintessential civil servant Sir Humphrey Appleby constantly thwarts the more audacious plans of his political master by raising objections along the lines of "this is not the right time", "we need to do a feasibility study first", "there are too many legal complications", and "the plan is too expensive". The satirical television series makes a real-lift point: big ideas are always in danger of dying on the altar of bureaucratic immobilism. Refusing to accept this as a fact of political life, Trump and Hitler did everything to escape the clutches of their respective bureaucracies.

The very first page of *The Art of the Deal* has Trump saying: "Most people are surprised by the way I work. I play it very loose. I don't carry a briefcase. I try not to schedule too many meetings. I leave my door open. You can't be imaginative or entrepreneurial if you've got too much structure".[10] Trump's approach to the Presidency was a continuation of this basic conviction. Similarly, Hitler told his architect Albert Speer: "In the first few weeks [of my Chancellorship] every petty matter was brought to me for decision. Every day I found heaps of files on my desk, and however much I worked there were always as many again. Finally, I put an end to that nonsense. If I had gone on that way, I would never have accomplished anything, simply because that stuff left me no time for thinking. When I refused to see the files they told me that important decisions would be held up. But I decided that I had to clear the decks so I could give my mind to the important things. That way I governed the course of development instead of being governed by the officials".[11]

In order to make sense of their boss's approach to politics, Trump supporters such as Newt Gingrich and Cliff Sims have invoked Isaiah Berlin's famous 1953 essay *The Hedgehog and the Fox*.[12] The essay takes as its starting-point a line among the fragments of the Greek poet Archilochus (seventh century BC): "The fox knows many things, but the hedgehog knows one big thing".[13] Berlin then uses this distinction to divide people into two groups. Hedgehogs "relate everything to a single central vision, one system, less or more coherent or articulate, in terms of which they understand, think and feel", whereas foxes latch on to "the essence of a vast variety of experiences and objects [...] without, consciously or unconsciously, seeking to fit them into, or exclude them from, any one unchanging, all-embracing, sometimes self-contradictory and incomplete, at times fanatical, unitary inner vision".[14]

Drawing on Berlin's categorization, Newt Gingrich tweeted during the 2016 Presidential campaign: "Clinton is a fox who knows many things you can fact check. Trump is a hedgehog who knows one very big thing: We need change".[15] Cliff Sims concurs: "Trump is a hedgehog, viewing all of the world's problems through the lens that he is the agent who will deliver the needed change. [...] Trump had a certain single-mindedness about him. The left derided this as ignorance, even stupidity. But in my experience it was, for lack of a better word, hedgehoggishness".[16] Sims goes on to compare this approach to that of policy wonks such as Republican politician Paul Ryan: "Trump was the guy who punched his ultimate destination into the GPS, then sat back and turned on the radio. Paul Ryan was the computerized voice in the GPS, reciting every detail of every exit, turn, and lane change".[17]

Such a defence of Trump strikes me as reasonable, at least as far as it goes. What it obscures is that ignorance is still ignorance; that lack of consultation is unlikely to improve policy; and that autocracy—one person determining the country's "ultimate destination"—is incompatible with democracy. But Gingrich's and Sim's argument does explain well why at least some of the criticism of the executive hands-off approach is misguided.

There is another reason why it is inaccurate (and dangerous) to regard Trump and Hitler as lazybones: not having regular working hours does not equal being idle. Indeed, one might go so far as to say that both men were busy all the time. They had no office hours—but no free time either—because there was no dividing line between their private and their political existence. Trump always had to be "Trump", whatever situation he found himself in, just as Hitler always had to act "Hitler". Their most powerful asset was their so-called charismatic personality—what I analysed in the first chapter as their *aura*. Fostering this aura was a 24/7 job. Both politicians were forever selling themselves, checking and controlling their media image, and devising new ways of self-staging. At the same time, they were constantly thinking up new action plans and seeking to convince others of the desirability of these ventures.

Trump had been a monomaniac ever since he decided to follow in the footsteps of his father, the real-estate developer Fred Trump. Norma King describes in her biography of Donald Trump's first wife how "[Ivana's] life became a whirlwind of activity" [18] after she had tied the knot with the entrepreneur. Overnight, her private existence all but evaporated. "It was a rare Saturday night meal that was not interrupted by at least a half dozen telephone calls—every single one of them crucial".[19] Trump's architect Der Scutt recalled that his boss thought "nothing of calling me at seven a.m. on a Sunday and saying, 'I've got an idea. See you in the office in forty minutes'".[20] And when Donald Trump Jr—who by then was working for the Trump Organization—wanted to go on holiday to Africa for two weeks, his father reprimanded him "because you can come back and your business is no longer there".[21] That was the advantage of golf: "you play for three hours and you come back to the office".[22] This boundless energy was reportedly sustained by the use of pep pills, a habit that Trump appears to have continued into the White House.[23]

Hitler was even more of a monomaniac than Trump. He had no family life, no real friends, and no hobbies (unless one counts his occasional bowling).[24] His press secretary, Otto Dietrich, wrote after the war how the Führer "seemed unable to distinguish between his official and his private life. He carried out official business in the midst of his private life" and because he never really involved other people in his decisions "lived a private life in the midst of his public affairs".[25] Politics—his work, his "mission"—was his *raison d'être*. Without political success Hitler was a nobody, and he knew it. This placed enormous pressure on him, especially after he had started the Second World War. From late 1936 onwards, his personal physician, Dr Theodor Morell, had been providing him with a steady supply of uppers and downers in the form of injections, pills, and drugs. When the war began to turn sour, the doses increased, as did their frequency, though not—as is sometimes thought—to the extent of turning the Führer into a toxin-addled wreck.

Hitler was an essentially lonely man, but he was not a loner. "In fact"—Otto Dietrich observes—"he could not bear being by himself. His fear of solitude was striking. It often seemed to me that he was afraid of facing himself".[26] His relationship with Eva Braun, which he kept hidden from the outside world, was patriarchal and not without serious ups and downs. But it was not artificial, abusive, or otherwise abnormal. Nor does their sex life appear to have been out of the ordinary. Accusations of perversion—such as Hitler's alleged predilection for "golden showers"—came from his opponents and belong to the standard repertoire of political vilification. (Trump had to face the same allegation when he was

President.) Both in Munich and at the Berghof the Führer surrounded himself with all manner of companions ranging from chauffeurs and bodyguards to supporters and cronies as well as their wives and children. With them, he could be charming, jolly, and—occasionally and to a limited degree—even jokey.[27]

Inevitably, all of this was also work. Hitler continued to sell himself as "Hitler". With the possible exception of Eva Braun, his friends (if that is the right word) invariably fulfilled a professional role in his life. The Führer's relationship with his companions was almost entirely transactional. They got fame, fortune, and glory out of him; he got political support and loyal service out of them. Being the narcissist that he was, he also fed on their admiration and sycophancy.

After the war, there emerged a picture of Hitler's life at the Berghof as a largely unpolitical *dolce far niente*. That was a myth, as historians such as Heike Görtemaker have shown.[28] It was a myth propagated by the memoirs of the surviving members of Hitler's court, who were retrospectively seeking to distance themselves from their boss's racist, militaristic, and genocidal policies. In reality, Hitler took most of his major decisions at the Berghof, and his entourage—who knew about these decisions, supported them, and often helped carry them out—were fully complicit in the crimes that ensued.

Moreover, Hitler was working incessantly. One of his former valets, the erstwhile SS officer Heinz Linge, has provided what is probably the most realistic post-1945 picture of his boss's use of time at his so-called holiday retreat. Hitler "did more to tire himself out on the Berg than anywhere else. Looking at me he asked: 'Linge, you have seen me for ten years now. Haven't I always been a glutton for work?' I had to agree, for I had never seen him loafing. Lazybones Hitler, who killed time travelling, chatting, listening to records, watching films and sleeping, is a character of fantasy in some of the biographies of him. He was in reality a workhorse with limitless energy, a person who even at table had only work in his head".[29] During the war, the Führer desperately tried to find ways to take his mind off things. He seldom managed. Even when "hold[ing] forth on some question 'nothing to do with the war' he would be thinking all the while how he could bring this or that operational change into play at the front".[30] It was always about work, always about winning.

Emotional Distance

Despite his active social life and personal affability, the Führer ultimately remained a distant figure even in private. His interactions never filled the void of his inner life. In many ways, Hitler was an emotional as well as a moral vacuum. He never really opened up to anyone. Albert Speer was arguably closer to him than anyone else with the exception of Eva Braun. Following his twenty-year incarceration in Spandau Prison for war crimes and crimes against humanity, the former Nazi architect and Armaments Minister asked himself why he had been unable to see himself as Hitler's friend. What was missing? "Everything was missing. Never in my life have I met a person who so seldom revealed his feelings, and if he did so, instantly locked them away again. During my time in Spandau I talked with [fellow prisoner and former Deputy Nazi Party Leader Rudolf] Hess about this peculiarity of Hitler's. Both of us agreed that there had been moments when we felt we had come close to him. But we were invariably disillusioned. If either of us ventured a slightly more personal tone, Hitler promptly put up an unbreakable wall".[31]

Hitler was a pathological case—a genuine psychopath. Trump was not. Yet he, too, ultimately remained distant. He never slept in the same room as his spouses. To Marla Maples, his second wife, her husband was "a man obsessed with business to such a degree that he was emotionally detached from loved ones, including his four children".[32] She deplored how little he had been present in their lives: "I would have loved to have seen him be the kind of dad that would take us all to Disney World and sit around the dinner table without having to have the financial news on".[33] He had a great many associates and acquaintances, but virtually no real friends. And he seldom betrayed his state of mind. From an early age, he never let his guard down. "It was like he had this defensive wall around him, and he wouldn't let anyone get close",[34] a former schoolmate recalled. Only Trump knew what went on in Trump's mind—and that was exactly the way he wanted it.

Trump's supporters believed that he understood them, that he truly cared about them. Maybe he did. But many of his critics, including supporters-turned-critics who knew him well, have suspected that the empathy was fake. "Donald Trump's single greatest character flaw as a leader and human being", *The Apprentice* contestant and former Assistant to the President Omarosa Manigault Newman writes, "is his complete and total lack of empathy".[35] Trump simply possessed "no empathy or pity for anything or anybody",[36] the President's former Chief of Staff Reince Priebus (or someone familiar with his thinking) told Bob Woodward.

Crucially, this emotional distance was not merely a psychological disposition. It was also the conscious projection of an *auratic* personality. In the first chapter, I defined the Leader's so-called charisma with reference to Walter Benjamin's concept of the aura—the unique appearance of a distance, however close it may be. The populist leader is close to us (he shakes our hand and takes selfies with us, he fights for us, he is our voice), yet he remains far away (he is somehow different and cannot be appropriated, he moves in higher spheres, he is our Saviour). He is both like all of us and unlike any of us. This aura, I explained following Benjamin, is fake. It is the product of calculated behaviour and cunning PR that play to a certain receptivity on the part of the audience. Hitler and Trump could only be *the unique appearance of a distance* if they staged themselves as mysterious, ineffable, and hence at least to some extent as unapproachable. They understood this, if not intellectually then certainly intuitively, and acted accordingly.

Follow the News: Shape the Narrative

It is unsurprising that Trump spent so much time following the news. The President watched hours of cable television per day not for fun, but to keep tabs on his public image—his aura—with a view to maintaining and indeed enhancing it. He read the newspapers so assiduously for the same reason. In addition, the news gave him insights into the public image of other politicians and provided him with ammunition for his criticism—or mockery—of their perceived weaknesses.

The same can be said of Hitler. His former Press Secretary Otto Dietrich has described the Führer's approach to the news in detail: "All through the day, from noon to past midnight, Hitler insisted on having the latest [radio] broadcasts and the most recent items from the foreign press. The reports were delivered in writing to his personal servant, who always remained close by him and kept them ready at hand for him. In the morning they had to be at his bedroom door, in case Hitler awoke early. There has probably never been a head of government who was so swiftly and completely informed on public opinion throughout the world as Hitler".[37] The importance the Führer attached to such reports is also apparent from the form in which he wished to receive them: "He did not want summaries; he had to have the original news items, word for word. In addition he was kept posted on the newspaper opinion of almost every country; editorials were telephoned to Berlin several times a day, and from Berlin transmitted to wherever Hitler happened to be staying at the moment".[38]

Moreover, Hitler used newspapers, as well as magazines and popular non-fiction books, as sources of learning. Specialist literature was not his thing, unless it concerned weaponry or other technical topics. He was a typical autodidact, who acquired knowledge not by reading academic studies and listening to expert opinion, but through journalistic accounts and popularizing overviews. These he read voraciously, but also unsystematically and always with a view to their political utility.

In *Mein Kampf*, Hitler seeks to provide a justification for this type of knowledge acquisition. "I know people who 'read' enormously, book for book, letter for letter, yet whom I would not describe as 'well-read'. True, they possess a mass of 'knowledge', but their brain is unable to organize and register the material they have taken in. [...] For reading is no end in itself, but a means to an end. It should primarily help to fill the framework constituted by every man's talents and abilities; in addition it should provide the tools and building materials which the individual needs for his life's work [...]; secondly, it should transmit a general world view".[39] What this means, of course, is that reading is only there to ground and strengthen your preconceptions and prejudices and enable you to translate these into concrete actions. For Hitler, reading is not about what others—say, academic specialists and scientific experts—think, and then learning from them. It is about you, and how to use (or abuse) the insights you have acquired. Your existing picture of the world should always remain intact. Any reader who approaches the matter differently—Hitler writes in an attempt at wit—will only be "growing more and more removed from the world until, not infrequently, he ends up in a sanitarium or in parliament".[40] By all accounts, Trump had the same unsystematic and indeed blinkered—or, if one wished to be generous, "hedgehoggish"—approach to knowledge.

Hitler largely ignored the views of intellectuals, the "eggheads". So did Trump. Similarly, both men had little time for official reports, especially those coming from their respective foreign offices. In Trump's opinion, State Department officials merely generated spurious subtlety, fake expertise, and red tape. As Michael Wolff puts it in *Fire and Fury: Inside the Trump White House*: "The old foreign policy was based on the idea of nuance: facing an infinitely complex multilateral algebra of threats, interests, incentives, deals, and ever evolving relationships, we strain to reach a balanced future. In practice, the new foreign policy, an effective Trump doctrine, was to reduce the board to three elements: powers we can work with, powers we cannot work with, and those without enough power whom we can functionally disregard or sacrifice".[41] Hitler had an equally disparaging view of what he considered the intellectualism and timidity of the German foreign-affairs establishment. He despised all bureaucracies, but especially the *Auswärtiges Amt*, the German Foreign Office. As early as the 1920s, he castigated the blindness and elitism of Germany's "diplomatic guild", and he never revised that opinion.[42]

Career diplomats stood for everything the Führer looked down on (and felt insecure about): breeding, education, and social graces—often combined with a certain aristocratic snobbishness—as well as internationalism, worldliness, and a tendency towards conciliation and compromise. From Hitler's perspective, these qualities equated to over-sophistication, lack of patriotism, and cowardice. In addition, there was the diplomat's obsession with protocol. Above all, Hitler felt, the *Auswärtiges Amt* and its ambassadors were living in a bubble—"a very small circle sufficient unto itself, a world entirely cut off from reality, without any idea of what is happening around them. The less they know, the more they talk. They never do anything, they never learn anything".[43] Their reports were little more than a collage of excerpts from foreign newspapers—delivered two weeks late.[44] "What did our diplomats report before the [first] world war? Nothing! During the world war? Nothing!

After the world war? Nothing!"[45] It was this disdain for foreign-policy professionals that led Hitler to appoint the wealthy wine merchant Joachim von Ribbentrop as Foreign Minister.[46]

While considering reading official reports largely a waste of time, both Trump and Hitler devoted a great deal of time to their own messaging. Trump's main method of communication with the American people were his Tweets. Contrary to what is often assumed, he crafted them with extraordinary care. More often than not, he typed them himself or dictated them word for word to someone else. Cliff Sims has described the process: "During the day, he would often call Dan [Scavino, the administration's Director of Social Media] into the Oval to dictate tweets, complete with punctuation instructions—dash, dash, 'sad', exclamation point—and his own unique way of capitalizing seemingly random words for emphasis".[47] At other times, his staff made suggestions for Tweets, but these always had to be submitted to the boss for approval: "Trump would approve them, disapprove them, or make tweaks, but you can rest assured that he wasn't letting anything go out without his sign-off".[48]

Hitler's main medium were his speeches. While he often spoke without notes (he had an unusually good memory), the most important speeches were delivered with a manuscript in front of him. He invariably composed the text himself. Each speech went through multiple drafts— "a labour which never ended",[49] as his former secretary Christa Schroeder puts it in her memoirs. "After every assault on [yet another draft] the modified version had to be retyped. More than once I had to run to his car to hand over the last pages".[50] For Hitler, as for Trump, there was nothing more important than his self-staging.

Informal Decision-making, Opportunism, Social Darwinism, and the Power of the Will

From the perspective of the Leader, an informal decision-making process has the advantage that he can always stand away from the outcome if things go wrong—if, say, there are unexpected legal or political complications, or if there is a public outcry. Management through informal instructions, indirect orders, suggestions, and hints creates plausible deniability. The lack of a paper trail significantly minimizes the Leader's political liability (though not, of course, his moral responsibility). This approach inevitably produces a power struggle among the underlings, which in its turn has a clear advantage for the Leader: any time he is disinclined or unable to impose his will, all he has to do is let his willing executioners fight it out and then he can come down on the winning side. That way, he never loses face.[51]

Informal decision-making both generates and requires a certain openness of policy. This, too, is advantageous to populist leaders. As the British historian Laurence Rees puts it with regard to Hitler's political programme in the 1920s: its "vagueness [...] offered maximum flexibility for him to interpret Nazi policy as he liked [...], and it allowed the Nazis to position themselves as a 'movement' rather than a run-of-the-mill political party tied down in formulating and agreeing detailed policy. It also permitted a broad range of people to profess support for the Nazis, since the proposal, for example, to 'remove the Jews' could be interpreted in a large number of ways—from legislation to prevent Jews entering certain professions to the forced expulsion of Jews from Germany to something worse altogether".[52] This does not mean that the Nazis never developed specific policies: they obviously ended up pursuing a number of very concrete and clearly defined military and genocidal objectives. And of course, once taken, some policy decisions—such as the invasion of Poland, which triggered the Second World War—turned out to be irreversible. Yet there was also a pragmatic, or rather opportunistic, side to Hitler.

Adolf Hitler was an ideological fanatic—a convinced racist and virulent anti-Semite. But he was also capable of shameless opportunism when it came to official National Socialist ideology, or at least certain aspects of it. Here, a comparison with Heinrich Himmler is instructive.

SS leader Heinrich Himmler was a firm believer in the great Aryan past that National Socialism propagated, as well as in various forms of occultism. He supported a number of anthropological expeditions to far-flung places across the globe in the conviction that such explorations would produce scientific evidence of this Germanic primal culture. Thor's hammer, for example, was for him not mythological fiction, but prehistorical fact: "Himmler"—his biographer Peter Longerich remarks—"believed this weapon had actually existed and had really been in the hands of gods or godlike beings".[53] The Reichsführer-SS even set up a range of institutes—combined into the Forschungsgemeinschaft Deutsches Ahnenerbe, or Research Association German Ancestral Heritage—to conduct studies into the origins and superiority of the "Aryan race".

Himmler's fantasies were not just a personal quirk. In Peter Longerich's words, they were also meant "to secure for the SS a lasting role at the ideological heart of National Socialism as preserver of the Germanic heritage and its interpretation".[54] Yet there is no doubt that Himmler believed he was dealing in empirical reality. This belief even extended to pseudo-sciences such as astrology and parapsychology.[55] The best example of Himmler's ideological credulity is his reliance on the self-proclaimed medium Karl Maria Wiligut, known as Weisthor. Refusing to see Wiligut for what he was—a combination of conman and crackpot—the SS leader frequently drew on Weisthor's "occult knowledge". Their official collaboration ended only when it became known that Wiligut had spent several years in a mental asylum.[56]

Adolf Hitler was too much of a conman himself to fall for people like Wiligut. Nor did he buy into Himmler's elaborate Germanic mythology. "For the Romans"—he said—"being transferred to Germania was like what it used to mean to us to be sent to Posen: one big quagmire and nothing but rain. [...] At a time when other peoples already had paved roads, we possessed nothing of any real cultural significance".[57] Injecting his reflections with a dose of racism, he added scornfully: "Those people in Northern Europe were on the same cultural level as the Maori!"[58] To Hitler, Himmler's pseudo-historical and pseudo-scientific preoccupations were nothing but "mysticism" and "cultic nonsense".[59] The Führer believed in Aryan superiority as a soon-to-be-realized ethnic fact: thanks to him, the German people would *prove* to be the fittest race because they *were* the fittest race. The actual past of the so-called Aryans was therefore, in a sense, irrelevant. What counted was its propaganda value as a collection of motivational stories—its narrative utility, not its historical truth.

This combination of conviction and cynicism, of fanaticism and opportunism, went hand in hand with an unbounded belief in the power of the will. For Hitler, history was not simply a series of racial struggles in which the superior race would automatically gain the upper hand. In order to come out on top, the superior race required a superior leader. History was therefore always also the history of great men capable of moulding their people in their own image. (Women, or indeed people of any non-male gender, played no role in his world view.) Victory was always also a victory of the will. The titles *Mein Kampf* and *Triumph of the Will*—the most famous propaganda film celebrating the Führer—say it all.[60]

The following passage from the chapter "Nation and Race" in *Mein Kampf* is emblematic of Hitler's social Darwinism: "all culture depends on men and not conversely; hence [...] to preserve a certain culture the man who creates it must be preserved. This preservation is bound up with the rigid law of necessity and the right to victory of the best and stronger in this world. Those who want to live must fight, and those who do not want to fight in this world of eternal struggle do not deserve to live".[61] Endlessly reproduced in the form of bookmarks and postcards, the final sentence became a well-known slogan in the Third Reich. Yet however exceptionally great the Aryan race was—Hitler believed—it still required the leadership of an exceptionally great man to be victorious. And it was Hitler's absolute conviction that he was that man. He alone could guide the German people into their glorious future and enable them to become what they were destined to be, the master race. His will to power would give form and forward thrust to their inchoate desires and transform their latent superiority into real-world domination.

Hitler's desire for dominance knew no bounds and brooked no contradiction. Giving up, yielding to others, or even merely acknowledging mistakes was simply an impossibility, both in terms of his psychological disposition and in terms of the public persona he had created. "There were occasions"—Otto Dietrich writes—"when he would refrain from answering pertinent objections right off in his usual domineering fashion because at the moment he had no counterarguments. But in such cases he would return to the subject again and again, with incredible stubbornness, until he had his way".[62] As a result, the Führer was essentially "unteachable".[63] Moreover, anyone working for him who did not support him unquestioningly "was branded a defeatist or saboteur".[64] At the same time, Hitler looked down on people whom he considered pliant and accommodating. "'Hard' men enjoyed his respect; humane, 'soft' people were never in his favor".[65] It is this cast of mind that gave rise to Hitler's view of history as the preserve of great men who impose their will both internally (on their own people) and externally (on other nations and races) and in doing so determine the course of events.

There can be no question of attributing the same racial view of history to Donald Trump. Trump was constantly pushing against the boundaries of American democracy and systematically played to white-nationalist sentiments, but he was not an ideological racist. Yet in his own way he, too, was a social Darwinist and a believer in the power of the will.

"Man is the most vicious of all animals", Trump once told a reporter, "and life is a series of battles ending in victory or defeat".[66] In other words, you are either a winner or a loser. There can never really be a win-win situation: compromise is not an option. You can only win if others lose; and if others lose, you win. Even more worrying was Trump's conviction that the ability to win is biologically determined. "I believe in hard work", he said to one of his biographers. "I believe in being prepared and all that stuff. But in many respects, the most important thing is an innate ability".[67] His own success too—he felt, ignoring his privileged background and a host of other social factors—was ultimately due to genetic superiority.[68]

As with Hitler, Trump's biological determinism was intermixed, in a manner not easily understood, with a near absolute belief in the power of the will. Whatever the problem, he was convinced he could solve it through sheer force of personality, subduing anyone who stood in his way. As biographers such as Michael D'Antonio have highlighted, this belief—or rather illusion—owed much to the philosophy of the Reverend Norman Vincent Peale, author of the 1952 mega-bestseller *The Power of Positive Thinking* and the young Trump's pastor. It was, in D'Antonio's words, "a kind of magical thinking", yet Trump "subscribed to [Peale's] view all of his life".[69]

Norman Vincent Peale was one of the most important Christian preachers of 1950s and 1960s America and as famous as that other evangelist superstar, Billy Graham.[70] Nicknamed "God's salesman", he was a one-person industry. His sermons at Marble Collegiate Church on

Manhattan's Fifth Avenue were so popular they necessitated the use of two overflow halls where the congregation followed the service on closed-circuit television. In addition, the hyperactive "jet propulsion man"[71] travelled all over the country to speak at more worldly gatherings ranging from graduation ceremonies to business banquets. He wrote books, magazine articles, and newspaper columns as well as selling LPs and his own range of postcards. He regularly appeared on radio and TV. Peale even founded his own magazine—*Guideposts*—offering *Reader's Digest*-like collections of inspirational stories along the lines of his peculiar reading of the Scriptures, which can be summarized in one sentence: believe in yourself. This, for him, was the essence of Christianity: God helps those who help themselves.

The Power of Positive Thinking offers the best exposition of this creed. It aims to encourage its readers to replace defeatism with positive thinking: "It is appalling to realise the number of pathetic people who are hampered and made miserable by the malady popularly called the inferiority complex. But you need not suffer from this trouble. When proper steps are taken, it can be overcome. You can develop creative faith in yourself—faith that is justified".[72] Accordingly, Peale redefines religious faith as "a scientific procedure for successful living".[73] Positive thinking is "applied Christianity".[74]

The book proceeds largely by exemplification. It tells the stories of unsuccessful people who turned their lives around by putting their faith in God, or rather in themselves: for the two ultimately come down to the same thing. Believing in God is believing in your own potential. These stories are combined with an array of practical rules, such as: "Never think of yourself as failing; never doubt the reality of the mental image"; "Depreciate every so-called obstacle"; "Make a true estimate of your own ability, then raise it 10 per cent"; and "Attitudes are more important than facts".[75] Taken together, these stories and rules show that you "need be defeated only if you are willing to be. This book teaches you how to 'will' not to be".[76] In other words, your success has little or nothing to do with objective social circumstances. It is how you deal with them that counts.

Peale has been called "a conman" and "a charlatan".[77] Whatever one thinks of such criticism, it is clear that the Reverend's message is only loosely connected to the gospel it is supposed to be based on. His ideas are unashamedly materialistic. The focus is on economic success; the majority of his inspirational stories are about businesspeople. Jesus may have thrown the merchants and moneylenders out of the temple, but Peale is quite happy to use the Bible as a business manual. "God helps me sell vacuum-cleaners", a saleswoman and Peale follower declares in *The Power of Positive Thinking*.[78] The foundation of her success, Peale tells us, was her belief in St Paul's "If God be for us, who can be against us?" (Romans 8:31). Other key tenets of Christianity are likewise translated into the vocabulary of personal development and thus robbed of their transcendent meaning. The problem of evil is reduced to a set of obstacles we can deal with if we just try hard enough. Sin and forgiveness have become missed opportunities and second chances. The penitent knowledge that even the most devout believer is still a sinful being inclined towards all evil—"If we say that we have no sin, we deceive ourselves, and the truth is not in us" (1 John 1:8)—is not part of Peale's world view. There is no sense of human finitude or moral ambiguity and no sense of tragedy. All things in life are capable of solution.

These are the things Donald Trump took from Peale: the existential importance of success; a highly personalized view of society and social relations; and a fanatical belief in the power of the will. All three dogmas were continually on display when Trump was in the White House. There was nothing more important to him than success. Those who failed to achieve it were (in Peale's words) "pathetic people" or (in the President's jargon) "losers". Moreover, as Cliff Sims observes in his memoir of his time with the President: "Everything was personal to Trump— *everything*".[79] From Trump's relations with his staff to his dealings with foreign leaders and indeed foreign policy generally, it was always a battle of wills. That is why Trump, like Hitler, adhered to the great-men theory of history.

There is a further similarity between the two leaders: their unyielding stance was a public-relations tool as well as a character trait. This explains why Trump, too, could never acknowledge that he was wrong and why he, too, remained in essence unteachable. Anyone working for the businessman or the politician Trump found out that contradiction only stiffened his resolve, if indeed they dared question his authority in the first place. "It was hard"—Gwenda Blair writes in *Donald Trump: The*

Candidate—"to have a different opinion, much less a debate, with a man who presented such an impenetrable, invincible image [...] and seemed touched with gold".[80] As with Hitler, Trump's aura of invincibility was both one of his strongest assets and one of his biggest weaknesses. It generated a kind of semi-religious faith on the part of his followers, but it also tended to make him blind to real-world constraints and deaf to sensible objections.

Divide and Rule

Hitler's and Trump's management style was based on their dog-eat-dog view of life. Both men took a brutal divide-and-rule approach to leadership, creating a highly competitive work environment in which—they believed—the best and strongest of their subordinates would come out on top. The result was a toxic culture of infighting, backstabbing, and shifting alliances among their staff. Cliff Sims has described the people working for Trump as a "team of vipers".[81] The phrase is also an apt description of Hitler's willing executioners.

Looked at from a traditional management perspective, this kind of statecraft is "not always a pretty picture", as Sims puts it euphemistically.[82] It is also, I believe, ultimately counterproductive—a recipe for institutional chaos rather than a source of superior policy. Yet Trump's and Hitler's unwillingness to intervene in their staff's supposedly creative conflicts was not a sign of the two men's managerial impotence, but a highly conscious strategy.

As early as the late 1970s, when he converted New York's failing Commodore Hotel into the glittering Grand Hyatt (his first major business success), Trump deliberately pitted his two architects—Der Scutt and Jordan Gruzen—against each other. He even created a competitive atmosphere between his wife Ivana, who was a business partner of sorts, and his father, who provided financial support. By asking now the one, then the other for advice, he reduced his dependence on both. The basic idea, which Trump also applied when he was in the White House, was to create overlapping areas of authority. That way, his subordinates would continually try to outperform each other, while he himself remained out of the firing line—the unchallenged leader whom everyone was seeking to please.

Hitler had the same modus operandi. Instead of a clear hierarchy, he consciously established a labyrinthine network of overlapping jurisdictions. The result was an "utterly wild confusion of leadership", as his former Press Secretary Otto Dietrich puts it in his memoirs.[83] There was a Chief of the German Press Organization (Joseph Goebbels), a Reich Head for the Press (Max Amann), and a Reich Press Chief (Otto Dietrich). The Labour Minister worked alongside, and feuded with, the Leader of the German Labour Front and the Commissioner General for Manpower. The Minister of Justice vied for authority with the Head of the German Legal Front. It was the same in all other areas of government and even in the armed forces: unclear jurisdictions, competing bureaucracies, and personal rivalries.

This administrative chaos—the point bears repeating—did not come about by accident. Hitler was not a weak leader, unable to impose himself on his fellow Nazis. "There was", as Otto Dietrich puts it, "a method in the madness".[84] The Third Reich's organization, or disorganization, was a strategic choice on the part of the Führer. "It was not negligence, not excessive tolerance and consideration which prompted Hitler, ordinarily so ready to cut across complexities, to create a tangle of struggles for position and conflicts of authority among the top men of the National Socialist State. [...] He could ensure the execution of his plans by playing one man off against the other or showing preference to one rather than another. His method systematically disorganized the objective authority of the higher departments of government—so that he could push the authority of his own will to the point of despotic tyranny".[85]

Accordingly, political advancement in the Third Reich was ruled by the law of the jungle. Success depended on a kind of natural selection of the wiliest and toughest schemers rather than on administrative competence. Power had to be *taken*, if need be by stabbing others in the back. "Might"—the British historian Richard Overy writes in his biography of Hermann Göring—"was right. Nazi political morality was derived entirely from this central premise".[86] The way to achieve power was, first and foremost, to win Hitler's favour. As a result, everyone was desperate to "work towards the Führer" (as one Nazi official called it)[87] by anticipating his wishes and picking up on his hints and suggestions. The more Hitler liked you and trusted you, the more you could achieve. Conversely, if you lost Hitler's trust, you also lost your authority, leaving a power vacuum that would immediately be filled by your political rivals. As Richard Overy puts it: "Nazi leaders rose and fell not because of incompetence or electoral defeat, but because they lost out in the personal, and even physical, contest for power and the restless efforts to provide Hitler with what he wanted".[88] The same was true of Trump's subordinates. This, according to his former campaign advisers Corey Lewandowski and David Bossie, was "the most valuable lesson you can learn about working with Donald Trump: Proximity to the boss is power".[89]

This, then, is what the Leader gets out of his chaotic, seemingly method-less management system. He secures the absolute loyalty of his collaborators, who are all trying to outdo each other in their efforts to please him. The system also provides him with plausible deniability if they fail or do something unpopular: because his orders so often remain implicit, the Leader is usually in a good position to distance himself from policy mistakes or untoward behaviour. Moreover, leaving the political daily grind to others allowed Hitler and Trump to concentrate on the thing they were best at and liked most: self-staging and propaganda. (When Hitler reached beyond that and began acting as a military leader, things soon turned sour.) Finally, with his subordinates constantly at loggerheads with each other, the Leader's position at the top remains virtually unchallenged.

Collaboration, Loyalty, and Self-denial

What do the Leader's collaborators get out of him? How do they feel about working for a man who—as Hitler and Trump tended to do—brands them "idiots", "defeatists", or "saboteurs" if they are not sufficiently obeisant?[90] How can strong characters—and many of them were—continue to muster such sycophancy when they see how easy it is to fall out of favour and be replaced by someone else? The answers to these questions reveal a more complex picture of Hitler's and Trump's faithful than one might expect.

One answer is obvious: ambition. To a much greater extent than conventional political operators, the Leader's collaborators appear driven by careerism, a lust for power, and a desire for prominence. Anti-establishment politicians attract people who, for all their skills, have not made it into the mainstream and are desperate for recognition. Before joining the Nazi party, Joseph Goebbels was a failed journalist and would-be public intellectual, while Heinrich Himmler was a lowly office worker with dreams of greatness. Hermann Göring meanwhile, a highly decorated ex-fighter pilot of an air force now banned by the Treaty of Versailles, was reduced to earning his living as a commercial-airline pilot. Joining the Leader's movement, they hoped, would put them on the national map and gain them the respect and influence they felt they deserved. The same—one suspects—is true of someone like Steve Bannon, who was the executive chairman of the far-right website Breitbart News before becoming Donald Trump's chief political strategist. Of course, I am not arguing that Bannon ended up plumbing the same criminal depths as Goebbels, Himmler, and Göring. That would be patently absurd. The point I am making is that part of his motivation, too, is likely to have been a yearning to move from obscurity into the limelight, from marginality into a position of power.

The Leader's associates also possess a real desire for social change. They are not mere careerists. Their marginality may be the result of their opposition to existing society; or, conversely, their opposition to existing society may result from their marginality. In either case, their anti-establishment position makes them receptive to the Leader's extremism. They embrace his populist message because what they are after is not reformism, but a revolution. Laurence Rees has called this "the lure of the radical"[91]—the temptation to do away with things as they are and wipe the slate clean. This radicalism is of crucial importance to the Leader's associates. Without it, they would be able to champion his cause only with complete self-denial and cynicism. Radicalism is what they themselves are looking for. It is what they think "the people" are looking for. And it is what they find in the Leader—the power to transform society root and branch.

This takes us to a further reason why gifted people with strong ambitions of their own are so keen to put themselves in the service of the Leader: their very real adulation of him. They believe he can move mountains. This belief is at least in part compensatory in nature. However wily and ruthless the Leader's associates may be, they lack—and know they lack—his aura. They pin their hopes on the Leader because they are absolutely convinced he will be able to push their ideas through. In this regard, they are as much the victims, or rather willing co-creators, of the Leader's image as are his ordinary followers.[92]

There is usually an element of projection involved in such semi-religious faith. Just as the Leader's run-of-the-mill followers, his associates tend to ascribe their own ideas to the boss. In the 1920s, virulent anti-Semites may have viewed Hitler above all as the man who would deal with the so-called Jewish question, but National Socialists of a (relatively speaking) moderate hue considered his anti-Jewish stance largely rhetorical. Similarly, Steve Bannon managed to convince himself that Trump was "really" an economic nationalist: Trumpism's ethno-nationalism would simply come out in the wash. "Asked [...] about the racist element found in many far-right parties"—Joshua Green writes in *Devil's Bargain*—"Bannon replied that 'over time it all gets kind of washed out'. He seemed to regard it as an unavoidable evil, a kind of way station on the path to populist triumph".[93]

Conventional politicians may harbour fewer illusions about the Leader and yet put their weight behind him. This can be out of careerism, but also out of a belief that they will be able to guide him in the right direction. The scope of such belief is wide and ranges from "only we can save the Leader from his worst instincts" to "this man will do our work for us". Thus, when Franz von Papen had engineered Hitler's Chancellorship in late 1932, he told his conservative friends: "We've hired him".[94] Even Germans who were more than a little sceptical about the Führer's suitability for office thought that since the new government as a whole comprised so many "quite reasonable people", Hitler "couldn't do much harm".[95] The general feeling was that the newly appointed Chancellor, constrained as he was by the rules of the democratic process, posed no real threat. To many, it therefore seemed logical to work with or for, rather than against, him.

Similarly, the many traditional Republican politicians who opted to work with or for President Trump thought he could be contained within the framework of American liberal democracy. They were going to be the adults in the room, counteracting his autocratic tendencies and compensating for his political naïvety with their superior wisdom. More than that, he was going to be their tool—the blunt instrument with which they would beat their political opponents out of the way and get their own policies over the line.

With the exception of Trump's appointments to the Supreme Court, this was largely an illusion. The Republican establishment had not co-opted him—he had co-opted them. It soon became clear that supporting the President required an ideological volte face, or rather several such about-turns: on free trade and free-trade agreements, on America's role in the world and the importance of NATO, on the danger of strongmen such as Vladimir Putin, on the need to respect one's political opponents and indeed the political process as a whole, as well as, quite simply, on one's attachment to empirical reality. In consequence, supporting the President also required a significant amount of self-denial and hypocrisy on the part of his moderate, or rather erstwhile moderate, Republican collaborators.

You are either with the Leader or against him. There is no middle way, no room for criticism or compromise. Any attempt to use the Leader for your own ends is doomed to failure. As John F. Kennedy said: if you seek power by riding the back of the tiger, you will end up inside.[96]

As we saw in the very first chapter of this book, Hitler and Trump were exceptionally good at playing to the strengths and weaknesses of their collaborators. They invariably did so in a highly personal manner that generated the impression of a real rapport. This was one of the most powerful weapons in their conman arsenal—the ability to fake an exclusive relationship with every single person working for them. As a result, each of their collaborators felt uniquely valued: "the Leader may look down on the others, and perhaps criticize or even ridicule me from time to time, but ultimately I am the one he really trusts (or likes, or needs, and so on)". This I-am-special feeling is yet another reason why so many people remain loyal to the Leader. The awakening usually comes only after the collaboration has come to an end. As Cliff Sims, one of the more lucid of

Trump's former staff members, puts it in the final sentence of *Team of Vipers*: "I had let my personal relationship with the President blind me to the one unfailing truth that applied to anyone with whom he didn't share a last name: we were all disposable".[97]

There is another thing the Leader does for his collaborators: his attitude enables them to repress any scruples they may have. The Austrian-American psychoanalyst Fritz Redl called this the *infectiousness of the unconflicted personality on the conflicted one*.[98] The idea is as follows. The Leader's collaborators find themselves in a double bind. On the one hand, they have a number of anti-social drives; say, the desire to ignore political conventions or even legal requirements. On the other hand, part of them realizes that this is wrong. The result is anxiety and guilt. The Leader, by contrast, experiences no such moral conflict. He simply does not care. It is this attitude that absolves his associates. They need to find a way to make their scruples go away (or, in psychoanalytic terms, to satisfy the demands of their superego). The Leader renders this possible by making them feel good about their negative impulses: "if the Leader is OK with it, it cannot be bad".

This psychological process is more subtle than it appears. It is not simply a matter of an order is an order—that would generate far too much moral resistance. The process works, first of all, because it is largely unconscious. There is no actual weighing up of options: for this, precisely, is what is rendered superfluous. Second, the process works because it is a group phenomenon. In chemical terms, it is autocatalytic; it works on and reinforces itself. In a social context, we are familiar with this dynamic from witch hunts and other forms of mass hysteria. This is the kind of contagion we are dealing with here—the rapid spread of new moral values and behaviour from one person to another. Finally, this phenomenon is most likely to occur in undemocratic and non-deliberative groups that are highly dependent on a leader from above who enjoys an almost superhuman status.

A special case is what Fritz Redl called the *exculpatory magic of the initiatory act*. Here, the Leader does play an active role in saving his collaborators anxiety and guilt. By autocratically initiating a particular—often dangerous or illegal—course of action and taking full responsibility for it, he achieves two things. He puts any inhibitions on the part of his collaborators out of force; and he burdens himself, not them, with the risk of failure. As a result, the Leader's collaborators feel exonerated in advance, which has a liberating effect on them.

The psychological roots of this phenomenon go deep. Children—Redl observes—often justify misbehaviour by pointing the finger at someone else. "*He* did it first", they say by way of excuse. Even their parents are not immune to this sentiment: if someone else's child started it, their own offspring—they feel—is at least partly exonerated. Likewise, most of us feel that we are not really to blame for the mess caused by a superior's wrong decision, however much we were involved in its implementation.

It is not Redl's aim to posit some kind of moral equivalence between the Leader and his associates. He wishes to draw our attention to the *psychological attraction* of the initiatory act. "Critics of Hitler"—he writes—"repeatedly ridicule the extent to which totalitarian leaders emphasize the fact that they are going to take 'all responsibility upon themselves'. These critics argue that it is absurd to 'assume responsibility' when there is no one to challenge their statements claiming it. The arguments of these critics are only logically correct. Group-psychologically speaking, those leaders know the importance of the 'magic of the initiatory act' and know, better than their critics, what dynamic power lies in it".[99]

Conventional politicians and functionaries as a rule retain certain reservations when serving the Leader. His immediate associates, by contrast, are true believers. Yet from time to time even they have doubts and disappointments. They would not be human if it were otherwise. Why do such sentiments rarely prompt the Leader's willing executioners to abandon their boss?

There are, of course, the various motives we have just looked at: ambition, a sense of mission, and so on. But I believe that the real reason lies elsewhere. It is to be found in the fact that everyone opting to collaborate with a populist rabble-rouser sooner or later reaches a point of no return, not simply in career terms, but on a much deeper existential level. To acknowledge that the Leader is not the political superman he pretends to be is to acknowledge that you were childishly naïve when you aligned yourself with him. It is to acknowledge that you fell for the fake charisma of a political conman. So what do you do? You *repress* any doubts and disappointments you may experience.

A penetrating description of the psychological process at issue can be found in Paul Nizan's novel *La conspiration* (The Conspiracy, 1938). Reflecting on the political attitude of the French soldiers who had been seduced by their country's nationalist propaganda in 1914, the narrator writes: "Ten years after [the 1918 Treaty of] Versailles, almost all the men who had returned from the front, saved at the last instance when the clarion of the Armistice sounded, still hesitated to unmask the meaning of the rhetorical inventions for which they had fought: rarely does a person have the courage to retreat and cry from the rooftops that he once took the word of liars; it is necessary to be strong indeed for such public confessions—people would rather have been accomplices than dupes".[100] This is why it is so much harder to give up on the Leader than not to join him in the first place: abandoning him is tantamount to abandoning your view of yourself as a mature, rational human being. It is to surrender your sense of self-worth. So you stick with the Leader and nip any sense of unease in the bud by transforming your doubts and disappointments— as the psychoanalyst Erik Erikson puts it, citing *Cyrano de Bergerac*—into "a thousand little disgusts that never add up to one big regret".[101]

Notes

1. See the *Morning Joe* edition of 11 February 2019 (available on YouTube). As in the other chapters, all general historical and biographical information on Hitler and Trump comes from the texts listed in the Select Bibliography.
2. Bob Woodward, *Fear: Trump in the White House* (London etc.: Simon & Schuster, 2018), p. 299.
3. Woodward, *Fear*, p. 299.
4. The promise was made at Trump's official welcome ceremony on 19 January 2017, one day before his inauguration.
5. Cf. Daniel Dale and Holmes Lybrand, "Fact Check: Trump Has Spent Far More Time at Golf Clubs Than Obama Had at Same Point", *CNN*, 25 May 2020).

6. Cliff Sims, *Team of Vipers: My 500 Extraordinary Days in the Trump White House* (New York: Thomas Dunne Books, 2019), p. 83.
7. Cf. Alexi McCammond and Jonathan Swam, "Scoop: Insider Leaks Trump's 'Executive Time'-Filled Private Schedules", *Axios*, 3 February 2019.
8. Ian Kershaw, *Hitler 1889–1936: Hubris* (London etc.: Penguin, 2001; first published 1998), pp. 343–44.
9. Cf. Chap. 2.
10. Donald J. Trump, with Tony Schwartz, *The Art of the Deal* (London: Arrow Books, no year; first published 1987), p. 1.
11. Albert Speer, *Inside the Third Reich*, trans. Richard and Clara Winston (London: Weidenfeld & Nicolson, 1995; first published in German 1969), p. 70.
12. See Sims, *Team of Vipers*, pp. 112–14, and Isaiah Berlin, *The Hedgehog and the Fox: An Essay on Tolstoy's View of History* (revised [1978] version Chicago: Elephant Books, 1993; first published 1953).
13. Cited in Berlin, *Hedgehog*, p. 3.
14. Berlin, *Hedgehog*, p. 3.
15. Newt Gingrich's Tweet was published on 25 September 2016. Harold Meyerson had earlier made the same observation about Hillary Clinton in his article "Bernie and Hillary, the Hedgehog and the Fox", in *The American Prospect*, 18 January 2016. In his book *Understanding Trump*, Gingrich puts forward a comparable argument about Trump's critics by drawing on Nassim Nicholas Taleb's concept of the IYI, or Intellectual Yet Idiot—someone who is highly educated, but has insufficient real life experience and lacks common sense. See Newt Gingrich, *Understanding Trump* (New York: Hachette, 2018; first published 2017), pp. 62–77. Taleb's original essay "The Intellectual Yet Idiot" can be found in his *Skin in the Game: Hidden Asymmetries in Daily Life* (Harmondsworth: Penguin, 2019; first published 2018), pp. 123–27, and is reproduced in Gingrich's book on pp. 296–301.
16. Sims, *Team of Vipers*, p. 113.
17. Sims, *Team of Vipers*, pp. 113–14.
18. Norma King, *Ivana Trump: A Very Unauthorized Biography* (New York: Carroll & Graf, 1990), p. 80.
19. King, *Ivana Trump*, p. 81.
20. Cited in Michael Kranish and Marc Fisher, *Trump Revealed: The Definitive Biography of the 45th President* (London etc.: Simon & Schuster, 2016), p. 84.

21. Cited in Robert Slater, *No Such Thing as Over-Exposure: Inside the Life and Celebrity of Donald Trump* (Upper Saddle River, NJ: Prentice Hall, 2005), p. 24.
22. Cited in Slater, *No Such Thing as Over-Exposure*, p. 24.
23. Cf. Gwenda Blair, *Donald Trump: The Candidate* (New York etc.: Simon & Schuster, 2015), p. 143, and Michael Wolff, *Siege: Trump under Fire* (London: Little, Brown, 2019), p. 54. According to Wolff, the upper was Provigil (the brand name of the wakefulness-enhancing drug Modafinil). There has been extensive discussion on social media as to whether Trump used the amphetamine Adderall while in office. It remains unclear if he did. Also, some commentators have suspected that the President was suffering from attention-deficit-hyperactivity, a condition often treated with Adderall. Cf. Benjamin Fearnow, "Adderall Trends after Kevin McCarthy Says Biden Lacks Energy of Trump, Needs More Sleep", *Newsweek*, 15 May 2021, as well as (on Trump's possible ADH) Blair, *Donald Trump*, p. 17, and Michael Kruse, "Donald Trump's Shortest Attribute Isn't His Fingers", *Politico*, 8 September 2016.
24. On Hitler's fondness for bowling, see Chap. 2.
25. Otto Dietrich, *The Hitler I Knew: Memoirs of the Third Reich's Press Chief* (New York: Skyhorse Publishing, 2014 [no translator mentioned]; first published in German 1955), pp. 111–12.
26. Dietrich, *The Hitler I Knew*, p. 112.
27. Tellingly, Hitler had a predilection for sarcastic and outright black humour. An example can be found in the memoirs of his personal photographer: "On one occasion, when Goebbels was paying Hitler a visit, the Propaganda Minister noticed among the paintings one by [Wilhelm] Löwith [1861–1932], which, Hitler told him, had been a present from me. […] 'A fine picture, mein Führer', Goebbels said, with a malicious glance in my direction. 'And I don't wonder, for Löwith, of course, was one of the most talented among the Jewish painters!' 'Quite!' retorted Hitler with a laugh. 'That's why it was such a good idea to hang him here!'. See Heinrich Hoffmann, *Hitler Was My Friend: The Memoir of Hitler's Photographer*, trans. H. R. Stevens (London: Frontline Books, 2014; first published 1955), p. 179 (translation modified).
28. See Heike Görtemaker, *Hitler's Court: The Inner Circle of the Third Reich and After*, trans. Geoffrey Brooks (Barnsley: Pen & Sword, 2021; first published in German 2019), especially pp. 100–01, 134, and 238–40.

29. Heinz Linge, *With Hitler to the End: The Memoirs of Adolf Hitler's Valet*, trans. Geoffrey Brooks (London: Frontline Books, 2009; first published in German 1980), p. 169.
30. Linge, *With Hitler to the End*, p. 170.
31. Speer, *Inside the Third Reich*, p. 156.
32. Michael D'Antonio, *The Truth about Trump* (new ed. New York: Thomas Dunne Books, 2016; first published 2015 as *Never Enough: Donald Trump and the Pursuit of Success*), p. 237.
33. Cited in D'Antonio, *Truth about Trump*, p. 237.
34. Ted Levine, cited in Blair, *Donald Trump*, p. 13.
35. Omarosa Manigault Newman, *Unhinged: An Insider's Account of the Trump White House* (London etc.: Simon & Schuster, 2018), p. 144.
36. Woodward, *Fear*, p. 235.
37. Dietrich, *The Hitler I Knew*, p. 115.
38. Dietrich, *The Hitler I Knew*, pp. 115–16.
39. Adolf Hitler, *Mein Kampf*, trans. Ralph Manheim (Boston and New York: Houghton Mifflin Company, 1999), p. 35. For the original German, see Adolf Hitler, *Mein Kampf. Eine kritische Edition*, ed. Christian Hartmann, Thomas Vordermayer, Othmar Plöckinger, and Roman Töppel (Munich and Berlin: Institut für Zeitgeschichte, 2016), vol. 1, p. 165.
40. Hitler, *Mein Kampf*, p. 36 (English) and vol. 1, p. 167 (German).
41. Michael Wolff, *Fire and Fury: Inside the Trump White House* (London: Little, Brown, 2018), p. 227.
42. Cf. Hitler, *Mein Kampf*, pp. 128 and 576 (English) and vol. 1, p. 377, as well as vol. 2, p. 1459 (German). Hitler's phrase "diplomatic guild"— in full, *blindgeborene hohe Diplomatenzunft*—comes from the *Völkischer Beobachter* of 6 March 1921; cited in the editorial commentary in the 2016 German edition of *Mein Kampf*, vol. 1, p. 376, note 22.
43. Adolf Hitler, *Monologe im Führerhauptquartier 1941–1944. Die Aufzeichnungen Heinrich Heims*, ed. Werner Jochmann (Hamburg: Albrecht Knaus, 1980), p. 254 (entry of 2 February 1942, afternoon). Other National Socialists felt the same way. Hermann Göring, for example, said about the diplomatic corps: "They spend the morning sharpening pencils and the afternoon at tea parties"; cited in Roger Manvell and Heinrich Fraenkel, *Goering: The Rise and Fall of the Notorious Nazi Leader* (London: Frontline Books, 2011; first published 1962), p. 143.

44. Cf. Hitler, *Monologe*, p. 117 (entry of 30 October 1941, evening).
45. Hitler, *Monologe*, p. 254 (entry of 2 February 1942, afternoon).
46. The appointment took place in 1938, after Hitler had for several years put up with the career diplomat Konstantin von Neurath (appointed 1932) so as to simulate a reassuring continuity in Germany's foreign policy.
47. Sims, *Team of Vipers*, p. 84.
48. Sims, *Team of Vipers*, p. 84.
49. Christa Schroeder, *He Was My Chief: The Memoirs of Adolf Hitler's Secretary*, trans. Geoffrey Brooks (Barnsley: Frontline Books, 2012; first published in German 1985), p. 57.
50. Schroeder, *He Was My Chief*, p. 57.
51. Cf. Kershaw, *Hitler 1889–1936*, p. 346.
52. Laurence Rees, *The Dark Charisma of Adolf Hitler: Leading Millions into the Abyss* (London: Ebury Press, 2013; first published 2012), pp. 38–39. Specifically, Rees is referring to the NSDAP's 25-point programme, which I touched on in Chap. 3.
53. Peter Longerich, *Heinrich Himmler*, translated by Jeremy Noakes and Lesley Sharpe (Oxford: Oxford University Press, 2012; first published in German 2008), p. 266.
54. Longerich, *Heinrich Himmler*, p. 274.
55. Cf. Eric Kurlander, *Hitler's Monsters: A Supernatural History of the Third Reich* (New Haven and London: Yale University Press, 2018; first published 2017).
56. The official collaboration of the two men lasted from 1934 to 1939, but Himmler continued to consult Wiligut occasionally even after the latter had been forced to take early retirement from his official SS duties.
57. Hitler, *Monologe*, p. 263 (entry of 4 February 1942, evening).
58. Hitler, *Monologe*, p. 264 (entry of 4 February 1942, evening).
59. Speer, *Inside the Third Reich*, p. 147, and Joseph Goebbels, *Die Tagebücher von Joseph Goebbels*, ed. Elke Fröhlich (Munich: Saur, 1993–2008), vol. 3/I, p. 279 (entry of 21 August 1935).
60. On *Triumph of the Will*, see Chap. 1.
61. Hitler, *Mein Kampf*, p. 289 (English; translation modified) and vol. 1, p. 753 (German).
62. Dietrich, *The Hitler I Knew*, p. 7.
63. Dietrich, *The Hitler I Knew*, p. 8.
64. Dietrich, *The Hitler I Knew*, p. 10.

65. Dietrich, *The Hitler I Knew*, p. 11.
66. Cited in D'Antonio, *Truth about Trump*, p. 154.
67. D'Antonio, *Truth about Trump*, p. 326.
68. Cf. D'Antonio, *Truth about Trump*, p. 327.
69. D'Antonio, *Truth about Trump*, p. 327.
70. The following account is based on Carol V. R. George, *God's Salesman: Norman Vincent Peale and the Power of Positive Thinking* (second ed. Oxford: Oxford University Press, 2019) and Douglas T. Miller, "Popular Religion of the 1950's [sic]: Norman Vincent Peale and Billy Graham", *Journal of Popular Culture*, 9.1, 1975, pp. 66–76.
71. George, *God's Salesman*, pp. 99 and 126.
72. Norman Vincent Peale, *The Power of Positive Thinking* (London: Vermillion, 1998; first published 1952), p. 1.
73. Peale, *Power of Positive Thinking*, p. 66.
74. Peale, *Power of Positive Thinking*, p. x.
75. Peale, *Power of Positive Thinking*, pp. 17–18 and 14. The final rule is a citation from the Austrian psychiatrist Karl Menninger. See Karl A. Menninger (with the collaboration of Jeanetta Lyle Menninger), *Love against Hate* (San Diego, New York, and London: Harcourt Brace Jovanovich, 1970; first published 1942), p. 245.
76. Peale, *Power of Positive Thinking*, p. viii.
77. See the contemporary criticism of Peale summarized in George, *God's Salesman*, pp. 136–44 and 195–99. A particularly severe example is William Lee Miller, "Some Negative Thinking about Norman Vincent Peale", *The Reporter*, 13 January 1955, pp. 19–24. Cf. Daniel Burke, "The Guilt-Free Gospel of Donald Trump", *CNN*, 24 October 2016. The characterization "charlatan" is used by Mary L. Trump (Donald Trump's niece) in her book *Too Much and Never Enough: How My Family Created the World's Most Dangerous Man* (London etc.: Simon & Schuster, 2020), p. 37.
78. Peale, *Power of Positive Thinking*, p. 130.
79. Sims, *Team of Vipers*, p. 100.
80. Blair, *Donald Trump*, p. 141.
81. Sims, *Team of Vipers*. The designation aims to evoke Abraham Lincoln's "team of rivals".
82. Sims, *Team of Vipers*, p. x.
83. Dietrich, *The Hitler I Knew*, p. 96. The following examples come from pp. 95–96 in Dietrich's book.

84. Dietrich, *The Hitler I Knew*, p. 96.
85. Dietrich, *The Hitler I Knew*, pp. 96–97.
86. Richard Overy, *Goering: Hitler's Iron Knight* (new ed. London and New York: I. B. Tauris, 2012; first published 1984), p. 17.
87. The phrase comes from a speech delivered on 21 February 1934 by Werner Willikens, State Secretary in the Prussian Agriculture Ministry: "Very often, and in many places, it has been the case that individuals, already in previous years, have waited for commands and orders [from the Führer]. Unfortunately, that will probably also be so in future. Rather, however, it is the duty of every single person to attempt, in the spirit of the Führer, to work towards him"; cited in Kershaw, *Hitler 1889–1936*, p. 529.
88. Overy, *Goering*, p. 17.
89. Corey R. Lewandowski and David N. Bossie, *Let Trump Be Trump: The Inside Story of His Rise to the Presidency* (New York: Hachette, 2017), p. 74.
90. Cf. Wolff, *Fire and Fury*, p. 11, and Dietrich, *The Hitler I Knew*, p. 10.
91. Rees, *Dark Charisma*, p. 156.
92. On the co-creative role that the Leader's followers play in his self-staging, see Chaps. 1 and 5.
93. Joshua Green, *Devil's Bargain: Steve Bannon, Donald Trump, and the Nationalist Uprising* (new ed. New York: Penguin, 2018), p. 213, citing J. Lester Feder, "This Is How Steve Bannon Sees the Entire World", *BuzzFeed*, 15/16 November 2016. Cf. the Munk debate *The Rise of Populism: Stephen K. Bannon vs. David Frum*, ed. Rudyard Griffiths (Toronto: Anansi, 2019). Other Trumpists have likewise ignored the fact that the object of their admiration systematically played to white-nationalist sentiments. Newt Gingrich, for example, claims—somewhat inconsistently—that, when running for President, "Trump was drawing crowds with an anti-PC message that was an explicit rejection of identity liberalism and a laser focus on the economic concerns of the working class that [Hillary] Clinton and the Democrats were ignoring. [...] His patriotic call to make America great again overwhelmed [their] explicit appeals to race, gender, and sexual orientation" with an appeal to one's identity "of being an American". See Gingrich, *Understanding Trump*, pp. 113–14.
94. Cited in Kershaw, *Hitler 1889–1936*, p. 421.

95. Herbert Richter, cited in Rees, *Dark Charisma*, p. 104. Richter had come across Hitler in a Munich café in 1921 and had remained entirely unimpressed. Hitler—he felt—was "creepy", while his ideas were "really, really simple" (*Dark Charisma*, p. 37).
96. The phrase comes from John F. Kennedy's 1961 inaugural address and reads literally and in context: "To those new states whom we welcome to the ranks of the free, we pledge our word that one form of colonial control shall not have passed away merely to be replaced by a far more iron tyranny. We shall not always expect to find them supporting our view. But we shall always hope to find them strongly supporting their own freedom—and to remember that, in the past, those who foolishly sought power by riding the back of the tiger ended up inside". See John F. Kennedy, "The Torch Has Been Passed to a New Generation of Americans", in *The Penguin Book of Modern Speeches*, ed. Brian MacArthur (fully revised and updated ed. London etc.: Penguin, 2017), pp. 298–302 (299).
97. Sims, *Team of Vipers*, p. 338.
98. See Fritz Redl, *When We Deal with Children: Selected Writings* (New York: The Free Press, 1966). The following account is based above all on the essays "Group Emotion and Leadership" (pp. 155–96) and "The Phenomena of Contagion and 'Shock Effect'" (pp. 197–213). My attention was drawn to this work by Rees, *Dark Charisma*, p. 205. Redl's ideas are an extension of Freud's *Group Psychology and the Analysis of the Ego*, which I touched on in Chap. 4.
99. Redl, *When We Deal with Children*, p. 179.
100. Paul Nizan, *The Conspiracy*, translated by Quintin Hoare (updated ed. London and New York: Verso, 2011; first published in French 1938), p. 41.
101. Erik H. Erikson, *Childhood and Society* (new ed. New York and London: W. W. Norton, 1993; first published 1950), p. 269, citing Edmond Rostand's 1897 play *Cyrano de Bergerac* (act V, scene 2). I have modified Erikson's translation.

7

Speeches, Lies, and Narrative (Un-)Truth

Why was Adolf Hitler so successful as a speaker? Watching clips from his speeches today, we see someone barely able to contain himself, a man ranting and raving in the most primitive way. There is nothing even remotely seductive about him or his oratory. Indeed, if one abstracts from the crude racism and over-the-top nationalism, there is just superficiality and shouting, or so it would appear. Why, then, did his rhetoric resonate with so many people? Were the appeal for "racial purity" and the promise to make Germany great again really that powerful by themselves? Or is there more to it?

It is equally difficult to see how Donald Trump struck a chord with his audience. Trump's speeches, too, were as devoid of social analysis as they were lacking in sophistication. He, too, appeared to offer little more than empty slogans: "Build the wall!", "Drain the swamp!", and, referring to his opponent Hillary Clinton, "Lock her up!". The remainder of his speeches seemed just a series of ramblings, an oddly meandering stream of grievances about Mexican immigrants (dangerous), the mainstream media (fake news), the Clintons (corrupt), the Democrats (taken over by left-wing extremists), Robert Mueller's investigation into possible links between the 2016 Trump election campaign and Russia (out to get me), China (exploiting us), and so on. Yet Trump, like Hitler, generated wild enthusiasm at his rallies.

What are we to make of this? The first thing to note is that the two men's seemingly direct, unfiltered way of speaking was by no means a matter of simple-mindedness. They knew exactly what they were doing. We saw in the first chapter that in private conversations and interviews Trump effortlessly employed an altogether different rhetorical style, with longer sentences and a measured voice. The only audio record of Hitler in unofficial conversation—the Mannerheim recording—shows that the Führer's private voice was equally calm.[1] In June 1942, Hitler paid a visit to Marshal Carl Gustav von Mannerheim, supreme commander of the Finnish armed forces (the Finns were reluctant allies of Nazi Germany). A Finnish sound engineer secretly taped the first eleven minutes of the conversation, revealing a perfectly composed, almost soothing Hitler. Not that the Führer was any more truthful than in his speeches: he lied about his attack on the Soviet Union as being pre-emptive in nature, about the number of Soviet tanks, and about other things. But he sounded entirely reasonable.

Trump and Hitler pretended to speak from the heart. This "authenticity" was part of their appeal. Yet they spent an inordinate amount of time preparing their messaging, as we saw in previous chapters. Their artlessness was artifice. In *Mein Kampf*, Hitler leans heavily on the central role of spontaneity in speech-making, stressing that "a brilliant popular orator [...] will always let himself be borne by the great masses in such a way that instinctively the very words come to his lips that he needs to speak to the hearts of his audience".[2] This statement provides a very incomplete picture of Hitler's actual oratory. He did thrive on—and was well able to respond to—the vibes his listeners gave off, but he was nothing if not prepared. "Hitler was not an emotional orator, as so many people (especially among his opponents) believed", former Gauleiter Albert Krebs wrote in his memoirs. "He constructed his speeches systematically and always knew exactly what he was saying and what effect he intended with his words".[3] Indeed, *Mein Kampf* also highlights the crucial importance of choosing the right venue, time of day, lighting conditions, and other highly practical conditions of public speaking. The Führer reportedly even had his suit jackets tailored to allow for his theatrical hand and arm movements.[4]

Speaking as Performance

In the 1932 Presidential elections, the Führer did something no German politician had ever done before: he used a plane to go from campaign venue to campaign venue. Heavily advertised as "Hitler über Deutschland" (Hitler over Germany), these speaking tours were a huge success, with thousands and thousands of people—some already committed to the cause, others simply curious—waiting for hours to witness the arrival of this superstar politician. Three years later, the Nazis used the same aeronautical image—a symbol evoking both technological modernity and the heavenly power of a saviour from above—at the start of the propaganda film *Triumph of the Will*.[5] Trump likewise had his election plane, his name blazoned across the fuselage. He, too, was no ordinary candidate, but a celebrity; no mere mortal, but a messiah.

Hitler employed a further pre-speech stratagem. He would invariably—and absolutely deliberately—arrive late. His rallies never started on time. He could be half an hour late, an hour, two hours: he always kept his audience waiting, wanting, wondering. Even at his first public appearance after his appointment as Chancellor, he did not start right away. Standing in front of an audience of thousands in the Berlin Sportpalast and with millions glued to the radio, the Führer at first just stood there, his arms crossed, observing his audience for well over a minute. In this hyped-up setting, the minute seemed like an eternity. More than any other politician of the day, Hitler knew about the power of silence.[6]

Nine days earlier, on 1 February 1933, Hitler had delivered a nationwide radio address, the "Aufruf der Reichsregierung an das deutsche Volk" (Appeal of the Reich Government to the German People). Unaccustomed to the new medium and without direct contact with his audience, he was sweating and shaking, speaking in a nervous, monotonous voice. As with Trump reading from a teleprompter, such static events were not his forte. Trump and Hitler were political performance artists with all the qualities of experienced showmen. They knew how to make an entrance, and they knew how to turn their speeches into spectacles. However well prepared both men invariably were, they needed a real audience to interact with.

Their oratory was the linguistic counterpart to this showmanship. Trump, a conservative journalist observed, "doesn't speak like a writer speaks. Obama was a writer, and he talks like one. Trump speaks to be heard rather than to be read. There's a huge difference between the two".[7] Hitler, too, was fully alive to this crucial distinction. In *Mein Kampf*, he devotes several pages to it, arguing that the written word only rouses intellectuals, whereas the spoken word moves the masses. Speech—and speech alone, Hitler believes—touches the people on a genuinely emotional, visceral level. "What has won the millions of workers for Marxism is less the literary style of the Marxist church fathers than the indefatigable and truly enormous propaganda work of tens of thousands untiring agitators, from the great agitator down to the small trade-union official and the shop steward and discussion speaker".[8] Such oratory, moreover, has its own—pragmatic—criteria. It cannot be judged against the requirements of academic discourse. By way of example, Hitler mentions the attempt to subject "the speeches of [British politician David] Lloyd George, who [during the Great War] was still munitions minister, to the magnifying glass, only to arrive at the brilliant discovery that they were intellectually and scholarly inferior products and hackneyed to boot".[9] As live performances, these speeches were "wonderful" and their impact "truly powerful".[10] One "*must not measure the speech of a statesman to his people by the impression which it leaves in a university professor*", Hitler concludes, "*but by the effect it exerts on the people*".[11]

What matters is to be *heard*—and, of course, *seen*. Both Trump and Hitler were visually highly expressive speakers; and research shows that the wider the range of a politician's facial expressions and gestural movements, the more responsive the audience tends to be.[12] Indeed, the American President and the German Führer were skilled comedians, not just in their ability to use humour and mockery (which I will explore in the next section), but also in their physical eloquence. One of Hitler's early supporters, the Harvard-educated part-American Ernst Hanfstaengl, compared the Führer's speech-body coordination to "the thrusts and parries of a fencer, or the perfect balance of a tightrope walker".[13] Hitler's gestures, Hanfstaengl commented admiringly, were "an integral part of his method of exposition. [...] It had something of the quality of a really great orchestral conductor who instead of just hammering out the downward beat, suggests the existence of hidden rhythms and meaning with the upward flick of his baton".[14] As we saw in the first chapter, Hitler practised his body language in front of the mirror and even had his personal photographer take pictures of him trying out different facial expressions and gestures as well as different attires.

Trump, too, often projected more the image of a Rowan Atkinson-like physical comedian (though without the British comic's subtlety) than that of a respectable politician. "He used his rubbery face to communicate disgust, anger, rage, and self-satisfaction", the journalist Michael D'Antonio writes in his analysis of Trump's 2016 Presidential campaign. "And he used his body to illustrate points he wanted to emphasize. When discussing a reporter who happened to be disabled, he mocked him by imitating the man's movements. To punctuate his charge that another candidate, [Florida governor] Marco Rubio, sweated during a debate, he splashed water around and then pretended to gulp from a plastic bottle".[15] He even sent his opponent a well-publicized gift to "help" him—a care package with towels and a bottle of Trump Ice Natural Spring Water.

Like Hitler, Trump employed this strategy quite deliberately. He knew that it is easier to retain visual impressions than discursive information (which is why most of us are so much better at remembering faces than names). He also knew that the same applies to entertainment—to fun events, but also to gossip and scandals. This explains his comparison of the two Fox News anchors Lou Dobbs and Sean Hannity. Speaking to Dobbs, he said: "Honest to God, Lou, I think you're the best who's ever done it. [...] Now you know Hannity—Sean is wonderful, so good. But I honestly think you may be better. And you know why? It's not just information, Lou. It's great information but it's more than that; it's entertainment. People forget about that. You can't just inform them. They won't listen to you for long if you put them to sleep! You've got to entertain them".[16] One of the ways in which both Trump and Hitler achieved this was the use of jokes and personalized invectives.

Jokes and Insults

Donald Trump's use of jokes and personal insults has become legendary.[17] He destroyed 2016 Republican Presidential candidate Rick Perry as a terrible governor (of Texas) who should take an IQ test before being allowed to enter a political debate. "He put glasses on, so people will think he's smart. It just doesn't work. You know, people can see through the glasses". (Perry's case was not helped when, during one of the Republican debates, he failed to remember the three government departments he would like to see abolished—he only got as far as two.)[18] Democratic contender senator Elizabeth Warren, who somewhat problematically claimed Native American heritage, was denigrated as "Pocahontas" and "Fauxcahontas". Trump's numerous other invectives included "Little Marco" (Marco Rubio) and "Lyin' Ted" (Texas senator Ted Cruz) as well as the devastating "Low Energy Jeb" (Jeb Bush, the former Florida governor and son of George H. W. Bush) and "Crooked Hillary" (Hillary Clinton). Often, Trump would test a sobriquet at campaign rallies, while also making sure that sound and spelling (*lyin'*, not *lying*) "flowed".[19] His punchy epithets resembled the nicknames of comic-book villains and Wrestlemania performers; and as expressions—or imitations—of mass culture, they possessed significant popular appeal.[20]

When dealing with women, Trump frequently resorted to outright sexism. "If Hillary Clinton can't satisfy her husband", he tweeted, "what makes her think she can satisfy America?" His attack on his 2016 Republican co-contender Carly Fiorina was equally chauvinist: "Look at that face!", he said. "Would anyone vote for that? [...] I mean, she's a woman, and I'm not s'posedta say bad things, but really folks, come on. Are we serious?" This was not a new modus operandi for Trump. Arianna Huffington, founder of *The Huffington Post* (which initially covered Trump's Presidential campaign not in the politics but entertainment section), had received the same treatment a few years earlier: "@ariannahuff is unattractive both inside and out", Trump tweeted in 2012. "I fully understand why her former husband left her for a man—he made a good decision".[21] Much of Trump's misogyny was strikingly visual in nature. He literally exposed the women he attacked, much like Richard Nixon had infamously characterized his political opponent Helen Gahagan Douglas as a pinko, "pink right down to her underwear".[22]

Hitler was likewise not averse to exposing women in this way. Here is how former Gauleiter Albert Krebs relates the Führer's take-down, in the late 1920s, of Mathilde Ludendorff, the second wife of World War One hero Erich Ludendorff and the driving force behind the Tannenbergbund, an extremist right-wing veterans' organization that competed with the NSDAP. "Hitler spent about twenty minutes describing how Mathilde Ludendorff, before she married the General, had tried to infatuate Hitler into marrying her. Whether this was a true story, or was only an attempt to ascribe personal motives to the attacks on the Nazi Party that the Tannenberg League had just initiated, is neither here nor there. In any case it disclosed Hitler's ability to put things both wittily and maliciously. He peeled off, so to speak, all the high lady's priestly, philosophical, scholarly, erotic, and other skins until all that was left was an evil, sharp onion".[23] Hitler could be equally vicious towards men. Thus, the centrist politician Matthias Erzberger, who in 1918 had signed the armistice between Germany and the Allied powers, would soon not even be able to find employment "as a schoolteacher in [his birthplace of] Buttenhausen", Hitler jibed on 13 November 1919.[24] In the same speech, he combined personal insult with another crowd-pleaser, anti-Semitism. The government, he said, displayed "astonishing energy" in prosecuting the little guy who hamstered a few eggs, but showed no such zeal "if the hamster's name is [...] Isidor Bach", a reference to a well-known Munich entrepreneur.[25] He then supplemented this slur with an ironic attack on Jewish immigrants: "The workers are always told to emigrate to Russia. Wouldn't it be more practical if the Eastern Jews stayed there, if there's so much work over there?"[26]

Hitler was extremely adept at negative messaging. He learned early on that "going negative", combined with relatively vague statements about Germany's future greatness under the National Socialists, was more likely to get the masses behind him than was putting forward specific policy proposals. After all, it is much easier to agree on what you are against than on what it should be replaced by. Moreover, we seem to derive more pleasure from seeing people we dislike being humiliated than from seeing people we like being praised (which explains much of the toxic nature of social media).[27] Scapegoating, Hitler found out, was particularly popular: it was his attacks on the various groups and persons supposedly responsible for the country's ills—such as the "traitors" who had signed the armistice and the Treaty of Versailles, the communists, and the Jews, as well as their individual "representatives"—that earned him the most applause.

Hitler as a rule attacked his opponents with biting irony and outright sarcasm. He was less good at softer jokes; his witticisms tended to be on the dark side. His most effective use of mocking humour was his response to Franklin Delano Roosevelt's long letter of 15 April 1939, in which the American President warned Germany not to occupy any more territories in addition to Bohemia, which the Reich had just annexed. In his Reichstag speech of 28 April, Hitler ridiculed Roosevelt's warning by repeating the entire list of countries the President had provided—a list so implausibly long (or so it seemed at the time) that Hitler's calculated repetition of it had the Reichstag deputies in fits of laughter. "Mr. Roosevelt demands finally that we 'give assurances that your armed forces will not attack or invade the territory or possessions of the following independent nations', and he mentions: Finland, Latvia, Lithuania, Estonia, Norway, Sweden, Denmark, the Netherlands, Belgium, Great Britain, Ireland, France, Portugal, Spain, Switzerland, Liechtenstein, Luxembourg, Poland, Hungary, Romania, Yugoslavia, Russia, Bulgaria, Turkey, Iraq, Arabia, Syria, Palestine, Egypt, and Iran".[28] The Führer then proceeded to demolish Roosevelt's demands point by point, stating among other things:

> I took the trouble to ask the afore-mentioned states, first, whether they feel threatened and, second, whether Mr. Roosevelt's letter was initiated by them or at least written with their consent. The responses I obtained were in the negative throughout, and in part even marked by outright indignation. Mind you, some of these states could not forward their response to us because, like Syria for example, they are presently not in the possession of their liberty since their territories are occupied by the military forces of the democratic states that have robbed them of all their rights. [...] In addi-

tion, I must draw Mr. Roosevelt's attention to a few other mistaken historical notions. For instance, he mentions Ireland and requests assurances that Germany will not attack Ireland. Now, I have just read a speech by the Irish Prime Minister de Valera in which, contrary to Mr. Roosevelt's view, he oddly enough does not accuse Germany of oppressing Ireland and instead reproaches England for the persistent aggression under which his state suffers. Despite Roosevelt's great insight into the needs and concerns of other states, it can safely be assumed that the Irish Prime Minister knows better what threatens the safety of his country than the President of the United States does. Equally, it appears to have slipped Mr. Roosevelt's mind that Palestine is not being occupied by German troops but by English ones. By brute force, England is curtailing Palestinian freedom and is robbing the Palestinians of their independence to the advantage of Jewish intruders for whose cause the Palestinians suffer the cruelest of abuses. The Arabs living in this territory assuredly have not complained to Roosevelt of German aggression.[29]

The speech is a masterpiece of irony. It also demonstrates Hitler's ability to develop a focused and coherent argument if he thought it was needed.

In the early days of the National Socialist movement, the Führer even embraced the jokes people made at his expense. "At that time", he writes in *Mein Kampf*, "I adopted the standpoint: It makes no difference whatever whether they laugh at us or revile us, whether they represent us as clowns or as criminals; the main thing is that they mention us, that they concern themselves with us again and again, and that we gradually in the eyes of the workers themselves appear to be the only power that anyone reckons with".[30] As late as 1933, he authorized the publication of a collection of cartoons about him, *Hitler in der Karikatur der Welt* (Hitler as Caricatured by the World), edited by Ernst Hanfstaengl. At this stage, though, he was no longer prepared to let the jokes stand. Each "caricature" is accompanied by a commentary pointing out the cartoonist's "lies". Hence the book's subtitle, *Tat gegen Tinte* (Action versus Ink). The cover shows a huge, imposing Hitler in SA uniform being attacked by three much smaller figures throwing quill-shaped spears at him.[31]

Violence and Strategic Controversy

Early on, Hitler wanted above all to be noticed. His rallies were aimed to attract controversy. If this resulted in violence, so much the better. After all, what more effective way was there to get into the news? By contrast, the meetings of traditional political parties—Hitler writes witheringly in *Mein Kampf*—were "more like a yawning bridge club", with the speakers doing everything they could "to preserve this peaceful mood".[32] These events were formal, reserved, dignified, and utterly boring. The committee—Hitler went on, describing one such meeting in his usual stylized manner—would sit on the platform. "To the left a monocle, to the right a monocle, and in between someone without a monocle. All three in frock coats, so that you got the impression either of a court of justice planning an execution or of a solemn baptism, in any case more of a religious solemnity. The so-called speech, which might have cut a perfectly good figure in print, was simply terrible in its effect. After only three quarters of an hour the whole meeting was dozing along in a state of trance".[33] Such events, Hitler realized, would generate neither significant attention on the part of the media nor much interest on the part of the electorate.

Trump had learned the same lesson. "Controversy", he wrote in *The Art of the Deal*, "sells".[34] As one of his earliest biographers, Robert Slater, observes about Trump the entrepreneur, "negative publicity bestowed on him an aura of celebrity that defined him and gave him an advantage in negotiating business deals".[35] Hence the title of Slater's book, *No Such Thing as Over-Exposure*.[36] Trump carried this belief in the power of controversy over into the Presidency. When attacking Mexican immigrants or clamouring for the seeming need for a border wall, he was—former *Apprentice* contestant and Trump supporter-turned-critic Omarosa Manigault Newman writes—"intentionally pitting races against each other for political gain, just as he'd pitted races against each other on *The Apprentice* for ratings".[37] The so-called "Muslim ban" (the executive order prohibiting people from a number of Muslim-majority countries from entering the United States) that Trump instituted soon after assuming office, as well as its chaotic implementation (on a Friday and with several legal unclarities), was almost certainly aimed to generate conflict from the very start of the administration. It was a media bait. The nation-wide controversy it was inevitably going to generate would tell all Trump supporters: look at how far we are willing to go to protect you, "the people".

Just as Hitler did, Trump welcomed violence at his rallies; he even seemed to encourage it actively. At a really in November 2015, he demanded that an unruly protester be thrown out: "Get him the hell out of here, will you, please?" When speaking to Fox News the day after, he almost regretted that there had been no real violence: "Maybe he should have been roughed up". Early on in the next year, he said from the podium: "If you see somebody getting ready to throw a tomato, knock the crap out of them, would you", adding that he himself would pay the legal fees. At another rally the same month, Trump once again deliberately stirred up his audience (and, of course, the media) by bemoaning the quietist nature of contemporary politics: "I love the old days. You know what they used to do to [disruptive] guys like that when they were in a place like this? They'd be carried out on a stretcher, folks. [...] I'd love to punch him in the face, I'll tell you".[38] While in these cases the objects of Trump's ire were in all likelihood real protesters, he was by no means above using stooges. Many of the audience members clapping enthusiastically when he announced his candidacy in 2015—investigative journalist David Cay Johnston reports—"were actors paid fifty bucks apiece".[39]

Donald Trump and Adolf Hitler were only too happy to give the media a little help. They broke the traditional campaign mould because they understood the dilemma that the press was in: not talking about the populist leader's distortions and lies would give his campaign free reign; doing the opposite and addressing them would provide his campaign with free publicity. Moreover, as political performance artists the two men knew that "the press thrives on confrontation", as Trump puts it in *The Art of the Deal*.[40] No media outlet, however principled and responsible, can afford to leave political scandals and conflicts unreported. The populist's political opponents find themselves in the same quandary. The following passage from *Mein Kampf* describes this double bind with regard to Hitler's communist competitors:

Sometimes they tried to kill us by silence. Then they discovered the uselessness of this effort and tried the opposite approach. Every day we were "mentioned" somewhere, usually with the intent of convincing the workers of the completely ridiculous nature [*unbedingte Lächerlichkeit*] of our existence. But after a certain time they could not help but feel, not just that this did us no harm, but that it actually benefited us, since naturally people were asking themselves why so much space was being devoted to a phenomenon which was supposed to be so ridiculous. The people became curious. Then there was yet another sudden shift, and they began for a time to treat us as humanity's biggest criminals. Article upon article in which our criminality was explained and proved again and again, as well as sensational stories [*Skandalgeschichten*] fabricated from start to finish, were expected to do the rest. But after a while they seem to have realized that these attacks too were futile and in fact drew even more public attention to us.[41]

Hitler's and Trump's campaign rhetoric was intended to cause outrage. By being strategically controversial, both men sucked the air out of the media atmosphere, leaving their opponents, desperate to catch up, gasping for air.

Entertainment, Community, and Individual Empowerment

Hitler's and Trump's rallies were big spectacles. However distasteful they may seem to us (they certainly do to the present author), to their supporters they were—I do not believe that the word is out of place—*fun*. Pop star David Bowie was on to something when, after having watched *Triumph of the Will* with Mick Jagger, he remarked that "Hitler was one of the first great rock stars. [...] He was no politician, he was a great media artist. How he worked his audience! He made women hot and sweaty and guys all wished they were the ones who were up there. [...] He made an entire country a stage show".[42] Commenting on Bowie's remarks, the cultural historian Frederic Spotts adds that "at the simplest level Hitler was providing the sort of excitement and pageantry that was totally lacking in the Weimar Republic".[43] This is not to say that Hitler's (and Trump's) rallies were *only* a form of entertainment, but that they were *also* a form of entertainment. The rallies provided a counterweight to the economic hardship and social marginalization that so many people faced—a provocative, politically incorrect, outrageous amusement park away from their drab and often depressing existence. Whatever else he represented, Hitler was also a consumer good: like Trump, he was "the greatest show on earth".[44]

Trump's and Hitler's "political fireworks"[45] were a form of entertainment, but they were not empty entertainment. Their recreational dimension possessed a deep emotional potency: it had the power to bind people together. Just as team sports create a feeling of camaraderie, so Trump's and Hitler's rallies, too, engendered a sense of community. That is to say, even beyond their actual content there was an existential depth to them: in sharing specific moments of intensity—anger, aggression, schadenfreude, and joy—the participants became almost like a family. The cultural theorist Hans Ulrich Gumbrecht has discussed this effect as the "production of presence".[46] On the one hand, there are—he says—ways of being and doing (and accompanying social realms) that are primarily based on propositional content and rational insight. On the other hand, there are ways of being and doing (and accompanying social realms) that are primarily based on one's experience in and of the event itself, on an intensification of feeling that emerges in the moment. According to Gumbrecht, the first variety is typical of modern societies (which he calls "meaning cultures"), while the second variety is characteristic of medieval societies ("presence cultures"). By way of example, he suggests that "parliamentary discussions are a ritual that fits [...] meaning cultures, whereas the Eucharist is a prototypical ritual for presence cultures".[47]

I would argue that a crucial feature of Trump's and Hitler's rallies is the production of *presence effects* in Gumbrecht's sense. There are three interrelated aspects to this. First, these gatherings generate moments of intensity that are not easily found elsewhere in society. Second, because the experience is a shared one, it produces a sense of togetherness—a community.[48] Third, the presence effects occur in a setting that is normally reserved for serious matters. Traditional political meetings may involve the odd joke and (especially today) a fair amount of cheering and occasionally even booing; but, ultimately, ordinary politicians do not want their gatherings to be like rock concerts: they are focused on their policies above all and value a certain decorum. Thus, when Presidential hopefuls John McCain and Barack Obama were running against each other, they would call any supporter to order who overstepped the mark and insulted or racially abused the other side. Trump and Hitler had no such scruples. To them, decency and civility were irrelevant and indeed counterproductive. They prioritized the fact that the opportunity just to feel and let go, and to do so together with other people, as a group, created a stronger bond among their supporters (as well as a greater attachment to the Leader) than any policy-based rational agreement ever could.

Let me stress again—the point bears repeating—that I am not saying that there was no political content to Trump's and Hitler's rallies, or that this content was somehow unimportant to the Leader and his followers (or, for that matter, to those affected by their respective political programmes). There obviously was such a content. What I am saying is that there is *also* a sense in which these gatherings transcended—were located at a level beyond—the ideological message that was being put forward. On this level, they worked simply by virtue of being performed. The experience itself was the message. To the extent that—again, on this level—there was a content-based message at all, it was more like a revelation. "For a presence culture", Gumbrecht writes, "legitimate knowledge is typically revealed knowledge. It is knowledge revealed by (the) god(s)".[49] Moreover, it is to a large extent, if not outright irrational, then at least non-conceptual in nature: it is less a form of knowing than of feeling. This is why his rallies are the perfect place for the Leader to expound—"reveal"—his narrative (un-)truth, or truth as gut feeling, to which I will turn in the latter half of this chapter.

There is a final aspect of Trump's and Hitler's rallies that we must look at. They were mass events and yet empowered the individual, at least in the individual's own perception: I am not alone, I am many. We see ourselves, but a hundred, a thousand times stronger. Of course, such empowerment is a feature of all political parties and social movements: of Anonymous ("We are Legion"), for example, or Extinction Rebellion ("Rebel together because together we are irresistible"). With Trump's and

Hitler's rallies, however, this empowerment was achieved—and hence effectively negated—by the individual's abandonment of critical thought and submission to the Leader.[50] As Michael D'Antonio puts it with regard to Trump, it is not just the crowd that is an "extension of the self" and as such enables us to "to escape feeling insignificant"—it is the Leader himself who is "us writ large".[51] The crowd's members identify with each other, and together they identify with the crowd's leader. This is the psychological mechanism that populists exploit when they claim that they are the people's voice.

We should not allow ourselves to be deceived by Trump's and Hitler's rowdiness, sloganeering, and seeming superficiality. Their understanding of mass psychology as well as of the media may have been intuitive rather than scholarly, but this does not mean—let me say it once more—that they did not know exactly what they were doing. Hitler even discusses the mass effects of his rallies quite openly in *Mein Kampf*. He writes:

> The mass meeting is [...] necessary for the reason that in it the individual, who at first, while becoming a supporter of a young movement, feels lonely and easily succumbs to the fear of being alone, for the first time gets the picture of a larger community, which in most people has a strengthening, encouraging effect. [...] But the community of the great demonstration not only strengthens the individual, it also unites and helps to create an *esprit de corps*. The man who is exposed to great tribulations, as the first advocate of a new doctrine in his factory or workshop, absolutely needs that strengthening which lies in the conviction of being a member and fighter in a great comprehensive body. And he obtains an impression of this body for the first time in the mass demonstration. When from his little workshop or big factory, in which he feels very small, he steps for the first time into a mass meeting and has thousands and thousands of people of the same opinions around him, when, as a seeker, he is swept away by three or four thousand others into the mighty effect of suggestive intoxication and enthusiasm, when the visible success and agreement of thousands confirm to him the rightness of the new doctrine and for the first time arouse doubt in the truth of his previous conviction—then he himself has succumbed to the magic influence of what we designate as "mass suggestion".[52]

How, then, did the two men play to the psychological disposition of their respective audiences? And what rhetorical devices did they use to convince their supporters of the Cause? These are the questions to which we must now turn.

Simplicity, Repetition, and Interpretative Openness

Perhaps more than any other politician, Adolf Hitler and Donald Trump were conscious of the power of words.[53] As we saw in the first chapter, Hitler was influenced above all by the populist rhetoric of Vienna's anti-Semitic mayor Karl Lueger, while Trump honed his oratory first as a salesman and then a television entertainer. The most fundamental features of their way of speaking were simplicity and repetition. This not only made their speeches much easier to understand, remember, and retell than those of their opponents. It also enabled the two men to establish a rapport with their audience, who perceived them as honest and authentic precisely because what they said seemed straightforward, obvious, and sensible.

The establishment politician's discourse is highly constructed, often evasive, and invariably prudent. By contrast, the populist leader "speaks from the heart". His language is our language; he does not feign, prevaricate, or stall. This is the reason why so many people feel that the Leader takes them seriously. He is not pompous or patronizing; he does not talk down to us. He is real. Of course, this feeling is entirely illusory. As former Gauleiter Albert Krebs puts it with regard to Hitler, "his great success with the masses depended on his art of addressing them—that is, of awakening in them the impression that they were being taken completely seriously. This was probably a very consciously developed art with him. It achieved its surety of method precisely because there was no inner conviction or sympathy involved. It was solely a matter of cool calculation".[54] The same is true of Trump. By contrast, "Hillary Clinton"—David Cay Johnston writes—"spoke at, but not to, the 90 percent of America whose incomes have been flat for almost a half century".[55] As a result, her honest policy proposals were perceived as a form of lying ("she is only saying these things because she is ambitious and wants to be President: she does not really care about us"), while Trump's lies were seen as the words of someone "telling it as it is".[56]

Obviously, this was not true across the board. There were plenty of ordinary people who saw Hitler for what he was. The Social Democrat Josef Felder, for example, who attended one of the Führer's speeches in the early 1920s, realized "that he was working in an extraordinarily demagogic fashion" and that many of his claims "were in no way valid".[57] The veteran Herbert Richter saw Hitler around the same time. He, too, was not impressed with the Führer's "really, really simple" sloganeering (he also disliked his moustache).[58] Trump likewise had at least as many opponents as supporters. We encounter here the same phenomenon that we observed when exploring the Leader's charisma, or aura, in the first chapter: he only impresses those who already broadly agree with his overall world view. This is why his supporters hear their own voice when they are listening to him. As the philosopher Ernst Bloch puts it in a perceptive 1936 essay on National Socialist propaganda: "Most people like listening to themselves best. This is not only true of chatterboxes and narcissists, but also of good listeners, people who are able to hear and respond to what others tell them. To get their attention, the speaker must grab them by their situation, as it were, by reflecting their own perception of their condition back to them".[59] In this sense, the Leader is always—as Michael D'Antonio says apropos of Donald Trump—"a walking inkblot test".[60]

Trump and Hitler deliberately played to this need for ideological affirmation. They knew that they would attract many more voters if, instead of offering detailed policy proposals, they kept to general statements that a large proportion of the electorate could agree with. Thus, Trump's promise that no one "would be tougher on ISIS" and his pledge to replace Barack Obama's "very bad" Patient Protection and Affordable Care Act (known as Obamacare) with "something terrific" were impossible to refute other than with specific—and hence invariably divisive—counterproposals.[61] Who does not want a tough leader or a terrific healthcare system? Hitler's declared objectives before 1933 were likewise short on specifics. Besides vague promises of strong leadership, social justice, and the restoration of national pride, his election pitches were "essentially a matter of directed hatreds, seldom the advocacy of clearly defined policies", as the historian Michael Lynch puts it. "It mattered more to him that people knew what the Nazis were against than what they were for".[62]

Moreover, Trump and Hitler consciously sought to attract very different groups of voters. Their meandering way of speaking—shifting from topic to topic, blaming first one, then another, then yet another enemy for the country's ills—was in reality a deliberate attempt to appeal to different electoral constituencies, such that each would recognize itself in the orator's words. The approach had the added benefit of tarring a variety of scapegoats with the same brush, tying them together into one somewhat unspecific, but satisfyingly universal conspiracy theory.[63] Here is how Ernst Hanfstaengl describes this modus operandi when discussing Hitler' oratory from the early 1920s:

> He scored his points all round the compass. First he would criticize the Kaiser as a weakling and then he rounded on the Weimar Republicans for conforming with the victors' demands, which were stripping Germany of everything but the graves of her war dead. There was a strong note of appeal to the ex-serviceman in his audience. He [critically] compared the separatist movement and religious particularity of the Bavarian Catholics with the comradeship of the front-line soldier who never asked a wounded comrade his religion before he sprang to help him. He dwelt at length on patriotism and national pride and quoted approvingly the rôle of Kemal Ataturk in Turkey and the example of Mussolini, who had marched on Rome three weeks earlier [i.e., in late October 1922]. He stormed at war profiteers, and I remember him getting a roar of applause when he criticized them for spending valuable foreign currency on importing oranges from Italy for the rich, when gathering inflation was facing half the population with starvation. He attacked the Jews, not so much on a racial basis, as accusing them of black marketeering and waxing fat on the misery round them [...]. Then he thundered at the Communists and Socialists for desiring the disruption of German traditions.[64]

Hitler's and Trump's lack of detailed policy could not be maintained once they were in power, at least not to the same extent. Decisions had to be taken; laws had to be passed. The President and the Chancellor dealt with this challenge by staying as much as possible above the fray of the day-to-day running of the country—an approach we already explored in previous chapters. Each had created a movement rather than building or rebuilding a traditional political party. Once in office, they continued to play the people's tribune, passing the nitty-gritty of administrative policy and the specifics of implementation (as well as any criticism in case things went wrong) on to their underlings.

Making the Country Great Again

Speech has the power to make us see the world in a certain way. Far from merely describing things as they are, it frames them and hence steers our perception of them.[65] On an abstract level, we know this; in real-world situations, many of us are still taken in by the power of words. The Brexit debate is a good example. The United Kingdom's departure from the European Union was always going to be no more and no less than a transition from one set of treaties, agreements, and interdependencies to another set of treaties, agreements, and interdependencies. Yet the Leave campaign's slogan "Take back control" powerfully conjured up the image of a Britain in the clutches of the EU from which it would have to wrestle itself free in order to become an independent nation "again". Instead of reframing the issue, the Remainers made the fatal mistake of trying merely to nuance this basic picture. Their argument along the lines of "Yes, the EU needs reforming, but …" acted to confirm rather than undermine their opponents' claims. Incapable of proposing a genuinely different way of seeing things, the Remain campaign was doomed from the start.

The same applies to the discussions surrounding the exact nature of Brexit. The more extreme Brexiteers successfully launched the distinction between a hard and a soft Brexit, suggesting that advocating a radical break with the European Union was equivalent to being strong, tough, virile ("hard"); accepting anything less was being weak, pliable, impotent ("soft"). Other ways of framing the issue—say, a distinction between a no-jobs and a pro-jobs Brexit—never got off the ground. Equally influential was the extremists' suggestion that "no deal [with the EU] is better than a bad deal". Once again, the Remainers failed to counter this perspective by putting forward an alternative slogan, or even simply by pointing out that what their opponents were saying was tantamount to "getting none of what you want is better than getting some of what you want". Finally, the framing of Brexit in terms of a divorce—instead of viewing it, say, as a disgruntled member's decision to leave a club—conjured up an image of the European Union as a mean-spirited spouse whose unfair demands any reasonable person would resist.

Hitler's and Trump's political framing rested largely on the oppositions then/now and us/them. In olden times, the country was unified, prosperous, and powerful; today, undermined and exploited by enemies at home and abroad, it is teetering on the brink of collapse, such that we—ordinary, decent, hardworking citizens—and our entire way of life are threatened with extinction. These oppositions are absolute: they lack any kind of nuance. Yet they also possess sufficient interpretative openness to accommodate the Leader's strategy of reaching out to highly diverse constituencies. Many of Hitler's potential supporters preferred the past to the present, but there was little agreement on what exactly it was that made the past so much better. Was it the Empire's hierarchical political structure, the prevalence of law and order, or had the country actually been woefully anti-meritocratic? Was it the Empire's economic success, or had this wealth been distributed unfairly? Was it the country's now lost international standing, or was it precisely its bellicosity that had plunged it into war and chaos? Hitler made sure to play to all these sensibilities, in effect offering something for almost everyone. The same applies to his against-ism: potential followers could all recognize "the enemy"—that is to say, one or more of their enemies of choice—in his meandering list of charges against the Allies, France, the Treaty of Versailles, the Jews (or "merely" some particularly powerful Jews), international finance capitalism, communism, political cliques, gangs, and so on. The successful populist Leader is above all a cunning public-relations manager who is able to combine extremist propaganda with strategic ambiguity.

Of course, on becoming Chancellor, Hitler also immediately set about transforming Germany into a dictatorship, and he ultimately instigated both the Second World War and the Holocaust. Yet even at the heart of these uniquely evil crimes was his self-perception as the country's propagandist in chief. In Ian Kershaw's words, from the very start "politics to

7 Speeches, Lies, and Narrative (Un-)Truth

Hitler—and so it would in all essence remain—*was* propaganda: ceaseless mass mobilization for a cause to be followed blindly".[66]

Both before and after their accession to power, Hitler and Trump complemented their against-ism with a healthy—or rather unhealthy—dose of part nostalgic, part utopian patriotism. Their promise to make the country great again was the logical counterpart to their picture of the country's current deplorable state and exploitation by foreign powers. This is how the historian Reginald H. Phelps summarizes Hitler's earliest speeches: "The role of the Jews is the paramount issue, followed by [...] the politics of the day and current events that demonstrate Germany's weakness since its defeat in the Great War. The present appears as a grotesque horror painting compared to the wondrous, ivy-covered past. [...] The old, glorious days, the mighty Empire before the war, outwardly strong, inwardly stable, concerned only for its citizens' welfare, surrounded by envious dwarfs. [...] And how does the country look today? Broken promises, powerless parties and politicians, a corrupt bureaucracy, a corrupt press, economic deprivation, political and social division, dishonesty, immorality".[67] And finally the pledge to do away with all this and achieve "Germany's liberation".[68]

In his first speech following his appointment as Chancellor well over a decade later, Hitler used the same framing. As is customary for inaugural addresses, the "Appeal of the Reich Government to the German People" struck a more conciliatory note, omitting any reference to the divisive topic of the Jews. Yet the text is still centred on the contrast between a glorious past and a disastrous present, coupled with the pledge to restore the country to its former greatness:

> More than fourteen years have passed since that unhappy day when the German people, blinded by promises from foes at home and abroad, lost sight of the most valuable possessions of our past, of our empire, of its honor and freedom, and thus lost everything. [...] With profound distress millions of the best German men and women from all walks of life have seen the unity of the nation vanishing away, dissolving in a confusion of political egotism, economic interests, and ideological differences. [...] The disintegration of the unity of spirit and will of the people at home was followed by the disintegration of its political standing in the world. [...] The

misery of our people is horrible to behold! Millions of the industrial proletariat are unemployed and starving; the whole of the middle class and the small artisans have been impoverished. [...] Fourteen years of Marxism have ruined Germany; one year of Bolshevism would destroy it. [...] The task that we must accomplish is the hardest which has fallen to German statesmen within the memory of man. But we are filled with unbounded confidence for we believe in our people and its imperishable virtues. [...] The national government will therefore regard it as its first and foremost duty to revive in the nation the spirit of unity and co-operation. It will preserve and defend those basic principles on which our nation has been built. It will protect Christianity as the foundation of our morality, and the family as the nucleus of our people and state. [...] It will establish reverence for our great past and pride in our old traditions as the basis for the education of our German youth. Thus it will declare a merciless war against spiritual, political, and cultural nihilism. Germany must not and will not drown in anarchistic Communism. [...] In terms of foreign policy, the national government regards preserving the right to live and thus regaining the freedom of our nation as its highest priority. [...] As great as is our love for our Army as the bearer of our arms and the symbol of our great past, we would be happy if the world, by limiting its own armaments, would never again make it necessary for us to increase ours. [...] We recognise no classes, we see only the German people, millions of peasants, bourgeois, and workers who will either overcome together the difficulties of these times or be overcome by them. [...] May God Almighty give our work His blessing, strengthen our purpose, and endow us with wisdom and the trust of our people, for we are fighting not for ourselves but for Germany.[69]

Trump's inaugural address of 20 January 2017 was framed in a very similar way:

> We, the citizens of America, are now joined in a great national effort to rebuild our country and to restore its promise for all our people. [...] For too long, a small group in our nation's Capital has reaped the rewards of government while the people have borne the cost. Washington flourished—but the people did not share in its wealth. Politicians prospered—but the jobs left, and the factories closed. The establishment protected itself, but not the citizens of our country. [...] Mothers and children trapped in poverty in our inner cities; rusted-out factories scattered like

tombstones across the landscape of our nation; an education system, flush with cash, but which leaves our young and beautiful students deprived of knowledge; and the crime and gangs and drugs that have stolen too many lives and robbed our country of so much unrealized potential. This American carnage stops here and stops right now. [...] The wealth of our middle class has been ripped from their homes and then redistributed across the entire world. [...] From this moment on, it's going to be America First. [...] We must protect our borders from the ravages of other countries making our products, stealing our companies, and destroying our jobs. [...] We will reinforce old alliances and form new ones—and unite the civilized world against Radical Islamic Terrorism, which we will eradicate completely from the face of the Earth. At the bedrock will be a total allegiance to the United States of America, and through our loyalty to our country, we will rediscover our loyalty to each other. [...] The Bible tells us, "How good and pleasant it is when God's children live together in unity". [...] We will be protected by the great men and women of our military and law enforcement and, most importantly, we are protected by God. [...] A new national pride will stir our souls, lift our sights, and heal our divisions. It is time to remember that old wisdom our soldiers will never forget: that whether we are black or brown or white, we all bleed the same red blood of patriots, we all enjoy the same glorious freedoms, and we all salute the same great American flag. [...] Together, we will make America strong again. [...] And, yes, together we will make America great again! Thank you! God bless you! And God bless America."[70]

Some of Trump's (as well as Hitler's) statements are, of course, staples of inaugural speeches: the appeal for unity, for example, or the promise to look after the interests of the country and its citizens. The fact that there are no attacks on the two men's favourite scapegoats—Mexican immigrants and the Jews, respectively—is likewise unsurprising in this context (both leaders would resume the assault on their main targets soon after). What is striking is the extent to which Hitler and Trump lean into the country's current misery. In the case of Germany, this is perhaps understandable. Following the Wall Street Crash of 1929, the Weimar Republic was indeed in dire straits. In the case of America, it is harder to understand, especially given the country's proverbial optimism. It was in all likelihood Trump's heavy emphasis on "this American carnage" that caused former President George W. Bush to comment on Trump's speech with the words "That's some weird shit".[71]

Franklin Delano Roosevelt in his 1933 inaugural address (best known for the phrase "the only thing we have to fear is fear itself") both acknowledged "the dark realities of the moment" and expressed the belief that "[c]ompared with the perils which our forefathers conquered [...] we still have much to be thankful for".[72] Hitler and Trump displayed no such sense of nuance. To them, the present was nothing short of a nightmare. A more sophisticated framing of the situation would not have been sufficient to justify their respective anti-centrist brands of politics. It is only extreme peril that justifies perilous extremism (or seems to do so anyway). If, for example, Hitler, had acknowledged that between 1924 and 1929 Germany had been well under way to recovery (hence the phrase *die Goldenen Zwanziger*, the Golden Twenties), he would not have been able to sell his strongman radicalism as the only realistic political option.

Another thing that strikes one about Hitler's and Trump's speeches is how dishonest they were: the promise of social harmony and equality was entirely mendacious. Hitler said he recognized no classes, but only Germans. Yet only two months later he introduced the Law for the Restoration of the Professional Civil Service, which barred thousands of Jewish Germans from holding positions as government officials, judges, professors, or teachers.[73] While Trump (obviously) never did anything as remotely evil as that, he too did little to make his promise of national unity come true. Equally inauthentic, finally, was Hitler's appeal to Christian values: while in no sense a believer himself, he realized that he needed the backing of traditional believers to build and foster a strong national movement, and that Church support would help legitimize his leadership.[74] One suspects that Trump's motivation was not entirely free of such considerations either. He himself claimed: "I am a religious person. [...] I'm Protestant, I'm Presbyterian, and I go to church, and I love God, and I love my church".[75] Others disagree. Thus, Michael Cohen, Trump's long-time personal lawyer, has stated that his former boss "possessed precisely zero personal piety in his life".[76] Describing a meeting Trump had with some of America's best-known evangelical leaders (such as Creflo Dollar, Jerry Falwell Jr., and Paula White), a meeting that included a laying-on of hands ceremony, Cohen writes: "Watching

Trump, I could see that he knew exactly how to appeal to the evangelicals' desires and vanities—who they wanted him to be, not who he really was. [...] Trump's answers to their questions were compassionate, thoughtful, Godly, in a way that I knew in no way reflected his beliefs or way of seeing life".[77] After the encounter, Trump commented on the ritual and the evangelicals with the words: "Can you believe people believe that bullshit?"[78] McKay Coppins for his part—to give only one further example—reports that Trump tended to mock believers and only saw prosperity preachers as kindred spirits, frequently expressing "a game-recognizes-game appreciation for their hustle".[79]

Emotions and Dreams

Hitler and Trump consciously played to people's pre-existing world view. They did so not simply on a rational but an emotional level. They knew that the way we look at the world is as much a matter of hopes and fears as of convictions and values. Indeed, while both men were capable of reasoned argument, they preferred emotive oratory. Hitler states in the chapter on propaganda in *Mein Kampf*: "The art of propaganda lies in understanding the emotional ideas of the great masses and finding, through a psychologically correct form, the way to the attention and thence to the heart of the broad masses. [...] The people in their overwhelming majority are so feminine by nature and attitude that sober reasoning determines their thoughts and actions far less than emotion and feeling".[80] In a later chapter, he makes the same point: "In a mass meeting of all classes the best speaker is not the one who is intellectually closest to the members of the intelligentsia that are present, but he who conquers the heart of the masses".[81]

Rationally, there was no need to be concerned about the role of Jewish Germans in the Weimar Republic, or to think that Mexicans entering the United States, whether legally or illegally, posed a threat to the American way of life. All the same, many people did feel that way. Hitler and Trump seized on this fear and then heightened it. Theirs was a two-part approach, which—broken down analytically—went something like this: "You think that some Jews (or Mexicans) are exploiting us? That we have let them for too long? That now they have become a problem? You're absolutely right. In fact, they are the most important problem our country faces. If we solve this problem, if we deal with the Jews (or Mexican immigrants), as well as with the politicians and other establishment figures and institutions protecting them, then our country will be ours again". The Leader's potential followers are first confirmed in their prejudices and then taken way beyond them: a perceived problem becomes a real problem and then *the* problem, while "some Jews" morphs into "the Jew".[82]

Hitler and Trump seized on very concrete negative emotions, such as the strong animosity many felt towards Jews or Mexicans. They also capitalized on a more indistinct existential malaise generated—as we saw in earlier chapters—by a variety of social strains. It is this free-floating anger that they managed to direct against "the system" and the "liberal elite". What is often overlooked, or at least underestimated, is the extent to which they also played to positive emotions, to people's hopes and dreams. Moreover, they were much more successful at this than many other politicians because of their overblown way of speaking. What they offered was not the implementation of realistic policy proposals, but a radical transformation of society—a revolution. They promised people the moon.

Already Trump the entrepreneur knew about the power of dreams. "I play to people's fantasies", he wrote in *The Art of the Deal*. "People may not always think big themselves, but they can still get very excited by those who do. That's why a little hyperbole never hurts. People want to believe that something is the biggest and the greatest and the most spectacular. I call it truthful hyperbole. It's an innocent form of exaggeration—and a very effective form of promotion".[83] The quote from the *New York Times* that adorns the cover of some editions of *The Art of the Deal* fits this marketing strategy perfectly: "Trump makes one believe for a moment in the American dream again". Unashamedly applying his concept of "truthful" hyperbole to hard facts, the master builder presented the 26-floor Grand Hyatt hotel (his first significant business success) as having 34 floors and—equally mendaciously—its ballroom as the largest in New York. He used the same ploy with Trump Tower, stretching the building's 58 stories to 68 through some creative floor numbering. "From day one"—he later wrote in *The Art of the Deal*—"we set out to sell Trump Tower not just as a beautiful building in a great location but as an event. We positioned ourselves as the only place for a certain kind of very wealthy person to live—the hottest ticket in town. We were selling fantasy".[84]

Trump the politician continued in the same vein, promising his followers that he would "make every dream you've ever dreamed for your country and your family come true".[85] He would restore their dignity and hope: "You're gonna be so proud of your country if I get in. [...] Because we're gonna turn it around. And we're gonna start winning again. We're gonna win so much. We're gonna win at every level. We're gonna win economically [...], we're gonna win with the military, we're gonna win with healthcare and for our veterans. We're gonna win with every single facet. We're gonna win so much you may even get tired of winning".[86] Characteristically, he managed to top even this excessive pledge with an almost Messianic one: "Politicians have used you and stolen your votes. They have given you nothing. I will give you everything. I will give you what you've been looking for for 50 years. I'm the only one".[87]

More than anyone else, it is the Jewish German philosopher Ernst Bloch who has drawn attention to National Socialism's hijacking of people's hopes and dreams. Bloch fled his home country in 1933—first to Switzerland, then Austria, Czechoslovakia, and ultimately the United States—and returned to Europe in 1949.[88] During his Swiss exile, he published *Erbschaft dieser Zeit* (Heritage of Our Times, 1935) and a significant proportion of this book is devoted to the Nazis' dreamscape. "There have been crooks at work, and how", Bloch writes, "but one must keep a close eye not only on the crook's fingers but also on that which he holds in them. Particularly if he has stolen it, if the soiled object was once in better hands".[89]

Bloch stresses the complex, heterogeneous nature of the Weimar Republic as a period in which the new and the old intersected. Weimar Germany's reality and mentality were simultaneously capitalist and feudal, internationalist and nationalist, urban and rural, feminist and patriarchal, individualistic and hierarchical. As Bloch puts it in his idiosyncratic style: "Not everyone exist[ed] in the same Now".[90] This was true of other Western European countries and America as well, but only Germany had to contend with a huge military defeat, a humiliating peace treaty, punishing reparations, economic misery, and political instability. As a result, the fault lines in German society were much more acute, while the hope for deliverance took on an almost religious—one is tempted to say eschatological—dimension. This is the area the Nazis moved into.

The very name *Third Reich*, Bloch writes, revives age-old image images while stirring dreams of a better life: "a mere number in a historical count (old Reich, Kaiserreich, Third Reich) is connected with the very familiar triple character of the fairytale (which with the number three always also contains the decision, the end, the happiness ever after)".[91] In addition, it evokes Christian expectations of ultimate salvation in the third stage of the triadic view of history propounded by medieval theologians: "After the gospel of the Father in the Old Testament, after the gospel of the Son in the New Testament, will come the third gospel, that of the Holy Spirit: this is how the abbot Joachim of Fiore [...], and indeed even Origen, the Church Father, heralded the better future".[92] Such expectations lived on—partly in religious and partly in secularized forms—into the twentieth century, which enabled Hitler to sell himself as a latter-day Messiah who would bring about this new era. As for ordinary non-Jewish Germans, they were given a renewed sense of self-worth by the Nazis' racist anthropology. They could again be proud Germans, since they were not Jews, Polish immigrants, Slavs, or other "subhumans". Their so-called Aryan status marked them out as members of a new nobility. "The little man likes to feel noble, that makes up for the lack of something to spread on his bread. He feels considerably better behind his desk and shop counter since he is Nordic or at least recognized in his blondness as regards his blood. Looking down on others, he equally looks up to himself".[93] Moreover—Bloch continues—in an increasingly divided, fast-changing, and frightening world, National Socialism offered a reassuring rootedness and a re-assertion of traditional values: a "blood-based, tangible life in small groups, with a known leader" based on "manly qualities, [...] strength, openness, decency, purity".[94] Presenting itself as a bulwark against both communism and international finance capitalism, it held out the promise of a return to the (largely imaginary) era of small-business early capitalism. And it revalorized rural life and long-established customs as against urban atomism and modern permissiveness.

According to Bloch, the fatal mistake made by Hitler's opponents was that they tried to counter this emotive and exuberant rhetoric with "all too abstract" policy proposals and hence "undernourished the imagination of the masses".[95] They talked about unemployment but did not give the unemployed their self-worth back. They praised the benefits of international cooperation and came across as un-patriotic. They ridiculed the appeal to Blood and Soil but overlooked people's very real attachment to tradition and yearning for community that such language exploited. Above all, they ignored the (twisted) synthesis of old certainties and new hopes that Hitler offered: "The wish for happiness was never painted into an empty and completely new future. A better past was always to be restored too, though not a recent past, but that of a dreamed-after, more beautiful age. And this golden age was not only to be renewed but also surpassed by an as yet nameless happiness".[96]

Extremism and Exaggeration

Hitler and Trump liked to talk big. They were gigantomaniacs in their speeches as well as in their ways of thinking and architectural preferences. Everything they did had to be, and in their own description was, the biggest and the best. By the same token, everything their opponents did was the worst, a mortal threat to the soul of the nation. This way of speaking reflected the two men's personalities, but it was also a consciously adopted rhetorical strategy.

Exaggeration has a venerable literary tradition. It is a well-known device in parody and satire, for example. It was a staple of medieval literature, used to underline the extraordinary nature of a person or event. Thus, Brünhilde would be described as the most beautiful woman who ever lived, and on the next page it would be said of Kriemhild that there never was a woman more beautiful than her. (German literary theory has dubbed this the *Einzigartigkeitstopos*, the uniqueness or singularity trope.) In political rhetoric, exaggeration is usually employed for less innocent purposes.

The most straightforward political aim of exaggeration is to attract attention. Wishy-washy pronouncements often get ignored; and so, sadly, do reasonable and fact-based statements. Truthful—that is to say, untruthful—hyperbole is much more likely to garner people's interest. This was the case in Hitler's time, and things have only got worse since then, especially with the advent of social media. Lying and insulting generates more clicks than truth-telling and civility; wild overstatement is more popular than reasoned argument. This is not merely a matter of noticing a particular message as opposed to not noticing it. Exaggeration also produces discussion: it formats public discourse. A politician says something that is outrageous or wildly inaccurate; people notice it and start pointing it out; and before you know it an entire debate ensues about the politician's honesty and suitability for office as well as about the statement's ("deeper") truth.

In this way, exaggeration can serve as a persuasion technique: it can help convince people that a particular topic—say, the Jews or Mexican immigrants—is the outstanding issue of their time. Scott Adams gives an example in *Win Bigly: Persuasion in a World Where Facts Don't Matter*. Zooming in on Trump's promise to build a wall between the United States and Mexico, Adams writes: "Common sense tells you that solid walls are not the best solution for all types of terrain. In many locations, the most cost-effective solutions might include wire fences, or digital monitoring of various types, or something else. […] By continuing to call it a 'wall' without details, [Trump] caused the public and the media to view that as an error. So they argued about it. They criticized Trump for not understanding that it couldn't be a 'wall' the entire way. […] And when they were done criticizing Trump for the 'error' of saying he would build one big solid 'wall', the critics had convinced themselves that border security was a higher priority than they had thought coming into the conversation".[97] The reason for this, Adams continues, is that the things that tend to concern us most are those that—however irrationally—are at the forefront of our mind. "And Trump made us think about the wall a lot".[98]

Moreover, extreme statements force people to take sides. You can no longer sit on the fence but have to come down on one side or the other. Reasoned argument at best invites reflection and at worst leaves you cold. Wild exaggeration tends to work more like propaganda: more often than not, it becomes an exhortation to rally behind the Leader and the Cause.

While antagonizing some people (most of all those would never have supported the Leader in the first place), such rhetorical extremism unites his followers even more, welding them together in their resistance against "the enemy's" fierce attacks on the Leader as someone who does not know what he is talking about, who is unable to separate fact from fiction, and hence is unfit for office. This is all the more likely to happen in a country that is politically divided and experiencing a culture war in one form or another.

Exaggeration, just as absolutism, is a vital ingredient in the Leader's ceaseless efforts at self-staging. When Barack Obama said of his Affordable Care Act that it was "not [...] going to go perfectly right away" and that it "doesn't solve the whole problem, but it moves us in the right direction", he was being realistic and reasonable.[99] Yet the people he needed to convince saw not pragmatism, but the implicit acknowledgement that the Act simply was not very good. Obama may have been trying to lower expectations (a conventional politico-rhetorical strategy), but to many he just came across as weak. After all, why propose a plan that you admit is going to be problematic from the start and is not even going to solve the issue it addresses? By contrast, Trump's unrealistic and unreasonable exaggerations with regard to, say, immigration made him sound like the strongest voice on the issue.[100] Whereas other politicians were, or looked as if they were, hedging, Trump—many felt—was the decisive Leader the country needed.

Last but not least, rhetorical exaggeration can be used to talk something into existence, as it were. Take the stock market. If enough people believe that prices will go up (or come down), this is exactly what is likely to happen. Unscrupulous speculators can try and get this process started by launching rumours about the "terrific" (or "terrible") state a particular company is in. One might call this Norman Vincent Peale-ing. The Reverend Norman Vincent Peale was the young Trump's pastor and the one who, in 1977, married the up-and-coming entrepreneur and Ivana. As we saw in the previous chapter, Peale's influence was less in the area of religion than in that of business. What Trump took away from the Reverend's teaching was that you can only be successful if, first, you believe in yourself and, second, you sell yourself accordingly. As Peale put it in *The Power of Positive Thinking*: "Make a true estimate of your own ability, then raise it 10 per cent".[101] This was the gospel that became Trump's personal philosophy and public-relations strategy: if you tell yourself and others how great you are (and how terrible your competitors are), reality will follow. Hitler, for his part, may not have had his Norman Vincent Peale, but he too was a strong believer in "the triumph of the will", as have seen throughout this study. And he too consistently employed rhetorical extremism not merely because this reflected his way of thinking, but also to manipulate reality.

Twitter

In a dictatorship, the Leader control the media. Not so in a democracy. How, then, did Donald Trump get his message across in a non-mediated way? The answer is: through Twitter.[102] Commentators dubbed him the "Twitter candidate" and subsequently the "Twitter President". From his candidacy announcement in June 2015 to the midterm elections in November 2018, Trump wrote 13,714 Tweets (roughly 11 per day on average), amassing over 61 million followers in the process. In Neal Gabler's succinct summary: "What FDR was to radio and JFK to television, Trump [was] to Twitter".[103] Yet whereas Roosevelt and Kennedy availed themselves of modern media above all to inform and reassure the public, Trump put Twitter to a very different use.

Trump's heavy reliance on Twitter must be seen against the backdrop of a traditional media landscape that inspired little confidence in the accuracy of news reporting and was highly divided to boot. Trust in the mainstream press had been steadily eroding since the Nixon era. (The same is true of trust in mainstream politicians and political parties.) This development began to accelerate in the 1980s with the arrival of cable-news networks, which often generated alternative narratives. The process reached new heights in the twenty-first century with the increased use of the Internet and subsequently the spread of social media such as Facebook and Twitter. The increasingly divided—and divisive—nature of political news and analysis intensified now that potentially all voters were able to go online and not only participate in constructive public discourse, but also disseminate their own "facts" and indeed full-blown conspiracy theories.

Twitter enabled Trump to bypass both the mainstream media and the multitude of highly partisan fringe media. This "disintermediation"[104] significantly enlarged his audience. It also allowed him to communicate in a highly direct and (as we will see further down: seemingly) unfiltered manner. Paradoxically, his disintermediation strategy received succour from the very media he was circumventing, for no self-respecting news outlet could ignore his controversial Tweets. "Controversy [...] sells", the master builder already observed in *The Art of the Deal*.[105] Tweets like "The FAKE NEWS media (failing@newyorktimes, @NBCNews, @ABC, @CBS, @CNN) is not my enemy, it is the enemy of the American People!"[106] not only appealed to the more anti-intellectual (or anti-"elitist") section of the electorate. They also triggered an immediate response by the offended party, such that Trump dominated the news cycle yet again. After all—to cite *The Art of the Deal*—"the press thrives on confrontation".[107] As a result, Trump received a good deal more free coverage than any other candidate (and subsequently President). In the era of big-budget campaigns, this was yet another significant political advantage.

Twitter perfectly accommodates the features of populist rhetoric we explored in the previous sections. To begin with, its 140-, later 280-character limit (including spaces) demands the very simplicity that was the hallmark of Trump's political communication.[108] This size restriction has given rise to such witty books as Alexander Aciman's and Emmett Rensin's *Twitterature* ("@Montague, @Capulet: Can't we all just get along?").[109] Yet its real-world consequences are deadly serious. At best, it reduces political discourse to sloganeering; at worst, it encourages verbal violence and extremism, as we will see further below. On Twitter, reasoned argument—the cornerstone of the enlightened public sphere on which philosophers such as Jürgen Habermas have pinned their political hopes—is a structural impossibility.

"Keep it short, fast, and direct", Trump wrote about messaging in *How to Get Rich*.[110] His Twitter language did exactly that. But it did more. Trump intuitively—but almost certainly consciously—mimicked what Marco Morini has called the *language of the home*: "It is how people speak in daily talks, in many family contexts. It is the language used in informal conversations with friends, in bars and cafés".[111] Twitter-speak is by its very nature informal. Yet most politicians still preserve a certain decorum even on social media. They sanitise their language, or have staffers do so; and one can sense their polls-driven desire to stay on message and—if they are running for the highest office in the land—be "Presidential". Trump took the opposite approach and he did so for a reason. By presenting himself as unscripted, he projected an image of himself as authentic, real. The retention of his longstanding username, @realDonaldTrump, fitted this strategy perfectly. When we are with our family or friends, we constantly emote, let off steam, and exaggerate ("He's worse than Stalin", "This new watch? Best decision ever") and we all tell multiple lies per week.[112] We use invectives, ignore stylistic subtleties, and make grammatical mistakes. Trump tweeted in that language of the home. As a result, many saw him as a straight-talker, a what-you-see-is-what-you-get kind of guy. In an era of deep scepticism vis-à-vis traditional—polished and pre-packaged—politicians, this was a major electoral advantage.

There is more. Twitter has the potential to change people's view of factuality, transforming the notion of truth in the process. Social media engenders a veritable army of lay producers of news and social commentary. In itself, such popular engagement is a good thing. But because there are no editorial standards and because few "citizen journalists" (as they are sometimes optimistically called) possess the requisite expertise, political discourse tends to collapse into mere emoting and venting. Fact becomes feeling; feeling becomes fact. Besides its character limit, this is arguably Twitter's most pernicious feature. As Michael Mario Albrecht puts it: "Twitter offers the possibility to conflate personal communication with public communication; it conflates the backstage persona with the frontstage persona and renders the potential contradictions between the truths inconsequential".[113] What counts is to tell "your truth". Speaking authentically, or appearing to do so, begins to encroach on factuality ("she is speaking from a place of truth") and ultimately annexes it altogether ("this is her perspective, her story, her truth").

Twitter helped Trump sell his lies as (felt) truth. It also enabled him to build a community of followers united in their sense of a shared "truth", one that was different from that of the other politicians and the mainstream media with its supposedly self-serving, hypocritical, and mendacious news about, say, Hillary Clinton's suitability for office (whereas in reality—so Trump's supporters felt—she is totally corrupt), the FBI's integrity (which is a fiction: the deep state is obviously trying to take down the only politician who really cares about us), and Trump's sexism (which is just locker-room talk and in any case Bill Clinton was much worse). Trump cultivated this dedicated following, often connecting with them direct through Tweets such as: "I truly LOVE all of the millions of people who are sticking with me despite so many media lies. There is a great SILENT MAJORITY looming!" and "Wow, Hillary Clinton was SO INSULTING to my supporters, millions of amazing hard working people. I think it will cost her at the Polls!".[114] His supporters' ability to participate in this conversation (if that is the right word) and to create hashtags and memes strengthened their sense of community even further.

There is another device that Trump employed to cultivate his online followers—the use of jokes and insults. This we already explored in an earlier section: shared entertainment binds people together. By tweeting politically incorrect jokes and insults, Trump created an in-group as well as establishing an empathetic rapport with his audience. While many of his Tweets were quite vicious in nature, Trump occasionally showed himself capable of irony, too: "History lesson: There is a big difference between Hillary Clinton and Abraham Lincoln. For one, his nickname is Honest Abe".[115] Such attacks also distracted attention away from concrete policy proposals (or the lack of them) by transforming complex political questions into personality issues—a key populist stratagem, as we have seen throughout this study.

Trump's *ad hominem* attacks and indeed his (Twitter) rhetoric in general relied heavily on various forms of linguistic extremism and exaggeration. The words he tweeted at his opponents most often were *weak, dishonest, terrible, dumb, fool, loser,* and *lightweight.*[116] Another favourite was *the worst,* which he applied to almost anything he disliked (or pretended to dislike) from supposedly counterproductive trade agreements to certain television shows. By contrast, anything he liked—starting with his own personality and abilities—was *the best.* This binarism is another a staple of populist rhetoric: whereas "nobody does it better than me", establishment politicians "don't have a clue". Trump's Twitter language heightened such linguistic superlativism even further through the frequent use of capital letters and exclamation marks.

In his extremism and exaggeration, Trump was the conscious successor to the jock shocks of the 1980s.[117] Talk-radio hosts such as Rush Limbaugh and Howard Stern offered their listeners a mixture of politically incorrect social commentary and equally politically incorrect comedy. Their main target was the so-called liberal establishment with its perceived superciliousness and oversensitivity, especially with regard to issues of gender and race. They ridiculed and insulted the objects of their scorn through outrageous banter, offensive jokes, and invectives such as *feminazi*, a term that Limbaugh popularized. Their main audience were the—overwhelmingly white and male—culturally alienated Americans who no longer felt at home in the modern world.[118] It is unclear what, if anything, such radio hosts actually believed. Their approach may well have been as much about ratings and revenues as about political convictions. But there can be no doubt about their influence on Donald Trump. Trump was a guest on *The Howard Stern Show* dozens of times; as President, he awarded Rush Limbaugh the country's highest civilian honour, the Presidential Medal of Freedom. His business career taught him how to sell himself; *The Apprentice* instructed him in the art of popular entertainment. The shock jocks showed him how these skills could be harnessed for a politics of grievance. By emulating their outrageous performances—combining political incorrectness with personal insults, transforming existential angst into establishment-bashing, and presenting himself as the defender of the common people—he managed to appeal, if not to a silent majority, then at least to a very sizeable minority of Americans who felt that their country was going downhill fast. Twitter was the ideal medium for this. Like radio, it put Trump in direct contact with his audience; and its stylistic features—simplification, emotionality, and a frequent lack of civility—were the main constituents of his political rhetoric.

Finally, Twitter offered Trump the perfect vehicle for strategic ambiguity: by retweeting particularly offensive statements, he was able to express loathsome views without stating them himself. This way of making a point while denying that one is making it is called paralepsis or paralipsis (from the Greek *paraleipsis*, "omission"). It is common in everyday language: "I'm not saying he's dishonest, but ...". Trump frequently availed himself of this device when trying to cast doubt on Barack Obama's citizenship status.[119] He also used it in his Tweets, as in the following take-down of a well-known journalist: "I refuse to call Megyn Kelly a bimbo, because that would not be politically correct. Instead I will only call her a lightweight reporter!".[120] *Retweeting* something put him at an additional remove from the content. This was particularly helpful to him with issues of race. In Jennifer Mercieca's words, retweeting "allowed Trump to recirculate white nationalist racist sentiment without having to take responsibility for being a racist".[121] In this way, he kept the overt racists on his side, while offering his followers who were not—or at least not consciously—bigoted, an excuse to continue to support him.

Narrative (Un-)truth

The number of misleading, inaccurate, and outright mendacious claims that Donald Trump has made over the years is astounding. After exactly three years of his Presidency—the fact-checker team at *The Washington Post* reported in 2020—"the count stood at 16,241. That works out to about 15 claims per day".[122] Of course, Trump the politician had begun bending the truth well before he took the oath of office, starting with his suggestion that the majority of Mexican immigrants were criminals: "They're bringing drugs. They're bringing crime. They're rapists. And some, I assume, are good people", he alleged in his candidature announcement speech.[123] Having left office, he continued to tell lies, notably what some media outlets have called the *big lie*, the false claim that the 2020 elections were rigged and that it was really he, not Joe Biden, who had won.

The idea behind the concept of the big lie is that if an untruth is sufficiently extreme, people are likely to accept it if only because they cannot bring themselves to believe that anyone could lie in such an outrageous manner. It was Hitler who came up with the concept, writing in *Mein Kampf* that "the great masses of the people [...] more easily fall victim to a big lie [*große Lüge*] than to a little one, since they themselves lie in little things, but would be ashamed of lies that were too big. Such a falsehood will never enter their heads, and they will not be able to believe in the possibility of such monstrous effrontery and infamous misrepresentation in others".[124] Ironically, he then goes on to accuse "the Jews" of being the most ardent practitioners of what he calls this "sound principle" of successful propaganda.[125] Sixteen years later, Nazi Propaganda Minister Joseph Goebbels put forward his own version of the concept, one that highlights the importance of repetition. In the article "Aus Churchills Lügenfabrik" (From Churchill's Lie Factory, 1941), he wrote that the British Prime Minister "was a true John Bull. Having told a lie, he would always stand by it, letting nothing and nobody stop him from repeating it over and over until he himself eventually believed that it was true. This is an age-old contrivance of British politics with which the whole world is now familiar. […] The English proceed on the principle that if you lie, then you should do so properly [*grundsätzlich*] and, more than anything else, stand by whatever you claimed was true!"[126] While accusing others of being inveterate liars, the real manipulators of the truth were, of course, Hitler and Goebbels themselves.

All politicians distort the truth from time to time, but populists tend to do so more frequently and in a more thoroughgoing fashion. In the previous sections, we looked at the reasons for this, such as the Leader's need to project a Messianic image while simultaneously presenting himself as a man of the people, an un-spindoctored "guy like us" who is "telling it as it is". What we have not so far explored is the question of how the Leader's supporters view his extremist statements, excessive promises, and flat-out lies. Do they actually believe them in a straightforward manner? Do they fall for them? Or is there more to it?

When Trump announced in June 2015 he was running for President, few respectable journalists and politicians took him seriously. He was, after all, a mere businessman and television personality. Politically, he was a nobody. In any case—so the conventional wisdom went—his oratory was too overblown to win him much support. New York's *Daily News*, his hometown paper, greeted his candidature with the headline "Clown Runs for Prez: Trump Throws Rubber Nose in GOP Ring", while the *Huffington Post* initially covered his campaign in the entertainment section.[127] It took the critics several months before they realized that while they took Trump literally but not seriously, the growing number of his supporters did the opposite: they took him seriously but not literally.

Much the same can be said about Hitler. For a long time, his critics, too, viewed him as a clown or a crank while overlooking the fact that many ordinary Germans—and even many National Socialists—did not take the Führer *à la lettre* and hence did not see him as an unsupportable madman. In an earlier chapter, I cited the example of the industrialist Fritz Thyssen, who for several years backed the Nazis financially before courageously turning against them. He did not take Hitler's rhetoric literally, he explained around 1930, because "a leader of the masses on the make has to say many things".[128] The British historian Laurence Rees, who interviewed a number of former Nazi supporters and sympathizers, cites one of them, the economist Johannes Zahn, as saying that "reading *Mein Kampf* was exactly like belief in the demands of the Bible. These are demands, but nobody believed they would be fulfilled one hundred per cent".[129] Even Germans who were deeply sceptical of the Nazis often did not take Hitler's extremist message literally. Herbert Richter, for example, whose dislike of the Führer's simplistic oratory I mentioned earlier on in this chapter, thought that the ideas expressed in *Mein Kampf* were just crazy rhetoric that could legitimately be ignored.[130]

How are the Leader's supporters able to take him not literally but nonetheless seriously? One way in which they manage to do so is by interpreting his—excessive, extremist, and mendacious—statements as what Scott Adams has called *directionally accurate*. Adams provides the following example: "Let's say you hire a personal trainer who promises to get your body fat down from 35 percent to 15 percent. You work together for a few years and get your body fat down to 20 percent. Technically, your trainer was wrong. You might even say your trainer lied. But the trainer was directionally accurate".[131] The reason this kind of speaking works, he goes on to say, is that in politics and indeed in life as a whole factuality is seldom a strong motivator. More often than not, what moves us, what we are looking for, is directional truth—a statement that may not be empirically accurate, but which confirms us in our basic pre-existing convictions (and in that sense is seen as true) and which precisely because it is not a dry fact takes on inspirational force (suggesting as it does a direction of travel that we feel is right even as we are on some level aware of the statement's lack of factuality).

Take Trump's remarks about immigration. I doubt if many of his supporters believed that the overwhelming majority of Mexican immigrants were drug traffickers and rapists, that Trump was going to build one big solid stone wall, and that Mexico would pay for that wall. That is why crime statistics and other empirical data were never going to undermine their trust in Trump. What they did believe is that immigration was a serious problem, that this problem should be addressed, and that the existing political system was failing to do so. A significant number of them were probably also biased against Mexicans or non-white people generally. What they heard Trump expressing was not a series of facts (or lies), nor even a series of concrete policy proposals, but directional or inspirational truth—a statement that said: yes, you're right, there is a real problem here, and no one is doing anything about it, but I will. Applying a similar psychological translation process, many people listening to Hitler were likewise able to take the Führer seriously but not literally. As Laurence Rees puts it, "whilst there is no evidence that most Germans would have supported in the 1920s the seemingly wild beliefs Hitler expresses in *Mein Kampf*, there is plenty of evidence that many Germans, like Johannes Zahn, thought that Jewish influence had 'gone too far' in Germany, and, like Herbert Richter, that the settlement at the end of the First World War had been too harsh on Germany and that the territory lost—particularly in the East—should be returned. So in calling for the persecution of the Jews and land to be seized in the Soviet Union, Hitler was [...] voicing in extreme form beliefs that existed amongst many Germans in more moderate form".[132]

Directional or inspirational truth is like a football manager's pep talk. Straightforward factuality does not come into it. Your belief in your team is not going to be affected by whatever the referee or your opponents say, however much you may on a semi-conscious or unconscious level be aware that they are in the right factually. Thus, even an obvious foul by one of your team's players is "clearly not a free kick", if only because one of the opposite team's players did "exactly the same" ten minutes ago and that was not a free kick according to the referee, so this one is "never a free kick" either. This comparison is not meant to provide a justification for accepting excessive, extremist, or mendacious statements by politicians. What is innocuous in one area is not necessarily so in another. Denying, say, the legitimacy of an election has far greater social implications than disagreeing with a referee's decision. The amount and duration of self-deception involved are likewise much greater. Still, the comparison goes some way in explaining how the Leader's supporters manage—unconsciously or semi-consciously—to convert some of his lies into what they perceive as a kind of truth.

Sometimes, a conversion process is not even needed. This is the case when people simply do not care enough whether a statement by the Leader is empirically true or false. The most obvious example is Trump's denial of the allegation that he paid off the porn star Stormy Daniels: few if any of his supporters appear to have been particularly worried as to the veracity of that denial. Now, one might say that they ought to have cared, and in a way this is true. After all, the President was a married man and, in addition, the allegation involved a possible violation of campaign-finance laws. Yet in another way it is naïve—that is to say, counter-factual—to demand such Mr Spock-like rationality of human beings. It may be the right thing to do from a moral perspective, but it does not help us understand the psychological mechanism involved.

An analytically more useful way of approaching the matter is by distinguishing between *hot cognition* and *cold cognition*—a distinction that has its origins in psychological and neurological research and which has found particularly fruitful applications in theology. Hot cognition involves statements that are deeply felt to be true and are an integral part of an individual's personal belief system; say, "God loves me" or "The Lord will give me strength". Hot cognition is knowledge that is emotionally valent: it possesses existential value and inner force. In a political context, many people have hot cognitive convictions (which they experience as "the truth") about such issues as abortion, affirmative action, and gay marriage. Hence, they will find it hard to support any politician who views these issues differently than they do. Cold cognition, by contrast, involves propositional content that has no immediate relevance to one's personal life: "Jesus was born of a virgin" or "He walked on water". Of course, what is and what is not emotionally valent will differ from person to person. Most Christians believe in God while happily disbelieving or simply ignoring the dogma of creation, according to which the world was made in six days, whereas for the small minority of creationists it is a different story. Returning to politics, we can say that for most ordinary voters only a politician's statements that touch on hot cognitive convictions have electoral relevance.[133]

The distinction between hot and cold cognitions also helps us understand why Trump's supporters kept defending him in public (say, when interviewed by a journalist) even in the face of his most outrageous statements. When it comes to hot conviction, this is obvious: they are heavily emotionally invested. But there is often a kind of existential meaning to cold cognition, too. As the theologian Alister McGrath puts it with regard to a typical instance of cold cognition, Church dogmas: "they arise in a social context, and fulfil a social function. [...] Christian dogmas define agreed community 'belief statements'" and as such "can be thought of as group identity markers".[134] Professing that one believes these doctrines (*creatio ex nihilo*, the virgin birth, and so on) is tantamount first and foremost to expressing one's affiliation to and support for a particular group, such as the Church, one's congregation, or the local community. I suspect that the same psychological mechanism is behind many statements of support for Trump's "dogmas". Moreover—and paradoxically—such statements are all the easier to make precisely because they are not deeply felt to be true (or untrue). In McGrath's words: "People may be prepared to assent to propositional contradictions [...] and counterfactual belief statements [...] precisely because the cognitive processes associated with their personal religion [or politics; HdB] are not taking place at this [cold cognitive] level at all, but at an intuitive level that is not easily amenable to description in propositional terms".[135]

In many cases, converting the Leader's untruth into perceived truth will involve illogicalities and contradictions. The Canadian writer and journalist Jeet Heer has given a good example of this. Referring to four consecutive Tweets by Trump about the 2016 election, he writes: "The first tweet read: 'So much time and money will be spent [on the recount; JH]—same result! Sad'. The subsequent tweet read: 'In addition to winning the Electoral College in a landslide, I won the popular vote if you deduct the millions of people who voted illegally'. And the next two tweets formed a single thought: 'It would have been much easier for me to win the so-called popular vote than the Electoral College in that I would only campaign in 3 or 4 states instead of the 15 states that I visited. I would have won even more easily and convincingly (but smaller states are forgotten)!'".[136] Heer then goes on to say: "What's interesting about these [...] tweets is that [...] Trump's second point contradicts both his first and third assertions. For if Trump truly *did* win the popular vote despite massive fraud (as alleged in point 2), then a recount *wouldn't* give the same result, as he's asserting in the first tweet. And saying that Trump is already the *real* popular-vote winner flatly goes against saying he would have been the popular-vote winner if that had been his goal".[137] In explaining this inconsistency, Heer refers to what has come to be known as *kettle logic*, a way of arguing first discussed by Freud in *The Interpretation of Dreams* and then, in essentially identical terms, in *Jokes and Their Relation to the Unconscious*. Freud writes: "A. borrowed a copper kettle from B. and after he had returned it was sued by B. because the kettle now had a big whole in it which made it unusable. His defence was: 'First, I never borrowed a kettle from B. at all; secondly, the kettle had a hole in it already when I got it from him; and thirdly, I gave him back the kettle undamaged'. Each one of these defences is valid in itself, but taken together they exclude one another".[138]

Heer is right when he makes the point that engaging in kettle logic allowed "Trump to appeal to different audiences".[139] He is wrong, it seems to me, when he maintains that in doing so Trump was "making a raw assertion of power".[140] That is to say, the psychological mechanism involved was not, as Heer thinks, akin to the "pure authoritarianism" that broke Winston Smith in George Orwell's *Nineteen Eighty-Four*, "the practice of a big brother who wants his followers to repeat 2+2=5".[141] Rather, Trump's supporters wanted him to be in the right from the very start, such that they were at least as much self-deluded as other-deluded. How is this to be understood?

Dreams—Freud says—are wish-fulfilments characterised by the absence of empirical logic. Much the same is true of politics and indeed of life in general. This, precisely, is the principal insight of psychoanalysis: reason and logic are neither the strongest forces operative in us nor even independent ones. All mental life and all behaviour involve a mixture of conscious, semi-conscious, and unconscious motivations, with the unconscious winning out more often than we would like to believe. Even the most formal settings—say, police investigations, or scientific research—are as a rule shot through with all manner of implicit bias. What human beings are particularly good at is keeping contradictory ideas in their minds: say, thinking of themselves as non-racists while continuing to support a candidate who consistently makes racist remarks. We may—and should—deplore such lack of self-reflection and try to do something about it, but that does not alter the fact that if people's wishful thinking is strong enough, their perception of reality and blindness to empirical facts will follow. They actively *want* to believe and are only too happy to buy into lies that accord with and amplify their prejudices. That is why authoritarianisms are so often embraced from below (as well as being forcibly imposed from above, which outright dictatorships certainly are).

Narrative (Un-)truth, Continued: Truthiness and Group Identity

It is a fundamental lie, Hitler asserts in the chapter on "Nation and Race" in *Mein Kampf*, "that the Jews are not a race but simply a religion".[142] On this lie—he goes on to say—"further lies are based. Among them is the lie with regard to the language of the Jew. […] When he speaks French, he thinks Jewish; and when he turns out German verses, he only exposes the essence of his own people [*das Wesen seines Volkstums*]".[143] Hitler concludes this argument (if one can call it that) as follows: "How much the existence of this whole people is based on a continuous lie is shown with incomparable accuracy by *The Protocols of the Elders of Zion*, which are so vehemently repudiated by the Jews. They are supposed to be based on a 'forgery', [or so] the *Frankfurter Zeitung* moans and screams every week— the best evidence that they are genuine [*echt*]. What many Jews may do unconsciously is here consciously exposed. And that is what matters. It is irrelevant from what Jewish brain these disclosures originate; decisive [*maßgebend*] is that they reveal, with positively terrifying accuracy, the Jew's essence and activity and expose how these interconnect and what they are ultimately aimed at. The best criticism applied to [the *Protocols*], however, is reality. Anyone who examines the historical development of the last hundred years through the lens of this book will immediately understand the screaming of the Jewish press: the moment the book's content has become common knowledge, the Jewish peril may be considered banned".[144]

What is striking about this argument is the approach to historical reality. *The Protocols of the Elders of Zion* constitute a kind of master plan for Jewish world domination, supposedly hatched at a number of behind-the-scenes meetings during the First Zionist Congress held in Basel in 1897. They are, of course, a forgery: while the congress was a real event, the supposed secret meetings never took place and hence no minutes—no "protocols"—were ever written. Moreover, when Hitler was writing *Mein Kampf* the *Protocols* were widely known to be fake.[145] Yet for Hitler this obvious forgery is still accurate, its content still true. How is that possible?

Hitler transposes the notion of truth from the realm of historical fact to that of felt conviction. The empirical question of who composed the *Protocols* when and why is seen as relating to mere surface phenomena, petty details in the face of a deeper reality—the "truth" that the Jews aspire to world domination. The text—this is Hitler's warped view—is the perfect expression of an inner certainty and therefore it is true in a very real sense regardless of its status as a historical document. Thus, the *Protocols* are a double lie—the text is a forgery, and the idea of a Jewish world conspiracy is pure fiction—but they are perceived as accurate because they agree with a strongly experienced gut feeling.

In 2005, the American comedian Stephen Colbert, referring to then US President George W. Bush's loose handling of facts, launched the term *truthiness* for this kind of inner (un-)truth.[146] "It used to be, everyone was entitled to their own opinion, but not their own facts", he subsequently explained in an interview. "But that's not the case anymore. Facts matter not at all. Perception is everything. It's certainty".[147] He then points to "another part of truthiness", which is the rejection of any authority other than that which one has chosen to embrace, such as a particular political leader or news organization: "It's not only that I *feel* it be true, but that *I* feel it to be true. There's not only an emotional quality, but there's a selfish quality".[148] These are important observations, but we need to delve deeper if we are to understand the phenomenon of truthiness in its full complexity.

First, the gut-based perception of a lie as expressing some deeper truth does not necessarily involve the embrace of the lie in all its literalness. In the case of the *Protocols*, for example, it was entirely possible for anti-Semitic Germans to view the text as truthfully revealing the nature of "the Jew"; but there was considerable variation as to the contours and ramifications of this so-called Jewish essence. Some Germans believed that the Jews aspired to full-blown world-domination, other Germans "merely" questioned their patriotism. Some Germans felt that the Jews were trying to take over the press (or had already done so), others "merely" that there were too many powerful Jewish journalists.[149] We looked at milder instances of this phenomenon earlier on—the way Trump's supporters interpreted his statements about Mexican immigrants and about the wall, for example. Truthiness, or gut (un-)truth, is not simply an emotional, straightforwardly counter-factual perception of reality. More often than not, it involves a process of de-literalization, which in its turn creates an interpretative openness that allows different groups to embrace the same lie as (their) truth.

Second, truthiness is as a rule not an individual but a group phenomenon. It is not simply *I* but *we* who feel it to be true. Truthiness is based on shared perception. Without such commonality in outlook, my felt truth is at best an idiosyncrasy and at worst a sign of mental illness. What makes truthiness persuasive is that others feel like me. Moreover, because this kind of "truth" is a matter of shared perception, it is also a matter of shared narratives. For we experience ourselves and the world around us in and through stories, as we saw in an earlier chapter. Human beings are *homines narrantes*. The mind thinks in stories, or at least that is its default position. Stories impose structure on a chaotic, unpredictable, and often frightening world, not least by distinguishing between what is the case and what is not, between what is true and what is false.

Let us look at an example. Many Trump supporters believed and continue to believe his lie that he and not Joe Biden won the 2020 election. Does this mean they are completely blind to empirical reality? Are they that dull-witted? Or have they been brainwashed to such an extent that they simply accept anything he says, even if he told them—in true Orwellian fashion—that two plus two equals five? I do not think that this is plausible. Rather, what happens here, I would suggest, is two things.

First, Trump's false claim about vote numbers is (unconsciously or semi-consciously) converted into a statement about the election's fairness. Second, this statement—that the election was rigged—is embraced because *that* feels accurate. After all, how could there have been a level playing field, what with the left-wing establishment and the biased mainstream media? Thus, what is arguably Trump's biggest lie comes to be experienced as true because it accords with the overarching narrative of America as country in the tentacles of a power-hungry liberal elite. Mathematically, Trump may not have received more votes than Biden, but that is not what matters to his supporters: decisive is that "the deck was stacked against him" and in that "deeper" sense his lie is "true".

Narrative (un-)truth is so potent precisely because it is not about statistical facts. It works as a story interlinked with and underpinned by the stories of me as a member of a particular group, which can be any collective from local communities to nations. Narrative (un-)truth is about the story of us, of our past, present, and future. This is why the falsehood that Barack Obama was not born in the United States got traction. Birtherism resonated because it was interlinked with and underpinned by the myth of America as an essentially Anglo-Saxon country. In such a country—"our country", the country of white folk—a black President has to be illegitimate. Truthiness, then, is narrative truth; and narrative truth is existential truth. As a result, it is almost impossible to dislodge.

There is another reason why narrative (un-)truth is so powerful. Like classic stories and full-blown conspiracy theories, it tends to take archetypal forms.[150] It is a tale of good against evil, heroes against villains, and rebels against the establishment. Its plot is one of continuous challenges and tasks to be accomplished, of persecution and resistance, of struggle and victory (or undeserved defeat). This is how Hitler (taking inspiration from Karl May and Richard Wagner) and Trump (benefiting from his reality-television experience) told their respective political fables, as we saw in previous chapters. It is also the way the mind at its most primitive experiences the world. Thus, the more hostile, frightening, and unjust the world appears to us, the more likely we are to embrace fairy tales.

Finally, people assess the validity of a story not by confronting it with the facts, but by comparing it to other stories. Is climate change a reality? I, for one, am not in a position to establish this empirically. I believe climate change is real because my view—my story—of the society I live in includes a significant amount of trust in science and in the scientific community. By the same token, I trust my country's election results because I accept the overarching story that its political and legal systems guarantee free and fair elections. If such trust breaks down, however, even the most basic facts will come to be questioned and people will start casting about for a different explanatory framework; that is to say, for a story that will give new meaning to the old facts, explain them away, or make them seem irrelevant.

It is precisely such a breakdown in social trust within their respective societies that Trump and (in a much more extreme fashion) Hitler managed to exploit. This book has examined the manifold ways in which they did so. Not least, it has shown how their auratic self-staging and rhetorical strategies connected with the hopes and fears, the naïve beliefs and noxious prejudices of ordinary people. In this sense, it is as much a study of human frailty as of political cunning.

Notes

1. The recording is available on YouTube. See, for example, "Hitlerin salaa tallennettu keskustelu Suomessa" and "Hitler's Secretly Recorded Conversation in Finland".
2. Adolf Hitler, *Mein Kampf*, trans. Ralph Manheim (Boston and New York: Houghton Mifflin Company, 1999), p. 470, and Adolf Hitler, *Mein Kampf. Eine kritische Edition*, ed. Christian Hartmann, Thomas Vordermayer, Othmar Plöckinger, and Roman Töppel (Munich and Berlin: Institut für Zeitgeschichte, 2016), vol. 2, p. 1193.
3. Albert Krebs, *The Infancy of Nazism: The Memoirs of Ex-Gauleiter Albert Krebs 1923–1933*, trans. William Sheridan Allen (New York: New Viewpoints, 1976; first published in German 1959), p. 152.
4. See Christa Schroeder, *He Was My Chief: The Memoirs of Adolf Hitler's Secretary*, trans. Geoffrey Brooks (Barnsley: Frontline Books, 2012; first published in German 1985), p. 47.

5. See the analysis in Chap. 1. Hitler's campaign was even turned into a film documentary, and Heinrich Hoffmann produced a photo book of the event.
6. A similar scene—this time with the Führer addressing a television audience—is used to great effect in the 2015 black comedy *Er ist wieder da* (Look Who's Back), which sees Hitler "wake up" in the twenty-first century and start a career as a populist politician. Based on Timur Vermes's eponymous novel of 2012 and directed by David Wnendt, the film—paradoxically—paints a much more realistic picture of Hitler's appeal than do more serious cinematic representations of him.
7. Tucker Carlson, cited in Allen Salkin and Aaron Short, *The Method to the Madness: Donald Trump's Ascent as Told by Those Who Were Hired, Fired, Inspired—and Inaugurated* (New York: All Points Books, 2019), p. 128.
8. Hitler, *Mein Kampf*, p. 472 (English) and vol. 2, p. 1197 (German).
9. Hitler, *Mein Kampf*, p. 476 (English; translation modified) and vol. 2, p. 1205 (German).
10. Hitler, *Mein Kampf*, p. 476 (English) and vol. 2, p. 1205 (German).
11. Hitler, *Mein Kampf*, p. 477 (English) and vol. 2, p. 1207 (German).
12. See, for example, the television documentary *Coupez le son! Le charisme politique*, presented by the political scientist and body-language expert René Zayan (dir. Thierry Berrod; Mona Lisa Productions / Ina, 2007). Zayan also discusses the importance of cultural differences in this context.
13. Ernst Hanfstaengl, *Hitler: The Memoir of a Nazi Insider Who Turned against the Führer*, trans. John Willard Toland (New York: Arcade Publishing, 2011, first published in German 1957), p. 35.
14. Hanfstaengl, *Hitler*, p. 68.
15. Michael D'Antonio, *The Truth about Trump* (new ed. New York: Thomas Dunne Books, 2016; first published 2015 as *Never Enough: Donald Trump and the Pursuit of Success*), p. xii.
16. Donald Trump, cited in Cliff Sims, *Team of Vipers: My 500 Extraordinary Days in the Trump White House* (New York: Thomas Dunne Books, 2019), p. 273.
17. See, for example, Marcus Gilmer et al., "Insult after Insult: All of Trump's Ugly Campaign Rhetoric in One Place, *Mashable* (no date given), and Kevin Quealy, "The Complete List of Trump's Twitter Insults", *The New York Times*, 19 January 2021.

18. The one he forgot was Energy, the very department President-elect Trump would later ask him to lead. Perry was confirmed as Secretary of Energy in March 2017. Trump's attacks on Perry's intellect were made in a Tweet of 16 July 2015 and at a campaign rally in Bluffton, South Carolina, on 21 July 2015.
19. See Mark Leibovich, "Donald Trump Shares His Opponent-Branding Secrets", *The New York Times Magazine*, 9 May 2016.
20. Cf. Leibovich, "Donald Trump".
21. The three statements come from a (later deleted) re-Tweet of 16 April 2015, Paul Solotaroff's report "Trump Seriously: On the Trail with the GOP's Tough Guy" in *Rolling Stone* of 9 September 2015, and a Tweet of 28 August 2012.
22. Cited in Greg Mitchell, *Tricky Dick and the Pink Lady: Richard Nixon vs. Helen Gahagan Douglas—Sexual Politics and the Red Scare, 1950* (New York: Random House, 1998), p. 170. Nixon launched this attack during his 1950 Senate campaign and hence against the backdrop of the rise of McCarthyism.
23. Krebs, *Infancy of Nazism*, pp. 154–55. The Tannenbergbund was banned in 1933.
24. Adolf Hitler, *Sämtliche Aufzeichnungen 1905–1924*, edited by Eberhard Jäckel in collaboration with Axel Kuhn (Stuttgart: Deutsche Verlags-Anstalt, 1980), p. 93. Erzberger had been a schoolteacher before entering politics. The jibe reminds one of Donald Trump's Tweet of 1 July 2015 that former New York governor George Pataki, who had criticized Trump's comments about Mexican immigrants, "couldn't be elected dog catcher if he ran again".
25. Hitler, *Sämtliche Aufzeichnungen*, p. 110.
26. Hitler, *Sämtliche Aufzeichnungen*, p. 110.
27. Cf. Chaps. 3 and 4.
28. Max Domarus, *The Essential Hitler: Speeches and Commentary*, edited by Patrick Romane (Wauconda, Illinois: Bolchazy-Carducci, 2007), p. 697 (translation modified). The German original can be found in Adolf Hitler, *Reden 1920–1945* (no date and publisher given): speech of 28 April 1939 (no page numbers given). This part of the speech can also be found on YouTube; see "FDR and Policing the World: Hitler's Threat". Later on in his reply, Hitler used the same rhetorical device when listing the numbers and types of weaponry Germany had destroyed following the Treaty of Versailles.

29. Domarus, *Essential Hitler*, pp. 698–99 (translation modified), and Hitler, *Reden 1920–1945* (no page numbers given).
30. Hitler, *Mein Kampf*, p. 485 (English) and vol. 2, p. 1229 (German).
31. The book's main text actually uses the word *Tatsache* (fact), not *Tat* (deed, action); in Trumpian translation, the subtitle might be rendered as *Fact versus Fake News*. The book was reissued in 1934 and, in a mass-market edition that omitted the editor's name, 1938 (having become increasingly critical of National Socialism, Hanfstaengl had fled Germany in 1937). See Claudia Schmölders, *Hitlers Gesicht. Eine physiognomische Biographie* (Munich: Beck, 2000), pp. 125–26, and Cris Whetton, *Hitler's Fortune* (Barnsley: Pen & Sword, 2004), pp. 266–67.
32. Hitler, *Mein Kampf*, pp. 480–81 (English) and vol. 2, pp. 1217–19 (German).
33. Hitler, *Mein Kampf*, p. 481 (English) and vol. 2, p. 1219 (German).
34. Donald J. Trump, with Tony Schwartz, *The Art of the Deal* (London: Arrow Books, no year; first published 1987), p. 176.
35. Robert Slater, *No Such Thing as Over-Exposure: Inside the Life and Celebrity of Donald Trump* (Upper Saddle River, NJ: Prentice Hall, 2005), p. 122.
36. Cf. Gwenda Blair, *Donald Trump: The Candidate* (New York etc.: Simon & Schuster, 2015), p. 226: "When he was asked if he worried about overexposure, he seemed almost baffled by the question. He didn't believe there was any such thing as overexposure".
37. Omarosa Manigault Newman, *Unhinged: An Insider's Account of the Trump White House* (London etc.: Simon & Schuster, 2018), p. 74.
38. The four statements come from a campaign rally in Birmingham, Alabama (21 November 2015), an interview with Fox News (22 November 2015), and campaign rallies in Clinton, Iowa (1 February 2016) and Las Vegas, Nevada (22 February 2016).
39. David Cay Johnston, *The Making of Donald Trump* (Brooklyn and London: Melville House, 2017; first published 2016), p. xx.
40. Trump, *Art of the Deal*, p. 304.
41. Hitler, *Mein Kampf*, p. 485 (English; translation modified) and vol. 2, pp. 1227–29 (German).
42. Cited in Frederic Spotts, *Hitler and the Power of Aesthetics* (new ed. New York: The Overlook Press, 2018), p. 56.
43. Spotts, *Hitler and the Power of Aesthetics*, p. 57.
44. Cf. Chap. 1.

45. This is the phrase that Ian Kershaw uses apropos of Hitler's political meetings. See Ian Kershaw, *Hitler 1889–1936: Hubris* (London etc.: Penguin, 2001; first published 1998), p. 152.
46. See Hans Ulrich Gumbrecht, *Production of Presence: What Meaning Cannot Convey* (Stanford: Stanford University Press, 2004).
47. Gumbrecht, *Production of Presence*, p. 85. The distinctions are, of course, ideal types in Max Weber's sense: we are not dealing with either/or, but with more/less.
48. This aspect remains marginal in Gumbrecht's study, which focuses largely on the individual.
49. Gumbrecht, *Production of Presence*, p. 80.
50. This is not to say that he mass behaviour of other groups is immune to this danger: see the discussion of Twitter witch hunts in Chap. 4.
51. D'Antonio, *Truth about Trump*, p. 346. Cf. my discussion of Freud's view of mass psychology in Chap. 4.
52. Hitler, *Mein Kampf*, pp. 478–79 (English) and vol. 2, pp. 1209–11 (German). Hitler's ideas on mass psychology were heavily influenced by Gustave Le Bon's *Psychologie des foules* (The Crowd: A Study of the Popular Mind, 1895).
53. Classic texts on Hitler's use of language include Kenneth Burke, "The Rhetoric of Hitler's *Battle*" [1939], in *The Philosophy of Literary Form: Studies in Symbolic Action* (Baton Rouge, LA: Louisiana State University Press, 1941), pp. 191–220, Victor Klemperer, *The Language of the Third Reich: LTI—Lingua Tertii Imperii: A Philologist's Notebook*, translated by Martin Brady (London: Bloomsbury, 2013; first published in German 1946), Josef Kopperschmidt (ed. in collaboration with Johannes G. Pankau), *Hitler. Der Redner* (Munich: Fink, 2003) Albrecht Koschorke, *Adolf Hitler's "Mein Kampf". Zur Poetik des Nationalsozialismus* (Berlin: Matthes & Seitz, 2016), Reginald H. Phelps, "Hitler als Parteiredner im Jahre 1920", *Vierteljahrshefte für Zeitgeschichte* 11.3, 1963, pp. 274–330, Othmar Plöckinger, *Reden um die Macht? Wirkung und Strategie der Reden Adolf Hitlers im Wahlkampf zu den Reichstagswahlen am 6. November 1932* (Vienna: Passagen-Verlag, 1999), Felicity Rash, *The Language of Violence: Adolf Hitler's "Mein Kampf"* (New York, NY: Peter Lang, 2006), and Lutz Winckler, *Studien zur gesellschaftlichen Funktion faschistischer Sprache* (Frankfurt am Main: Suhrkamp, 1970). A recent bibliography is Heidrun Kämper, *Sprachgebrauch im Nationalsozialismus* (Heidelberg: Winter, 2019). On

Trump's use of language, see, for example, Scott Adams, *Win Bigly: Persuasion in a World Where Facts Don't Matter* (New York, NY: Portfolio Penguin, 2017), Michael Mario Albrecht, *Trumping the Media: Politics and Democracy in the Post-Truth Era* (New York etc.: Bloomsbury Academic, 2023), Oliver Jones, *Donald Trump: The Rhetoric* (London: Eyewear, 2016), Michele Lockhart (ed.), *President Donald Trump and His Political Discourse: Ramifications of Rhetoric via Twitter* (New York and London: Routledge, 2019), Jennifer Mercieca, *Demagogue for President: The Rhetorical Genius of Donald Trump* (College Station: Texas A&M University Press, 2020), Marco Morini, *Lessons from Trump's Political Communication: How to Dominate the Media Environment* (London: Palgrave Macmillan, 2020), Peter Osborne and Tom Roberts, *How Trump Thinks: His Tweets and the Birth of a New Political Language* (London: Head of Zeus, 2017), and Bérengère Viennot, *La langue de Trump* (Paris: Les Arènes, 2019).
54. Krebs, *Infancy of Nazism*, p. 159.
55. Johnston, *Making of Donald Trump*, p. 214.
56. This is one of the things that Steve Bannon emphasized vis-à-vis Trump before being made chief strategist of the 2016 election campaign. Bannon—Bob Woodward reports—stressed that Trump "spoke in a voice that did not sound political", whereas Hillary Clinton "spoke like the trained politician she was. [...] Even when telling the truth, she sounded like she was lying to you. [...] It was a mechanical way of speaking, right out of the polling and focus groups, answering the questions in political speak". See Bob Woodward, *Fear: Trump in the White House* (London etc.: Simon & Schuster, 2018), p. 16.
57. Cited in Laurence Rees, *The Dark Charisma of Adolf Hitler: Leading Millions into the Abyss* (London: Ebury Press, 2013; first published 2012), pp. 36–37.
58. Cited in Rees, *Dark Charisma*, p. 37.
59. Ernst Bloch, "Sokrates und die Propaganda [1936]", in *Vom Hasard zur Katastrophe. Politische Aufsätze aus den Jahren 1934–1939* (Frankfurt am Main: Suhrkamp, 1972), pp. 103–11 (103).
60. D'Antonio, *Truth about Trump*, p. 13.
61. The first statement comes from Trump's Presidential announcement speech of 16 June 2015, while the second one comes from his interview with CNN's Dana Bash of 30 July 2015. In subsequent speeches and interviews, Trump refused to reveal the details of his "absolute way of

defeating ISIS" because—he claimed variously—his political opponents might steal his ideas, or because he did not want ISIS to know the plan in advance, or because in politics it is always better to remain unpredictable (see, for example, his interview with Fox News' Greta Van Susteren of 27 May 2015). When explaining his plan for a better healthcare system to Bash, Trump did not venture beyond "We're gonna have to work out some very, very smart deal with hospitals around the country".

62. Michael Lynch, *Hitler* (London and New York: Routledge, 2013), p. 93.
63. For a detailed discussion of conspiratorial thinking, see Chap. 3.
64. Hanfstaengl, *Hitler*, pp. 34–35. The subclause I have omitted reads "a charge it was only too easy to make stick", a gloss that shows that even after having abandoned his National Socialist sympathies Hanfstaengl had not fully shed his anti-Semitism.
65. For a good introduction to issues of political framing, see George Lakoff, *The All New Don't Think of an Elephant* (White River Junction, Vermont: Chelsea Green, 2014). Other useful overviews include Hans de Bruijn, *Political Framing: How Politicians Convince Us That They Are Right* (Amsterdam: Amsterdam University Press, 2019), Frank Luntz, *Words That Work* (New York: Hyperion, 2007), Steven Poole, *Words Are Weapons* (London: Abacus, 2007; first published 2006), and Elisabeth Wehling, *Politisches Framing. Wie eine Nation sich ihr Denken einredet—und daraus Politik macht* (Ullstein, 2019; first published 2016).
66. Kershaw, *Hitler 1889–1936*, p. 170; cf. pp. 156–57 and 185.
67. Phelps, "Hitler als Parteiredner", pp. 283–84.
68. Phelps, "Hitler als Parteiredner", p. 284.
69. Adolf Hitler, *The Speeches of Adolf Hitler 1921–1941* (no date and publisher given): speech of 1 February 1933 (no page numbers given; translation modified); also in Domarus, *Essential Hitler*, pp. 209–14. The German original can be found in Hitler, *Reden 1920–1945* (no page numbers given).
70. Donald J. Trump, *The Essential Speeches, Remarks, and Addresses of the Fifty-Fourth President of the United States of America*, ed. by Anthony Raymond Michalski (Wilkes-Barre, PA: Kallisti, 2020), pp. 56–63. The Biblical citation is from Psalms 133:1.
71. Cited in Michael Wolff, *Fire and Fury: Inside the Trump White House* (London: Little, Brown, 2018), p. 44.
72. Franklin Delano Roosevelt, "The Only Thing We Have to Fear Is Fear Itself" [1933], in Brian MacArthur (ed.), *The Penguin Book of Modern*

Speeches (London: 4th, revised ed. Penguin, 2017), pp. 129–33 (129–30).

73. The "Gesetz zur Wiederherstellung des Berufsbeamtentums" of 7 April 1933 also applied to members of communist organizations and a number of other groups. Initially, the law made various exceptions—for former frontline soldiers, for instance—but such "loopholes" were soon closed.
74. For a good short overview of Hitler's opportunistic approach to matters of religion and faith, see Ian Kershaw, *The "Hitler Myth": Image and Reality in the Third Reich* (new ed. Oxford: Oxford University Press, 2001), especially pp. 105–20, and Rees, *Dark Charisma*, pp. 112–13 and 136–39.
75. Trump made this statement in an interview with Frank Luntz, held during the Family Leadership Summit at Iowa State University on 18 July 2015.
76. Michael Cohen, *Disloyal: A Memoir* (New York, NY: Skyhorse Publishing, 2020), p. 125.
77. Cohen, *Disloyal*, pp. 127–28.
78. Cohen, *Disloyal*, p. 133.
79. McCay Coppins, "Trump Secretly Mocks His Christian Supporters", *The Atlantic* of 29 September 2020. See also David Cay Johnston, "What He Really Thinks: Trump Mocks Christians, Calls Them 'Fools' and 'Schmucks'", *Salon* of 11 September 2020.
80. Hitler, *Mein Kampf*, pp. 180 and 183 (English) and vol. 1, pp. 501 and 507 (German).
81. Hitler, *Mein Kampf*, p. 342 (English; translation modified) and vol. 1, p. 889 (German).
82. Cf. Laurence Rees's 2016 Tans lecture and his conversation with Atticus Mullikin (both available on YouTube).
83. Trump, *Art of the Deal*, p. 58.
84. Trump, *Art of the Deal*, p. 181.
85. Donald Trump in a Tweet of 7 November 2016 (one day before election day). He used an almost identical phrase at a campaign rally in Melbourne, Florida, on 27 September 2016.
86. Donald Trump at a campaign rally in Albany, New York, on 19 February 2016. He used the getting-tired-of-winning phrase at various other campaign rallies as well.
87. Donald Trump at a campaign rally in Bismarck, North Dakota, on 26 May 2016.

88. On Bloch's biography, see Cat Moir, "Ernst Bloch: Life—Work—Reception", in: *Rethinking Ernst Bloch*, ed. by Henk de Berg and Cat Moir (Leiden: E. J. Brill, 2023), pp. 10–50.
89. Ernst Bloch, *Heritage of Our Times*, translated by Neville Plaice and Stephen Plaice (Oxford: Polity Press, 1991; first published in German 1935 and—in an extended edition—1962), p. 117, and *Erbschaft dieser Zeit* (Frankfurt am Main: Suhrkamp, 1985), p. 126.
90. Bloch, *Heritage*, p. 97 (translation modified), and *Erbschaft*, p. 104.
91. Bloch, *Heritage*, p. 57, and *Erbschaft*, p. 63. The Nazis adopted the name from Arthur Moeller van den Bruck's *Das Dritte Reich* (The Third Reich, 1923).
92. Bloch, *Heritage*, p. 57 (translation modified), and *Erbschaft*, p. 63.
93. Bloch, *Heritage*, p. 44 (translation modified), and *Erbschaft*, p. 49.
94. Bloch, *Heritage*, p. 99, and *Erbschaft*, p. 105–06.
95. Bloch, *Heritage*, p. 135, and *Erbschaft*, p. 149.
96. Bloch, *Heritage*, p. 128, and *Erbschaft*, p. 140. Bloch also established a link between the narrative structure of certain manifestations of popular culture (such as Karl May's adventure stories) and that of National Socialist ideology, a link similar to the one we explored in Chap. 1. See Bloch, *Heritage*, pp. 154–64, and *Erbschaft*, pp. 169–81.
97. Scott Adams, *Win Bigly: Persuasion in a World Where Facts Don't Matter* (New York: Portfolio / Penguin, 2017), pp. 21–22.
98. Adams, *Win Bigly*, p. 22.
99. Barack Obama, "Statement by the President", delivered at the Fairmont Hotel in San Jose, California, on 7 June 2013.
100. Cf. Adams, *Win Bigly*, p. 22.
101. Norman Vincent Peale, *The Power of Positive Thinking* (London: Vermillion, 1998; first published 1952), p. 18.
102. The following account draws above all on the studies by Albrecht, Lockhart (ed.), Mercieca, Morini, and Oborne and Roberts listed in note 669. All numerical data come from these sources.
103. Neal Gabler, "Donald Trump, the Emperor of Social Media", *BillMoyers.com* of 29 April 2016, cited in Morini, *Lessons*, p. 6.
104. On this term, see Morini, *Lessons*, pp. 1–26.
105. Trump, *Art of the Deal*, p. 176.
106. Tweet of 17 February 2017. For a database of Trump's Tweets, see the *Trump Twitter Archive* at www.the trumparchive.com.
107. Trump, *Art of the Deal*, p. 304.

108. The 280-character limit was introduced in November 2017.
109. Alexander Aciman and Emmett Rensin, *Twitterature: The World's Greatest Books Retold through Twitter* (London: Penguin, 2009), p. 51.
110. Donald J. Trump with Meredith McIver, *How to Get Rich: The Secrets of Business Success from the Star of The Apprentice* (London: BBC Books, 2004), p. xii.
111. Morini, *Lessons*, p. 88.
112. Cf. Ian Leslie, *Born Liars: We All Do It But Which One Are You: Psychopath, Sociopath or Little White Liar?* (London: Quercus, 2011).
113. Albrecht, *Trumping the Media*, p. 99.
114. Tweets of 29 July 2015 and 10 September 2016.
115. Tweet of 9 October 2016.
116. This is in the period from his candidature announcement in June 2015 until the midterm elections in November 2018. See the table in Morini, *Lessons*, p. 74.
117. On this topic, see Brian Rosenwald, *Talk Radio's America: How an Industry Took Over a Political Party That Took Over the United States* (Cambridge, Mass., and London: Harvard University Press, 2019), as well as Albrecht, *Trumping the Media*, pp. 39–61.
118. On the issue of national and cultural identity, see Chap. 5.
119. See Gregory Krieg, "14 of Trump's Most Outrageous 'Birther' Claims—Half of Them from after 2011", *CNN*, 16 September 2016.
120. Tweet of 27 January 2016.
121. Mercieca, *Demagogue for President*, p. 90. Among the best-known of such saying-it-without-saying-it messages is Trump's (later deleted) retweet of 28 June 2020, which included a link to a video of someone shouting "White power! White power!". For further examples, see Mercieca, *Demagogue for President*, pp. 89–98.
122. Glenn Kessler, Salvador Rizzo, and Meg Kelly, *Donald Trump and His Assault on Truth: The President's Falsehoods, Misleading Claims and Flat-Out Lies* (New York, etc.: Scribner, 2020), pp. x-xi.
123. See Chap. 3.
124. Hitler, *Mein Kampf*, p. 231 (English; translation modified) and vol. 1, p. 617 (German).
125. Hitler, *Mein Kampf*, pp. 231 and 232 (English) and vol. 1, p. 617 (German).
126. Joseph Goebbels, "Aus Churchills Lügenfabrik" [1941], in *Die Zeit ohne Beispiel. Reden und Aufsätze 1939/40/41* (Munich: Zentralverlag

der NSDAP. Franz Eher Nachf., 1941), pp. 364–69 (364–65). In her September 1990 *Vanity Fair* article "After the Goldrush", Marie Brenner cites ones of Trump's lawyers as saying: "Donald Trump is a believer in the big-lie theory [...]. If you say something again and again, people will believe you". Trump's response—she adds—was: "I think if one of my lawyers said that, I'd like to know who it is, because I'd fire his ass. I'd like to find out who the scumbag is!"

127. Cf. the photo section in D'Antonio, *Truth about Trump*, between pp. 138 and 139.
128. R. G. Waldeck, *Meet Mr. Blank* (New York: G. P. Putnam's Sons, 1943), p. 49, cited in James Pool, *Who Financed Hitler: The Secret Funding of Hitler's Rise to Power, 1919–1933* (rev. and updated ed. New York etc.: Pocket Books, 1997), p. 121.
129. Cited in Rees, *Dark Charisma*, p. 63.
130. See Rees, *Dark Charisma*, p. 64.
131. Scott Adams, *Loserthink: How Untrained Brains Are Ruining the World* (New York: Portfolio / Penguin, 2019), pp. 87–88.
132. Rees, *Dark Charisma*, pp. 64–65.
133. Of course, to a certain type of voter a candidate's factual accuracy may be emotionally valent, too. On the whole, though, most voters appear to be unconcerned about cold cognitive untruths.
134. Alister McGrath, with Joanna Collicut McGrath, *The Dawkins Delusion? Atheist Fundamentalism and the Denial of the Divine* (London: SPCK, 2007), p. 37.
135. McGrath, *The Dawkins Delusion?*, p. 37.
136. Jeet Heer, "Trump's Lies Destroy Logic As Well As Truth", *The New Republic* of 28 November 2016, referring to Tweets of 27 November 2016.
137. Heer, "Trump's Lies".
138. Sigmund Freud, *Jokes and Their Relation to the Unconscious*, translated by James Strachey (Harmondsworth: Penguin, 1976), p. 100; cf. pp. 266–67. See also *The Interpretation of Dreams*, translated by James Strachey (Harmondsworth: Penguin, 1976), p. 197.
139. Heer, "Trump's Lies".
140. Heer, "Trump's Lies".
141. Heer, "Trump's Lies".
142. Hitler, *Mein Kampf*, p. 307 (English; translation modified) and vol. 1, p. 799 (German).

143. Hitler, *Mein Kampf*, p. 307 (English; translation modified) and vol. 1, p. 799 (German).
144. Hitler, *Mein Kampf*, pp. 307–08 (English; translation modified) and vol. 1, pp. 799 and 803 (German).
145. On the conception and history of the *Protocols*, see Wolfgang Benz, *Die Protokolle der Weisen von Zion. Die Legende von der jüdischen Weltverschwörung* (third, rev. ed. Munich: Beck: 2017), Norman Cohn, *Warrant for Genocide: The Myth of the Jewish World Conspiracy and the Protocols of the Elders of Zion* (Harmondsworth: Penguin, 1967), Richard J. Evans, *The Hitler Conspiracies: The Third Reich and the Paranoid Imagination* (London: Allen Lane, 2020), especially pp. 13–45, and Eva Horn and Michael Hagemeister (eds.), *Die Fiktion von der jüdischen Weltverschwörung. Zu Text und Kontext der "Protokolle der Weisen von Zion"* (Göttingen: Wallstein, 2012).
146. He did so on the very first episode of his television comedy show *The Colbert Report*, broadcast on 17 October 2005.
147. Nathan Rabin, "Stephen Colbert", *The A. V. Club* of 25 January 2006.
148. Rabin, "Stephen Colbert".
149. This interpretative latitude was aided by what Richard J. Evans has called the text's "[r]ambling, chaotic and unstructured" nature. Interestingly, as Evans also notes, a number of standard anti-Semitic notions are not in the document. This includes the idea of "typically Jewish" physical characteristics and the supposed danger of racial intermixing. See Evans, *Hitler Conspiracies*, p. 17.
150. On conspiracy theories, see Chap. 3; on classic story-telling, see Chap. 5.

Correction to: Trump and Hitler

Correction to:

H. de Berg, *Trump and Hitler*, https://doi.org/10.1007/
978-3-031-51833-1

The original version of this book has been revised. The end notes were moved to respective chapters and the missing numbers have been added to the text in the relevant chapters. The movement of end notes had affected the pagination throughout the book.

The updated version of this book can be found at
https://doi.org/10.1007/978-3-031-51833-1

Select Bibliography

This bibliography lists the studies from which the historical and biographical background information not referenced in the main text has been taken. The more specialized publications on which I have drawn can be found in the endnotes.

Barrett, Wayne, *Trump, the Greatest Show on Earth: The Deals, the Downfall, the Reinvention* (new ed. New York: Regan Arts, 2016; first published 1992 as *Trump: The Deals and the Downfall*).

Blair, Gwenda, *The Trumps: Three Generations That Built an Empire* (New York etc.: Touchstone, 2000).

Blair, Gwenda, *Donald Trump: The Candidate* (New York etc.: Simon & Schuster, 2015).

Bracher, Karl Dietrich, *The German Dictatorship: The Origins, Structure and Consequences of National Socialism*, trans. Jean Steinberg (Harmondsworth: Penguin, 1973; first published in German 1969).

D'Antonio, Michael, *The Truth about Trump* (new ed. New York: Thomas Dunne Books, 2016; first published 2015 as *Never Enough: Donald Trump and the Pursuit of Success*).

Evans, Richard J., *The Coming of the Third Reich* (London etc.: Penguin, 2004; first published 2003).

Evans, Richard J., *The Third Reich in Power, 1933–1939* (London etc.: Penguin, 2006; first published 2005).

Evans, Richard J., *The Third Reich at War* (London etc.: Penguin, 2009; first published 2008).
Groenhuijsen, Charles, *Donald Trump* (Amsterdam: Balans, 2015).
Haberman, Maggie, *Confidence Man: The Making of Donald Trump and the Breaking of America* (London: Mudlark, 2022).
Hamann, Brigitte, *Hitler's Vienna: A Portrait of the Tyrant as a Young Man*, trans. Thomas Thornton (new. ed. London: Tauris Parke Paperbacks, 2010; first published in German 1996).
Hauner, Milan, *Hitler: A Chronology of His Life and Time* (second, rev. ed. Houndmills, Basingstoke, and New York: Palgrave Macmillan, 2008; first published 2005).
Johnston, David Cay, *The Making of Donald Trump* (Brooklyn and London: Melville House, 2016).
Kershaw, Ian, *Hitler 1889–1936: Hubris* (London etc.: Penguin, 2001a; first published 1998).
Kershaw, Ian, *Hitler 1936–1945: Nemesis* (London etc.: Penguin, 2001b; first published 2000).
King, Norma, *Ivana Trump: A Very Unauthorized Biography* (New York: Carroll & Graf, 1990).
Kranish, Michael, and Marc Fisher, *Trump Revealed: The Definitive Biography of the 45th President* (London etc.: Simon & Schuster, 2017; first published 2016).
Longerich, Peter, *Hitler: A Life*, trans. Jeremy Noakes and Lesley Sharpe (Oxford: Oxford University Press, 2019; first published in German 2015).
Lynch, Michael, *Hitler* (Oxford and New York: Routledge, 2013).
McDonough, Frank, *Hitler and the Rise of the Nazi Party* (second ed. London and New York: Routledge, 2014; first published 2012).
McDonough, Frank, *The Hitler Years: Triumph 1933–1939* (London: Head of Zeus, 2019).
McDonough, Frank, *The Hitler Years: Disaster 1940–1945* (London: Head of Zeus, 2020).
Melching, Willem, *Hitler. Opkomst en ondergang van een Duits politicus* (Amsterdam: Prometheus, 2019).
Moorhouse, Roger, *The Third Reich in 100 Objects: A Material History of Nazi Germany* (Barnsley: Greenhill Books, 2017).
O'Brien, Timothy L., *TrumpNation: The Art of Being The Donald* (new ed. New York and Boston: Grand Central Publishing, 2016; first published 2005).

Overy, Richard, *The Dictators: Hitler's Germany, Stalin's Russia* (New York: W. W. Norton, 2004)
Simms, Brendan, *Hitler: Only the World Was Enough* (London: Allen Lane, 2019).
Slater, Robert, *No Such Thing as Over-Exposure: Inside the Life and Celebrity of Donald Trump* (Upper Saddle River, NJ: Prentice Hall, 2005).
Thamer, Hans-Ulrich, and Simone Erpel (eds.), *Hitler und die Deutschen. Volksgemeinschaft und Verbrechen* (Dresden: Sandstein, 2011).
Ullrich, Volker, *Hitler: Ascent 1889–1939*, trans. Jefferson Chase (London: The Bodley Head, 2016; first published in German 2013).
Ullrich, Volker, *Hitler: Downfall 1939–45*, trans. Jefferson Chase (London: The Bodley Head, 2020; first published in German 2018).
van Capelle, Hendrik, and Arie Pieter van de Bovenkamp, *Hitler 1889–1945. Een tiran in beeld* (new, revised and extended ed. Ede: De Lantaarn, 2019).
Weber, Thomas, *Hitler's First War: Adolf Hitler, the Men of the List Regiment, and the First World War* (New York etc.: Oxford University Press, 2011; first published 2010).
Weber, Thomas, *Becoming Hitler: The Making of a Nazi* (Oxford: Oxford University Press, 2017).

Index[1]

A

Abramowitz, Alan, 108
Absolutism, 17–19, 293
Aciman, Alexander, 295
Adams, John, 131, 151n12
Adams, Scott, 292, 301
Adolf-Hitler-Spende der deutschen Wirtschaft, 84
Adversaire repoussoir, 122
Affect heuristic, 177
Against-ism, 136, 207, 282, 283
Aggregation-and-disaggregation, 129, 130
Aggregation fallacy, 172
Ahnenerbe institute, 241
Ailes, Roger, 36, 63n161
Alberta, Tim, 23
Albrecht, Michael Mario, 296
Aldrin, Buzz, 143
All Marketers Are Liars (Godin), 194
Alternative facts (Conway), 180, 182
Althusser, Louis, 160
Aly, Götz, 127
Amann, Max, 66n205, 85, 247
American dream, 196–198, 200, 206, 288
Anger (as strategy), 15–17, 22, 126
Apprentice, The (TV show), 14, 21, 22, 41–43, 66n198, 208, 236, 272, 298
Archetypes, 219
Archilochus, 231
Aristotle, 192–194, 207
Armstrong, Neil, 143
Art of the Deal, The (Trump / Schwartz), 13, 231, 272, 273, 288, 295
Aschheim, Steven, 137

---

[1] Note: Page numbers followed by 'n' refer to notes.

As I Lay Dying (Faulkner), 146
Assassination attempts, 16, 20, 90
Ataturk, Kemal, 280
Atkinson, Rowan, 267
Aufführungszwang, 54n22
"Aufruf der Reichsregierung" (Hitler), 265
Aura (Benjamin), 54n23, 236
"Aus Churchills Lügenfabrik" (Goebbels), 300

B

Baarová, Lída, 97, 98
Baby, It's Cold Outside (song), 214
Bach, Isidor, 269
Bajohr, Frank, 105, 117n92
Bambi (Salten), 32
Bannon, Steve, 3, 13, 14, 36, 110n6, 111n20, 208, 215, 216, 224n47, 249, 250, 315n56
Barlow Palace, 80
Barthes, Roland, 198
Bash, Dana, 315n61, 316n61
Basic trust vs. basis distrust (Erikson), 149, 155
Battle for America (dir. Bannon), 208
Bechstein, Carl, 81, 88
Bechstein, Helene, 81
Beinart, Peter, 107, 108
Ben-Ghiat, Ruth, xi
Benjamin, Walter, 5–7, 36, 54n23, 236
Berghof, 88–91, 93, 94, 97, 100, 229, 234
Berlin, Isaiah, 122, 167, 231
Berliner Illustrirte Zeitung, 14
Berlusconi, Silvio, xi
Bettelheim, Bruno, 176

Biden, Joe, 299, 308, 309
Big Brother (TV show), 207
Big lie, 299
Birtherism, 66n194, 121, 138, 214, 309
Bismarck, Otto von, 40, 52, 212, 317n87
Bismarck (dir. Wolfgang Liebeneiner), 40, 41
Black Lives Matter, 214
Blade Runner (dir. Scott), 190, 220n2
Blair, Gwenda, 23, 245
Blake, Jacob, 178
Bloch, Ernst, 279, 289–291, 318n96
Border War (dir. Knoblock), 208
Boris III, 93
Bormann, Martin, 85, 87, 89, 90, 101, 113n43, 114n55, 181
Bossie, David, 2, 248
Bowie, David, 274
Bracher, Karl Dietrich, 216–218
Braun, Eva, 46, 76, 85, 88, 97, 115n70, 117n87, 233–235
Breitbart News, 143, 208, 249
Breker, Arno, 89
Brenner, Marie, ix, xiiin1, 320n126
Brexit, 281, 282
Brown House, 17, 80
Bruckmann, Elsa, 81
Brynner, Yul, 205
Bürgerbräu beer hall, 20
Bush, George W., 268, 286, 307
Bush, Jeb, 43, 268

C

Cagliostro, Alessandro, 28
Caligula, 123

Cameron, David, 54n27
Capricorn One (dir. Hyams), 143
Carinhall, 98, 99, 116n83
Carter, Miranda, 51
Case of Wagner, The (Nietzsche), 27
Celebrity Apprentice (TV show), 21, 42
Chamberlain, Neville, 56n43, 93, 115n69
Chaplin, Charlie, 50, 89
Charisma (Weber), 4, 5, 7, 54n22
Childhood and Society (Erikson), 155
Chotiner, Isaac, xi
Christianity, 4, 31, 64n166, 219, 244, 245, 280, 284, 293, 304, 306, 317n74
Christie, Agatha, 207
Churchill, Winston, 71, 300
Chyrons, 46
Ciano, Galeazzo, 93
Cleese, John, 175
Clifford, Stephanie, see Daniels, Stormy
Clinton, Bill, 7, 297
Clinton, Hillary, 43, 73, 108, 138, 148, 149, 231, 255n15, 260n93, 263, 268, 278, 297, 313n38, 315n56
Clooney, George, 95
CNN, 146, 174, 180, 295, 315n61
Cohen, Michael, 49, 74, 107, 108, 286
Cohn, Gary, 3, 13
Colbert, Stephen, 178, 307
Colbert Report, The (TV show), 321n146
Comey, James, 138
Commodore, The (hotel), 246

Communist Manifesto, The (Marx / Engels), 159
Conspiracy theory, 79, 121–149, 194, 224n43, 280, 295, 309
Container approach, 135–141, 209
Conway, Kellyanne, 180, 187n65
Coppins, McKay, 287
Corruption, 8, 27, 69–109, 139, 141, 148, 157
Cox, Archibald, 131, 151n12
Cranach the Elder, Lucas, 87
Crowd psychology, see Group psychology
Cruise, Tom, 16
Cruz, Ted, 23, 43, 268
Culture wars, 107, 179, 192, 208, 293
Cusanus, see Nicholas of Cusa
Cyrano de Bergerac (Rostand), 254

D

Dadaism, 192
Daniels, Stormy, 49
D'Antonio, Michael, 12, 243, 267, 277, 279
Das Buch der Deutschen (dir. Richard Skowronnek), 77
Das österreichische Antlitz (Salten), 32
Das Testament des Dr. Mabuse (dir. Lang), xivn14
Davies, William, 179–181, 187n64
Davis, David, 54n27
Davos, 157, 216
Death of Expertise, The (Nichols), 175
Debord, Guy, 193, 221n8
De la démocratie en Amérique (Tocqueville), 169

Delgado, Alois, 91
Der Bolschewismus als Aktion einer fremden Rasse (Rosenberg), 117n88
Der ewige Jude (dir. Hippler), 124
Der große König (dir. Harlan), 41
Der Mythus des 20. Jahrhunderts (Rosenberg), 117n88
Derrida, Jacques, 148
Der Sumpf (Rosenberg), 105
De totalitaire paradox (van Ree), 131
Deutsche Arbeiterpartei (DAP), 35, 36, 128
Deutscher Hof (hotel), 38, 39
Devotions upon Emergent Occasions (Donne), 187n58
Dick, Philip K., 220n2
Dietrich, Otto, 9, 19, 233, 236, 242, 247
Dignity, xiii, 30, 203–207, 213, 215–217, 289
    See also Identity; *Thymos*
Diplomats, 11, 89, 238, 258n46
Directional accuracy (Adams), 301
Disagreeing with the facts (Spicer), 182
Disintermediation (Morini), 295
Disintermediation (Rauch), 172, 173
Displacement, 126
Do Androids Dream of Electric Sheep? (Dick), 220n2
Dobbs, Lou, 267
Dolchstoßlegende, 209
Dollar, Creflo, 286
Donald Trump in Historical Perspective (ed. Harvey), xi
Donne, John, 178
Dowd, John, 13

Downfall (dir. Hirschbiegel), 3
Doyle, Jim, 151n12
Drexler, Anton, 35, 78
Dr. Mabuse (dir. Lang), xivn14
Durkheim, Émile, 64n166

E

Eagle's Nest, *see* Kehlsteinhaus
Ebert, Friedrich, 14
Edward VIII, 93
Eher (publishing house), 83, 85
Einsatzstab Rosenberg, 101
Eliot, T. S., 106
Elites, 98, 134, 155–182, 209, 211, 216, 309
Emotion *vs.* reason, 28
Engel, Gerhard, 103
Engelhard, Julius, 117n87
Engels, Friedrich, 159, 160, 182n9
Erbschaft dieser Zeit (Bloch), 289, 318n89
Erikson, Erik H., 155, 254
Er ist wieder da (Vermes), 311n6
Er ist wieder da (dir. Wnendt), 311n6
Erzberger, Matthias, 269, 312n24
Establishment-bashing, x, 162–166, 298
Evans, Alex, 200
Evans, Richard I., 219
Evans, Richard J., xi, 321n149
Exaggeration, 13, 35, 126, 288, 291–294, 297, 298
Exculpatory magic of the initiatory act (Redl), 252
Expertise-bashing, 181
Extremism, 19, 144, 230, 249, 286, 291–295, 297, 298

F

Falwell Jr., Jerry, 286
"Fascinating Fascism" (Sontag), 37, 63n159
Faulkner, William, 146
Feder, Gottfried, 34
Felder, Josef, 279
Fenestra caeli, 39
Feuerbach, Anselm, 92
Fick, Roderich, 91
Finchelstein, Federico, xi
Fiorina, Carly, 268
Fischer, Joschka, 172, 185n41
Fisher, Marc, 24
Floyd, George, 178
Flynn, Gillian, 146
Flynn, Michael, 73
Ford, Henry, 79
Foucault, Michel, 183n17
Fox News, 36, 107, 146, 267, 273
François-Poncet, André, 11
Frederick the Great, 1, 41, 212
Freikorps, 34
Freud, Sigmund, 147, 148, 170, 185n31, 261n98, 305
Frey, Alexander Moritz, 50, 66n204
Freyend, Ernst John von, 16
Friends (TV show), 207
From Fascism to Populism in History (Finchelstein), xi
Frum, David, 108, 109
Führer Museum, 95
Fukuyama, Francis, 204, 205
Fuqua, Antoine, 223n39
Future of Freedom, The (Zakaria), 171

G

Gabler, Neal, 294
Gaddafi, Muammar, xi
Gaha, Eden, 21
Gahagan Douglas, Helen, 269
Gall, Leonhard, 92
Ganz, Bruno, 3
Garner, Eric, 178
Gefühlsgemeinschaft, 165
General will (Rousseau), 132, 166
Generation Zero (dir. Bannon), 208
German Dictatorship, The (Bracher), 217
German Ideology, The (Marx / Engels), 160
Gesamtkunstwerk, 7, 27, 80
Gesundes Volksempfinden, xii, 181
Gingrich, Newt, 231, 232, 255n15, 260n93
Girtherism, 65n194
Givhan, Robin, 74
Goda, Norman, 102
Godard, Jean-Luc, 193
Godin, Seth, 194–196
Godwin, Mike, x
Godwin's law, x
Goebbels, Joseph, ix, 1, 2, 15, 18, 44, 47, 76, 96–101, 161, 247, 249, 256n27, 300
Goebbels, Magda, 97
"Golden showers" accusation, 233
Golf, 14, 227, 228, 233
Gone Girl (Flynn), 146
Gone with the Wind (dir. Fleming), 214
Göring, Hermann, 2, 15, 33, 48, 57n63, 76, 90, 98–101, 115n72, 247, 249, 257n43
Görtemaker, Heike, 234
Gottschall, Jonathan, 193, 194
Gove, Michael, 175
Graham, Billy, 243
Gramsci, Antonio, 183n17

Index

Grand Hyatt (hotel), 246, 288
Great Again (Trump), 211
Great Dictator, The (dir. Chaplin), 89
Green, Joshua, 224n47, 250
Green Party (in Germany), 172
Gruzen, Jordan, 246
Guderian, Heinz, 104
Guideposts, 244
Gumbrecht, Hans Ulrich, 275, 276

H

Haby, François, 51
Hall, Wynton, 17, 43
Hamann, Brigitte, 25, 31
Hanfstaengl, Ernst, 81, 82, 266, 267, 271, 280
Hanfstaengl, Helene, 81
Hannity, Sean, 2, 267
Harrer, Karl, 35
Harvey, Michael, xi
Hauer, Rutger, 190
Haus Wachenfeld, 82, 88
Heß, Rudolf, 36, 38, 77, 82, 85
Hedgehog and the Fox, The (Berlin), 231
Heer, Jeet, 304, 305
Hegel, Georg Wilhelm Friedrich, 204
Heidemann, Gerd, 100
Herz, Rudolf, 48
Hewitt, Hugh, 109
Hicks, Hope, 2
Hidden hand, 142
Himmler, Heinrich, 240, 241, 249
Hindenburg, Paul von, 51, 84, 103
Hitler, Adolf, ix–xiii, xiiin1, xivn13, 1–5, 7–20, 23–26, 28–31, 33–42, 44–48, 50–52, 52n1, 52n3, 54n22, 56n43, 58n74, 58n83, 60n109, 60n110, 62n147, 65n185, 65n187, 76–106, 113n39, 113n42, 115n63, 115n70, 115n72, 117n87, 121, 123, 124, 127, 128, 131, 134–137, 142, 156, 161, 164–166, 174, 181, 196, 203, 206–213, 215–220, 224n42, 224n50, 228–243, 245–251, 254n1, 256n27, 258n46, 261n95, 263–267, 269–280, 282, 283, 285–288, 290–292, 294, 299–302, 306, 307, 309, 310, 311n5, 311n6, 312n28
Hitler, Alois, 50
Hitler at Home (Stratigakos), 91
"Hitler diaries," 100
Hitler in der Karikatur der Welt (ed. Hanfstaengl), 271
Hitler née Dowling, Bridget, 50
"Hitler über Deutschland" campaign, 265
Hitler wie ihn keiner kennt (Hoffmann), 86
Hoffman, Jenn, 14
Hoffmann, Heinrich, 11, 20, 44–48, 85–87, 91, 100
Hoffmann, Henriette, 114n44
Holocaust, ix, 3, 8, 282
Horcher (restaurant), 100
Hot cognition *vs.* cold cognition, 303, 304
Howard Stern Show, The (radio show), 298
How Fascism Works (Stanley), 107

How to Get Rich ((Trump / McIver), 43, 295
Huffington, Arianna, 268
Huis clos (Sartre), 190, 192, 205
Humour, *see* Jokes
Hyperinflation, 79, 203

Ice Bucket Challenge, 14
Identity, 108, 155, 156, 162, 163, 168, 178, 182, 189–220, 220n1, 260n93, 304, 306–310
See also Dignity; *Thymos*
Identity heuristic, 178
Ideological state apparatuses, 160, 161
"Idéologie et appareils idéologiques d'État" (Althusser), 183n12
Ideology, x, 29, 35, 39, 121, 127, 133, 141, 161, 167, 170, 240
"I Have a Dream" (King), 197, 199
Illustrierter Beobachter, 85
Inaugural address, 261n96, 283, 284, 286
Infectiousness of the unconflicted personality (Redl), 252
In Geschichten verstrickt (Schapp), 191
Insults, xi, 268–271, 297, 298
International Jew, The (Ford), 79
Interpretation of Dreams, The (Freud), 305
Interpretative openness, 146–147, 278–282, 308
Iser, Wolfgang, 144, 145, 147
ISIS, 124, 136, 279, 316n61
"I Talked to Hitler" (Lloyd George), 115n67

Jackson, Andrew, xi
Jackson, Ronny, 65n194
Jagger, Mick, 274
James, William, 222n10
Jaubert, Alain, 50
Jaws (dir. Spielberg), 140, 141
Jesus, 4, 39, 245, 303
JFK (dir. Stone), 143
Johnston, David Cay, 273, 278
Jokes, 31, 266–271, 297, 298
Jokes and Their Relation to the Unconscious (Freud), 305
Josefine Mutzenbacher (Salten), 32
Joseph, Franz, 32
Jung, Carl Gustav, 43, 219

Kagan, Robert, x
Kahneman, Daniel, 177
Kaiserbart, 51, 52
Kampfzeit, 210
Kandinsky, Wassily, 83
Kapp-Lüttwitz putsch, 202–203
Kapp, Wolfgang, 202
Kehlsteinhaus, 90
Keitel, Wilhelm, 94, 104
Keller, Gottfried, 88, 114n53
Kelly, Megyn, 299
Kennedy, John F., 7, 147, 251, 261n96, 294
Kershaw, Ian, 4, 5, 35, 38, 54n22, 80, 208, 228, 282
Kettle logic, 305
Khomeini regime, 132
Kim dynasty, xii
King, Martin Luther, 197, 199
King, Norma, 232

King, Rodney, 193
Kipling, Rudyard, 199
Kislyak, Sergey, 73
Kleider machen Leute (Keller), 88, 114n53
Klein, Ada, 51
Koch, Robert, 40
Koepnick, Lutz, 29, 39
Koffler, Keith, 216
Kojève, Alexandre, 122, 204, 223n38
Kranish, Michael, 24
Krause, Karl Wilhelm, 87, 88
Krebs, Albert, 16, 17, 264, 269, 278
Krupp von Bohlen und Halbach, Gustav, 84
Kubizek, August, 25
Kujau, Konrad, 100, 117n87
Kurosawa, Akira, 146
Kushner, Charles, 71
Kushner, Jared, 71–73

L

La conspiration (Nizan), 254
Lakoff, George, 206
"La moustache d'Adolf Hitler" (Jaubert), 50
Landsberg Prison, 77, 82
Lang, Fritz, xivn14
Lang, Jochen von, 89, 113n43
Language of the home (Morini), 295
Last Year in Marienbad (dir. Resnais), 192
Law for the Restoration of the Professional Civil Service, 286
Leadership style, xi, xii, 71, 227–254
Lechfeld, 35
Leeb, Wilhelm Ritter von, 104
Leerstellen, 145

Legitimation through procedures (Luhmann), 168
Lenin, Vladimir Ilyich, 182n9
Leonardo da Vinci, 87
Le Pen, Marine, xi
Les chiens de garde (Nizan), 160
Les formes élémentaires de la vie religieuse (Durkheim), 64n166
Lewandowski, Corey, 2, 248
Lichtdom, 26
Life of Brian (dir. Jones), 175
Limbaugh, Rush, 298
Lincoln, Abraham, 259n81, 297
Linge, Heinz, 16, 234, 257n29
Littleton, Cynthia, 42
Lloyd George, David, 93, 115n67, 266
Longerich, Peter, 116n75, 241
Love Island (TV show), 208
Löwith, Wilhelm, 256n27
Ludendorff, Erich, 269
Ludendorff, Mathilde, 269
Ludwig III, 34
Lueger, Karl, 30–33, 40, 278
Lügenpresse, 134, 135, 151n21, 209
Luhmann, Niklas, 168, 176
Lure of the radical (Rees), 249
Lüttwitz, Walther von, 202–203
Lynch, Michael, 280

M

Mackensen, August von, 103
MAGA baseball cap, 133, 150n9
Magnificent Seven, The (dir. Fuqua), 205
Magnificent Seven, The (dir. Sturges), 205, 207
Manafort, Paul, 73, 74

Management style, *see*
    Leadership style
Manifest destiny, 200, 205
Manigault Newman, Omarosa, 21,
    236, 272
Mannerheim, Carl Gustav von, 264
Mannerheim recording, 264
Many-willed-ness (Nietzsche),
    134, 151n19
Mao Zedong, xi
Marc, Franz, 83
Marx, Karl, 159, 160,
    182n9, 223n34
Marxism, 137, 159, 167, 266, 284
Matisse, Henri, 96
Mattis, Jim, 3
May, Karl, 8, 9, 20, 43, 83,
    309, 318n96
May, Werner, 129, 212, 213, 215
McCain, John, 276
McCarthy, Joe, 142
McCarthyism, 312n22
McDougal, Karen, 74
McGahn, Don, 72
McGrath, Alister, 304
Meaning cultures (Gumbrecht), 275
Mein Kampf (Hitler), 29, 31, 35, 36,
    42, 66n205, 77–79, 82, 83,
    105, 136, 137, 209, 211, 237,
    242, 257n39, 264, 266,
    271–273, 277, 287, 299, 301,
    302, 306, 307
Menninger, Karl, 259n75
Mercieca, Jennifer, 299,
    318n102, 319n121
Meyerson, Harold, 255n15
Military parades, 212
Miller, Jason, 2, 23

Mills, Charles Wright, 161, 183n16
"Minority Report, The"
    (Dick), 220n2
Minority Report (dir.
    Spielberg), 220n2
Misogyny, *see* Sexism
Miss Universe, 41
Mitchell, Paul, 49
Mitford (later Mosley), Diana, 93
Mitford, Unity Valkyrie, 93, 115n70
Molotov-Ribbentrop pact, 41, 45
Mondrian, Piet, 193
Monet, Claude, 96
Montgomery, Bernard, 100
Monuments Men, The (dir.
    Clooney), 95
Moorhouse, Roger, 58n83
Morell, Theodor, 233
Morini, Marco, 295, 318n102
Mosley, Oswald, 93
MS-13, 124
Mueller, Robert, 138, 263
"Muslim ban," 272
Mussolini, Benito, xi, 11,
    14, 93, 280
My New Order (Hitler), ix, xiiin1
Myth, 18, 29, 189–220, 234, 309
Myth gap, 199–220
Myth Gap, The (Evans), 200
Mythologies (Barthes), 198

Narrative paradox, 144, 145, 147
Narrative (un-)truth, 135,
    200, 263–310
National Bolshevism, 62n147
Nazaryan, Alexander, 75, 111n26

Negative partisanship, 108
Nepotism, *see* Corruption
Nervous States (Davies), 179
Neurath, Konstantin von, 258n46
Nicholas of Cusa, 187n68
Nichols, Tom, 175
Niekisch, Ernst, 62n147
Nietzsche, Friedrich, 27, 28, 67n207, 151n19
Night of the Long Knives, 91, 92, 103
Nineteen Eighty-Four (Orwell), 305
Nixon, Richard, xi, 63–64n161, 131, 143, 268, 294, 312n22
Nizan, Paul, 160, 183n10, 254, 261n100
Noske, Gustav, 14
Nouveau roman, 192
Novanglus Essays (Adams), 151n12
Nationalsozialistische Deutsche Arbeiterpartei (NSDAP), 36, 40, 77–79, 82, 84, 85, 96, 101, 104, 105, 128, 217, 218, 228, 258n52, 269
Nuremberg rallies, 25, 26, 36

O

Obama, Barack, 73, 107, 121, 180, 214, 227, 266, 276, 279, 293, 299, 309
Obamacare, 279
O'Brien, Timothy L., 12–13
Ocasio-Cortez, Alexandria, 138–140
Odeonsplatz, 45
Of Beards and Men (Oldstone-Moore), 52, 67n206
Oldstone-Moore, Christopher, 52, 67n206

Omar, Ilhan, 138–140
Omarosa, *see* Manigault Newman, Omarosa
Opponentism, *see* Against-ism
O'Reilly, Bill, 2
Orwell, George, 305
O'Shaughnessy, Nicholas, 196, 210, 211, 224n50
Othello (Shakespeare), 148
Overy, Richard, 116n80, 247, 248

P

Papadopoulos, George, 73
Papen, Franz von, 250
Paralepsis, 298
Paris Bordone, 92
Participatory authoritarianism, 130–135
Pascal, Blaise, 50
Pataki, George, 312n24
Patient Protection and Affordable Care Act, *see* Obamacare
Peale, Norman Vincent, 243–245, 293, 294
Pensées (Pascal), 66n201
Perot, Ross, 41
Perry, Rick, 268, 312n18
Phelps, Reginald H., 283
Phipps, Eric, 99
Plato, xi, 204
Politics as entertainment, 24, 26
Politischer Katechismus (May), 129, 212, 215
Politics *vs.* grassroots democracy, 167, 168
Politophobia, 174
Pool, James, 87
Populism, xivn13, 18, 29, 30, 32, 39, 47, 69, 76, 86, 121, 122,

Index 337

125, 130–136, 140, 157, 159, 161, 162, 164, 171, 200, 210, 211, 214
Power Elite, The (Mills), 161
Power of Positive Thinking, The (Peale), 243–245, 293
Presence cultures (Gumbrecht), 275, 276
Pressley, Ayanna, 138
Price, Tom, 75
Priebus, Reince, 236
Principles of Psychology, The (James), 222n10
Projection, 25, 40, 85, 126, 156, 198, 219, 236, 250
Protocols of the Elders of Zion, The, 306, 307
Pruitt, Bill, 42
Pruitt, Scott, 75, 76
Putin, Vladimir, 251
Pyta, Wolfram, 27, 28

R

Raffendes Kapital vs. schaffendes Kapital, 225n64
Rashomon (dir. Kurosawa), 146
Räterepublik, 34
Raubal, Geli, 82, 113n38
Rauch, Jonathan, 172, 173, 186n46
Reaction-formation, 126, 127
Redl, Fritz, 252, 253
Reductio ad Hitlerum, x
Rees, Laurence, 1, 18, 52n1, 181, 196, 240, 249, 301, 302
Reform Party, 41
Reichsparteitag, see Nuremberg rallies
Reign of suspicion, 141, 152n26

Religion, see Christianity
Rembrandt, 87
Rensin, Emmett, 295
Repressive state apparatuses, 160
Republican Party, 19, 106, 216, 228
Resistance (as psychological mechanism), 27, 143, 147, 252
Resnais, Alain, 192
Retrospective utopianism, 213
Reventlow, Ernst zu, 17
Ribbentrop, Joachim von, 100, 239
Richter, Herbert, 261n95, 279, 301, 302
Richthofen, Manfred von, 57n63
Ridley, Matt, 223n34
Rienzi (Wagner), 25, 60n107, 208
Rivera, Christian, 107, 108
Röhm, Ernst, 92, 98, 115n63
Roller, Alfred, 25, 26, 60n110
Romney, Mitt, 54n27
Roosevelt, Franklin Delano, 7, 71, 270, 271, 286, 294
Rosenberg, Alfred, 101, 105, 117n88
Rostand, Edmond, 261n101
Rothko, Mark, 193
Rousseau, Jean-Jacques, 132, 166
Rubio, Marco, 43, 267, 268
Russell, Bertrand, 178, 187n56
Ryan, Paul, 232

S

Sachs, Jonah, 196, 199
Salkin, Allen, 41
Salten, Felix, 32, 33
Santilli, Ray, 144
Sartre, Jean-Paul, 160, 189–192, 195, 205

Scapegoating, x, 125, 127, 129, 130, 219, 270
Scarborough, Joe, 227
Scavino, Dan, 239
Schacht, Hjalmar, 11
Schapp, Wilhelm, 191
Schiller, Friedrich, 40
Schiller, Keith, 2
Schirach, Baldur von, 114n44
Schmölders, Claudia, 48
Schönerer, Georg von, 31, 42
Schröder, Gerhard, 185n41
Schroeder, Christa, 16, 19, 50, 239
Schuschnigg, Kurt, 94
Schwartz, Tony, 13, 22
Schwarzwäller, Wulf, 95, 112n31
Schwerin von Krosigk, Lutz, 10, 11, 20
Scott, Ridley, 190
Scruton, Roger, 172
Scutt, Der, 233, 246
Seeßlen, Georg, 44
Selling Hitler (O'Shaughnessy), 196, 210, 224n50
Sexism, 191, 268, 297
Seyß-Inquart, Arthur, 94
Shock jocks, 298
Short, Aaron, 41
Simpson, Wallis, 93
Sims, Cliff, 24, 42, 46, 228, 231, 232, 239, 245, 246, 251
Slater, Robert, 21, 22, 272
Smith, Liz, 12
Social Darwinism, 239–246
Society of the Spectacle, The (Debord), 193
Sonderauftrag Linz, 95, 101
Sonnemann (later Göring), Emmy, 99

Sontag, Susan, 37
Spaun, Fridolin von, 1
Speeches, ix, 17, 26, 29, 31, 45, 46, 51, 82, 99, 138, 164, 181, 199, 212, 213, 239, 263–310
Speer, Albert, 3, 11, 12, 15, 16, 18, 20, 25, 90, 91, 96, 101, 231, 235
Spicer, Sean, 14, 180
Spione (dir. Lang), xivn14
Spitzweg, Carl, 83
Spotts, Frederic, 26, 274
Sprague, Blanche, 21
Stab-in-the-back legend, *see* *Dolchstoßlegende*
Stalin, Josef, 45, 71, 122, 123, 131, 136, 149n2, 296
Stanley, Jason, 107, 108
Statues, 213, 214
See also War memorials
Stegemann, Bernd, 163, 165
Stern, Howard, 298
Stone, Oliver, 143
Stormy Daniels, 49, 74, 303
Story-telling, 217, 220n1
Storytelling Animal, The (Gottschall), 193
Strategic controversy, 272–274
Stratigakos, Despina, 91–93
Strauss, Leo, x
Strongmen (Ben-Ghiat), xi

T

Tag der Freiheit (dir. Riefenstahl), 38
Taleb, Nassim Nicholas, 255n15
Talk-radio, 298
Tannenbergbund, 269

Tea Party, 200, 208
Thatcher, Margaret, 7
Thinking, Fast and Slow
  (Kahneman), 177
"This Is How Fascism Comes to
  America" (Kagan), x
Thomas theorem, 80
Thymos, 204
  See also Dignity; Identity
Thyssen, Fritz, 80, 81, 85, 301
Tibbetts, Molly, 107, 108
Tietjen, Friedrich, 50
Tillerson, Rex, 3
Time to Get Tough (Trump /
  Hall), 43
Tlaib, Rashida, 138–140
Tocqueville, Alexis de, 169
"Too Close for Comfort"
  (Chotiner), xi
Toothbrush moustache, 50–52
Treaty of Versailles, 134, 202, 249,
  254, 270, 282
Trevor-Roper, Hugh, 117n87
Triumph of the Will (dir. Riefenstahl),
  26, 36–38, 44, 242, 265, 274
Troost, Gerdy, 91
Trump, Donald J., ix–xiii, xiiin1,
  xivn13, 2–5, 7, 8, 10, 12–15,
  17, 19–24, 36, 41, 42, 44,
  46–49, 52n1, 59n86,
  65–66n194, 66n198, 69–76,
  84, 102, 105–109, 109n2,
  121–125, 129–131, 135, 136,
  138–140, 142, 143, 146, 149,
  156, 163–166, 174, 177,
  179–181, 184n22, 184n23,
  187n64, 196, 200, 205–220,
  224n42, 224n45, 224n50,
  227–233, 235–236, 238, 239,
  243, 245, 246, 248–252,
  254n1, 255n15, 256n23,
  260n93, 263–268, 272–280,
  282–289, 291–300, 302–305,
  308–310, 312n18, 312n24,
  315n56,
  315–316n61, 320n126
Trump, Eric, 70
Trump, Fred, 232
Trump, Ivanka, 70–73
Trump Jr., Donald, 70, 233
Trump née Zelníčková, Ivana, ix,
  xiiin1, 13, 232, 246, 293
Trump Organization, 70,
  109n2, 233
Trump Tower, 43, 44, 288, 289
Truthful hyperbole, 13, 288
Truthiness, 178, 306–310
"Twenty-Five Point Programme,"
  128, 258n52
Twitter, 70, 133, 139, 170,
  227, 294–299
Twitterature (Aciman/Rensin), 295

V

Valera, Éamon de, 271
Valkyrie (dir. Singer), 16
van Gogh, Vincent, 96
van Meegeren, Han, 115n72
van Ree, Erik, 131–133
Van Susteren, Greta, 316n61
Verjudung, 137
Vermeer, Johannes, 115n72,
  193, 221n7
Vermes, Timur, 311n6
Vernunftrepublikaner, 202

Völkischer Beobachter, 78, 85
Volksgemeinschaft, 35, 38

W

Wagener, Otto, 1
Wagner, Richard, 24–29, 33, 43, 81, 89, 208, 309
Wagner, Siegfried, 208
Wagner, Winifred, 60n110, 81
Waldeck, Rosie, 81
Wallace, Edgar, 83
Wall (between Mexico and the US), 121, 272, 292, 302, 308
Wall Street Crash, 107, 140, 203, 206, 285
Ward, Vicky, 71–73, 111n14
War memorials, 213
  See also Statues
A Warning (Taylor), 3
Warren, Elizabeth, 268
Watteau, Antoine, 87
Weber, Max, 4, 5, 7, 54n22, 165
Weber, Thomas, 35
Webster, Steven, 108
Weimar Republic, 5, 14, 105, 140, 201, 202, 209, 215, 275, 285, 287, 289
Weisselberg, Allen, 70
Weisthor, *see* Wiligut, Karl Maria
Welles, Sumner, 99
Whetton, Cris, 88

White, Paula, 286
Wiedemann, Fritz, 181
Wilhelm II, 51
Wiligut, Karl Maria, 241, 258n56
Willikens, Werner, 260n87
Wilson, Robert Kenneth, 144
Win Bigly (Adams), 292
Winning the Story Wars (Sachs), 196
Wnendt, David, 311n6
Wolff, Michael, 20, 238, 256n23
Woodward, Bob, 227, 236, 315n56
"Work of Art in the Age of Technological Reproducibility, The" (Benjamin), 54n23
World of Warcraft, 192, 208, 224n47
WrestleMania, 41, 268

Y

Yanukovich, Viktor, 74
Yes, Minister (TV show), 230
Yes, Prime Minister (TV show), 230

Z

Zahn, Johannes, 301, 302
Zakaria, Fareed, 171
Zayan, René, 61n130, 311n12
Zigarettenbilder, 65n184
Zinke, Ryan, 75, 76
Žižek, Slavoj, 140, 141, 152n25

SPRINGER NATURE

GPSR Compliance

The European Union's (EU) General Product Safety Regulation (GPSR) is a set of rules that requires consumer products to be safe and our obligations to ensure this.

If you have any concerns about our products, you can contact us on ProductSafety@springernature.com

In case Publisher is established outside the EU, the EU authorized representative is:

Springer Nature Customer Service Center GmbH
Europaplatz 3
69115 Heidelberg, Germany

The manufacturer's authorised representative in the EU is Springer Nature Customer Service Centre GmbH, Europaplatz 3, 69115 Heidelberg, Germany. If you have any concerns regarding our products, please contact ProductSafety@springernature.com

Printed and bound by CPI Group (UK) Ltd, Croydon, CR0 4YY

25/03/2026

02078179-0005